Research Series on the Chinese Dream and China's Development Path

Project Director

Xie Shouguang, President, Social Sciences Academic Press

Series Editors

Li Yang, Chinese Academy of Social Sciences, Beijing, China
Li Peilin, Chinese Academy of Social Sciences, Beijing, China

Academic Advisors

Cai Fang, Gao Peiyong, Li Lin, Li Qiang, Ma Huaide, Pan Jiahua, Pei Changhong,
Qi Ye, Wang Lei, Wang Ming, Zhang Yuyan, Zheng Yongnian, Zhou Hong

D1694658

Γ awing on a large body of empirical studies done over the last two decades, this S ies provides its readers with in-depth analyses of the past and present and fo casts for the future course of China's development. It contains the latest res ch results made by members of the Chinese Academy of Social Sciences. This seri n invaluable companion to every researcher who is trying to gain a deeper unde ng of the development model, path and experience unique to China. Thanks he adoption of Socialism with Chinese characteristics, and the implementa of comprehensive reform and opening-up, China has made tremendous a ements in areas such as political reform, economic development, and social cons tion, and is making great strides towards the realization of the Chinese dream of al rejuvenation. In addition to presenting a detailed account of many of these ements, the authors also discuss what lessons other countries can learn from 's experience.

More information about this series at http://www. r.com/series/13571

Qiang Li

China's Development Under a Differential Urbanization Model

Qiang Li
Faculty of Social Sciences
Tsinghua University
Beijing, China

Translated by He Gan

Sponsored by the Chinese Fund for the Humanities and Social Sciences.

ISSN 2363-6866   ISSN 2363-6874   (electronic)
Research Series on the Chinese Dream and China's Development Path
ISBN 978-981-13-9453-9   ISBN 978-981-13-9451-5   (eBook)
https://doi.org/10.1007/978-981-13-9451-5

Jointly published with Social Sciences Academic Press, Beijing, China
The printed edition is not for sale in the Mainland of China. Customers from the Mainland of China
please order the print book from Social Sciences Academic Press.

This Springer imprint is published by the registered company Springer Nature Singapore Pte Ltd.
The registered company address is: 152 Beach Road, #21-01/04 Gateway East, Singapore 189721,
Singapore

Series Preface

Since China's reform and opening began in 1978, the country has come a long way on the path of Socialism with Chinese characteristics, under the leadership of the Communist Party of China. Over 30 years of reform, efforts and sustained spectacular economic growth have turned China into the world's second largest economy, and wrought many profound changes in the Chinese society. These historically significant developments have been garnering increasing attention from scholars, governments, and the general public alike around the world since the 1990s, when the newest wave of China studies began to gather steam. Some of the hottest topics have included the so-called "China miracle", "Chinese phenomenon", "Chinese experience", "Chinese path", and the "Chinese model". Homegrown researchers have soon followed suit. Already hugely productive, this vibrant field is putting out a large number of books each year, with Social Sciences Academic Press alone having published hundreds of titles on a wide range of subjects.

Because most of these books have been written and published in Chinese, however, readership has been limited outside China—even among many who study China—for whom English is still the lingua franca. This language barrier has been an impediment to efforts by academia, business communities, and policy-makers in other countries to form a thorough understanding of contemporary China, of what is distinct about China's past and present may mean not only for her future but also for the future of the world. The need to remove such an impediment is both real and urgent, and the *Research Series on the Chinese Dream and China's Development Path* is my answer to the call.

This series features some of the most notable achievements from the last 20 years by scholars in China in a variety of research topics related to reform and opening. They include both theoretical explorations and empirical studies, and cover economy, society, politics, law, culture, and ecology, the six areas in which reform and opening policies have had the deepest impact and farthest-reaching consequences for the country. Authors for the series have also tried to articulate their visions of the "Chinese Dream" and how the country can realize it in these fields and beyond.

All of the editors and authors for the *Research Series on the Chinese Dream and China's Development Path* are both longtime students of reform and opening and recognized authorities in their respective academic fields. Their credentials and expertise lend credibility to these books, each of which having been subject to a rigorous peer review process for inclusion in the series. As part of the Reform and Development Program under the State Administration of Press, Publication, Radio, Film, and Television of the People's Republic of China, the series is published by Springer, a Germany-based academic publisher of international repute, and distributed overseas. I am confident that it will help fill a lacuna in studies of China in the era of reform and opening.

Xie Shouguang

Acknowledgements

After a relatively short gestation period, the *Research Series on the Chinese Dream and China's Development Path* has started to bear fruits. We have, first and foremost, the books' authors and editors to thank for making this possible. And it was the hardwork by many people at Social Sciences Academic Press and Springer, the two collaborating publishers, that made it a reality. We are deeply grateful to all of them.

Mr. Xie Shouguang, president of Social Sciences Academic Press (SSAP), is the mastermind behind the project. In addition to defining the key missions to be accomplished by it and setting down the basic parameters for the project's execution, as the work has unfolded, Mr. Xie has provided critical input pertaining to its every aspect and at every step of the way. Thanks to the deft coordination by Ms. Li Yanling, all the constantly moving parts of the project, especially those on the SSAP side, are securely held together, and as well synchronized as is feasible for a project of this scale. Ms. Gao Jing, unfailingly diligent and meticulous, makes sure every aspect of each Chinese manuscript meets the highest standards for both publishers, something of critical importance to all subsequent steps in the publishing process. That high-quality if also at times stylistically as well as technically challenging scholarly writing in Chinese has turned into decent, readable English that readers see on these pages is largely thanks to Ms. Liang Fan, who oversees translator recruitment and translation quality control.

Ten other members of the SSAP staff have been intimately involved, primarily in the capacity of in-house editor, in the preparation of the Chinese manuscripts. It is time-consuming work that requires attention to detail, and each of them have done this, and is continuing to do this with superb skills. They are, in alphabetical order: Mr. Cai Jihui, Ms. Liu Xiaojun, Mr. Ren Wenwu, Ms. Shi Xiaolin, Ms. Song Yuehua, Mr. Tong Genxing, Ms. Wu Dan, Ms. Yao Dongmei, Ms. Yun Wei, and Ms. Zhou Qiong. In addition, Xie Shouguang and Li Yanling have also taken part in this work.

Mr. Tong Genxing is the SSAP in-house editor for the current volume.

Our appreciation is also owed to Ms. Li Yan, Mr. Chai Ning, Ms. Wang Lei, and Ms. Xu Yi from Springer's Beijing Representative Office. Their strong support for the SSAP team in various aspects of the project helped to make the latter's work that much easier than it would have otherwise been.

We thank He Gan, Li Ting, Tang Yan, Zhou Jian, Liu Nan, Liu Hong, Wen Shengfang, Liu Jia, Lv Xue, Sun Liheng for translating this book and Mr. Elliot Munden for his work as the polisher.

Last, but certainly not least, it must be mentioned that funding for this project comes from the Ministry of Finance of the People's Republic of China. Our profound gratitude, if we can be forgiven for a bit of apophasis, goes without saying.

Social Sciences Academic Press
Springer

Contents

Chapter 1
Urbanization Since 1949: History, Current State and Problems

1.1 Introduction: Urbanization with Chinese Characteristics

China, a country with a 5000-year history of civilization, is one of the countries that developed the earliest urban areas, having the largest size and number of cities in the world. However, urban development in China lagged behind the industrially-advanced countries since the nineteenth century. After the founding of the People's Republic of China in 1949, urbanization process in China was full of twists and turns. In the approximately 30 years before the initiation of the reform and opening policy, the pace of urbanization in China was rather slow, whereas after the reforms were launched, urbanization accelerated with an unprecedented large scale and speed in human history. Urbanization proceeded more rapidly in China than in most other countries that have undergone the process.

Urbanization trend is independent of man's will. Urban society has a good many obvious advantages relative to the traditional rural society. Land use, production and consumption, population, and energy are centralized, thus creating numerous and varied job opportunities and providing efficient model of economic development. The development of nonagricultural sectors after reform and opening-up especially the development of industry and rapid economic growth have already started up the urbanization process on large scale in Chinese society.

Urbanization in China is both unique and complex. On one hand, China is the most populous developing country with government-guided economic reform. She should neither copy nor blindly follow other countries' development model and experiences without modification. On the other hand, China covers a vast area of territory with the uneven pattern of regional development. Different cities have distinctive development paths and life cycles. If a one-size-fits-all urbanization model or path is enforced across the board, it would likely create intractable social

© Social Sciences Academic Press 2020
Q. Li, *China's Development under a Differential Urbanization Model*,
Research Series on the Chinese Dream and China's Development Path,
https://doi.org/10.1007/978-981-13-9451-5_1

problems or even knotty obstacles for future economic development. Therefore, urbanization in China should have Chinese characteristics and reflect actual conditions of the country.

Urbanization in China has increased in speed over the past three decades and is now at a crucial stage marked by intensification of social conflicts. According to the current pace of economic development and the tendency of industry reform, three hundred million people are expected to move from rural to urban areas over the next two decades. More cities and towns as well as larger intake capacity are required for such a huge population migration. The climax of a new round of urbanization has arrived. In the process of such a large-scale social transformation, without a strategy suitable for China and scientifically-sound urban development plans that meet the needs of different regions, not only will the abovementioned problems in urban development persist but new conflicts and crises will also arise.

Urbanization is also a way of redistributing resources and wealth not only among different social groups but also within different geographical areas. Such redistribution involves rather profound industrial restructuring and entails changes in population and occupational structure. Urbanization also brings about fundamental changes in lifestyle. There is significant overlap among these changes, which also exert influence on one another. Against the backdrop of these interwoven transformations, rapid urbanization has brought sweeping changes to the society at large that are exceptionally drastic and profound. We cannot, therefore, afford not to treat potential social problems that might arise in this process with utmost seriousness. Neither developed countries nor developing countries have any experience with this particular form of social transition. The change from the planned economy to the market economy, the fast drive of social modernization, the overall social structural transformations and reorganization, the change of the organizing principles of social life from politics-dominated to economy and ethics-dominated ones, and the transformation from a "units" society to a civil society are interwoven together in the large-scaled social transitions in China. Against all these major social changes, the road of urbanization in China is inevitably a tough and innovative one with Chinese characteristics and suitable for China.

Conditions in China, a large developing country, are unique. There are vast interregional variations in population, resources, environment, social, and economic conditions. China is now at a critical stage of urbanization. We must pay close attention to such issues as how decisions should be made, what kind of general approach to adopt, the things to be taken into consideration, and planning strategies insofar as they bring the universal law of urbanization to bear. In sum, it is important for China to adopt a differential urbanization model with Chinese characteristics.

1.2 History of Urbanization in China

Urbanization in China in the twentieth century has gone through three major phases: the first phase spans from the beginning of the twentieth century to the eve of the founding of the People's Republic of China (from 1900 to 1949), the second phase goes up to the beginning of reform and opening-up (from 1949 to 1978), and the third phase covers the years of reform and opening-up (from 1979 till now).

1.2.1 From 1900 to 1949

Because the development of productivity was restrained by the feudal production relations for a long time, modern cities didn't actually appear in traditional China. In the opium war in 1840, western powers forced open the door of China with tough warships and weapons. In over 60 years since the signing of the Sino-British Treaty of Nanking, 104 port cities and towns in China was either forced to or voluntarily opened up.[1] While dumping foreign goods, the imperialists objectively brought capital and technology from the industrial revolution to China. It was the semicolonial and semifeudal trading port cities and towns took the lead in industrialization and urbanization in China. The Westernization Movement initiated in 1861 marked the beginning of China's autonomous modernization and urbanization. The large-scale exploration of industrial raw material, the establishment of big machinery factories and the development of railway and transportation stimulated the rise of an array of modern cities.

Between the Revolution of 1911 and the 1930s, China once witnessed a period of rapid growth of urbanization, which was referred in history as a period of working class formation in China.[2] Urbanization during this period bore the following characteristics: foreign capital invasion and rapid development, gradual expansion of national industries which brought migrants into cities, and declining handicraft industry in rural areas. In 1936, there existed ten large cities in China with a population of over 500 thousand. Shanghai was the largest city with a population of 3.48 million.[3] Urbanization during this period witnessed obvious development in South China. A typical case was the development of Shanghai. With the establishment of foreign Concessions and the blossom of Sino-foreign

---

[1]Tu (1996).

[2]Mao Zedong. *Analysis on Classes in Chinese Society*. 1925-12. "There are about two million modern industrial proletariats. Due to economic backwardness, they are few in number. Most of them come from the five industries of railway, mining, shipping, textile and shipbuilding. A large number of them are under the yoke of foreign industry. Industrial proletariat is not a large number, but it is representative of China's new productive forces and China's most advanced class, which becomes the leading force of revolutionary movement".

[3]Tu (1996).

trade, as well as the population flooding in from Jiangsu and Zhejiang provinces, Shanghai rapidly grew into a highly modernized big city. It was estimated that the entire population in Shanghai in 1933 reached 3.4 million, 2.7 times more than the population of 900 thousand in the First Sino-Japanese War in 1985. During the same period the total number of workers in Shanghai increased by 8.5 times from 37,000 to 3,500,000.[4] The average annual growth rate of industrial output value in Shanghai was 9.36% from 1895 to 1911, 12.05% from 1911 to 1925, and 6.53% from 1925 to 1936 in spite of a slow-down.[5] However, urbanization during this period was particularly featured by semifeudalism and semicolonialism, or semi-capitalism. Without the real independence of the country, a great many coastal cities had foreign Concessions and big cities became the place where foreign capital ad capitalism raced for. Therefore, the significance of the year 1949 lies in its national independence and it was since then that Chinese people started urbanization on their own.

Although urbanization before the founding of the People's Republic of China started early in the period of Westernization Movement in the mid-nineteenth century, the pace of urbanization was quite slow over nearly a century due to wars, revolutions, social unrest, and other upheavals and turmoils.

The population of the cities and towns in China in 1843, 1893, and 1949 was 20.7, 23.5, and 57.66 million, respectively, representing urbanization rates of 5.1, 6.6, and 10.6%, respectively.[6] Urbanization rate of 10.6% was on par with that in Britain in 1850, behind the west by a century. Within the Chinese territory, which covers 9.6 million km^2, there were only 136 large, medium and small cities and 2000 counties and designated towns, where cities and urban economy were far from prosperous. Clearly, China started urbanization later and from a lower developmental level than many other countries in the world.

1.2.2 From 1949 to 1978

In the early years of the People's Republic China, industrial development shifted rapidly to the heavy-industry-oriented strategic plan following a transient industrial start-up. Urban population grew rapidly in China based on the extensional expanded reproduction. But restricted by the cities' intake capacity and "the economic difficulties" occurred between the late 1950s and the early 1960s, the urban development policy of "controlling the size of big cities" was eventually formed. Meanwhile, rural–urban migration was strictly restricted by means of the household registration system, etc. Although the size of some cities had a relatively dramatic growth before reform and opening-up, it was mainly the result of the

---

[4]Zhang (1996).
[5]Xu et al. (1995).
[6]Zhao and Xie (1987, 1988).

high natural population growth rate. In the dimension of overall urbanization level, urban population growth before reform and opening-up was slow and with considerable fluctuations. Several important stages could be further divided into in this period of time.

1.2.2.1   From 1949 to 1957: Slow but Steady Progress

When People's Republic of China was founded in 1949, there were only 69 cities throughout the country with a rural population of 57.65 million. The urbanization level was only 10.64%.[7] Over the period of national economy recovery and the implementation of First Five-Year Plan, the large-scale economic development on the national level saw a rapid raise of industrialization level and the renovation of an array of old industrial cities. A large number of new and expansion industrial projects were carried out nationwide. City construction, economic, and service industry development became the industrial foundation for urbanization in China over this period. The need for labor force led to a mass rural–urban migration which speeded up the urbanization in China. The statistics in *China Compendium Statistics 1949–1998* shows that up till 1957, the number of the cities in China amounted to 176, which was 1.6 times more than that in the early days after the founding of the People's Republic of China, with an average annual increase of 12.42%. The rural population reached 99.49 million, with an average annual increase of 7.06%. The urbanization rate was 15.39%, which was 4.75% more than that in 1949, with an annual increase of 0.59% (see Fig. 1.1).

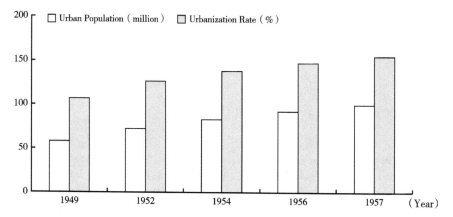

Fig. 1.1   Urbanization level in China 1949–1957. *Source China Compendium Statistics 1949–1998*, 1999

[7]*China Compendium Statistics 1949–1998*. China Statistics Press, 1999.

1.2.2.2   From 1958 to 1965: Ups and Downs

From 1958 to 1965, China's economy had experienced an uneven process including
the "Great Leap Forward" movement, three-year successive natural calamities in
1959, 1960, and 1961 and the adjustment in national economy. Urbanization in this
period also saw its ups and downs. From 1958 to 1960, the number of cities and
towns, urban population, and the urbanization rate increased rapidly. The population in cities and towns had increased from 99.49 million in 1957 to 130.73 million
in 1960, and the urbanization rate from 15.39 to 19.75%, with an annual average
increase of 1.45% points. Compared with the early days after the founding of PRC,
the speed of urbanization had a marked growth. However, from 1958, the rigid
urban–rural dual system took shape and the state urbanization policies were
adjusted. For example, in 1958, the strict household registration system was
implemented, tight restrictions were laid on rural–urban migration and China's
Construction Commission and the Ministry Urban Construction were abolished.
During that period, the economic strategy with the priority given to heavy industry
and the highly concentrated planned economy system made industrial construction
top priority in urban development. The construction of residential housing and
public facility in urban areas were suspended. Consumption cities shifted to production cities. Some new county-turned cities even became counties again and
some other prefectural-level cities were downgraded to counties.

Between 1961 and 1965, due to the severe natural calamities, the urban–rural
economic recession and changes in government policies, the number of cities and
towns and the urbanization rate fell abruptly. In the early 1960s, particularly, over
2.6 million urban inhabitants moved to rural areas as a result of staff cuts at
government organs and a batch of cities were administratively reclassified and were
no longer cities. As a result, only 171 cities remained by 1965. Despite the slight
growth of urban population, due to significant increases in the country's total
population, the urbanization rate dropped to 17.98%, a decrease of almost 2%
points (see Fig. 1.2).

1.2.2.3   From 1966 to 1978: Slowing Down

During the Cultural Revolution, which lasted from 1966 to 1976, urbanization
slowed down considerably, as did development in other areas. During that period,
political movement and campaigns took centerstage in the country. Industrial and
agricultural production was at a standstill and economic development suffered.
Starting from 1968, in the "Going to the Countryside" movement, large number of
educated urban youth, urban workers, and cadres moved to the countryside.
According to incomplete statistics, about 20 million educated youths were sent to
and resettled in the countryside during the Cultural Revolution. If we include urban
cadres, workers, and their family members, the total number of urban residents that
left the cities stands at approximately 30 million. The urbanization rate was 17.55%
in 1977, lower even than what it had been in 1965 (see Fig. 1.3).

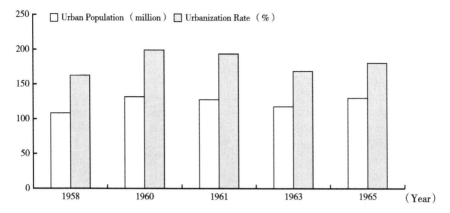

Fig. 1.2 Urbanization in China 1958–1965. *Source* China Compendium Statistics 1949–1998, 1999

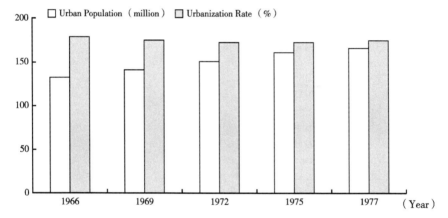

Fig. 1.3 Urbanization in China 1966–1977. *Source* China Compendium Statistics 1949–1998, 1999

What's worth mentioning is that this period laid the institutional foundation for the urbanization after the reform and opening up. During this period, the household registration system which controlled urban population and administrated urban and rural areas separately became the institutional starting-point of the following increasingly enlarged urban–rural gap. At that time, cities were undergoing a functional shift from centers of consumption to places of production, a process in which the "price scissors" between industrial and agricultural products helped advance industrialization. The result is the rudimentary form of a dual administrative system that bifurcated the county into rural and urban areas. This was an incremental process by which an agricultural country can develop into an industrial country with the right conditions for modernization.[8] At the same time, however, due to unevenness in economic development, something of a "city-phobia" developed, reflecting the idea among many that reducing urban population might offer a solution to urban problems. This led to many migrant workers being asked to return to their places of origin in the countryside, especially from cities that experienced economic difficulties. Meanwhile, the notion that "industrial and city construction is constrained in scale only by the amount of the surplus agricultural products (particularly grain and cereal) that can be made available to meet urban consumption demands began to take hold. The was an earlier formation of the widely accepted idea that "urban development can proceed no faster than is allowed by the supply of grain commodity needed to sustain urban population growth".[9]

1.2.3 From 1979 to the Present

Since 1979, with the acceleration of reform and opening up and industrialization, Urbanization in China entered a period of steady growing. Urbanization during this period can be roughly divided into the following stages:

1.2.3.1 Recovery: 1979–1984

During this stage, the urbanization was mainly pushed by rural system reform and agricultural modernization. The Third Plenary Session of the Eleventh Central Committee of the CPC held in December 1978 was the prelude of the economic system reform in rural areas. Agriculture in China hence embraced a concession of years of rapid growth, on which township enterprises and small quasi-city towns grew in high speed. The old dual structure which advocated "cities focus on industry and countryside focus on agriculture" was broken through, gradually being replaced by a new dual structure which emphasized both on urban industrialization and agricultural modernization.

In October 1980, the State Council approved the implementation of the basic principle of "controlling the scale of big cities, supporting the rational growth of moderate cities and advocating the development of small cities", which was proposed at the National Urban Planning Meeting. In 1983, Fei Xiaotong, a famous sociologist proposed that "rural surplus labor force should be mainly arranged by small quasi-city towns, and then by small, medium-sized, and big cities". This idea was widely acknowledged and became a chief policy concerning urban development in the following years (see Fig. 1.4).

---

[8]Hou (2010).
[9]Zhao (1988).

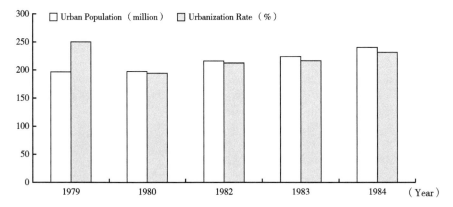

Fig. 1.4   Urbanization in China 1979–1984. *Source* China Compendium Statistics 1949–1998, 1999

1.2.4   Steady Development: 1985–1991

Urbanization at this stage witnessed the urban system reform and rapid growth of manufacturing industry. In October 1984, the Third Plenary Session of the Twelfth Central Committee of the CPC Passed the *Decision on Economic System Reform by the Central Committee of the CPC*, which signified China's entering into the stage of city-focused economic system reform. During this period, the central government continued the urbanization policy: Strictly controlled the expansion of big cities and encouraged the development of small and medium-sized cities especially small quasi-city towns. The aim was to absorb surplus rural labors so as to prevent problems that might arise due to over-expansion of big cities.

With the rapid growth of township enterprises, the notion of "developing small quasi-city towns" later became "a major strategy facilitating rural economic and social development". Since the mid-1980s, small quasi-city towns had greater development in China especially in densely populated areas—the south of the middle and lower reaches of the Yangtze River. From 1980 to 1991, the percentage of registered urban population in the national total population rose from 19.93 to 26.94%, an increase of about 7%. Small towns contribute greatly to that percentage by absorbing in quite a number of rural populations. In the 1980s, the policy of relaxing control over and revitalizing the circulation sector led to the prosperity of farmer's market. The enterprise reform removed the limit on labor market. The coexistence of different forms of ownership expanded the commodity market and unleashed the production factor market. All of them created more jobs for farmers.[10]

---

[10]Wang (2001).

However, some problems arose during the rapid growth of small quasi-city towns. For instance, a lot of small quasi-city towns or small cities scattered loosely, without distinct urban functions, proper management, and urban construction plan. They were simply an extension of the countryside. That was what we called the "county disease" in urban development. The low level of intensification, low-economic efficiency and high-energy consumption among other problems in the small quasi-city towns received some criticism.

1.2.4.1 Rapid Growth: 1992 to the Present

China entered a new era in its drive to urbanize in 1992. Deng Xiaoping's remarks on his South inspection tour in 1992 and the 14th National Congress of CPC in October opened a new chapter in the nationwide development of a socialist market economic system. With the deepening of the market economy reform and further opening up to the outside world, both industrialization and urbanization were given an enormous boost.

Over the last decade, the population density in cities continued to climb from year to year. In 1990, the population density in urban China was 279 persons/km^2 on average. In 1995, that number grew to 322, and then to 422 in 2000, 588 in 2001, 754 in 2002, and over 1000 in 2005. At the same time, the expansion and growth of big cities were spectacular. In 1993, there were only 68 cities with a population over 500,000, but by the end of 2002 that number sharply increased to 450 and the number of cities with a population over 1 million increased to 171 by the end of the same year. During the 9 years from 1999 to 2008, the percentage of urban population rose from 34.78 to 46.2%. Cities and towns experienced a large increase in number, which has plateaued. The number of cities increased from 193 in 1978 to 467 in 1990 and 663 in 2000. The number of towns rose from 2664 in 1982 to 9322 in 1990 and 19,692 in 2000. Meanwhile, the administrative area of some cities expanded. The increase in urban population from the mid-1980s to the 1990s was partly due to "reclassifying counties as cities" and "quashing villages and merger counties" policy.[11]

Urban development during this period was mainly the result of industrial development and marketization reform. The spatial layout of cities throughout the country and urban development model were more influenced by the market. For example, in coastal areas of southeast China, industrial parks, economic development zones, logistics parks, and other forms of concentrated industrial models expanded cities greatly, absorbing a large number of surplus labor from all over the country as well as transferring cities and urban populations to southeast China. For instance, the ratio of cities in eastern China to central China and to western China in 1978 was 1:2.2:0.6. However, in 1995, the ratio has changed to 1:0.8:0.4.

---

[11]Bai (2003).

Out-of-control and disorderly growth in land use in urban areas in recent years can be attributed to a number of factors, including local government policies, existing land tenure, household registration, and taxation systems and GDP growth-oriented development model. Recent years saw a rapid increase in cases violating the laws concerning land use in cities in China while the number of economic development zones at all levels and in all categories increased greatly. Researches showed that the planned construction area of all economic development zones together has exceeded the total area of land for national construction. It is very common to see "illegal land use" and "planning failure" caused by local-government-guided urban development model.[12]

Under market-oriented urbanization, small, medium-sized, and big cities all had strong development demand. Big cities aspire to become international metropolis while small and medium-sized cities wanted to grow bigger. A typical example would be central business district (CBD) that many cities in China have tried to build. Some estimate puts the number of Chinese cities with plans to build CBD at 40, which is larger than the number of CBDs in the US. Analyzing the internal relation between economic growth and business activities, that number is obviously unreasonably large. According to a classified survey on the "CBD bubble" done by state authorities, only 13 cities in China had the right condition for building CBD. Four out of the 40 cities which wanted to build CBD have fewer than 200,000 inhabitants. The construction of a CBD needs a lot of land and tens of billions of RMB and can take anywhere between 20 and 30 years to complete. It is a protracted process. And if anything should go wrong, the cost can be great.

As urbanization continues, urban development policies are also evolving. According to the report of the 16th National People's Congress of CPC held in 2002, the country must stay committed to coordinating the development of different sizes, and pursuing urbanization with Chinese characteristics. The government announced in its 11th Five- year Plan that construction of city cluster was to be given high priority. The goal, more specifically, was to realize a coordinated, effective, and sustainable urbanization spatial layout featuring major north–south rail lines such as those between Beijing and Guangzhou and between Beijing and Harbin, major east–west transport lines such as the Yangtze River and the Lanzhou–Lianyungang rail line, a number of massive city clusters, other cities and smaller towns distributed in the spaces between them, interspersed with permanent farmland and ecological protected areas". By far, three city clusters including the Pearl River Delta, the Yangtze River Delta, the Bohai Economic Rim, seven city belts along the Yangtze River and the Lanzhou–Lianyungang Railway, around Harbin, Changchun, Shenyang cities, and so on, and 50 big city circles with provincial capitals and prefectural level cities with strengths and specialty as the core, took initial shape in China. In the report made at the 17th National People's Congress of CPC, further requirement was made for the development of

---

[12]Li and Yang (2007).

urbanization in the future: "focusing on enhancing cities' carrying capacity, depending on megalopolis, forming city clusters with great radiation functions so as to foster new economic growth".

1.3   Current Conditions

According to the results of the Sixth National Census, the urbanization level in China maintains a momentum of fast growth since the founding of PRC, from 13.26% in the early days after the founding of PRC increased to 49.68% in 2010, an increase of 36.42% points. Especially since the 1990s, urbanization rate in China increased by 10% points every 10 years. According to statistics, since 1982, the speed of urbanization in China has stayed high, with an annual average increase of 0.7% point from 1982 to 1990, 1% point from 1990 to 2000, and of 1.36% points from 2000 to 2010 (see Fig. 1.5).

Since 2000, the urbanization rate in China had increased year by year, entering a stage of rapid growth. In recent 10 years, it grew from 36.09% in 2000 to 49.68% in 2010 (data not included in the figure), a growth exceeding 13% points. Namely, a yearly increase of more than 1% point, that is to say, at least 10–20 million people a year moved to cities on average, which was quite a large number (see Fig. 1.6). Urbanization in China proceeded with unprecedented speed and scale.

Since 2000, the annual growth of the urbanization rate in China declined by and large. That is to say, the acceleration of the urbanization rate slowed down on the

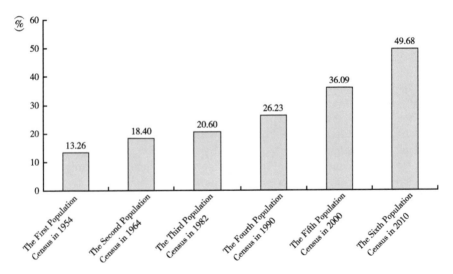

Fig. 1.5 Variation of urbanization rate in China in Six National Censuses. *Source The Six Bulletins of China National Census.* National Bureau of Statistics of the People's Republic of China

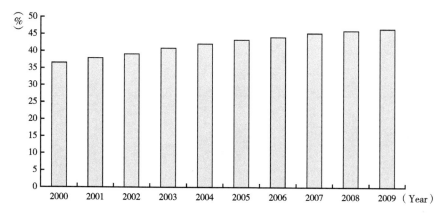

Fig. 1.6 Variation of urbanization rate in China (2000–2009). *Source* China Statistics Yearbook 2010

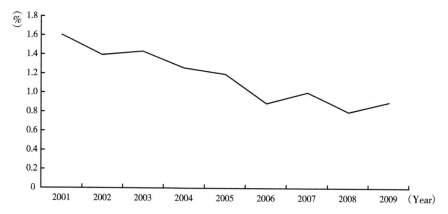

Fig. 1.7 Variation of urbanization growth rate in China (2001–2009). *Source* China Statistics Yearbook 2010

whole. According to statistics (see Fig. 1.7), the increasing amplitude reduced from 1.61% in 2001 to 0.90% in 2009, which indicated the growth did slow down. Especially from 2006 to the end of 2008 it was quite unsteady, reaching the bottom in 2008 and then bounced back.

At the end of 2008, in order to regulate the macro-economy and to mitigate the impact of the financial crisis, urbanization cannot but to restart in China, with large-scale investment and construction. The urban land expanded to some extent. As a result, the urbanization rate increased from 0.8% in 2008 to 0.9% in 2009.

From the distribution of the urbanization rate in provinces and cities throughout the country, the urbanization level varied significantly among regions (see Fig. 1.8). By region, it was 56.96% in eastern China, 44.68% in central China and 38.44% in western China.

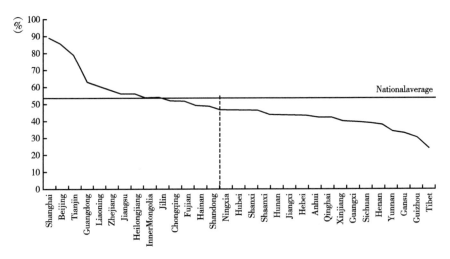

Fig. 1.8 Diagram of urbanization rate for 31 Provinces, autonomous regions and municipality directly under the Central Government (exclude: Hong Kong, Macao and Taiwan) in 2009. *Source* China Statistics Yearbook 2010

By province, the urbanization level can be divided into four tiers. To rank the urbanization level in China in descending order, the first tier included Beijing (85.01%), Tianjin (78.01%), and Shanghai (88.60%), ranking the top; the second tier (50–70%) included Guangdong, Liaoning, Zhejiang, Jiangsu, Heilongjiang, Inner Mongolia, Jilin, Chongqing and Fujian; the third tier (40–50%) include Hainan, Shandong, Ningxia, Hubei, Shanxi, Shaanxi, Hunan, Jiangxi, Hebei, Anhui, and Qinghai; the fourth tier (less than 40%) Xinjiang, Guangxi, Sichuan, Henan, Yunnan, Gansu, Guizhou, and Tibet.

1.4 Basic Problems

Just as many foreign scholars ranked the "urbanization in China" with the "High-tech in America" as the crucial factor that would shape the development of human society in the twenty-first century, urbanization in the next 50 years in the most populous developing country of China is destined to influence the global development significantly. While looking back over the China's urbanization process, it can be found that government-guided market economy system played a vital role. On one hand, it strongly stimulated the development of economy and became an important means of state's macroeconomic control. As a state-level developing program it effectively ensured the firm movement towards the urbanization targets. On the other hand, as power and market infiltrated with each other in the process of marketization, such social problems as land issue, environmental, and resource issues, city renewal and demolition, city over-expansion and sprawl, and the swell of floating population resulted from the rural–urban migration, etc. subsequently emerged.

The fundamental problems facing China in the urbanization process can be summarized as: the rural–urban segmentation system which had long handicapped the development of economy and society in China. In other words, China had to solve the problem of the dual status system that separated urban from rural residents, ultimately realize the urban and rural integration, make plans for both urban and rural as a whole, and subsequently blazing a trail with Chinese characteristics, by which urbanization, industrialization, and agriculture modernization would promote mutually and develop coordinately. The intention of this book is to study and analyze this problem from the perspective of strategic pattern.

To explore and solve the problems above, particular mention should be made to the following aspects.

First, the long-standing contradiction of the dual status system that separate urban from rural residents should be resolved. Urbanization in the world features population shifting from rural to urban areas. Although the same happened in China, it differs considerably from other countries. Because the separation of urban from rural residents was made by the household registration system, most of the farmers who moved into cities could not fully enjoy the urban residents' welfare. Consequently, most of the farmers or migrant workers have kept moving between cities and countries over the last 30 years of reform. Because the population shift from rural to urban areas in China is in extremely large quantities, the pressure China face is rarely seen. The system transformation is a very difficult task. Therefore, we should, on one hand, press ahead with urbanization and system reform; on the other hand, we must realize that there should be a buffer zone, for the reform cannot be accomplished in one move. The book, giving attention to the above two aspects of reform, analyzes the pushing strategies for the urbanization with Chinese characteristics such as, advancing urbanization by taking advantage of "Development Zones" and "Special Economic Zones", as well as the buffering and gradual means and methods.

Second, discussions are needed about the reform of household registration system. The household registration system, created within a particular historical context, is the most crucial cause of the rural–urban segmentation system. Since the beginning of reform and opening-up, governments at all levels have been trying to implement various reforms, but until now, the reform of household registration system, as an institutional overhaul, is still at the experimental and exploratory stage. Recently, the Ministry of Public Security has given permission to local governments to make experimental reforms on the household registration system tailored to suit local conditions. We will look more closely at these efforts later in the book.

Third, to change the status of farmers or migrant rural workers is an unprecedented challenge. The most distinctive feature of the household registration system is that it puts people in different categories according to where they are born and registered at birth. The two basic categories are urban residency status and rural residency status, between which there is a world of difference. The key factor here is the two different systems of public services in cities and countries. Generally speaking, urban citizens enjoy more public service resources than people living in rural areas. How farmers or migrant workers can officially become urbanites is a serious problem with no easy solution.

Fourth, the social integration of farmers, migrant workers, and floating population takes time and effort. The success of residency status change of the farmers or migrant workers doesn't necessarily mean that they could integrate into urban society. This book, then, examines at greater length how farmers integrate into cities, presents such issues as "semiintegration" and "nonintegration", explores the social distance between migrant workers and urban residents, and discusses the alternatives for the "migrant workers in New Era" and their children to integrate into cities, etc.

Fifth, the general strategy of adopting a differentialdifferential urbanization model should be recognized. As mentioned above, the diversity of urbanization models is not yet fully appreciated, and China went somewhat haphazardly from trying to build mega-cities, to building big cities, to limiting the size of big cities, to encouraging the establishment of "small quasi-city towns". Lack of recognition of developing medium and small cities in a long period has caused development imbalance among large, medium, and small cities, which restrains cities' ability to absorb migrants. Moreover, because of some restrictive factors, such as traditional planning model and investment threshold of infrastructure facilities, most big and medium cities choose to expand by sprawling to nearby districts. Center areas show a trend of high-density development in general, with the exposure of many problems, such as crowded dwellings, inadequate and low-leveled public facilities, insufficient afforesting areas and outdoor places for public activities, heavy traffic, awkward public transport, too many potential risks of disaster prevention, and security. Stimulated by the benefits of land development, urban fringe area presents a trend of hasty and disordered expansion, resulting in such problems as lacking intensification in land using, insufficient matched public facilities, etc. In addition, regardless of the requirement of industrial development and the characteristics of city development, some big and medium cities indiscriminately pursue "urbanization" and high-end urban district such as CBD, causing serious fault in urban development. What is mentioned here is related to the recognition and handle of overall strategy of urbanization in our country, which will be dealt with in more details in this book.

Sixth, how should we evaluate the important position and functions of the medium and small cities? At present, the development of small quasi-city towns in China is confronted with an awkward situation. Lack of organic coordination and cooperation among widely-scattered small quasi-city towns or between small cities, these small cities and towns do not possess distinctive urban functions, but disordered construction and management. Similar to enlarged villages, they suffered from "county disease" in the process of urban construction. Meanwhile, small cities have a relatively low level of intensification, low economic efficiency and high-energy consumption. Therefore, this book, from the dimension of overall development strategy, gives priority to the development of medium-sized cities, emphasizes the conception of county economy, attaching importance to the strategy of developing the county-economy-based medium-sized cities.

Seventh, the relationship between the urban and rural development should be well handled. For a long period, the transformation of traditional agriculture and agriculture modernization has not been included in the overall development plan of urbanization, neglecting the importance of lifestyle urbanization in rural areas. As a result, the faster the cities grow, the bigger the gap between cities and rural areas is. Meanwhile, large population shift from rural to urban areas causing the deterioration of employment, residence environment, etc. in some areas. However, urban development basically relies on taking land resource in rural areas. The Constitution of the People's Republic of China stipulates that the ownership of land in cities and rural areas is distinctively different, so urban expansion into rural areas aroused many social conflicts and problems. When analyzing the causation of frequent mass events, we can find that the primary incentive of those events is the land requisition, house demolition, and transformation in rural areas. Such contradiction and conflicts caused by them are always fierce. Therefore, how to deal with the land in rural areas, the farmers' land and realize urban–rural integration is another subject to be explored in this book.

Making a comprehensive view of the China's urbanization process over the last three decades, according to the analysis on the current situation of urbanization and the slowdown of urbanization growth rate, China has entered into a stable development phase of urbanization. Nevertheless, the foundation of system and the policy orientation are not free from the old patterns and inertia yet. Urbanization, considered and applied as a means of economy, is expected to solve "the problems facing China's agriculture, rural areas and farmers" as well as the problem of surplus rural laborers. Policies and measures are simply made according to present economic interests and development need.

Urbanization rate is one measure of a country's level of modernization. In the next 30 years, the urbanization rate in China will likely grow from 50 to 70%, an average annual increase of about one percentage point (or 10 million people out of rural areas and into urban ones). As a comprehensive and systematic process of modernization, urbanization has its own logic and direction, requiring more understanding of its significance over social progress and social structure transformation. When urbanization lags behind industrialization, as is what is taking place in China, not only are economic growth and structural adjustment hampered, but the country faces growing crisis in population, resources and environment.[13] It must be noticed that it is of great theoretical and practical significance for economic structure adjustment, boosting domestic demand, and creating new civic society to eliminate the confinement of urban–rural dual system and farmer residency status

---

[13]Bai (2003).

and deepen policy reform and system construction for urbanization have. When summarizing the process of urban development since the founding of PRC, we found the following:

First, the precondition of urbanization in China was national industrialization and modernization. Urbanization, as a kind of restricted factor, subordinated and gave way to the development of industrialization in a long period of time. Although it provided the essential basis for the accumulation of the country, it confined the economic stimuli and social resources for a long and sustainable development of the society. As a result, a basic pattern took shape: urbanization lagged behind industrialization.

Second, the structural framework of urbanization in China was established at the beginning of the foundation of PRC. On the one hand, it produced the urban–rural separation system; on the other hand, it set up a government-guided model of urbanization. This kind of structural framework still plays an important role nowadays, but we should be aware of that with the deepening of urbanization it has exerted negative influence on the balanced urbanization development of cities and regions, although it had relative advantages at the initial stage of the development.

Third, the urbanization process in China has become increasingly open and proactive and is creating cities of ever larger scales. Urban development in China has been influenced increasingly by globalization, regional economic integration, the rise of network society and civil society, etc. In order to deal with the economic and social problems caused by urbanization, it is quite necessary to make a comprehensive, systematic, forward-looking strategic plan with the overall situation being considered, to integrate and coordinate specified planning of different departments, and to set up urban administrative organizations with well-defined power and responsibility and coordinating and unifying functions.

Fourth, urbanization has become the core of and a crucial factor for advancing reform and opening up. The success of urbanization is related to the overall situation of reform, stability and development. With the proceeding of urbanization, the available land resources are decreasing steadily, urban expansion model based on land economy becomes unsustainable. Problems caused by the transformation of urban lifestyle, beliefs, and social structure are increasing. Therefore it should be taken into special consideration how to introduce social participation, realize social equity and justice in urban growth, and mitigate the adverse impact of social differentiation brought be rapid development, when making policies and working out solutions in the following period.

References

Bai, N. (2003). Urbanization in China. *Management World, 11*.

Hou, L. (2010). A new interpretation of the history of urbanization under the planned economy in China. *Urban Planning Forum, 2*.

Li, Q., & Yang, K. (2007). *Urban Sprawl*. China Machine Press.

Tu, W. (1996). Genering strategy on urbanization in modern China and modernization in urban area. *Jianghan Forum, 1*.

Wang, Y. (2001). Choice and obstacles: Urbanization in China. *Strategy and Management, 1*.

Xu, X., et al. (1995). Profile and statistics of the major sectors of modern Shanghai Industry. *Research on Shanghai, 10*, 137.

Zhang, Z. (Ed.). (1996). *Southeast coastal cities and modernization in China* (p. 429). Shanghai: Shanghai People's Publishing House.

Zhao, Y. (1988). Theoretical reviews and commentaries: Chinese pattern of urbanization. In W. Ye (Ed.), *Exploration of the urbanization in China*. China Zhanwang Press.

Zhao, W., & Xie, S. (1987). *Handbook of Chinese cities* (p. 796). Economic Science Press.

Zhao, W., & Xie, S. (1988). *A history of Chinese population* (p. 626). People's Publishing House.

Chapter 2
Theoretical Explorations of a Differential Urbanization Model

The particularities of China such as large population, vast territory, uneven development between east and west regions, and wide gap between urban and rural areas, determined the fact that the urbanization in China cannot easily and blindly follow one single pattern. During the rapid social and economic development, there was still a large room for promoting the urbanization rate of China which was 50% at present, in the next two or three decades. Different from market-oriented development model in the west, the government-guided administrative system played a very important role in China's urbanization process. Therefore, it deserved a deep and thorough exploration on issues such as what kind of urbanization models should be selected and what strategies should be adopted to push ahead with further urbanization.

First, this chapter analyses the particularities of the foundation and conditions of urbanization in China. Second, from the perspective of the "differentialdifferential sizes of towns and cities" and the "differentialdifferential driving forces", it reviewed the theory of "urbanization with a differentialdifferential process" and put forward the basic principles for carrying out the urbanization with a differentialifferential process. At last, it analyzed the overall strategic planning for advancing urbanization and explored the characteristics of a differentialdifferential urban society formed on the basis of urbanization with a differentialdifferential process.

2.1 The Particularities of the Foundations and Conditions of Urbanization in China

To under what makes China's urbanization unique, we must first understand the general background against which it is taking place. We would like to highlight the following are five aspects.

© Social Sciences Academic Press 2020
Q. Li, *China's Development under a Differential Urbanization Model*,
Research Series on the Chinese Dream and China's Development Path,
https://doi.org/10.1007/978-981-13-9451-5_2

First, China is the most populous country in the world. According to the Sixth Nationwide Census, Mainland China had a population of 1.34 billion. Rural population was still over 67.4 million, which includes the floating population that has resided in cities over the preceding 6 months. Urbanization meant scattered rural population would gradually move to urban areas. Such large population urbanization is unprecedented in world history, which requires massive infrastructure investment and construction and large-scale industrial restructuring to assimilate rural population. Urbanization also meant effort made by millions of population to embrace the modern lifestyle of urban civilization.

Second, the long-accumulated urbanization pressure is intense. Compared with countries at the same level of economic development, China apparently lags behind in urbanization rate. This is partly because, before reform and opening-up began in 1978, tight policies were in place that restricted urbanization. At one point, a policy was "counter-urbanization" (i.e., dispersing urban population) was adopted. After the start of reform and opening-up, China urbanized more slowly than it industrialized.[1] As a result, tensions have been building for a long time, putting the country under growing pressure to expedite the urbanization process in order to catch up with what process it has made in industrialization. In recent years, governments in different regions proposed to speed up urbanization in order to solve the long-accumulated contradictions in a short term. However, such methods often led to much more serious social contradictions and problems.

Third, the gap between rural and urban areas showed its own particularities. Through out the history, China was a country of great difference, especially the difference between rural and urban areas. In recent years, China's economy was developing rapidly and attracted the world's attention. However, the rapid development didn't narrow down the gap between rural and urban areas. Until now, the consumption level of urban residents was still three times more than that of rural areas.[2] The large cities in eastern China formed sharp contrast to those impoverished and backward rural areas in western China in terms of living standard, living style, infrastructure, and investment. Given such a wide gap between rural and urban areas, it was completely unrealistic to solve it in one action and in a short term by advancing urbanization.

Fourth, there was a household registration system in China. By far, a country with such a strict household registration system like China was rarely seen. After three decades' reform, many social welfare and security were gradually detached from the household registration system. But it was still closely linked to many resources such as the education resource of College Entrance Exam. In February 2012, the General Office of State Council promulgated "The Notice of Advancing Carefully the Reform of Household Registration System". The notice had two

---

[1]Li et al. (2009).

[2]"In 2009, the per capita consumption expenditure of urban and rural residents in China was respectively 12,265 and 3993 yuan." *China Statistical Yearbook (2010)*. Compiled by National Bureau of Statistics of People's Republic of China, China statistics press, 2010.

meanings. The first one was to vigorously advance the household registration system reform while the second one was to advance it carefully and properly. Though active measures should be taken to advance the reform, careful and proper methods must be emphasized. In other words, it would harm the interests of rural residents instead if their household registration status were changed from rural to urban, with an infringement of their cultivated and housing land.

Fifth, the development stages of urbanization were complicated. The path of urbanization in the developed countries showed clearly different stages. Generally, it underwent such stages as concentration, dispersion, gentrification, etc. However, due to the wide difference among regions, developed regions and the underdeveloped regions were on completely different stages. Developed regions such as Beijing, Shanghai, or Guangzhou had entered the second stage (dispersion) while most mid-western areas were still at the first stage (concentration). Gentrification also appeared in several cities. Therefore, China's urbanization was characterized by various development stages coexisting at the same time. Such complexity usually resulted in the failure of policies to reach every aspect of a matter. Policy regarding the first stage was bound to be contradictory to that of the second stage.[3]

2.2 One Size Fits All or Differentiated? A Question About Basic Approach

Given the unbalanced social development among different regions and areas in China, the path of urbanization should not follow one single pattern. Instead, principles taking into account the different situations in different regions should be adopted. Compatible urbanization strategies should be chosen according to different situations. As a result, the process of China's urbanization should be differentiated. Based on my own research, the consideration for urbanization in most cities of China was more or less uniform, mostly government-guided, with the standard of advancing urbanization being one that imposed uniformly in all cases. Some local government in certain areas even adopted aggressive measures to push forward in order to achieve higher urbanization level in a short time of a few years.

Nowadays, the government-guided urbanization model, on one hand, was related to the traditional centralized system in China, which was branded with all-embracing government. On the other land, it was also related to the strong motivation of local governments. Generally speaking, the developed areas showed more initiatives towards urbanization and their local governments had stronger guiding impetus. Judged by the problems in the process of urbanization, the impetus from government, to an extent, could compensate the imperfection of market economy, but the effect was limited. Defect and problem were inevitable for a uniform government-guided pattern, leading to numerous social contradictions

---

[3]Li (2004).

and conflicts. Given China's vast territory and complex, unbalanced development, a differential urbanization model should be taken into consideration.

The urbanization process was differential. Urbanization in developed countries underwent a concentration-dispersion path. Developing countries also had their own different levels and different paths of urbanization. From the experience of the western developed countries, the participants involved were differential and the development paths were different with their unique characteristics at different stages. None of them took a uniform process.

As is well-known, the differential urbanization model in the western countries was accompanied by a long evolution of cities and towns. Starting from the Industrial Revolution in Great Britain in the middle-eighteenth century, urbanization took several hundred years in western countries. The path with many factors involved, such as market and nongovernment forces, led to a slow pace of and dispersed urbanization. Especially when it came to spatial planning, it was hard to carry out due to people's conflicting opinions.

Therefore, the differential urbanization model in China should be suitable to the conditions in China, which means we cannot blindly follow or copy the model of urbanization in the developed western countries. In terms of social foundation, civic society was much more developed in western countries while China lacked the soil for NGOs. In the renovation project of the old town of Nanchizi in Beijing, the then vice mayor of Beijing, Zeng Guangshou, attempted to promote public participation, but failed due to the residents' lack of impetus of self-organization. So we should strike a balance between the differential models of the developed countries and traditional uniform model of China so as to explore an urbanization model suitable for China.

2.3   A Differential Urbanization Model

What was the model of urbanization with a differential process? There was no unified definition in the academic circle. Different perspective led to different understanding, for instance, the differential sizes of cities and towns, the differential development forms, the differential patterns of population mobility, the differential driving forces of urbanization, the differential leading industries of urbanization, etc.[4] However, discussion centered on two aspects—a differential urbanization model based on the scale of cities and towns and a differential urbanization model based on driving force.

---

[4]Yan (2004).

2.3.1 A Differential Urbanization Model that Factors in City Size

It had been a long time to explore the urbanization model from the perspective of the scale of cities and towns. According to the researches, it could be summarized as the following basic models at present.

The first one was small quasi-city town model. China was the most populous country with large surplus labor. Cities especially large ones can hardly accommodate such large population and offer them employment. The solution was then to develop small quasi-city towns, moving large number of farmers from countryside to the neighboring small quasi-city towns. The development of small quasi-city town emphasized on the population employment and the connection between cities and rural areas. This model was particularly suitable for the densely-populated Southern China, where considerable progress was witnessed, absorbing more than 100 million people. Moreover, small quasi-city town could serve as a transition during the process of urbanization. When condition permitted and reasonable planning made, small quasi-city town could upgrade to the next level— medium-size town. However, the small quasi-city town model had its own limitations. It might lead to small quasi-city town springing up all over the place and the waste of resources if the impetus for development was not sufficient. For less densely populated northern and mid-western areas, this model was not suitable.

The second one was medium-size town model. Reliance on small quasi-city towns or small cities was not a solution to the problem of surplus labor in rural China. Compared to the low profit of investment and the severe waste of land in small cities or small quasi-city towns, medium-size town with a population of around 500 thousand had its unique advantages—the aggregation effect of industrial production and the avoidance of the disadvantages of overpopulation in large cities or metropolis. Compared with investment returns of "small quasi-city town" developing strategy, funds put into certain numbers of medium-size cities would play a better role of absorbing population and change the irrational structure of cities in China. According to the city center geographic theory, the appropriate proportion of super city, large city, medium-size city, and small city was 1:3:9:27. However, in the Chinese city structure, the number of medium-size and small cities was relatively small. The unbalanced city structure undermined the aggregation effect of a certain area. According to the theory of central place, it was appropriate to develop 1300 medium and small-sized cities, which meant that half of 1635 unrecognized county towns should be developed into medium-size cities. The development of medium-size cities centering on the county towns was also convenient for the rural–urban population shift.

The third was large-city model. Large city usually had solid foundation of industry and municipal infrastructure and well-established public service facilities such as education and medical service. Swarming into large cities to work and live, people would benefit from the scale and aggregation effect of economy, turning the cities into the core of the area. The advantages of large city and super city were even more prominent in Asia. Asian countries were usually densely-populated with limited resource. Therefore, to develop large city and super city became an important option of urbanization for many Asian countries. For instance, in countries like Japan, South Korea, Thailand, etc., super cities were places where most population gathered, and Singapore and Hong Kong were areas where super cities aggregated.

The fourth was city group, city belt, and city circle model, an extension of super city. From the process of urbanization, city group, city belt, and city circle were at a more advanced stage of urbanization. With the benefits of institutional thickness, large city groups and belts were favorable to efficient allocation of resources, promoting the development of its surrounding areas and boost economic growth. In China, city-dense areas emerged with different characteristics such as the Beijing–Tianjin–Hebei city cluster group with Beijing and Tianjin as the core, Yangtze River Delta and Pearl River Delta characterized by dense city and town clusters.

The fifth was a model that could be called "urbanization of rural life". The basic meaning of urbanization was the aggregation of population and agricultural production transferring to nonagriculture industry. From the experience of developed countries, it was a period of middle-class aggregation and extending and moving to suburban areas. The fundamental social significance of which was lifestyle was no longer a traditional rural one. The suburban life had no difference from urban life. Therefore, in contemporary society, urbanization itself became a lifestyle, that was, a modern civilized lifestyle created by urban residents, which could be popularized in rural areas.

In conclusion, one of the most prominent features of Chinese society was the uneven development between regions. From the perspective of urbanization, such unbalance of economic development between different regions formed a differentialdifferential urbanization model. Therefore, no uniform standard should be enforced in urbanization in China. Specific conditions of particular areas should be taken into consideration and the related urbanization factors such as industry, land, natural resources, and population should be analyzed so that suitable urbanization models could be adopted by different regions and areas.

2.3.2 A Diversified Urbanization Process Based on Driving Force

The city and town scale mainly explored how city and town aggregated, a study on the development model of urbanization from objective and outcome. However, no matter what models were taken, the actual driving force was more concerned about the reality of the regional development. Therefore, it was of great importance to study the driving force.

Due to the particular situations in China, the driving force bore different features from that of western countries. Based on the comparison of domestic and international experience, this book put forwards the notion of the "driving force" of urbanization. In a word, the prominent feature of China's urbanization was government-guided, planning for large area, and integrated pushing, which were dealt with theoretically in Chap. 4 of Part Two of this book.

In China, we can identify seven types of driving force and spatial structure: establishing development zone, building new district and city, expanding city, renovating old city, developing CBD and industrialization of towns and villages. More details were discussed from Chaps. 5–11 of Part Two.

Besides the abovementioned seven driving forces of urbanization, it was necessary to fully recognize some special factors in the process of urbanization. (1) the radiate effect of the administrative center; given that the political and economic development was mostly state-guided in Chinese society, administrative center usually played an essential role to its surrounding cities and towns. (2) The driving force of large project; the construction of large national and provincial project had an immense influence on the development of cities and towns. (3) The stimulus of foreign capital; the influx of large amount of foreign capital in the coastal prosperous areas accelerated the progress of urbanization. (4) the initiative factors in the densely-populated areas; Due to the high density of population, rural labor voluntarily moved to cities and towns in the Yangtze River Delta area where the tradition of handicraft industry and business activity were long. Under the abovementioned factors, the model of China's urbanization demonstrated some important subtypes, for instance, key project-driven type, self-organized development type (typical examples was Southern Jiangsu Model and Wenzhou Model), external force-driven type such as foreign investment-driven type, border trade-driven type and tourism-driven type.

In the meantime, the abovementioned seven driving forces of urbanization were closely related to the urbanization models based on the differential scales of cities. Generally speaking, different urbanization strategies had their own driving forces and means, with certain corresponding relations between them. The stimulus and inducing factor of urbanization such as center-radiation, key project-driven, foreign investment-driven, and self-organized migration in densely-populated areas could be integrated and arranged into the driving forces of urbanization. Issues such as what the corresponding relation between the two factors was, whether certain derivative driving forces or subtypes would emerge in the actual progress of urbanization, what kind of combination between driving forces and pushing factors would emerge, and what kind of combination would generate better associative effects would be dealt with in Part Two. Moreover, it was certain that the misfit between driving force and urbanization model would lead to immeasurable loss. In that sense, the selection of driving force was an extension of the choice of the strategic model of urbanization.

2.3.3   The Basic Principles for Pushing Ahead
with the Diversified Process of Urbanization

While discussing the details of the abovementioned differential urbanization models, attention should be paid to the basic principles of pushing urbanization in China. The principles could be summarized as the following five relations.

The first was the relation between industrial model and urbanization model. From the driving impetus of urbanization, urbanization was the result of social and economic growth such as the spatial aggregation of industry. As industrialization proceeded rapidly, the concentricity and consistency of production and the commercialization of products made economic activities aggregated in geographic space. At different stages of industrialization, the structure transformation of industry carried different characteristics of urbanization. The rural and urban areas, and city and city interacted. Industry was the fundamental driving force of urban development. Different forms of industry and development features might lead to different urbanization models. Concentrated industrialization usually led to large-city model. For instance, the model of developing heavy industry at the early days after the founding of PRC led to rapid growth of large cities. While the industrialization based on industrial chains generally resulted in clusters of medium-size and small cities and towns, such as the urban development model in the Pearl River Delta and Yangtze River Delta. By the same token, other forms of industry would lead to different urban development models. Therefore, when determining the objective of urbanization model by a certain area, the types, characteristics, and development level of local industry should be considered prior to others.

The second was the relationship between government and market in urbanization. Market-only model or Laisser-faire urban development model usually led to the uneven development between regions, widening gap between urban and rural areas, inefficient land utilization, and lack of urban planning. But plan-only model often led to the rigidization and singularization of urbanization, insensitive to the ever-changing urbanization process, thus slowing down the speed of urbanization.

The third was the relation between urban and rural areas in urbanization. Appropriate choice of urbanization model should follow the principle of mutual development of modern city and agriculture. The modern agriculture, characterized by the increase in productivity, and countryside should transform synchronously and their corresponding rural lifestyle should be replaced by urban lifestyle, changing fundamentally the dual-structure relationship between urban and rural areas. The integrative development of urban and rural areas should be the core concept to be persisted in implementing the differential urbanization strategies.

The fourth was the relation between population intake capacity and rational city layout structure, which was closely linked to the first kind of relation. That's to say, different driving forces of industry would result in different population migrating models such as migrating locally or long distance migrating, etc. The factor of population mobility would to a large extent influence the city layout structure, the number and the scale structure of different types of city.

The fifth was the relation between urban development and resources utilization. It mainly included land resource and water resource, etc. The per capita area of cultivated farmland in China was half less than the average level in the world. Due to the lack of cultivated farmland and the fragile ecosystem, the lessons of "over suburbanization" and "over dispersed layout" should be learnt and increase the efficiency of land utilization in urbanization. In different framework of urbanization models, the major methods of intensive resources utilization would be different. The World Bank's report on China's urbanization gave a comprehensive analysis on the influence of China's urbanization and pointed out that the strategy of China's urbanization should take many factors into consideration and pay attention to the sustainable development and utilization of energy and resource and made it a national strategy.[5]

In conclusion, from the history and lessons of China's urbanization, the suitable urbanization path and model of a country or region depended on the characteristics of its industry, social development level, cultural environment as well as energy and resources.

2.4 Three Plan in One: Making Overall Plans Based on the Strategy of Urbanization with a Diversified Process

2.4.1 The Integration of the National Development Plan for Priority Zones, Land and Resources Plan and Urban Planning

In terms of national plans, the Development Strategy of City Agglomeration in the 12th Five-Year Plan and The National Development Plan for Priority Zones are compiled by the National Development and Reform Committee (NDRC) and released by the State Council. The latter had been included into the Development Strategy of City Agglomeration. The National Development Plan for Priority Zones (hereinafter "Planning") released by the State Council was a strategic, fundamental and binding plan for land and space resources utilization. Other similarly weighty plans included the Urban Plan by the Construction Department and Land Resources Plan by land and resources department. Besides, every five years NDRC would compile the "National Economic Development Plan". It can be concluded that the three above-mentioned plan were currently implementing in China. So far, these

---

[5]Shahid and Tony (2008).

plans were mainly governed by the State Council, while compiled, implemented and supervised by Ministries, departments and local government at all levels.

The four plans often conflicted with each other in implementation. These conflicts are partly attributable to complex historical factors, barrier between different departments and conflicting interest of divisions. First of all, urban planning, as the most important aspect for the development of a city, was attached with great importance. In their long-run working, the construction department had established comprehensive and systematic working system and manning. In comparison, the department of land and resource was relatively weak in terms of planmaking and personnel schedule. Their emphasis, for most time, was laid on monitoring the bottom line of land utilization and approving the change of land utilization. The plan made by NRDC paid more attention to economic development. However, the connection and coordination between the National Economic Development Plan. the Urban Plan and Land and Resources Plan still had much room for improvement. Although The National Development Plan for Priority Zones promulgated recently made its first step as the "top-level design" in national spatial planning,[6] there lacked sufficient administrative organizations with specific responsibilities to enforce these overall strategic planning. At the same time, there lacked corresponding, systematic and specific measures to integrate all the other planning.

2.4.2 Establishing an Overall Strategic Planning System for Land and Space Use

In order to build an effective, coordinated and sustainable pattern of land and space development, it was necessary to arrange and make an overall strategic planning for land and space, covering the Urban Plan, Land and Resources Plan and The National Development Plan for Priority Zones in operation, and strike a balance between local development planning in different regions. The top priority of constructing such a planning system, just like the establishment of constitution and general laws and regulations, was to straighten out relation between different planning. Only the well-coordination between top-level design and low-level planning could eradicate the system of "numerous planning coexisting" with conflicting standards.

An overall strategic planning for land and space should coordinate with the national economy development plan and have an important and equal position. An overall strategic planning for land and space should be the spatial implementation of national economic development. Therefore, it would be necessary to set up an administrative organization with comprehensive management capacity and

---

[6]"State Council 2010: No. 46," that is *The Program of National Development Priority Zones, 2010-12-21.* In which, it was made clear the aim of the program was to build efficient, coordinated and sustainable national land and spatial development patterns.

specified power to prepare the planning, organize, and train qualified personnel. It was necessary to transfer the personnel from the existing construction sectors, land and resources sectors, the National Development and Reform Commission (NDRC) and local governments to set up a new organization—Land and Space Planning and Management Department. Only in this way, would the "planning" have well-defined subject of legal responsibility, and an effective, coordinated, and sustainable planning system with specified power and responsibility would be established.

When making an overall strategic planning for land and space, the concrete methods of pushing urbanization should be considered comprehensively according to the strategy of urbanization with a differential process and the development conditions in different areas and regions. The planning should not just be confined to an overall strategy, it should move further to the controlled planning of certain professional fields, such as ecological protection, afforestation, and so on. More effort should be made to establish and improve the national, regional and urban planning and index package, statistic system and dynamic supervisory system. For instance, as the implementation of city groups strategy and priority zone strategy, China was pursuing or intended to pursue the urbanization model that several key city circles merged into super city groups and city belts. This kind of urbanization model would unavoidably encounter with different regions, departments and interest groups with their corresponding demands and claims in terms of profit distribution and cost compensation. To meet these demands and claims, how to establish a coordinated profit and distribution system in an overall way, how to coordinate different interest groups and achieved an overall maximization of profits, and eventually turned them into the common interest of all the people, should be considered so that the present overall strategic planning system would be further improved, specified and more enforceable. For instance, in the implementation of Bohai city agglomeration strategy, how to implement and coordinate the development planning with environmental protection and ecological construction deserved a thorough research and exploration. On one hand, the environmental protection and ecological construction carried obvious externality and would not pay off in a short term. On the other hand, though different regions and departments had made their own conservation planning regarding urban afforestation, environmental protection, and water resource protection, in recent years, mass events caused by environment deterioration increased rapidly. In terms of development planning, on one hand, it needed to be improved and specified. On the other hand, it was necessary to integrate all kinds of planning, establish administrative organizations, and systems at regional level, and made further controlled planning.

It would take a long way to change from "multiple planning coexisting" to "a singular master plan". It would also take great efforts to establish and improve the planning system and its staff functions. To select a suitable development model according to actual economic, social, and cultural conditions, and the carrying capacity of energy, resources and environment, was the prerequisite of making an overall strategic planning, establishing and improving planning system and staff functions, enhancing well-coordinated urbanization, and effectively managing urban development. We should make an overall strategic planning for land and space according to the strategy of urbanization with a differential process, integrate all existing planning, tolerate different interest groups, ease conflicts through negotiation, establish a dynamic planning system, and place urban development in the framework of laws and regulations so as to form a sustainable, long-term and dynamic development system. Only in this way could we make the key step to the last gateway on China's path to modernization—the becoming of new urban society.

2.5 Formation of a Diverse Urban Society

2.5.1 Social Structure Transition: A Differential Urbanization Model and the Formation of Urban China

The renowned scholar Kingsley Davis pointed out that it marks a new and fundamental step in the evolution of human society when the majority of a population lives in urban areas. He described with S-curve the urbanization of western society from the Middle Ages to 1960s–1970s and indicated that when the urbanization rate reached 60%, it would slow down and stay more or less constant.

With regard to the urbanization rate in China, different scholars held different opinions. By far, the estimation made by the Ministry of Construction in 2004 was positive, holding that by 2020, the urbanization rate in China would be 60%. At least, the urbanization rate of China in 2013 surpassed 50%, and theoretically could be defined as urban society. According to The Sixth National Census in 2010, the urbanization rate of China was 49.68%. Hereby, if the urbanization rate was underestimated due to the household registration factor, it would be of no doubt that the urbanization rate of China had surpassed 50%. In other words, the goal of China's urbanization rate had achieved 3 years ahead of time than estimated 2003. Thereby, it could be asserted that, at least theoretically, urban society had formed in China and an urban China was born.

Modern urban society was a society of high degree of complexity, which was mainly reflected in the" rationalization" tendency of capitalist development in city operation. Max Weber held that modern city was a social form in essence allowing maximally individuality and peculiarity. He then, called city the tool of historical change and believed that city was a series of social structures encouraging individuality and social innovation, and facilitated various lifestyles.[7] While German

---

[7]Richard (1969).

sociologist Georg Simmel emphasized the complexity of urban life—to cope with the complexity of urban life, people would rather live in an unemotional, rational, and functional social relation.[8]

In urban study, Chicago School believed that the rational urban society gave birth to urbanism processed by cities, telling countryside from cities. Louis Wirth named "Urbanism - as a way of life". And he believed that was resulted from the city scale, density, and heterogeneity.[9] Reviewing on the classic theories of urban study, we reached a basic consensus that urban society was a new-type of social pattern, in which coexisted a series of social structures such as rationalization versus marketization, social isolation versus social innovation, and diversity versus complexity.

As to the urbanization process in contemporary China, the concurrence of urbanization and social structure transformation is particularly noteworthy. With the deepening of urbanization, the formation of urban society implied the transformation of social structure was accomplished or tended to be accomplished. The emergence of new-types of cities and mega-cities induced by the urbanization with a differential process meant that the socio-organizing form became more complicated and systematic. In the process of transformation, great changes would take place in people's concept and lifestyle. In order to adapt to these changes, superstructure had to change accordingly.

From a broader historical perspective, China's urbanization process has been accompanied by a spiral rising route, in another word, urbanization stimulated the transformation of social structure, exerting more pressure on the changes of superstructure. With the reform at the system level, new urban culture as well as the new systems and social structure based on it was formed.

For instance, the last urbanization in China took place from the end of the nineteenth to the early twentieth centuries. Joseph W. Esherick believed that after the Sino-Japanese War of 1894–1895, the country gentries moved to cities and established modern schools, industries and business because of the pressure from outside.[10] John K. Fairbank, the renowned China scholar, pointed out that the urbanization tide led by the rural gentry was the result of rural elites moving into cities for education and wealth.[11] This urbanization at the turning point of the twentieth century was an oxytocic for the birth of new social structure, the disintegration of patriarchal clan, the growth of entry capitalism, the rise of cities and the following short-term change—the disintegration of Qing Dynasty.[12] During this process of urbanization, the main participants involved were rural elites or local gentry. What deserved mentioning was, this urbanization laid the social groundwork for the later New Culture Movement, promoted the development of localism,

---

[8]Richard (1969).

[9]Louis (1938).

[10]Zhou (1980).

[11]John (2006).

[12]Jin and Liu (2010).

collapsed the central authority, and disorganized the clan, the cell of patriarchal society. The large scale urbanization at the early twentieth century gave birth to the mega-cities like Wuhan and Shanghai, brewing the later New Culture Movement which was the cultural consciousness of the emerging urban class. The impact of this round of urbanization on the Chinese social structure was significant and far-reaching.

The urbanization we were experiencing at present was the second round of urbanization in China. From the beginning of 1990s, with the establishment of socialist market economy, the urbanization process accelerated. Compared with the previous "gentry urbanization", this round of urbanization could be called as "farmer urbanization". Large numbers of young and middle-aged rural laborers flooded into cities, draining the rural labor force while disrupting the rural social order at the grass-roots level. Some were so concerned as to claim that "Agriculture is in danger!" Urban problems became increasingly serious. On the one hand, the integration of urban society was difficult. Urban–rural gap existed and identity discrimination were prevalent. Great number of migrant workers traveled back and forth between cities and rural areas. On the other hand, cities rapidly expanded and grew both in scale and in density, fostering structural tensions in urban areas. The whole society was in a state of angst and instability. From 1995 to 2008, social conflicts rose from thousands per year to eighty thousand per year. According to Yu Jianrong, most of the conflicts were caused by land and demolition, etc., many over labor disputes.[13]

Generally speaking, after 30 years of reform and opening up, especially nearly 20 years of marketization, urban society was taking shape or at least had its initially form. The model of urbanization with a differential process and its differential driving forces would directly decide the types of urban society to be formed. From "rural China" to "Urban China", the model of urbanization with a differential process would have a far-reaching influence on the long-term development of Chinese society.

2.5.2 Disputing Over Urban Society: Diversified Urban Society and its Influence

Our knowledge about urban society was primarily based on our understanding about cities and urbanization. The most basic attributes of cities—sociality, complexity, and diversity—were often ignored by cities or urbanization. Lack of understanding of sociality resulted in social polarization, inequity and injustice in city planning and management. Lack of understanding of the issue of complexity led to simplistic thinking about city development, uncontrolled sprawling, insufficient supply of public services, appearance slums and rising crime rates. The

---

[13]Yu (2009).

ignorance of city diversity contributed to uniform and homogeneous city construction, difficult integration of migrant workers into urban society, intolerance towards different cultures, and absence of coordination mechanism that tolerated the pursuit of personal benefits by different individuals. The models of urbanization under observation till now all had defects of one kind or another as well as experiences and lessons to be learnt. Therefore, the only feasible option for China is to pursue urbanization with distinctly Chinese characteristics suitable to the country.

Contemporary urban society is a social form characterized by high levels of risk, large information flow, and complicated, differential and globalized form of social organization. Firstly, urban society was a society of high risk. High density and mobility of urban society brought with them challenges and made city-swellers vulnerable to disasters. Cities also brought higher incidence of diseases, so public health rose in response. City brought in pollution, so environmental protection rose in response. City brought in poverty and ugliness, so city beautiful movement rose in response. The demand for energy and space, the pursuit of speed and efficiency in urban areas in turn brought in the increase of living costs and risks in human society. Secondly, urban society was a kind of "information society" or "network society". Urbanization, accompanied by digitalization, informatization, and network, was forming a kind of network society, in which interpersonal communication was much faster and more efficient, and meanwhile the complexity of social system was intensified. This new change accelerates the information flows on the one hand, and on the other hand brought uncontrollable risk and instability to society. The "Arabian Jasmine Flower Revolution" which wiped out the whole Arabian world exemplified the great influential power and basic feature of network society, judging by its expanding, spreading speed and cross-border transmission. The material basis and spatial place that network society relied on was city, while its social foundation was the urban society that was gradually taking shape in Middle Eastern countries. Finally, urban society was a kind of "global urban society" or "globalized society". The modernization process in world history was itself a process of a countries establishing domestic and international markets and molding world economy.[14] Globalization established the economic network linked by "Global cities", reaching across borders and forming a certain transnational organization or economy.[15] This process of economic globalization also gave rise to the need for social integration.

We believe that the formation of urban society in China would present five challenges:

First, it would be a challenge to the public governance structure. Large-scale population urbanization would change the governance at grass-roots level in cities

---

[14]Herman (2008).
[15]Saskia (2008).

and rural areas and promote the development of urban economy, producing greater social basic needs and presenting a big challenge to social public services and management.

Second, it would be a challenge to further marketization. One of the primary sign of the forming of urban society was the rise of urban middle class, which promoted the specialization of labor division. In accordance of the view of classic economist Adam Smith, the degree of specialization of labor division indicated the level of marketization. Then, the formation of urban society would place further requirements and challenge to the economic marketization in China.

Third, the formation of urban society would bring about the transformation of lifestyle and ideas, which would diversify people's thinking, and ultimately help shape the current ideological structure together with network technology and informationization. In reference to the current situation, "the new generation of migrant workers", were becoming more aware of their own rights, collective actions and social conflicts to protect their legal rights increased. The new comers in urban area would look for ways to express their interests.

Fourth, the formation of urban society would increase pressure on the environment and lead to energy source shortage. Cities were not only the places of environment and energy consumption, but also the location of various contradictions and where different interests of different groups of people clash. Social contradictions would be intensified for resource allocation. Meantime, such enormous gap of resource allocation resulted from personal lifestyle would constitute a big challenge to the sustainable development and utilization of energy and resources in China.

Fifth, urbanization was a process of space polarization, which would greatly challenge social mobility and capital. When large population lived in urban areas, the most distinctive characteristic in space was determining social space according to economic structure, which was pointed out by many western researchers. R. E. Parks's Urban Ecology Theory based on urban social space in Chicago and E. W. Burges' Concentric Zone Theory pointed out that lower class would gather together to shape residential areas according to the spatial location of industrial structure, so the suburbanization and gentrification of cities would be inevitable. Newly formed lower class residential areas tended to solidify social mobility and form "poverty culture". Based on this, the polarization of urban space, which coming from irresistible trend of globalization, would result in further isolation of social groups of lower class, which would become more and more distinct and worsen with the slowdown of economic growth. In addition to the spatial polarization within city, the urban system formed based on "shirt-county city" would transform into a new urban network based on economic and industrial division. Megacities, metropolises and big city belts would inevitably come into being; the second-tier cities and third-tier cities would become more and more homogeneity and finally form new urban systems featured by city agglomeration. This trend is now becoming increasingly evident.

References

Herman, M. (2008). State versus market: The emergence of global economy. In: Schwaz (Ed.) (p. 50) (J. Xu. Trans.). Jiangsu People's Publishing House.

Jin, G., & Liu, Q. (2010). *The transformation of Chinese society (1840–1956)—The fate of its ultrastable structure in modern times* (pp. 102–120). Law Press China.

John, K. F. (2006). *The Cambridge history of China* (Vol. 2, p. 643). Social Sciences Publishing House.

Li, Q. (2004). *Urban migrant workers and social stratification in China* (pp. 308–309). China: Social Sciences Academic Press.

Li, Q., et al. (2009). *Study on major issues an solutions in Chinese urbanization process* (pp. 2–3). Economic Science Press.

Louis, W. (1938, July). Urbanism: As a way of life. *American Journal of Sociology*, 1–24.

Richard, S. (1969). *Class essays on the culture of cities*. New York: Meredith Corporation.

Saskia, S. (2008). *Global city: London, New York and Tokyo*. Shanghai Academy of Social Sciences Press.

Shahid, Y., & Tony, S. (2008). *China urbanizes: Consequence, strategies, and policies*. Washington, DC: World Bank.

Yan, R. (2004). Diverse urbanization in Western China. *China Public Administration, 9*.

Yu, J. (2009). Mass disturbances in present China: Types and characteristics. *Journal of CUPL, 6*.

Zhou, X. (1980). *Reform and revolution in China—The 1911 revolution in Hunan and Hubei* (p. 80) (S. Yang, Trans.). Zhonghua Book Company.

Chapter 3
The Lessons and Experiences of Urbanization and Urban Development at Home and Abroad

The Industrial Revolution marked the beginning of the most spectacular development stage in human history, that is, the process of modernization. Since then,
across the globe, the economic systems, social structures, political systems, and
cultural patterns that constitute human society have undergone tremendous change
and progress. Urbanization and industrialization are the two most important aspects
of such modernization. These aspects invariably coincide with each another in
mutual support, promoting both the growth of global wealth, and unprecedented
alterations throughout society.

Patterns of urbanization across the globe can be divided into three levels. The
first level is typical of developed countries such as the US, Japan, Soviet Russia,
and most European countries. In these countries, the urbanization process has
reached a maturity. The main problem facing these countries, therefore, is the
regeneration of existing urban functions. The second level is typical of such
countries as the "Four Little Dragons" in Asia as well as numerous Latin American
countries (e.g., South South Korea, China Taiwan, Brazil, and Argentina). These
countries have basically completed the process of industrialization and urbanization. Their main problem is to strengthen the urban effects. The third level exists in
a vast number of developing countries, especially China, India, and South Africa.

"Learning lessons from others, one can find out advantageous and disadvantageous actions; taking warnings from history, one can understand the rise and fall of
civilizations". China's urbanization is the greatest economic and social project
witnessed by the world so far. China's vast population of rural farmers, equivalent
to the population of Europe, is undergoing a geographical and social transition
towards becoming urbanized and citizenized. Such an unprecedented deed will
inevitably face unparalleled difficulties and challenges. As such, both an exploration
of historical processes of and recent trends of urbanization in other countries are,
therefore, required in order to guarantee that China's own urbanization proceeds
successfully. Only by in-depth study of the developing urbanization process in

© Social Sciences Academic Press 2020
Q. Li, *China's Development under a Differential Urbanization Model*,
Research Series on the Chinese Dream and China's Development Path,
https://doi.org/10.1007/978-981-13-9451-5_3

other countries, and learning lessons from their experiences can the entire China's urbanization process be scientifically handled, and steadily pushed forward in a factualistic manner.

3.1 The Experiences and Lessons in Urbanization to Be Learned from Developed Countries

3.1.1 United Kingdom: Endogenous Urbanization

The model of urbanization in the United Kingdom was of a typical endogenous type. That is to say, industrialization and urbanization in the United Kingdom was a historical process initiated by continuous internally motivated and driven changes to social productivity. Such a model has led processes of urbanization throughout the world since. Urbanization in the United Kingdom was completed under no pressure or time constraints and with no previous precedents. As the first nation to achieve widespread industrialization, consequently, Britain took the lead in the mass urbanization of its own population while contributing greatly to urbanization across the globe.[1] In accordance with this trend setting, the UK was the first country to implement urban planning laws, establish garden and ecological cities, enact from-cradle-to-grave urban social security systems, construct satellite towns, and, finally, witness widespread "suburbanization". Britain's experiences and patterns of urban development gave rise to the benchmark for subsequent urban development and construction across the globe.

3.1.1.1 The Four Stages of Urbanization in the UK

Early in the Opium War, the British had already completed the process of the industrial revolution. After 115 years of development, they have achieved a highly sophisticated degree of urbanization. Therefore, a historical survey of the general features of the UK's successful urbanization process may be informative. This urbanization process can be divided into three periods: First, primary urbanization during the agricultural revolution; second, stable development throughout a period of commercial revolution; third, rapid development during the industrial revolution.

Primary Urbanization During the Agricultural Revolution

Revolution in the field of agriculture triggered urbanization in the UK, primarily in accordance with the following two developments:

---

[1]Ji (2004).

A. First, the marketization of agricultural products enabled the British to transcend small-scale, self-sufficient, and primarily sustenance farming activities and, in turn, nurtured conditions for commercial trading. Arable and pastoral farming in the UK gave rise to both domestic and overseas trade from a very early stage. Even as early as the mid-sixteenth century, most of the workable land, previously part of the estates of aristocratic manors, had been sold or leased to landlords and repurposed for market. The UK had cast away from small-scaled self-sufficient agriculture economy at a very early stage. Comparatively, after 115 years (during the Opium War), China was still an empire of small-scale farms with extremely strong social stability.

B. Second, the enclosure movement freedup a great deal of land and labor. At the cost of traditional small-scale production, this integral component of the agricultural revolution gave rise to large-scale pastoral farming and, shortly after, mass agriculture. Small holdings of land were enclosed into large-scale holdings and utilized to utmost effectiveness while also laying the foundations for agricultural mechanization.[2] In addition, the enclosure movement effectively transformed parts of the landed aristocracy into capitalists who leased their land to latifundium and, thereby, gave rise to early capitalist enterprises.[3] Small-scale land-holding farmers subsequently disappeared as rural peasants became agricultural wage workers or went to cities to become industrial workers. This revolutionary movement has a complex legacy, simultaneously characterized as, on the one hand, a period of "blood-and-tears" and, on the other hand, the birth of agricultural mechanization, the commercialization of agricultural products, abundant land resources,[4] capital,[5] and labor,[6] that is to say, the prerequisite of urbanization.

Urbanization During the Commercial Revolution

Columbus's voyage was the prelude to a major shift in the European economy. That is to say, capitalism acquired a new impetus:

A. Mercantilism became the dominant economic theory and practice, bringing with it a view, widely supported by the state and population at large, that currency (e.g., gold, silver) was the measure of national wealth.[7] Thus, foreign

---

[2]Ji (2004).
[3]Ji (2004).
[4]Ji (2004).
[5]Huang and Xie (2010).
[6]Shen (2001).
[7]Huang (2010).

trade and the accumulation of currency became a priority for the national agenda. As it emerged that legitimate trade was insufficient to meet the escalating demand for wealth, illegal trade, and inhumane colonialism were looked to as alternatives.

B. Those who followed the spirit of capitalism to lucrative overseas ventures found themselves richly rewarded. The seafaring nations of Spain, Portugal, Holland, and Britain, to name a few, branded in their nationality the trait of adventurism while utilizing newly opened sea routes to bring waves of European merchant fleets to every corner of the world. As a result of this adventurism, lucrative international trade grew exponentially.

C. Newly established colonial economies, spread across vast empires, now functioned as the basis of global commerce. Britain, meanwhile, obtained maritime supremacy, plundering capital and raw materials freely. Ultimately, trade in and with overseas colonies provided the conditions for Britain to complete its urbanization movement. With the expansion of colonial regions, British foreign trade increased six-fold in the eighteenth century and London became the center of world trade.

D. A consequence of the ongoing commercial revolution was the birth of commercial capitalists, who engaged in such profit-driven enterprises as trafficking, trade, the slave trade, piracy, plundering resources, and overseas mining activities. Mercantilist economic policy was prevalent during this period of time. To encourage trade voyage, even the British royal family invested in a large number of shares in order to publically demonstrate their support.[8]

Urbanization During the Industrial Revolution

Urbanization during the Industrial Revolution began in the 1760s while it was essentially completed by the late 1830s. The whole process took just 70–80 years. Urbanization initially took place in newly industrialized villages that were previously small marinas, small fishing villages, valleys, or simply untapped mineral-rich areas. In the late eighteenth century, Britain's industrial revolution and process of townization accelerated significantly. In 1775, for example, driven by the forces of commercialization and industrialization, large-scale population migration was witnessed as waves of laborers shifted from rural areas to newly industrial regions (industrialized villages). What had been mere industrial villages, subsequently, expanded into industrial towns while small cities grew into large cities and existing large cities gave rise to city-groups. By the late nineteenth century, 70% of the population lived in cities where industrial machinery in factories had already rendered previous styles of production by hand in workshops. Underpinning this industrial revolution was unprecedented scientific and technological developments,

---

[8]The United Kingdom, *The Rise of Great Nations*, CCTV documentary.

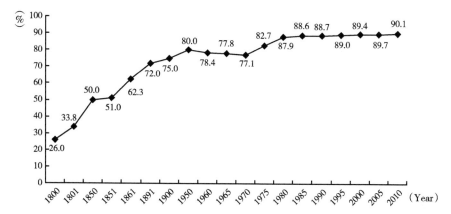

Fig. 3.1 The historical urbanization process in the UK (1800–2010, nonequal gap between years). *Source* According to data extrapolated from World Bank Open Data

as well as an almost simultaneous transportation revolution, all of which significantly increased the efficiency and profitability with which industrialists could exploit natural resources.

Towards this, from the mid-eighteenth century onwards, the population and geographical size of British cities expanded rapidly. By the 1830s, Britain could be characterized as the first country to have completed industrialization and urbanization (see Fig. 3.1). The impact of the Industrial Revolution on urbanization was decisive, that is to say, the former was, in fact, both a prerequisite to and an inevitable outcome of the latter. After all, the Industrial Revolution unquestionably enhanced both the social and economic status of cities, which became places where a myriad of public organizations and institutions, including trade centers, infrastructural projects, education and training facilities, and government administration congregated. Furthermore, transportation was becoming much easier in cities, facilitating their access to raw materials and cheap labor which, in turn, provided opportunities for manufactured goods to be sold to local residents. All in all, then, the transportation hubs of major cities were responsible for greatly increased domestic sales of goods which met the demands of not only urban residents but also villagers from surrounding areas. Urban agglomeration effect turned cities, towards which surplus rural labor from surrounding areas continued to gravitate, into cores of entire regions.

3.1.1.2 The Core Strengths of the British Model and the Internal Dynamic Mechanism

Urbanization in the UK offers many lessons that are still relevant today. Perhaps, most important is to explore the core strengths and intrinsic motivations of the period that were responsible for the UK's successful modernization. In particular, the factors considered below are especially noteworthy.

The Improvement of Agricultural Technology and the Commercialization of
Agricultural Products

Throughout the nineteenth century, the agricultural labor productivity of the UK
ranked highest in Europe. The growing consumption demands of urban life were
met through technological improvements and overall increases in agricultural
production (thanks to the Industrial Revolution). The percentage of the population
engaged in agriculture declined from 80% in 1520 to 35.9% in 1801, while agricultural productivity increased from 60 to 100%. The fact that newly established
larger farms as well as the modernization of agriculture enabled Britain to feed its
growing urban population with a declining agricultural population laid the necessary material foundations for a relatively smooth process of urbanization.[9] In
addition, the commercialization of agricultural products protected farming incomes
and the interests of, among other vulnerable groups, farmers. Comparatively,
farming technology in China underwent no qualitative changes in 50 years; the
biggest improvement, in fact, was simply replacing cattle with tractors.
Furthermore, primarily due to the consideration of costs to profits ration of agriculture, land abandonment around was a widespread phenomena across the
countryside.[10]

The Industrial Revolution Rapidly Turned Small Towns to Big Cities

Cotton and textile mills in the UK pioneered the application of machines to their
production process, which, consequently, not only expanded scales of production,
but also encourage cities and towns to expand rapidly, thereby leading to the
development of metropolises.[11] Glasgow, for example, was a small town at the end
of eighteenth century, yet by 1831 it had already become a large industrial city with
a population of over twenty million. Typical of cities across the UK, industrial
modernization in Glasgow underwent rapid development since the establishment of
its first factory in 1777. To further illustrate, by 1835 there were 1262 cotton mills
operating around the country. This establishment of factories, on such a large-scale,
meanwhile, was the principle cause of the UK's urbanization. Such a correlation
between industrialization and urbanization is typified by Manchester, the population
of which increased from 75,000 in 1801 to 351,000 in 1871.[12]

---

[9]Ji (2004).
[10]Feng (2011).
[11]Zhao (2008).
[12]Ji (2004).

The Industrial Revolution Changed the UK's Industrial Structures and
Promoted the Formation of Cities

In 1801, the UK's agricultural, industrial, and service sectors accounted for 32, 23,
and 45% of GDP, respectively, while in 1841, these figures altered to 22, 34, and
44%, respectively. The diminishing overall share of the labor force engaged in
agriculture, forestry, animal husbandry, and fishing is exemplified by the following
figures: from 40% **before 1801** to 35.9% in 1801; 21.7% in 1851; and, finally, 8.7%
in 1901. Employment in manufacturing, mining, and construction, meanwhile, rose
from 29.7% in 1801 to 46.3% in 1901. Massive portions of the urban-based
working population underwent the transformation from primary industry roles to
employment as part of the secondary and tertiary industries. Such shifts in production gradually centralized energy, means of production, sales-driven markets,
and basic service facilities, thereby equipping cities in such a way as to trigger
aggregation effects which, in turn, further promoted and accelerated urbanization in
the UK.

The Transportation Revolution Pushed the UK into a New Phase of
Urbanization

Britain's industrial revolution brought along with it a "transportation revolution"
comprised primarily of canals, steamboats, roads, and railways. Regarded the latter,
in 1836, the British Parliament approved the construction of 25 new railways, with
a total length of over 1600 km. What's more, by 1855, the total mileage of operational railways in the UK had reached 12,960 km. Consequently, a comprehensive
network of inland railways gradually formed (to serve the needs of the country's
growing population and industry). As for canals, since the first canal was built from
Worsley to Manchester in 1761, by 1842, Britain had proceeded to erect a further
3960 km of artificial canals. Manchester and Birmingham, in particular, became
hub for canal freight. Such a developed network of transportation links greatly
strengthened economic ties between rural and urban areas. The regions surrounding
these transport hubs, meanwhile, soon developed into cities or towns themselves,
likewise beginning to integrate commerce, industry, and services as a whole.[13]

Urban Expansion, Suburbanization, and City Clusters

The abovementioned technological advances to transportation were responsible for
further advancing urban sprawl and suburbanization. It was in 1825 that the British
built the world's first railway and by the mid-nineteenth century, a nationwide
railway network was basically complete. To put it another way, in the 1850s, trains

---

[13]Zhao (2008).

could reach all the UK's cities. Indeed, following the transportation revolution, coastal and inland cities, alike, were systematically connected by means of roads, canals, steamboats, railways, cars, buses, and so on. This comprehensive network of communication promoted the widespread circulation of commodities and the mobility of people while further driving the development of numerous industries. Sectors as widespread as construction, postal communication, commercial services, finance, insurance, science, education, and even the leisure industry all witnessed significant expansion throughout this period. Accompanying such industrial developments, extensive conurbation emerged in metropolitan areas, such as Newcastle, Gateshead, North Sheffield, South Sheffield, Wallsend, and Jarrow. In such cases, multiple, previously dispersed, smaller urban settlements, generally located around a central urban hub, expanded their borders towards one another to such a point that they all combined into a single large-scale conurbation. The outwards development of London is a case in point insofar as it engulfed neighboring Westminster, Southwark, Greenwich, Redbridge (乌利奇), and Deptford, thereby giving rise to a Greater London. In the mid-twentieth century, 15% of the British population lived in Greater London urban area.[14]

3.1.1.3 Problems Emerged in Urbanization in Britain

With no exception, various problems of urban society also occurred in Britain, who boasts both histories' first and longest process of urbanization. As it was so, it exposed fully all aspects of the problems, making it more valuable as regards its solution and counter-measures.

The Shortage of Housing and the Emergence of Slums

During the period of industrialization, large numbers of agricultural laborers relocated into cities, thereby triggering noteworthy housing shortages. Conditions were worsened insofar as factory owners were initially only concerned with maximizing output and profit, such that no attention was paid to the construction of infrastructure, public utilities or the improvement of worker's living conditions. As a result of this neglect, slums spread throughout the UK's industrial cities. In London alone, there were 20 slums, such as the "Lair of Cholera King", each of which housed over ten thousand people.[15] Living conditions in these slums were appalling, with low-quality housing including poor lighting, ventilation, and sanitary conditions. In the city of Manchester, for example, twenty thousand people, that is,

---

[14]Ji (2004).
[15]Engels (1957), quoted.

12% of the cities' workforce, lived in basements while in Liverpool, one in six people occupied cellars.[16]

Air and Water Pollution

Public health was another grave concern of urbanization insofar as severe air and water pollution as well as the lack of public health services gave rise to epidemics of assorted diseases, which was undesirable for the urbanization in British. Of particular concern to public health, especially from the perspective of disease control, was the contamination of rivers by runoff from domestic sewage and industrial waste. In London, the River Thames was contaminated by more than five-hundred-and-fifty sewage pipes. Unsurprisingly, then, slums became a breeding ground for various infectious diseases, such as fever, typhoid, and cholera. Waste collection and comprehensive sewage systems were not initially established in early cities, thereby leading to the mass dumping of garbage and fecal matter which presented a serious risk to the health of residents. Similarly, until 1830, half of the houses in Manchester and most of the houses in Liverpool had no drainage or sanitation systems. What drains there were generally discharged into small rivers and docks which, consequently, became putrid and foul smelling. Residents, meanwhile, had no choice but to fetch water from these contaminated rivers and surrounding wells. Diseases that spread through water-borne bacteria and viruses were, therefore, commonplace.[17] Glasgow, typical of industrial cities, had a worker's mortality rate of 2.8% in 1821, a figure which rose to 3.8% in 1838 and culminated at 4% in 1843.[18] All of this is to say that, throughout the nineteenth century, the average life of agricultural workers was, in fact, longer than that of industrial workers.

The Worker's Struggle and the Prevalence of "Sweatshops"

Throughout the early period of industrialization in the UK, only one-third of the working age population was fully employed while another third only held unstable temporary work, and the final third was unemployed altogether. Throughout the early period of urbanization, urban laborers had to endure shifts of at least 12 h, sometimes extending as much as 14 or 15 h.[19] Working conditions in most factories, meanwhile, were comparable to those of prisons, particularly, that is, under the supervision of a considerable number of strict overseers. For the vast numbers of women and children employed by factories, the situation was considerably

---

[16]Engels (1957), quoted.
[17]Mei (2001).
[18]Qian and Liu (1999).
[19]Li (2003).

bleaker. Female textile workers, for example, had to work in excess of 12 h and in repressive temperatures of 30–35 °C. Air quality, within such factories, presented a considerable problem, primarily because of abundant dust and textile debris which presented a serious risk to employee's respiratory health. British historian Eric Hobsbawm, for instance, commented: "By the standard of 1848, the UK's achievements were really great. But its emerging cities were fouler than elsewhere, and the conditions of the working class was shocking."[20]

The Lagging Behind of Urban Planning at Early Stages and Ugly Landscapes

Throughout the period of early urbanization, urban planning was simply unable to keep up with the accelerating pace of urban development which, consequently, proceeded in a blind and highly dispersed manner. The fact that unprecedented mass urbanization occurred in just a few decades precluded any such opportunity to establish, or follow, a rationale related to urban planning. As a result, of this haphazard management, the newly constructed streets and roads within developing cities were narrow and frequently congested, not to mention the landscape. For instance, when Alexis de Tocqueville dealt with the City of Manchester in 1835, he said: "It is from the filthy gutter that mankind's greatest industrial streams discharged, fertilizing the whole world and it was from the dirty sewer that pure gold out flew. Here humanity gained the fullest development as well as reached the most savage state. Here civilizations created a miracle while the civilized man had almost turned into a savage."[21] That is to say, urbanization essentially transformed Britain's cities into the most unfit places for human habitation in the whole of Europe. Manchester was labeled the "Black Country" while London often immersed in "Disastrous Smoke", was crowned as the "The Smoking Capital". All the while, so-called "The Tragedy of King Midas", a phenomenon marked by rampant material desires and shameless profiteering, eroded the moral and social fabric of numerous emerging cities such as Liverpool.[22]

3.1.2   United States: Market-Based Urbanization

The United States is among the most developed capitalist countries today as well as a typical example of a market-driven economy. Indeed, market factors consistently played a crucial role throughout the course of the US initial urbanization and subsequent urban development. In general, the economic and social development of

---

[20]Hobsbawm (2001).
[21]Owen (1981).
[22]Li (2003).

a country is closely interlinked with the ethos and spirit of its people. As such, an overview of the American national spirit and temperament allows for a deeper, more accurate understanding of urbanization in the United States. After all, this is what has helped Americans to persevere despite challenges and to continue to make progress in social, economic, and urban development.

3.1.2.1 The Historical Process and Developmental Stages of Urbanization in the US

After Columbus discovered the New World, Europeans initially immigrated to the North America to pursue agricultural activities. As the European colonial movement accelerated, however, early urbanization in the US quickly followed. Nevertheless, American urbanization was not a single, simple or isolated event, but rather represented the ups and downs the new nation faced and was inextricably linked with its ever-changing economic and social structures.

Urbanization in America can be divided into three periods: The early period (1609–1830); the interim period (1840–1960); and the current period (1970–2010). Urban development throughout the early period was especially difficult and slow. Over a period of 225 years (1605–1830), the urban population only increased from 8.3 to 8.8% and, indeed, frequently drifted below the 8% mark. In the interim period, urbanization accelerated significantly, growing from 10.8 to 70% during this 130 year interval. In the present 40-year period, American cities are highly developed, such that its overall pace of urbanization has entered a naturally slower period of growth—only increasing from 72 to 82% accordingly.

Needless to say, however, statistical analysis alone does not adequately portray the urbanization process in the US. The following discussion, therefore, will explore the three main periods, as well as the seven additional phases, of urbanization in the United States (see Fig. 3.2).

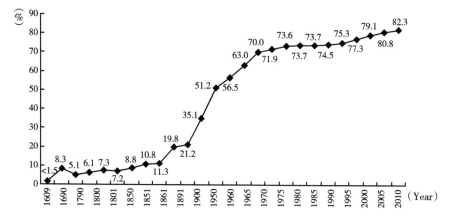

Fig. 3.2 The historical urbanization process in the United States (1609–2010, nonequal gap between years). *Source* According to data extrapolated from World Bank Open Data

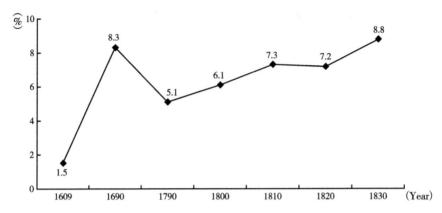

Fig. 3.3 The urbanization rate of the US (1609–1830). *Source* According to data extrapolated from World Bank Open Data

The Colonial Period to the Noncolonial Period (1609–1830)

The Colonial Phase of Trading Port Cities (1609–1776)

Prior to European colonization, the North American continent was home to pre-dominantly rural-based traditional, agricultural societies. As such, the colonial period represented the real beginning of urban development in America. From 1609 onwards, due to the influx of European immigrants, urban settlements initially developed along the east coast. Throughout this phase, American cities were limited both in scale and number while continued urbanization proceeded only at low developmental levels—never exceeding 9%. More specifically, the urbanization rate in 1609 was 1.5%, rising to 8.3% in 1690, yet, in 1790, declining again to 5.1% (see Fig. 3.3).

At this point, cities formed simply for the purpose of serving the colonial economy. Urbanization hadn't yet assumed any autonomy as an organic process, but rather remained contingent upon the needs of trade and the colonial activities of the mother country (suzerain state). What urban construction there was, meanwhile, simply replicated traditional European city planning including, among others, features such as latticed roads. At the time, these early cities simply functioned as ports for the import of manufactured goods and the export of raw materials, gen-erally to and from Britain itself. Unsurprisingly, then, trading port cities such as New York, Boston, Charleston, and Philadelphia were responsible for most of the urban development throughout this phase.[23]

---

[23]Xing (2011).

The Development of New Midwestern Towns in the Independence Phase (1776–1830)

This phase witnessed the initial introduction of systematic city construction and urbanization in America. From 1790 to 1830, the population of the US increased, from less than four million inhabitants, to over thirteen million. Urbanization levels, nevertheless, were still fluctuating unstably. In 1790, these rates regressed to their lowest level, however, in 1810, they rose again to 7.3% before falling again to 7.2% in 1820, and, finally, recovering to 8.8% in 1830. More specifically, in the US, throughout the 1830s, there were 90 cities with a population of over 2500 residents and an increasing rate of urbanization of 9%.

At this stage, the United States, although already independent, maintained intricate economic ties with Europe, especially Britain. The dynamics and motivating forces which underpinned America's subsequent urban development was closely related to the mother country (suzerain state).

First, the simple plantation-based agricultural economy of the southern states was transformed into a cotton-based export economy, the principle consumer of which was the UK. As southern cotton was generally shipped to the UK from New York, thereby rapidly raising the status of this city.

Second, the construction of America's transport network played an integral role in urban development. Initially, transportation was limited to natural rivers, but the construction of artificial canals followed soon after, before, finally, giving way to the construction of railways.

Third, the development of the Midwest constituted a significant part of the period's urban development. New towns in the Midwest were originally built by New England immigrants, aiming to restore the fading cultural traditions of England. Subsequently, developers who were responsible for constructing waterways, as well those using the canals for trade, further contributed to the growth of new towns. Throughout the 1820s and 1830s, for example, a significant majority of the residents of such towns were Irish workman employed in the field of constructing canals.

A Period of Accelerated Industrial Restructuring and Development (1830–1920)

By far the most important period in the American industrial revolution occurred as existing small-scale industrial activities were transformed into large-scale industrial activities. Following the American Civil War, in particular, the US economy developed at an unprecedented rate. Indeed, the Civil War itself functions as a useful division between two crucial developmental phases of urbanization in the United States.

*The Development of Regional Connections Prior to the Civil War
(1830–1860)*

In this phase, the number of cities with more than 2500 residents grew from 90 to 392, accompanied by an increasing urbanization rate—from 8.8% in 1830, to 19.8% in 1860 (see Fig. 3.4). Simultaneously, the number of cities with a population of more than 100,000 people grew from just one (New York) to a total of nine. Likewise, the overall national population increased exponentially, having reached 32 million by 1860.

At this stage, urban development in the United States exhibited four principle characteristics.

For one thing, the development of northeastern regions was consolidated. In this early stage, urbanization was primarily limited to northeastern areas in which industry was already conducted on a relatively large scale.

Second, regions in Midwest and surrounding the Great Lakes also witnessed substantial development. In particular, the discovery and subsequent mining of precious metals gave rise to an abundance of new settlements around San Francisco Bay and Pike's Peak in northern Colorado.

Third, the construction of America's modern transport system had profound effects on subsequent urban development. Indeed, this network was an essential prerequisite for the further development of the abovementioned Midwest and Great Lakes regions. The process of constructing a 4250 mile canal network had essentially finished before the outbreak of the Civil War in 1861. Nevertheless, these waterways were almost immediately replaced by railroads. In fact, the Americans were already constructing their first intercontinental railways in the 1850s and had, within a decade, constructed a network of over thirty thousand miles. As a result of these comprehensive links between the Northeast and the Midwest, the latter not only became the nation's second largest economic center, but also directly gave rise to the development of Chicago, that is, as the central railway hub for the Midwest region.

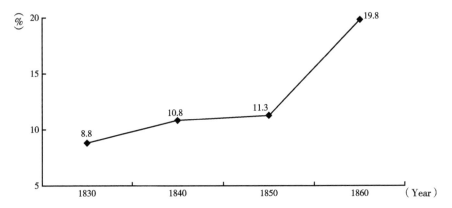

Fig. 3.4 The urbanization rate of US (1830–1860). *Source* Wang (2000b, p. 67)

Fourth, a clear division of regional economy developed. Industrialization transformed the manufacturing process, from one principally conducted in artisan workshops, to one conducted in large mechanized factories. Improved technological developments, as well as increased connectivity within regions, meanwhile, made total-factor allocation possible (gave rise to a greatly increased industrial output relative to levels of capital and labor input).

The Formation of a Belt of Industrial Cities Following the Civil War (1860–1920)

This was the most important period of America's industrial revolution and urban development as well as the period which gave birth to subsequent urban planning in the US. By 1860, the nation's population was more than 31 million, of which 20% was urban population. By 1920, America's population had exceeded one hundred million, over 50% of which was concentrated in urban areas. Unsurprisingly, then, urbanization proceeded at its quickest rate throughout this stage, with the urban population increasing from 19.8% in 1860, to 51.2% in 1920 (see Fig. 3.5).

At this stage, urbanization in America was characterized by a number of distinctive features.

First, the growth in the urbanized population depended above all else on a continued influx of immigrants which was, in turn, the principle cause of the country's population growth, accounting for no less than 40% of the growth between 1860 and 1920. While the passing of the "immigration law", effective 1918–1924, curtailed this number significantly, most immigration, at the time, was destined for New York as well as a select number of other big cities.

Second, this period gave rise to the formation of a manufacturing zone. Leading up to the 1890s, in accordance with the preliminary urban system already taking shape in the US, the development of numerous western settlements had entered a mature stage. Of particular importance was the extension of the territory of the US

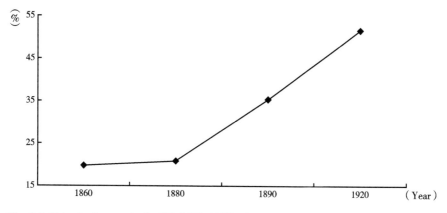

Fig. 3.5 Urbanization rate in the US (1860–1920). *Source* Wang (2000b, p. 89)

to the Pacific coast. Consequently, large-scale industrial centers transferred from the East Coast to central and western regions. This westwards shift of industrialization, subsequently, gave form to a considerable manufacturing belt which extended across the Northeast and Midwest regions concentrated around the Great Lakes. According to Weiss's study, relevant to this period, nearly 50% of the national workforce was engaged in manufacturing while the remaining 50% participated in the service industry. The proportion of those engaged in farming, meanwhile, was small.

Third, the abolishment of slavery in the south had profound consequences on the process of urbanization. After the Civil War, former slaves from the south, now freed, were responsible for an increase in population mobility bringing with it, gradually, economic vitality. Southern industrialization, as well as further urbanization, then commenced following a similar developmental pattern to that previously observed in the north.

Fourth, further construction of convenient methods of transportation extended the reach of urbanization. At this stage, the United States was engaged in building railroads which comprehensively connected the East and West and, therefore, promoted exchange and communications between the two, while also lending itself to the birth of new western cities and the overall expansion of America's urban network. Improvements to this railway network, especially the completion of the railway that connected the East and West, strengthened the economic ties between the East and West. As a result, more and more people, products, and capital traveled westwards, which promoted the westward expansion of both industrialization and urbanization.

Fifth, the model of urban structure, followed by most US cities, shifted from a single structure to polycentric structure. During World War I, the structure of urbanized areas in the United States generally conformed to a distinctive pattern. The city center, comprised primarily of high-rise buildings, was divisible into numerous clusters, each of which embodied the gathering of buildings which shared a particular function or industry sector (e.g., municipal, financial, commercial, medical). Residential areas, meanwhile, were generally located on the peripheries of these functional centers. That is to say, the development of cities, at the time, exhibited what could be described as a radial or polycentric pattern. While concentrated urbanization such as this was most readily observable in the Midwest, nationwide development did become more balanced along with the progress of communication and cooperation across the US.

Sixth, the process of suburbanization commenced. As the development of cities, each of which represented an agglomeration around a highly condensed centre, reached its peak, the phenomena of urban disease became increasingly widespread, thereby triggering waves of suburbanization. That said, cities remained the core of all economic, political, cultural, and social processes. Commence and population alike remained concentrated in these city centers while competition and mergers actually further increased the degree of centralization of America's industry.

The Period of the Maturation and Transition of Metropolises (1920–2011)

Mature metropolises are characterized by the widespread outwards growth of an urban area. This growth, which gives rise to substantially developed, suburban can be described as urban sprawl, that is, a phenomenon otherwise known as "suburbanization." Most significantly, throughout this process, previously rural areas are assimilated into urban sections while the differences between urban and rural regions shrink noticeably.

The Phase of Suburbanization and the Formation of Metropolitan Areas (1920–1960)

Since 1920, despite the government's moderately successful attempts to attract skilled workers, population growth began to slow in the United States, including both natural population growth and oversea immigration. However, rural-to-urban immigration increased. American migration, through this period, then, was increasingly characterized by migration between cities rather than immigration from overseas. At the same time, urban population growth reached its highest levels and regional population was redistributed. Consistent immigration to the United States prior to this period had, for the most part, resulted in a relatively even population distribution among the nations' developed regions (see Fig. 3.6).

The ongoing re-distribution of America's population could be characterized, principally, as "suburbanization" and an increasing concentration around the so-called "Sunbelt". Dissatisfied with increasingly serious urban problems, by the 1960s, much of the American middle classes gradually began to leave metropolitan areas in favor of suburban areas. Consequently, a great deal of the urban dwelling population dispersed from central city areas core to scattered suburban areas. This suburbanization, in turn, granted increasing political and economic independence to suburbs, many of which began to rival their city-centre counterparts. The second

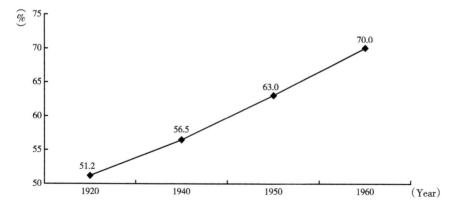

Fig. 3.6 Urbanization rate in the US (1920–1960). *Source* Wang (2000b, p. 134)

major process of population redistribution in this period was a widespread movement from the core area of the East and Midwest to less central areas of the west and south US, otherwise known as the "Sunbelt". Predictably, gradual population growth further accelerated as these regions began to accumulate economic opportunities.

From 1910 to 1960, however, migration, once again, changed direction, that is, insofar as Americans began to relocate from the south to the north and from rural to urban areas. The shortage of labor, triggered by World War II, in this period, created abundant new economic opportunities for black people and women. In 1910, almost all black people lived in the southern states, 72% of which resided in rural areas. This new demand for labor, however, resulted in the widespread movement of black people to heavily industrialized areas in the north. As a result, by 1960, only 60% of black people in the US still resided in the South. Population movements between different regions of the United States, such as this, gradually gave rise to increasingly balanced levels of development and uniform population distributions. Significantly, by 1920, the urbanization rate in the United States exceeded the 50% mark. Unsurprisingly, then, by 1940, as the urbanization rate further increased to 56.5%, the United States was a country dominated by major cities. Furthermore, after the 1920s, the popularity of cars resulted in the relative ease for those wishing to commute into the city from its outskirts, that is, in the different direction of the bulk of the rail transit at the time. The recession and war interfered with the process of suburbanization throughout the 1930s, however it resumed with fresh vigor in the postwar period.

The Phase of Metropolitan Areas Transforming into Mega-Cities (1960–2000)

Suburbanization resulted in the physical overlap of metropolitan areas, thereby giving rise to a new era of mega cities, the largest of which emerged as the Northeast Urban Corridor extending from the city of New York, and the Southern California Urban Corridor centered on Los Angeles. There were clear divisions in the status and role of the cities that make up these megalopolises, such that they were naturally characterized as either central cities or functional satellite cities.

Furthermore, the American baby boom commenced following World War II, subsequently reaching its peak in 1956. The population underwent rapid growth throughout this period, that is, as the birth rate, per 1000 women, reached as high as 123. Following the baby boom, the birth rate in US entered a period of decline. In 1976, for instance, the birth rate, per 1000 women, was as low as 65.8, approximately half that of in 1956. Yet, as the natural population growth declined, foreign migration increased accordingly. For a period of around 30 years, Mexico and Asia constituted the largest source of immigration to the US. This constant growth of the overall population functioned to consolidate and promote the urbanization process that might, otherwise, have stagnated. More specifically, during this period, the urbanization rate of the United States increased at a rate of around 10% (see Fig. 3.7).

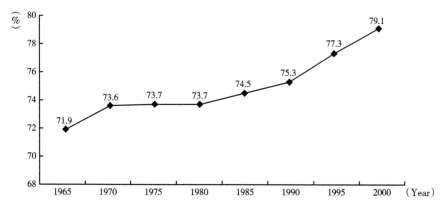

Fig. 3.7 Urbanization rate in the US (1960–2000). *Source* Wang (2000b, p. 159)

The Dilemma of Urban Hollowization in the US (2001–2011)

Urban Hollowization has always existed in America; however it only became a particular predicament in the twenty-first century. The factors responsible for this predicament are complex and varied.

Following World War II, economically, the United States took global centre stage, gradually gaining a broad lead in its competition with the Soviet Union up until the end of the Cold War. By the 1970s, the US boasted a highly developed information society and an advance tertiary industry, based on the information and high-tech sectors, proving to be its largest, most profitable, enterprise. Meanwhile, the United States began to organize its production on a global scale, encouraging, for example, that a great deal of manufacturing be transferred abroad. As a result of an increasing saturation of domestic market, as well as relentless industrial upgrades, the US looked towards the export of its industry, capital, and technology, thereby giving rise to the possibility of capital allocation at a global level and the rapid development of multinational corporations.

Continued developments to transportation methods, such as the construction and improvement of highways and the increasingly popularity and functionality of cars, as well as new means of digital communication, transformed the way in which Americans traveled and communicated in all aspects of their lives. These developments were, in no small part, responsible for further increasingly rapid suburbanization of cities.

Following the much encouraged global division of labor, America also witnessed a transformation of its domestic industry. In particular, narrowly profitable, environmentally damaging manufacturing (e.g., equipment manufacturing, light, and heavy industry) was outsourced to the developing world. Such globalization forced the US to focus domestically on the development of its information industry, exemplified by Silicon Valley; cultural industry, exemplified by Hollywood; creative industry, exemplified by Apple; high-end corporate services (e.g., lawyers), financial services (e.g., Wall Street), and a range of other lucrative fields. For a long

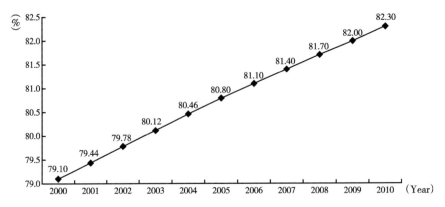

Fig. 3.8 Urbanization rate in the US (2000–2010). *Source* Wang (2000b, p. 172)

time, they benefited from cheap commodities imported from China, for instance, and other developing countries. Less beneficially, however, their dependence on foreign products and unwillingness to enhance the development of these industries domestically both increased accordingly.

Furthermore, two fatal blows weakened the strength of the United States, giving rise to a potential crisis for the faltering superpower. A combination of The September 11th terrorist attacks and 2008 international financial crisis drastically worsened the urban predicament faced by the United States.

American supremacy also faced a significant new challenge from rising countries. The multi-polarization of the world economy triggered an inevitable decline of America. Other BRIC countries, China and India, in particular, benefited from huge policy and cost advantages which, in turn, gave rise to their own rapid development, posing a threat to the status of the US as the centre of the global economy. Contributing to the problem, for years cities in the US had been hemorrhaging manufacturing jobs, causing both a rise in domestic unemployment and decreased revenue for local governments. Even the federal government itself was not immune, shut down on multiple occasions. By 2011, the US economy was still subject to a depression while the hollowization of American cities persisted. Consequently, the US enacted drastic adjustments to its future developmental. Among others, policies encouraging a "return to industry" and "increase savings" became widely applauded. A large number of major US companies recently withdrew their investment from overseas enterprises (Fig. 3.8).

3.1.2.2 Main Problems Facing Urbanization in the US

Under the political system in the US, urban planning and management are the responsibilities of local authorities, and the federal government has limited ability to exercise control in these matters. In the face of the powerful force of capital, the federal government did little to guide the urbanization process. This, resulted in haphazard development across the country, for which the US government and its people have paid a high price. One prominent problem is suburbanization, that is, the uncontrolled and unplanned construction that led to urban sprawl. Another consequence is increased social differentiation, and many related structural—both spatial and social—problems.[24]

Suburbanization

In the first half of the twentieth century, urbanization in the US witnessed rapid progress and, consequently, a range of challenges. These include increasing "traffic congestion in city centers, environmental degradation, housing shortages, and high crime rates. Wealthy families, subsequently, left their high-rise apartments in city centers in order to live in the suburbs, building their own single-family low-rise properties. Enabled by further economic development, as well as the popularity of automobiles, the majority of ordinary urban middle class residents soon followed suit also relocating to the suburbs. This trend gave rise to a spatial pattern of urban development characterized by constant low-density urban sprawl along highways. Cities, then, developed into metropolitan areas expanding over a great number of rolling cities and towns. In the end, by 1970, the US suburban population actually exceeded the population in the central cities and non-metropolises. According to statistics, from 1960 to 1985, the population of metropolitan New York increased by only 8%, whereas the geographical size of the urbanized area grew by 65%. Suburbanization on this scale had profound impact on socioeconomic development in the US. It reduced population density, and narrowed the gap between urban, suburban, and rural areas, which became increasingly integrated. The costs of suburbanization were, however, substantial, including serious waste of land resources, elevated economic costs, worsening environmental conditions, high level of energy and resource consumption and a whole host of social problems such as increasing gap between the rich and poor and increased crime rates."[25]

Since the 1990s, "government officials, academics, and even ordinary people in the US have become more aware of the disastrous consequences of suburbanization, and the concept of 'Smart development' was introduced. The idea is to increase land use efficiency, develop public transportation, create more space for pedestrians, make land use more functionally diverse and flexible, protect open spaces, improve the urban environments, and promote public participation. The overall goal is to achieve economic, environmental, and social justice by imposing limits, providing protection, and facilitating coordination. [The 'Smart Development' approach] is essentially an operationally feasible management

---

[24]Wang (2000a).
[25]Wang (2000a).

philosophy and model that is consistent with the requirements of sustainable development and meets scientific standards, and it was intended as a way to address the myriad of social and environmental problems brought about by suburbanization."[26]

The Problem of Social Differentiation

In the US, issues associated with social differentiation typically manifest themselves as "inner city" problems. As more members of the, predominantly white, upper and upper-middle classes moved to the suburbs, they found new and effective ways of securing the borders of these suburban areas,[27] which made them more isolated from the urban underclass. By contrast, within the city center areas, an "inner city" formed in which people of low income tended to concentrate, especially African Americans, Hispanics, and those from other minority groups This situation did not improve despite progress in economic development in the US. Economically, the "inner city" was locked in a state of isolation from the rest of the urban areas, and benefitted little if at all from the economic growth of the 1990s. Although poverty rates among African Americans declined since the 1990s, it became substantially more concentrated and noticeable within cities.

On the one hand, minority groups living within "inner city" areas of the United States were discriminated against by the majority population. Mexican Americans, for example, were frequently harassed by the police, a phenomenon that has been referred to as "legitimized oppression."[28] Reports in the mainstream media about the residents in such areas tended to be biased. Striking similarities exist between their experiences and those of slum dwellers in Brazil, India, and other developing countries. On the other hand, these "inner city" areas suffered from stubbornly high crime rates, as illustrated by drug trafficking and violent gang activities in cities like Cincinnati. All of these threatened the stability of the entire community.[29]

In addition to poverty and socioeconomic exclusion, belief in individualism and social Darwinism, which had long been culturally entrenched in the US, had even more devastating impact on these populations. These ideologies hold people personally responsible for their "being poor". So even when both the government and residents themselves would like to see inner-city conditions improved through government intervention, the support and justification needed to implement such measures are often lacking.

---

[26]Wang (2000a).

[27]Katz (2008).

[28]Duran (2009).

[29]Waymer (2009).

3.1.3 The Soviet Union: Urbanization Through Central Planning

Urbanization in the Soviet Union also proceeded on an equally grand, spectacular, and rapid scale. It had far-reaching consequences and was unmatched as a model for urban and industrial planning. The Soviet Union was the leader of the socialist camp and even post-Soviet Russia remained a major international power. Occupying this position, the Soviet Union made remarkable and great achievements in following its own process of urbanization. The Soviet model of central planning was a typical representation of the catch-up strategy. Under the strong leadership of the Soviet Communist Party (whose economic policies were centered on the Five-year Development Plans), urbanization advanced rapidly and steadily, accompanied by rapid social and economic social development and growth in GDP, which at some point reached second place in the world. However, as conditions changed, some of the defects and sources of tension inherent to the Soviet model became apparent. These not only slowed down, halted and perhaps even reversed the urbanization process but also contributed to the collapse of the Soviet Union itself. The political system of the Soviet Union was similar to that of China. As such, learning from history and carefully studying the case of the Soviet Union is of particular importance to Chinese thinkers.

3.1.3.1 The Historical Track of Urbanization in Soviet Russia

Soviet Russia is intricately tied to the previous Russian Empire, the wider Soviet Union and the subsequent Federal Republic of Russia. The urbanization process of the Soviet Union must, then, be observed from a historical perspective. The initial development of urbanization can be traced back as early as the Russian Empire. With the disintegration of the Soviet Union, which represented another major stage of Russian urbanization, the historical period of the Russian Federation began. Thus, the process of Russian urbanization can, at a glance, be divided into three periods: those of the Russian Empire (i.e., the onset of urbanization), the Soviet-era and, finally, the Russian Federation. Nonetheless, under closer scrutiny, the Soviet-era itself can, in fact, be divided into three periods: those of the newborn regime, of central planning and, finally, of in-depth development. This historical period, then, makes for a total of five periods.

The Initial Period of Urbanization in Russia (850–1916)

Russian urbanization has always been closely linked with the destiny of its host, experiencing the same long and turbulent historical upheavals as Russia itself (Table 3.1; Fig. 3.9). Dating back to the middle of the ninth century, Eastern Slavs, occupying the Eastern European Plains, established the Ancient Rus dynasty.

Thereafter, in the year 882, Prince Oleg moved the capital of the Rurik dynasty to Kiev, subsequently starting the reign of the Kievan Rus federation. During that time, the Slavs developed smooth trading relationships with the Byzantine Empire in the East, thereby giving birth to a number of commercial cities. Records indicate that from the ninth to tenth century there were, in fact, 25 cities in ancient Rus. The eleventh century saw in further developments of productivity, such that the cities' handicraft industries and commerce developed accordingly. These cities which began to function as the military and religious centers of feudal lords eventually increased in number to more than 80. From the mid-eleventh century onwards, however, following the invasion of the Mongols, as well as the split of numerous principalities, the Kievan Rus federation gradually dissolved. This triggered the virtual standstill of the Russian economy as well as the destruction of many commercial cities. Indeed, it wasn't until the fourteenth century that Russia gradually began to recover from the Mongol invasion. The northeastern cities of Russia, such as Novgorod, Pskov, Moscow, and Tver, in particular, witnessed significant development, no doubt due to an abundance of handicrafts and other prosperous commercial enterprises. In the late fifteenth century, Russia overthrew Mongol rule and established a unified centralized state. Subsequently, since the sixteenth century, urban development accelerated in Russia, which witnessed, among others, the flourishing of Novgorod and Pskov. After the second half of the seventeenth century, however, the entire Russian economy centered around Moscow gradually began to form. At that time, there were 200,000 people living in Moscow which was well equipped with trade routes leading to every region in the country, thereby enabling direct trade with over 150 other cities. Such economic success gave rise to an accumulative effect by which the number of cities in the country soon reached 234. It wasn't until the eighteenth century, in the reign of Peter the Great of Russia, in which the urbanization process and modernization really commenced. In 1719, an extensive administrative network, at provincial, state, and county levels, was established in order to further strengthen the grip of the absolute monarchy over the country's 50 provinces. Petersburg, as the country's new capital, developed rapidly and subsequently became the largest city in Russia.[30] The years between 1775 and 1785 were a period under the rule of Catherine the Great. Administrative reforms divided the nation into provinces and counties, the latter of which were managed and administrated from cities. Each of the country's 50 provinces contained a population of between 30 and 40 million while each county had a population of between 20 and 30 thousand. During the period of Yekaterina Alexeyevna, there were already 216 cities, yet, after the reform of the serf system in 1861, Russia entered a new stage of accelerated development. In 1901, most of Russia's 775 cities functioned as centers of handicraft, administration, and commerce. Some were military fortresses while there were also a small number of industrial cities.

---

[30]Ji (2002).

Table 3.1   Regime shift in Russia before the Soviet Union

Regime	Ancient Rus	Kievan Rus	Mongol annexation	Russian empire
Period	Around 850 AC	The year of 882/882 AC	Eleventh to thirteenth century	By the end of fifteenth century

Source Ji (2002)

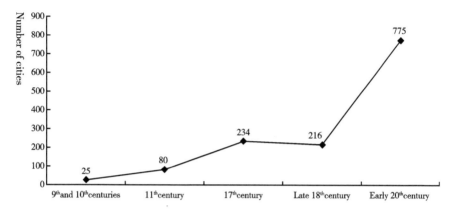

Fig. 3.9   The number of cities in Russia before the October Revolution

The Neonatal Period of the Soviet Union (1917–1926)

1917 saw the outbreak of the October Revolution in Russia. As a result of World War I and the subsequent Civil War, Russia's urban population declined sharply, to seven million people less than prewar levels. Prior to 1917, however, the urbanization rate had been gradually rising, that is, from 4%, in 1796, to 8%, in 1863, to 12.7%, in 1897, 16% in 1913 and, finally, culminating in 1917. Following the 1917 revolution, urbanization initially experienced a temporary drop, decreasing to 15.3% in 1920. At first, urbanization levels throughout the Soviet Union were markedly low. Nevertheless, the new Soviet regime abruptly consolidated its position, primarily by crushing all opposition, at home and abroad,[31] thereby avoiding the damaging effects of continued conflict. Even the economy was fully restored, helped, in particular, by the 1922 establishment of the Union of Soviet Socialist Republics (USSR or Soviet Union). Thereafter, the urbanization process advanced steadily, rising from 15.3%, in 1920, to 16.2%, in 1922, and, finally, to 18% in 1926.

A Period of Compulsory Central Planning (1926–1950)

The first of the Soviet Union's five-year plans gave rise to unprecedented leaps and bounds of urbanization. This process was promoted, in particular, by both the

---

[31]Cheng (1984).

collectivization of agriculture and the large-scale industrialization include in these centralized plans. Thereafter, urban populations essentially doubled as surplus rural laborers migrated into cities. As a result, the urban population, compared with that in 1928, increased by 14% in 1939 and subsequent growth rates exceeded 6.2%. For instance, urbanization rates reached 18% in 1926, 18.4% in 1929, 28.4% in 1937, 30% in 1939, 32.5% in 1940, and, finally 39% in 1950. Accordingly, one could conclude that the central five-year plans of the Soviet directly contributed to rapid urbanization.[32]

The Period of Deepening Urban Development (1951–1991)

After World War Two, the Soviet Union maintained the rapid development of its urbanized areas. Admittedly, the Second World War had resulted in the destruction of most of the Soviet Union's cities as well as a significant decline to the total population. Needless to say, then, the urbanization process in the Soviet Union did slow, however, it far from stalled completely. In order to meet the needs of war, the bulk of the Soviet's industrial enterprises had been relocated from the west to the east. Prior to the war's end, in 1945, more than 70 new cities emerged in the Urals and Siberia, thereby providing a platform for the rapid renaissance of urban development in the post-war period. In 1950, for instance, the urban population saw an increase of nine million compared to 1939 levels, that is, as the urban population increased to 39%.[33] Following 1950, the Soviets continued to emphasize the development of heavy industry and large-scale construction projects, particularly in the relatively wealthy areas around the Donets and the Dnieper. Nevertheless, the Soviet Union also began to towards a more rational location of its productive forces. To the east of the Urals, in Siberia, the precise configuration of productive forces was well planned. To name a few examples, Kazakhstan's coal reserves were utilized, a large hydropower station was constructed close to the University of Siberia, and oil fields in Tyumen underwent significant development. During this period, a very important factor in urbanization process planned by the Soviet Union was to promote a transition to conurbation.[34] A conurbation refers to the overall synthesis of an urban region, with a major city acting as the core of a system which is comprised of nearby suburbs, smaller cities, and, even, rural areas. Just as important as their physical proximity, is an extensively interconnected economy, labor force, culture, and daily life. The conurbation of Moscow, for instance, consisted of more than 180 distinct communities. In accordance with relevant Soviet planning, from 1970s to 1980s, city aggregations developed rapidly and the urbanization rate accelerated accordingly.

---

[32]Cheng (1984).
[33]Wang (1990).
[34]Wang (1990).

The Period of Stagnation and Wandering (1991–2010)

The character of Russian nation was radical and capricious. After the disintegration of the Soviet Union in 1991, the Russian nation introduced radical economic and social reforms, known as "shock therapy". As "shocking" as this strategy was, it did not fully resolve many of the deep-seated problems faced by the nation. Instead, their path to complete economic and social rejuvenation was both long and riddled with obstacles. Of particular concern was the relative weakness of Russia's industry. At the time, Russian industry was heavily dependent on energy resources, armaments production, heavy manufacturing and tourism. Compared with its European and American counterparts, the Russian economy was rather simple, lacking both competitiveness and technological progress. Besides, further contributing to its economic downturn, was Russia's lack of the low-cost, labor-intensive industries that were responsible for the economic boom of the other BRIC countries. During this period, urbanization, that is, a telling indicator of the Russian economy, underwent fluctuation and, in the end, stagnation. In fact, for many years, the level of urbanization actually dropped. According to data from the World Bank, for instance, from 1991 to 2000, urbanization levels in Russia maintained at around 73.4%. In 2001, however, they fell to 73.1%, 72.9% in 2004, and finally, in 2010, to 72.8%, that is, even lower than the Soviet period.

3.1.3.2 The Experiences and Lessons of Russian Urbanization

Most Eastern European countries followed in the footsteps of Soviet style urbanization, characterized, as it was, by rapid industrial development and a highly centralized economy. Under this system, local authorities functioned as the agents responsible for formulating and implementing social and economic programs, as well as the suitable allocation of investment, in accordance with the central planner's designs. Obviously, then, the policies of such local Soviet authorities were directly responsible for implementing and managing the process of urbanization. Unfortunately, however, mass industrialization and the subsequent massive waves of rural-to-urban migration were, particularly in the Soviet period, accompanied by a series of problems.

Acute Contradictions in Urban and Rural Housing Intensified

From 1918 to 1928, around three-quarters of newly constructed houses were erected in rural areas, that is, due to the relative impoverishment that characterized most urban regions. Nonetheless, following the rapid restoration and development of industry in the 1920s, urban population growths far exceeded the existent rates of urban housing construction. For example, from 1929 to 1937, the total area utilized for housing construction was just 61% of that in the years from 1918 to 1928, that is, despite a much higher demand during the former. From 1929 onwards, urban populations increased exponentially as urban areas witnessed a massive influx of agricultural workers. In fact, the urban population increased by 65% before the completion of the second Five-Year Plan, which meant, the rate of urban growth far exceeded the capacity of the five-year planning system to adapt accordingly, thereby triggering a long-term housing shortage. It was until 1989 that large-scale housing construction projects, initiated from 1959 onwards, finally, resulted in 83% of urban households being occupied by a single family. Prior to that, it had been common place for several families to share a house or live in shared dormitories.

A Serious Shortage of Urban Public Facilities

Entire suburban areas, as well as the residential areas of small cities and urbanized towns, were low-leveled by the construction of unsatisfactory public facilities. Poor quality housing composed of low-quality, inexpensive silicate bricks, and prefabricated components, for instance, were a common sight across the country. The same such standards were applied to the construction of public buildings and spaces, such that poor quality permeated every aspect of the urban environment and the life of urban residents. The extent and quality of urban drainage systems, for example, is a telling indicator of urban living quality. But by the end of twentieth century, in the European regions of Russia, however, two-thirds of the residences of over 100 cities lacked underground drainage systems.

The "Ruralization" and "Farmerization" of Russian Cities

Interestingly, a great number of heavily urbanized areas in Russia actually exhibited the characteristics of rural agricultural areas. For one thing, in accordance with the orders of central administrators, agricultural areas were integrated into the catchment areas of urban areas such that rural suburbs effectively became parts of cities. Nevertheless, the environment, housing style and the economic structure of these areas remain unchanged, thereby resulting in the so-called "agricultural city" and "rural area" in a city by which apparently urban areas exhibited predominately rural characteristics.

Just as importantly, the massive influx and settlement of rural laborers into cities soon outnumbered the number of indigenous urban residents. Cities, therefore, became massive aggregations of farmers that, until 1940s and 1950s, at least, effectively controlled and shaped the development of their new urban residences. For instance, according to statistics from the period, in 1946, 709 of the 855 cadres in the city of Minsk Oblast were former farmers while only 58 people were working-class. The first generation of Soviet leaders, during a period of revolution and civil war, had the highest proportion of members born in the city, that is, despite urban populations comprising only a fraction of the national population at the time. Later, however, despite unprecedented urban population growth, the number of party elites who were actually born in rural areas increased significantly.

From 1930 to 1989, only 7% of the party's top leaders were born in Moscow and Leningrad, while 18% were born in other major cities. A staggering 47.3%, however, were born in rural areas, as well as 27.2% born in small agricultural towns and cities.

What's more, farmers who poured into cities, while technically becoming urban residents, generally failed to immediately accustom themselves to city life and urban values. Consequently, in many cities, there appeared a transitional, marginalized group of "semi-urbanite-semi-farmers". They no longer maintained either a fully urban or a fully rural identity. Of course, as former farmers and their families took root in cities, they gradually integrated into urban society and all such transitional stages gradually diminished. Yet, it is widely held today, that the adaptation of the agricultural population in Russia and post-Soviet republics (except the three Baltic states) to urban lifestyles, culture, values, and code of conducts was far from completion. Such social upheaval may be describe as the grave consequence of the "sudden onset" of urbanization during the Soviet period. Perhaps it also contributed to mass ownership of second houses and villas in suburbs or rural areas by Russians that can be observed today. To some extent, this phenomenon also reflects the rural characteristics of urbanization in the Soviet Union.

A Series of Problems Brought About by Identity Restrictions

An "ID card system" was widely used throughout the Soviet Union and other Eastern European countries. For one thing, this ID card system limited the prospects of farmers insofar as the issuing of ID cards to rural populations was delayed until the Khrushchev period. As a result, rural populations were initially restricted from relocating to cities while even urban residents themselves could be restricted from moving between cities. Furthermore, such a system offers proof that Soviet administrators favored directly distribution rather than allowing indirect market mechanisms in social practice. The ID card system gave rise to a level of urban privilege by providing rights to free housing and various other benefits. While beneficial for some, this artificially gave rise to stratified levels of inequality within urban areas. Furthermore, the Soviet Union's urbanization was regarded merely a necessary byproduct of much coveted industrialization, that it, as a means of providing industrial labor. Therefore, although the social status of newly urbanized farmers was somewhat improved compared to their rural counterparts, they were still essentially regarded as a "screw" in the huge state apparatus. They did not, therefore, enjoy even some of the most fundamental rights of citizens such as the freedom of mobility and occupation. Consequently, an integral part of a smoothly functioning urban civil society was essentially absent during the Soviet period, which may have been an intrinsic factor of the turmoil and ultimate disintegration of the Soviet Union in the late 1980s.

3.1.4 Japan: Urbanization Promoted by the Government

Urbanization in Japan followed a model typical of that promoted by the government and one which varied significantly from market-based urbanization witnessed in the United States. From the point of the Meiji Restoration up until the contemporary period, the Japanese government dominated all economical and social affairs. Comprehensive plans, formulated by government functioned to introduce, lead and regulate the process of Japanese marketization. In fact, in a wide range of areas, Japan's experience of urbanization exemplified a number of innate advantages from which China could itself learn and apply towards its own process of urbanization. In terms of such urbanization, Japan and China expressed close similarities in at least three key aspects: First, the contemporary culture of both nations could be traced back to Confucian origins and, indeed, continued to be influenced by such roots. Second, urbanization in both countries was initially stimulated and further driven by external factors. Third, in both cases, government planning played a central role in guiding economic and social development alike. Therefore, any review of the successes and drawbacks of the urbanization process in Japan will, invariably, deliver important lessons for the Chinese process of urbanization.

3.1.4.1 The Historical Urbanization Process in Japan

Urbanization in Japan can be divided into four periods: a period of agricultural society (1603–1867); a preparatory period of pre-urbanization (1868–1920); a period of heavy industry and city circle (megalopolis) (1920–1950); a post-war period of rapid development (1950–1990); and, finally, a period of urbanization in the era of post bubble crisis (1990–2011).

A Period of Agricultural Society (1603–1867)

In the Tokugawa period (1603–1867), Japan was almost exclusively an agricultural country. The development of the country was largely inhibited by political turmoil and uncertainty as well as a poor basis of economic resources. Urbanization during this period underwent slow development at best. In 1680, the number of people engaged in the primary industry sector accounted for as much as 87.9% of total employment while as little as 4.1% were engaged in secondary industry. Japan's insightful people, including nationalists, diligently sought out methods of making the country prosperous. In 1853, Mathew C. Perry, the Commodore of the East India Fleet of the United States, reached the coast of Japan and asked Tokugawa Shogunate for opening negotiations. As a consequence of this, a Japan–US Treaty of goodwill was signed in 1854, namely the "Ansei Treaty", which opened the ports of Shimoda and Hakodate to the United States, which had previously been confined to Nagasaki. This treaty also effectively afforded the United States the status of Japan's "most favored nation". This event, referred to as the event of "Edo Bay", essentially marked the point at which Japan opened her doors to Western countries. This further led, in no small part, to the Meiji Restoration, effectively marking the onset of Japan's route to full capitalism. The "Edo Bay" event did, however, give rise to a national sense of shame, similar to that witnessed in China as a result of the Opium War. Nevertheless, in time, this sense of shame effectively gave way to a stronger sense of envy directed towards advanced Western technology and systems, and ultimately triggered the full implementation of modernization.

The Preparatory Period of Urbanization (1868–1920)

Japan's urbanization and industrialization commenced from the point of the Meiji Restoration in 1868. Following this, a series of agricultural policies were launched in an effort to promote the development of agriculture while seed capital for industrial development was raised by the imposition of elevated agricultural taxes. The main measures included[35] the following:

A. The abolition of a series of bans enforced during the Tokugawa period, as well as the reform of land ownership, that had previously been dominated by landlords, established a good environment for Japanese agricultural development and a rural labor transfer.

B. Japanese authorities also vigorously carried out a policy of "advising-farmers" in order to improve the agricultural technology being used, build irrigation systems, and promote the all round development of agricultural production.

C. Special emphasis was laid on the education and popularization of agricultural operation. In addition, the Government organized the construction of industrial infrastructure, starting to build, for instance, a nationwide rail network, giving preferential policies to the mining industry, the iron and steel industry and, finally, the manufacturing and mechanical industry. Light industry developed rapidly while the textile industry became a significant pillar industry. The fundamental purpose of all of these policies was to accumulate industrial capital in preparation for the massive industrialization to come. Likewise, by integrating previously dispersed rural farmland, Japanese policy made available an abundance of land and a great surplus of labor that could be put to use throughout the subsequent industrialization and urbanization process. Needless to say, the effectiveness with which this promoted industrialization and urbanization, thereby accelerating the transformation of Japan, from an

---

[35]Hao (2007).

agricultural country to an industrial one, cannot be overstated. From 1889 to 1920, for instance, the proportion of the population engaged in primary industry dropped to as low as 53.8% in city areas while those engaged by the secondary and tertiary industries increased to 20.5 and 23.7%, respectively.

The Heavy Industry and City Circle Period (1920–1950)

Primarily towards enhancing their wartime power and becoming strong, Japan attached great importance to the development of its heavy industry. Such manufacturing was mainly concentrated in and around major cities like Tokyo, Osaka, Nagoya and Fukuoka. "In 1960 four coastal industrial zones, which together occupied a mere 2% of Japan's land area, contributed more than 30% of Japan's gross industrial output, while its four metropolis, which occupied only 12% of its total land area, contributed the remaining 70% of Japan's gross industrial production. Significantly, while some parts of the production chain have been dispersed to other places, even today nearly 8% of Japan's GDP is still in fact concentrated in these four major metropolitan areas. The rapid industrial development witnessed in this stage was accompanied by an ever-increasing mass migration of rural populations to urban areas, especially heavy industrial cities. Japan's four famous industrial belts, that is to say the Keihin industrial zone, Chukyo Industrial Zone, Hanshin industrial zone, and the Kitakyushu industrial zone, gave rise to an area of "quadruple concentration". The overall rate of urbanization in this period, therefore, rose from just 18% in 1920 to as high as 33% in 1950".[36]

The Post-war Period of Rapid Development of (1950–1990)

After World War II, Japan experienced a devastating economic recession accompanied by shortages of basic materials, growing unemployment, inflation and declining living standard. In other words, the urbanization achievements since the Meiji Restoration came to naught. In 1950, however, the Korean War broke out and Japan, as the material base of the Western powers, witnessed a period of rapid revival including rapid economic growth which, among other things, accelerated its urbanization. This unexpected acceleration to Japanese industry in big cities, particularly within the four industrial zones, as well as a knock-on effect boost to related industries created abundant employment opportunities thereby attracting large numbers of labors to the cities and, in turn, giving rise to the three Metropolitan Areas: The Greater Tokyo Area, The greater metropolitan area of Keihanshin, and The Chukyo Metropolitan Area, with Tokyo, Osaka, and Nagoya as their separate centers (see Tables 3.2 and 3.3).

---

[36]Li (2006).

Table 3.2 Population in Japan's three major metropolitan areas and their proportion of the national total (1955–2005) (*Unit* 10,000, %)

Years	Nationwide	Three metropolitan total	Tokyo circle	Osaka circle	Nagoya circle
1955	9007	3321 (36.9)	1542 (17.1)	1095 (12.2)	683 (7.6)
1960	9430	3738 (39.6)	1786 (18.9)	1218 (12.9)	733 (7.8)
1965	9920	4293 (43.3)	2107 (21.2)	1390 (14)	801 (8. 1)
1970	10,466	4827 (47.8)	2411 (23)	1547 (14.8)	869 (8.3)
1975	11,194	5323 (47.6)	2704 (24.2)	1677 (15)	941 (8.4)
1980	11,706	5592 (47.8)	2870 (24.4)	1735 (14.8)	987 (8.4)
1985	12,105	5834 (48.2)	3027 (25.0)	1783 (14.7)	1023 (8.5)
1990	12,361	6046 (48.9)	3180 (25.7)	1811 (14.7)	1055 (8.5)
1995	12,557	6164 (49.1)	3257 (25.9)	1826 (14.5)	1080 (8.7)

Table 3.3 The increase of cities nationwide and in metropolitan areas in Japan (1955–2005)

Years	Nationwide	Tokyo circle	Osaka circle	Nagoya circle	Three metropolitan total
1955	496	57	45	51	153
1960	561	66	47	61	174
1965	567	71	47	62	180
1970	588	86	51	66	203
1975	644	109	56	71	236
2000	672	121	58	77	256
2005	751	118	69	85	272
1955–1975	148	52	11	20	83
1975–2000	28	12	2	6	20
2000–2005	79	−3	14	8	19

3.1.4.2 The Experiences of Japan's Urbanization Model

Attaching Importance to the Transformation of Agriculture and the Promotion of Agricultural Modernization

Agricultural development functioned as a prerequisite, as well as the material basis, for the growth of Japan's industrial sector. Due to Japan's limited land resources, successive Japanese governments attached utmost importance to agricultural development. The result of this was the continuous introduction of policies designed to significantly development of agriculture, in part, by intensifying the use of rural land and, therefore, establishing the preconditions for subsequent agricultural mechanization. In 1960, for instance, expenditure on agricultural machinery in

Japan was 84.1 billion yen, a figure that increased to 968.5 billion yen by 1975, that is to say, an increase of more than tenfold.[37] In the mid-1970s, Japan had already realized the comprehensive and spectrum-wide mechanization of its agricultural process, from ploughing, sowing, cultivating to harvesting. This, in effect, constituted the necessary preconditions for the development of industries and, ultimately, rapid urbanization itself.

Population Shifts Triggered by the Development of Manufacturing and the Tertiary Industry Sectors

The development of Japan's tertiary industry provided an abundance of new employment opportunities for the rural surplus labor force. As such, rural laborers began to rapidly concentrate around major cities. From 1950 to 1970, for instance, those employed within the primary industry sector decreased from 48.3 to 19.4%. In the same period, employment in the secondary industry sector increased from 21.9 to 33.9% while in the tertiary industry sector, employment rose from 29.8 to 46.7%.[38]

The Construction of an Adequate Transportation Network

From 1964 onwards, Japan's transportation infrastructure witnessed extraordinarily rapid development. Japan was already heavily engaged in the construction of a highly advance, nationwide Shinkansen railway network as well as a comprehensive network of roads and highways. Further propositions existed to the effect of connecting all of Japan's economically relevant islands such that they would all be within one day's reach of one another. Perhaps most significantly, the extent of the Shinkansen railway network increased from 515 km in 1970 to 2176 km in 2005. The mileage of Japan's high-speed railway network, meanwhile, increased from 638 km, in 1970, to 8744 km in 2005. Needless to say, such an advanced transportation system gave rise to numerous cities while further promoting the exchange of materials and information between cities as well as their rural peripheries.

Huge Uptake of Foreign Investment in Both Capital and Technology

Though Japan saw economic recession as well as low levels of productivity following World War II, the outbreak of the Korean War provided Japan with opportunities to absorb and use foreign investment for its development, thereby triggering period of rapid growth of the Japanese economy. One indication of such

---

[37]Sun et al. (2010).
[38]Sun et al. (2010).

growth was Japan's position at the forefront of purchasing advanced technology from overseas. From 1950 to 1973, for instance, Japan imported **2168** technologies, spending cumulatively 4.356 billion dollars. During which, the 1950s, for instance, witnessed an annual introduction of **233** significant new technologies, whereas the 1960s witnessed an annual introduction of **2157** technologies. Technology introduction triggered Japan's technological revolution.[39]

Strengthening the Construction of Rural Infrastructure

The construction of rural infrastructure was an important measure not only to narrow the urban-rural gap, but also to provide more employment opportunities in rural areas. Such increased investment successfully promoted economic development in rural areas, providing new employment opportunities and paving the way for the continued expansion of urbanized populations and industry. In 1988, for example, Japanese investment in rural infrastructure was as much as 1.091 trillion yen. This abundant investment and development functioned to strengthen the links between urban and rural areas; creating the conditions for the realization of urban and rural integration.

Prioritizing Education, Social Security, and the Public Good

After World War II, Japanese authorities attached great importance to the provision of basic education. In pursuit of universal basic education, the "Basic Education Act" and the "School Education Law" (1947) increased the duration of compulsory education from 6 to 9 years. Japan's investment in public education, however, continued to intensify further as, from 1963 to 1973, investment in public education saw an average annual growth of 17.6%, that is to say, a figure which exceeded the growth rate of the total economy. By the 1980s, meanwhile, Japan had successfully popularized high school education, even providing 40% of school-age students from rural areas with the opportunity to continue their studies at university. Among other social benefits, this substantially increased the quality of Japan's available workforce.[40] At the same time, Japan emphasized vocational training, specific to the skills required for certain occupations, for rural laborers: that was, the government and local businesses persevered to provide, along with the training, employment information and advice to these prospective workers. Such widespread training played a significant role in laying the foundation of agricultural mechanization and, consequently, increased labor productivity.

---

[39]Gao (2002).
[40]Yu (2007).

Industry Regurgitation-Feeding Agriculture

Japan's industrial progress revolutionized its agricultural processes in at least two ways. First, as was required in order to adapt to modern urban development, a series of agricultural policies were issued to promote rural land system reforms with a view to, in particular, further enhancing agricultural production. Second, the technological progress, as a result of Japan's rapid industrial development, led to widespread agricultural mechanization thereby greatly improving the productivity of land, and, ultimately, the agricultural development.

3.1.4.3 Lessons to Be Drawn from Japan's Model of Urbanization

Inadequate Housing and Serious Traffic Congestion

Of all the problems that resulted from industrialization in Japan, shortages of available housing in urban areas, due to the over-concentration of the population in these areas, was among the most testing. After the Meiji Restoration, a great deal of Japan's rural population concentrated, within a short timeframe, to Tokyo and Osaka, among other major cities, subsequently, resulting in the massive over-crowding of such destinations. Consequently, the growing ranks of poor residents within urban areas were restricted to living in slums that, needless to say, were notorious for their poor conditions. Even as late as the 1960s, by which point industrialization had reached its peak, a considerable number of people remained confined to relatively deprived residential areas. A combination of these cramped and poor conditions and the high cost of property and rent encouraged a great deal of people to move to cheaper land on the outskirts of cities. This, in turn, functioned to exacerbate the already serious traffic problems, thereby leading to unprecedented congestion in and around big cities.[41]

The Burst of Japan's Bubble Economy Caused by Inflated Urban House Prices

Land usage is among the most fundamental considerations of a successful city. Problems as far ranging as poor housing conditions, congested transportation, and environmental degradation can all be due to limited space. Law of supply and demand dictates, furthermore that an inadequate supply of land will invariably result in the rise of land prices. However, in Japan's, the inflation of land values was almost unprecedentedly high. In the 17 years from 1955 to 1972, for instance, land prices in Japan increased approximately 17.5 fold. Such an increase was practically incomparable with other countries at the time and was, in fact, one of the major

---

[41]Li and Zhong (2007).

causes of the bubble economy which, in turn, subsequently, triggered a long-term depression of the Japanese economy.[42]

Overloaded Cities and Declining Living Environments

With the rapid industrialization and urbanization, on the one hand, industrial pollutants, discharged from facilities heavily reliant on petroleum, increased dramatically while, on other hand, motor vehicle exhaust emissions surged significantly. Together, these substantially worsened the already degraded air quality within major urban centers. In particular, from the mid-1960s to the mid-1970s, Japan witnessed massive growth in the popularity and availability of motor vehicles. Yet, even a few years prior to this boom, air pollution was among the most serious problems faced by urban residents. Tokyo, as well as in Osaka, Yokohama, and a range of other concentrated cities, notices warning of dangerously poor air quality were issued dozens, even hundreds of times annually. By July 1992, the total number of vehicles on the Japanese home islands had reached 60 million. Such a large number of vehicles congested Japan's somewhat limited space, especially major cities, thereby leading to severe traffic congestion to accompany its poor air quality. Additionally, overpopulation resulted in worrying levels of urban waste, including domestic garbage, especially in big cities. Finally, the so-called urban heat island effect was also, a result of the concentration of large population.[43]

3.2 Experiences and Lessons from the Urbanization Process in Developing Countries

3.2.1 South Korea: Centralized and Decentralized Patterns of Urbanization

South Korea, as one of the "Four Asian Tigers", is a country that have, in recent history, successfully achieved industrialization. Since 1960, South Korea's economy developed considerably while, at the same time, urbanization rates proceeded at comparatively high levels. South Korea's occupation by Japan continued until the end of World War II. From 1945, however, South South Korea proceeded to depart from Japan's colonial rule and achieve independent sovereignty. It is a typical late-development economy. Furthermore, South South Korea's modernization process was delayed significantly by the outbreak of the South Korea South South Korean War afterwards. A truly modernized and industrialized urbanization began to emerge from the 1960s.

---

[42]Li and Zhong (2007).
[43]Li and Zhong (2007).

3.2.1.1   Phrases of Urban Development and the Distribution of Population Within South Korea

From the changes observed in the distribution of cities in South Korea since 1949, urban development can be informatively divided into the following phases.[44]

A Period of War and Subsequent Recovery (1949–1960)

The migration of population caused by war would usually leads to the reorganization of population, spatially and geographically, during war and after war. The outbreak of the Korean War (1950–1953) had a significant impact on the spatial and geographical distribution of population in South Korea.

First, the war led to population concentrations within urban areas. In order to escape from conflict, people abandoned their homes and naturally began to gather in urban areas. This was particularly common in the case of North Korean refugees who, insofar as they did neither own property nor other resources within rural areas, regarded cities as their best chance of finding shelter and residence. Urban areas were, at this point, characterized as centers of relief for the refugees who flocked there in large numbers, throughout the wartime period and during the postwar period. The urbanization rate, therefore, rose significantly, that is to say from 17.21%, in 1949, to 24.49% in 1955. Just as importantly, the war also led to regional space reorganization of South Korea's urban populations. From 1949 to 1960, South Korea's fast-growing urban population mainly concentrated in the following regions. The most significant was the southern region. From 1949 to 1953, the Korean War forced a great deal of the population of northern regions to flee southwards. This upheaval actually resulted in significant urban population growth, as well as the establishment of a number of cities across the southern regions of South Gyeongsang, North Gyeongsang, and South Jeolla. Partly as a consequence of such urbanization, these regions underwent a significant period of recovery after the War (1953–1960). Also noteworthy, the northern region of Gangwon, as well as the city of Seoul itself, witnessed unprecedented growth as wartime migrants returned northwards. As a result, Seoul and the Gangwon-do region enjoyed significant growth while the number of cities in the Gangwon-do region increased substantially.

South Korea's Economic Take-off (1960–1970)

From the 1960s, under the governance of Park Chung-hee, South Korea underwent a rapid drive towards industrialization. Initially, industry was heavily geared around textiles and basic commodities. The success of such enterprises was, meanwhile,

---

[44]Li (2008a).

comparatively dependent upon factors such as the labor market, commodity market, and transportation conditions. Considerations of this sort strongly favored the aggregation of industries and companies which, in turn, dictated that this early industrialization concentrated almost exclusively within large cities. The capital city of Seoul, with a population of more than two million, naturally, then, gave rise to a region where industrialization was notably accelerated. Encouraged by the abundant employment opportunities resulting from the development of industry in this region, the population of Seoul increased dramatically, from just 2.44 million, in 1960, to 3.79 million, in 1966, and, finally, 5.43 million in 1970. Relative to both the overall national population and the nationwide urban population, Seoul's growth was unprecedentedly dramatic. That said, the urban population in other regions continued to increase throughout the same period. Ultimately, however, these rates of growth were considerably smaller especially, that is, in the South Gyeongsang, North Gyeongsang regions. Despite significant urban development, urban population in these regions rarely increased throughout the 1950s while their share of the overall national total population even entered into short periods of decline.

The First Economic Adjustment and the Aggregation of Consumption (1970–1980)

From the late 1960s onwards, the massive influxes of manufacturers, who engaged in textile and other light industries in Seoul, triggered a localized surge in the value of fixed assets. As a result, the negative effects of aggregation increased, the input–output efficiency of industry declined, and economic growth slowed down. This, in turn, triggered the first round economic adjustment to the industrial structure and industrial spatial structure of South Korea. The clear logistical advantages of established cities that were adjacent to Japan, such as Busan, as well as those along the southeast coast, including, for instance, Ulsan, gave rise to new centers of manufacturing and industry. Consequently, the population of such southeastern coastal regions rapidly increased, particularly, within urban areas, making the region, a place in Korea, where population was growing fastest. Nevertheless, at the same time, as Seoul developed into a megalopolis, it provided a range of commodities and services that could not be found, at prices that were significantly lower than those available in other regions. Seoul, despite the economic slowdown, therefore, remained highly appealing for consumers in general. Consequently, the capital's population continued to be characterized by rapid growth. Such growth had, in return, a balancing effect by which a well-supplied labor market as well as demand for consumer goods bolstered regional industry, the tertiary sector in particular, and, thereby, rekindled Seoul's prosperity. The concentration of residents and manufacturers in the capital, interacted, and jointly promoted the further expansion of Seoul's population. Compared to the levels witnessed throughout the initial economic take-off, however, Seoul's population growth rate during this period was notably decreased. That is to say, while Seoul's population proportionate to the total national population continued to increase, it actually declined relative to overall urban population.

The Development of Satellite Towns and a Period of Balanced Development (1980–2005)

After the 1980s, the development of South Korean cities underwent major changes. On the one hand, since the late 1980s, democratic reforms were introduced in South Korea. Nationwide concern was shown over regions of South Korea that had been left behind by prior development. Accordingly, policies which promoted balanced development among regions came to forefront of the political discussion. Attention, the subsequent state policies, were directed, in particular, at underdeveloped central and southwestern coastal regions. Accordingly, the urban population in these areas increased substantially, as did both the size and number of cities. Throughout the mid-to-late 1990s, an agenda of balanced nationwide development was followed from strength to strength. Yet, after two decades of fast economic growth, from 1960s to 1970s, the savings and disposable income of Seoul's urban residents had, by the 1980s, reached considerable levels. This, in turn, fuelled and funded an appetite for improved living conditions that ultimately drove residents of Seoul towards the nearby Gyeonggi-do area. At this time, the South Korean government paid particular attention to the construction and improvement of Seoul's satellite cities. Consequently, the urban population in the Gyeonggi Province, including Incheon city, soared from 2.379 million, in 1980, to 11.07 million, in 2005. Its proportion of the total national population and the total urban population, meanwhile, increased from 6.36 and 11.1%, in 1980, to 23.0 and 25.85%, in 2005. In fact, the Gyeonggi Province was home to the fastest-growing urban population in South Korea. Other regions, too, witnessed continuously increasing urban populations, but their overall shares of the national urban population actually stabilized or declined in comparison.

   South Korea's urbanization process was shaped, above all else, by the above-mentioned regional characteristics. Cities and urban population were, for the most part, concentrated in two areas, that is, the Seoul metropolitan and in the North and South of the Gyeongsang region, stretching across the southeast coast. Urbanization, in general, consists in the spatial transfer of economic activity from rural to urban regions, the key of which was the widespread rural to urban population movement. This could be exemplified by the case of South Korea. Massive population moved towards the abovementioned two regions, speeding up the process of regional urbanization, as a result, metropolitan agglomerations came into being.

3.2.1.2 The Distribution of Cities by Size in South Korea

In the urban system of South Korea, the composition of different-sized cities varied greatly. In particular, cities were characterized in terms of their population, with five separate population categories: 50,000–100,000 inhabitants, 100,000–250,000, 250,000–500,000, 500,000–1,000,000 and, finally, those with over 1,000,000. In 2005, eight South Korean mega-cities, that is, less 10% of the total number of cities, contained more than one million people. Between them, these mega-cities held 53.8% of the total urban population, or in another word, more than half of the total national population. The scattergram of cities in the five population categories could be described as spindle-shaped. The majority of South Korea's cities, meanwhile, corresponded to the middle three population categories while there were relatively few cities that fit within the highest or lowest categories. However, in the distribution map of the population in five city categories, numerical increases could be witnessed between categories. The two largest categories, in particular, witnessed a shape division from one another, the difference was almost 40% points, thereby indicating a trend towards the development of major metropolitan areas in South Korea.[45]

Meanwhile, the distribution of different-sized cities in South Korea varied greatly across different periods of development. From 1960 to 2005, for instance, the number of cities with a population of more than one million increased from just two to as many as eight. The number of cities with a population of 500,000–1,000,000, meanwhile, increased from one to ten while cities with a population of 250,000–500,000 increased from two to twenty. Likewise, the number of cities with a population of 100,000–250,000 increased from four to thirty-three and, finally, the number with a population of 50,000–100,000 actually reduced from eighteen to thirteen. All of that is to say, with a 45 year period, the number of large and medium cities in South South Korea significantly grew whereas the number of small cities substantially shrunk.[46]

In sum, prior to 1980, urban growth in South Korea was largely concentrated around mega-cities such as Seoul. Since the 1980s, however, South Korea witnessed a typical model of population decentralization as small cities increased in number and population size. Developing small cities played a dominant part in urbanization in South Korea at that time. The 1990s, meanwhile, witnessed these small cities, those established in the 1980s, developing into medium cities, thereby effectively reducing both the number of small cities and the proportion of the population which now resided in small cities. Simultaneously, the number of larger cities and their relative share of the population rose sharply. The growth of medium cities was, therefore, the leading trend of urbanization at that time. In the twenty-first century, however, urbanization and urban population, once again, turned towards a process of decentralization which, in turn, favored the growth of smaller cities.

---

[45]Li (2008b, p. 241).
[46]Li (2008b, p. 243).

3.2.1.3 Enlightenment Gained from Urbanization in South Korea

South Korea's process of urban development clearly demonstrated that urbanization and economic development occurs in highly concentrated patterns when economic development is rapid and industrial performance strong. Decentralized economic development and dispersed urban development, meanwhile, corresponds with slower or stagnated economic growth. Therefore, the focus policies directed towards urban development must be to effectively induce aggregation effect and promote its development. At the same time, however, it is also noteworthy that, at different stages of development, the precise distribution of economic activities and the focus of concentration in urbanization process varied significantly. Throughout earlier stages of economic development, national and regional capitals functioned as the clear centers of economic activity and agglomeration. Nevertheless, at later stages of economic development, secondary peripheral cities witnessed significant economic growth and population aggregation. As such, policies, provided by South Korean government, directed at encouraging and restricting the growth of different tiers of cities are affected by and sensitive to different stages of overall economic and industrial development.

In addition, South Korea's experiences of urbanization demonstrate that the key to maintaining sustained rapid economic development is to ensure the dynamic regulation of the overall economy. One such example is South Korea's introduction of a policy allowing the free movement of its population. The large-scale population movements between regions, as well as the free flow of rural to urban migration, filled effectively the income gaps, caused by different levels of development, between different cities and between urban and rural areas. Compared with other countries' urbanization at the same stage, such dynamism facilitated nationwide rapid economic growth while also avoiding a deteriorated income distribution relation. Therefore, there comes the "Miracle on the Han River", an example of comparatively coordinated development.

Meanwhile, South Korea South South Korean authorities were particularly attentive to the options of micro-efficiency and macro-efficiency in urban development. On the one hand, throughout the entire process of urbanization, the government extensively intervened in the planning and development of urban areas. They had, for instance, highly exacting criteria for urban planning proposals relating to land as well as a strict system of oversight and approval relating to the conversion of agricultural land. Meanwhile, in order to implement the government's urbanization strategy, South Korean authorities selected a method of management for urban development that differed from those typical of other capitalist economies. In order to promote and effectively manage large-scale urban development, the South Korean government established a series of publically accountable corporations. Such corporations engaged in urban planning and large-scale urban development as well as the construction of key urban infrastructure. All of this was done strictly in accordance with the comprehensive planning of state territory and urban planning regulations, thereby effectively ensuring that the process of urban development abided by the necessary standards. Such a system, while highly conducive to the operation of large-scale projects, particularly the construction of new cities, was also coordinated in such a way as to avoid the duplication of constructed infrastructure between and within regions.

3.2.2   China Taiwan: Urbanization Driven by Industry

Urbanization process worldwide has shown that the precise course of urbanization may follow different paths, influenced primarily by differences in the level of economic development as well as preexisting levels of urbanization. A number of developing countries, or at least particular regions within such countries, have, for example, experienced a degree of "over-urbanization", which has, in turn, triggered a range of related problems. Economic development, for instance, may slow or even reverse while social unrest and insecurity are also possibilities. China Taiwan, a case in point, had a great deal of industry of population concentrated in a select few metropolitan areas. Nevertheless, Taiwan also spared no effort in terms of developing small towns and cities with a view to decentralizing some of its workforce in order to resolve some of the problems of excessive urban development.

3.2.2.1   Urbanization in Taiwan

Because of its unique historical circumstances, Taiwan's urbanization process has been influenced by a range of factors at each stage of its development. It was during the Japanese Occupation that Taiwan witnessed the beginning of its urbanization. Subsequent urban development has been obviously branded by the times, possessing the characteristic of larger discrepancy, thereby giving rise to a range of distinctive developmental phases.

From 1895 to 1950

During the Japanese Occupation and the subsequent period of recovery, impacted by the colonial rule and the wartime demand, limited by socioeconomic conditions at the early stage of recovery, urban planning in Taiwan was largely restricted to the development of a few towns and cities. Taipei city, that is, the only significant urban center of the period, and a relatively balanced distribution of small towns took shape accordingly.

The Late 1950s to the 1960s

As industrial development in Taiwan gradually accelerated, especially, that is, as assigned industrial zones matured, the focus of urban planners shifted towards large-scale regional planning. During this period, the urban population in Taiwan increased rapidly from 3.87 to 8.69 million,[47] while the nationwide urbanized population increased from 47.2 to 59.2%. It was a stage of rapid urbanization. At this stage, as industrial zones were developed and the agglomeration effects were generated, new industrial cities mushroomed and the number of cities increased to some extent. Nevertheless, with the inevitable formation of metropolitan regions that follows sustained economic development, Taiwan's population and economic resources became somewhat concentrated. A series of problems, therefore, resulted, such as the widening of the gap between urban and rural areas, urban overpopulation, housing shortages, congestion and environmental pollution. Needless to say, these had a major impact on sociopolitical and economic activities alike. At this begin, the administrative authorities of Taiwan were compelled to gradually reflect upon and review the urbanization process so far.

The End of 1960s to the Early 1980s

During this period, the urban population in Taiwan increased to as high as 15.09 million, a great concentration of who resided within large cities. Meanwhile, the proportion of the overall population within urban regions rose to 70.3%, thereby indicating a phase of city expansion.

The 1980s to the Mid-1990s

During this period, the population of satellite towns, surrounding major cities, increased rapidly. The Zhonghe and Yonghe regions in Taipei County, for instance, underwent significant growth. One significant cause of this phenomenon was the rapid rise of housing prices within the central areas of major cities. This effectively excluded ordinary working people from purchasing property in such locations. Furthermore, improvements to public transportation networks made possible the convenient movement between city centers and surrounding towns. People started to move to satellite towns. This, combined with the relatively stable cost of living there, resulted in an increase of urban population to 16.23 million while the proportion of urban population increased to 77.2%. In other words, Taiwan's suburbanization was well and truly underway.

---

[47]It should be noted that, the then large proportion of urban population in Taiwan had much to do with the migration of a large number of military and civilian population from the Chinese mainland to Taiwan and their concentration in urban areas. In 1947 the urban population in Taiwan was 2.57 million.

The Mid-1990s to the Early Twenty-First Century

During this period, Taiwan's urbanization reached new heights insofar as public facilities within urban areas were gradually constructed and improved. "The urban population effectively stabilized with only a slight downward trend. In 1997, for instance, the share of urban population stabilized at 77.1%, maintaining growth around 77–78%. Despite this stability, however, the trend of suburbanization became more evident. For one thing, the number of satellite towns increased from 417 in the mid-1980s to 441."[48] This indicated that Taiwan's urban development had, by now, gradually entered the post-urbanization stage.

Overall, however, the pace of urbanization in Taiwan remained very fast. According to CEPD (Council for Economic Planning and Development) measure standard, based on employment distribution across the primary, secondary, and tertiary industry sectors, Taiwan's urbanization rate was around 68% at this stage. In fact, in 2000, 78% of Taiwan's overall population resided in cities with populations of more than fifty-thousand. However, insofar as even those cities with less than fifty-thousand inhabitants had generally reached a highly urbanized post-agricultural stage, took this in consideration, the total urban population, in 1996, exceeded 81%. Taipei, Taichung, Tainan, and Kaohsiung, as Taiwan's four major metropolitan areas, became the focal points for further large-scale urban development. In comparison, the total urban population in the United States was 78% in 1990,[49] that is to say, urbanization level of Taiwan was roughly the same levels as the United States. However, the United States required 100 years to reach this level, whereas Taiwan managed it in 50. In general, the rate of urbanization not only coincides with accelerated industrialization development, but also constitutes a prerequisite for rapid economic take-offs. Urbanization speed, then, had, to a large extent, a direct impact on the social, political, and economic structure of a country.

3.2.2.2 The Features of Urbanization in Taiwan

The Appearance of Metropolitan Areas

The urbanization process in Taiwan began to expand significantly from the late 1970s. This was particularly evident as instances of metropolitan areas, with large cities at their core, gradually came into being. Such metropolitan areas invariably gained priority status in terms of resource allocation. The Taipei, Taichung, Tainan, and Kaohsiung metropolitan areas are among those areas that had profound and direct impacts on subsequent patterns of economic and social development in Taiwan Region.

---

[48]Sheng (2010).

[49]*Statistical Compilation of Metropolis and Regional Development in Taiwan*. Compiled by CEPD (Council for Economic Planning and Development) of Taiwan 2002, p. 12.

First, the formation of metropolitan areas represented a spatially industrial clustering. Throughout earlier stages of industrialization, due to abundant labor concentrated within dispersed rural areas, factories were spatially decentralized so that farmers could take part-time job there. This situation was, however, short lived as, from 1970 onwards, a production network gradually replaced the old organization structure of industrial production in Taiwan, in accordance with the needs of economic globalization and Taiwan's industrial division. The concentration of production within particular regions, therefore, became increasingly evident. Prior to the 1970s, in fact, most large corporations engaged in capital-intensive industry, in which labor demands were low in comparison to small companies. As such, the reliance of large corporations upon surplus laborers was limited at best. Therefore, large corporations were consistently predisposed to locate and concentrate within those specific metropolitan regions. This predisposition of big business functioned as a developmental impetus of metropolitan areas and surrounding towns, which evolved into economic complexes as a result, which gradually possessed a relatively full function of cities. This furthermore, encouraged population concentration and the self-perpetuated expansion of metropolitan areas.

Second, Taiwan's metropolitan areas showed significant prospects for continued development beyond levels already reached. "Such prospects consisted in the potential for Taiwan's metropolitan areas to undergo the process of internationalization including interwovening into the international urban network and being a link within the global economy and industry relocation. This potential was closely related to Taiwan's economy structure. Based on current situation, urbanization within Taiwan could, at this point, be said as entering an entirely new stage of 'top-down' urban development, which was globally driven, characterized by the professional division of labor and urban comprehensive service function oriented. Like most processes of urban development, this internationalization of metropolitan areas would further accelerate in accordance with economic factors, that is, in this case, the increasing internationalization of Taiwan's economy."[50]

The Choice to Develop Small Towns

While mapping out the precise details of its urbanization and industrialization, Taiwan's authorities selected to focus, to a large extent, on the growth of medium and small cities. The process of which was different from the modernization in Latin American and other Asian countries who had, to some extent, resulted in social inequality and metropolis over-expansion as a result of excessive rural-to-urban migration. Although there existed a gap between the development of urban and rural areas in Taiwan, this gap was not especially large and, what's more, the entire population of urban areas maintained steady growth rates and expansion only on a modest scale.

---

[50]Sheng (2010, pp. 57–63).

The urbanization past in Taiwan indicated that during the "climax" of Taiwan's industrialization, migration from rural to urban areas, as well as from southern to northern regions, did occur, thereby resulting in the fairly rapid expansion of cities. Due to relatively limited migrants, however, a relatively balanced patterns of regional development was ensured, including convenient transport facilities and a reasonable distribution of industry for all. There simply wasn't any massive population movement or subsequent population agglomeration within Taiwanese metropolises. On the contrary, small and medium towns across Taiwan did witness the most rapid growth. There were, for instance, only three big cities, which were located with the three major metropolitan areas of the northern, central and southern regions, respectively, with a population of greater than one million. There were, however, more than 40 small and medium cities. Such moderately populated urban centers, which generally had three to seven hundred-thousand inhabitants, essentially followed the same developmental patterns as the small and medium towns in mainland China throughout the 1980s.[51] Later on, during the late 1980s, along with increased economic globalization, the number and development of metropolitan areas continued to increase. Nevertheless, this did not fundamentally change the overall balance of Taiwan's urban development and layout.

3.2.2.3 The Factors Behind Taiwan's Urban Development

Since 1960, urban development in Taiwan has been driven, for the most part, by three forces. First, economic forces have played a central role. Globalization, for instance, contributed to restructuring the organization structure of Taiwan's industry in such a way that reinforced the urban agglomeration effects and furthered their comprehensive economic functions. Second, government policies drove forward urbanization. Such policies were industry-oriented, thereby consistently neglecting both the development of agriculture and farmers' earning. This led to serious imbalances between levels of urban and rural development. The third factor was Taiwan's increasing total population. As Taiwan's rural, agricultural population shrunk, the pressures of additional population growth fell onto cities. As a result, most economic and social resources were rapidly concentrated in urban areas, thereby resulting in "city disease" in big cities. In conclusion, the combined effect of the three abovementioned factors shaped the basic spatial pattern of metropolitan areas which formed in Taiwan throughout the late 1980s. In this process, the spatial agglomerating effects of economic and urban development exacerbated regional imbalances and widened the gap between urban and rural areas.

---

[51]Chen (1999).

Urbanization and Economic Development in Taiwan

Following the end of Japanese occupation, Taiwanese authorities looked towards import substitution as a means of furthering economic development. Based on land reforms, the strategy of "nurturing industry through agriculture and promoting agriculture through industry" was implemented, through which, the basic needs of the people's livelihood were met. In this way, Taiwan's economy and society achieved a degree of short-term stability.[52] At this stage, then, the economic was almost entirely driven by agriculture while the handicraft industry within small and medium cities played a supporting role. In fact, handicraft industry constituted the main role of economic exchange between urban and rural areas. Therefore, such small and medium cities boomed, which, to an extent, weakened the agglomerating effects in big cities. This phenomenon was, of course, partly inherited from the layout of urban functions during the Japanese occupation period. It was also inseparable from the widely enforced evacuation policy that had extended to most of Taiwan's cities. For these reasons, urbanization in Taiwan presented a clear trend of decentralization.

Throughout the late 1950s, however, the focus of economic policy shifted from import substitution to export orientation. Taiwan's economic development, therefore, witnessed accelerated integration with the global economy. Took the advantage of relatively low factor cost involved in production, Taiwan attracted a great deal of labor-intensive industries from Western nations to the island which, in turn, achieved rapid industrialization and an almost unprecedented economic take-off. Taiwan subsequently became one of the four so-called "Asian Tigers" and one of the few economic winners of East Asia. Needless to say, these timely adjustment of economic development policies, including significant successes within a short time span, had profound impacts on the subsequent urbanization process in Taiwan.

The sort of labor-intensive industries that would be instrumental to Taiwan's new export-oriented economy relied upon its abundant supply of low-cost labors and the fact that there had, up until then, been fairly stagnant development within rural regions. The emergence of such labor-intensive, export-orientated industries required the concentration of both social capital and the working population into the network of industry established by large entrepreneurial organizations. The city, meanwhile, which functions as a link in the network of a global economy, was destined to receive much of the transfer of international industrial capital and would, therefore, become the inevitable center of large enterprises. Under such circumstances, industrial aggregation zones, centered on Taiwan's big cities, began to form, gradually at first but with increasing acceleration. As a result, from the late 1970s to the late 1980s, Taiwan's annual economic growth exceeded 10%. This period, marked, as it was, by full economic take-off, big cities and their adjacent

---

[52]Ye (1990).

towns witnessed a greatly accelerated urbanization process driven by industrial agglomeration. And metropolitan areas began to take shape.[53]

Policy: The Prioritization of Urban Development at the Price of Rural Development

Since the start of industrialization in Taiwan in 1960, imbalanced agricultural policies caused the share of agricultural incomes to decrease from **0.65**, in 1966, to **0.5**, in 1973. As a result, it was difficulty for agricultural workers to improve their living standards simply through agricultural production, especially, that is, in comparison to the living standards of urban residents, thereby resulting in an overall decline of agricultural development and a growing gap between urban and rural development. That said, from the late 1960s onwards, Taiwanese authorities, with a view to raising agricultural incomes, had attempted to enact the policy of "agricultural renaissance", which consisted, primarily, of agricultural mechanization and increased scales of production. Nevertheless, the overall effects limited, gradually a great deal of farmers were encouraged into sideline employment and, ultimately, into the industrial sector altogether.

While urban and rural gap widened and regional imbalances gradually increased, problem arose in policies concerning the development of industrial zones, which exacerbated problems within urban regions themselves. Taiwan's economic take-off, throughout the 1960s, was characterized by accepting the transfer of international labor-intensive industries, which made full use of the availability of cheap labor to develop export processing industries. As a development state, key to Taiwan's industrial competitiveness was access to abundant low-cost land resources for industrial purposes. As it was, the industrial zones that came to occupy this land were, with the exception of a few private developers, were developed by these Taiwanese authorities. The Taiwanese authorities formulated plans for industrial development for particular regions based, to a large extent, on forecasted market prospects and existing land use within the region. They also established specialized agencies tasked with developing and managing land resources prior to transferring or leasing these resources to eligible manufacturers at relatively favorable rates. Nevertheless, this model relied almost entirely on the judgment of the relevant authorities through the logic rules of market. As a result of these limitations, it led to a range of inevitable problems, not least the worsening of industrial land wastage. Thus, something contradictory happened in the process of urban development in Taiwan. On the one hand, with the expansion of urban areas, land resources became increasingly scarce and land prices kept rising. This adversely affected both urban planning and the prospects for improving urban living environments. On the other hand, idle and wasted land within industrial development zones was endemic. In

---

[53]Sheng (2010, pp. 57–63).

fact, this contradiction was widespread, and detrimental to the long-term stability of urbanization, not only in Taiwan, but also throughout all of East Asia.[54]

3.2.3 Brazil: Urbanization Driven by External Factors

The total population and land area of Brazil both at ranked fifth in the world while Brazil's GDP ranked at seventh. Historically speaking, Brazil was first discovered as late as just 500 years ago. In comparisons to countries such as China, which have a long history of civilization stretching back to ancient times, Brazil was a nation of immigrants without a very long history. There were then, in one sense, few historic factors that could hinder the urbanization process in Brazil. The Nation of Brazil was, after all, originally composed of a combination of immigrants from five continents and indigenous peoples, all of who had integrated through a long process of communication and joint efforts in production. Since it was such a nation originally composed of a large number of foreign immigrants, Brazil, in the future, would never be a closed country, thereby giving it a distinct advantage in the processes of urbanization and globalization. Indeed, the manner in which Brazil, an almost uniquely exogenous nation, responded to the challenges of global trends such as urbanization and globalization, the specific challenges they faced and solutions they embraced, would function as a telling test, the details and outcomes of which might contribute to better understanding such processes in other developed and developing countries alike.[55]

3.2.3.1 Urbanization in Brazil

The history of population urbanization in Brazil is roughly divisible into the following stages.[56]

Pre-nineteenth Century Urbanization

Before the nineteenth century, urban development in Brazil was extremely slow, particularly because the influence of the Industrial Revolution had not yet arrived. Urbanization could be described as in gestation.

---

[54]Sheng and Hu (2009).
[55]Yanjun (2011, p. 5).
[56]Yanjun (2011, p. 9).

Urbanization from the Nineteenth Century to the Twentieth Century

The Early nineteenth century, however, witnessed a new stage of urbanization in Brazil. In the late nineteenth century, large-scale European immigration entered Brazil which, in turn, promoted urbanization within Brazil. Additionally, in the late nineteenth century and the early twentieth century, significant developments to Brazil's agricultural economy enhanced the process urbanization further.

Urbanization Since the Twentieth Century

It was, however, in the twentieth century that the true taking-off of Brazil's urbanization process could be witnessed. Brazilian industrialization, commencing from the 1930s, promoted the development of central cities. By the 1940s, Brazil's population accorded, for the first time, to a clear urban and rural separation. Its urbanization rate, throughout this period, was 31%. Moreover, from the 1940s to the 1980s, urbanization in Brazil entered into a period of unprecedented rapid development. As a result, by 1970, the overall urban population, which significantly exceeded the rural population, was 54%, rising again to 70% by 1984. After the mid-1980s, the pace of urbanization in general slowed down. The urbanization level of Brazil has since reached 84.2% and, according to figures released by the Brazilian National Geographic Bureau of Statistics, will rise again to 93.6% by 2050.

In other words, it took a little more than 40 years for Brazil's urbanization levels to reach 70%. This is significantly quicker than most developed countries. It took the United States and France, for instance, more than 130 years to do so while even Japan required more than 50 years. Of course, prior to the twentieth century, Brazil's urbanization was characterized by traditional urban expansion without the incubus of industrialization. Industrial development since the twentieth century, however, quickened the pace of urbanization. Like in the most countries, then, industrialization proved to be the main driving force behind urbanization, industrialization and urbanization, each promoting and influencing the other in profound ways.

The figures above indicate Brazil's urbanization levels were exceptionally high, even for a developing country. Especially from the 1950s to the 1980s, Brazil saw rapid urban development. Thus, to study the unique factors responsible for this rapid model and process of urbanization, could not only enrich our understanding of the law under urbanization process in general, but also draw on the experience and lessons of the Brazilian urbanization process.

3.2.3.2 Brazil's Urbanization Path

In order to urbanize the country, Brazilian authorities had to carefully manage the settlement of population flowing between rural and urban areas. That means in addition to the flow of people into city regions, in situ urbanization in rural areas must also be managed. In this way, Brazil could effectively increase its urbanization levels without creating serious divisions between rural and urban areas. Fortunately, effective measures were taken by Brazil authorities in handling this issue.

External Factors

Brazil's urbanization was driven, to a large extent, by external factors, that is, its rural population, immigrants and big businesses were all permitted a free mobility to move into concentrated urban areas.[57]

Indeed, the movement of rural populations into urban areas constituted the main driving factor behind Brazilian urbanization and the greatest increase to the overall urban population. It is estimated that, since the later half of the nineteenth century, especially after the 1930s, as much as 60% of Brazil's urban population resulted from internal migration. In 1870, for instance there were only 30,000 people in the city of Sao Paulo. By 1990, however, it had reached the status of a mega-city with more than ten million residents. Nowadays, it has a population of 17 million. The rapid expansion of such cities was due primarily to the inflow of rural populations. It is, therefore, possible to conclude that, generally speaking, urbanization in Brazil was driven by a process of rural populations shifting to urban areas and the subsequent growth of new cities.[58]

That said, the rapid development of Brazilian cities was also driven by the large influx of foreign immigrants, particularly from Europe. After the 1850s, many Latin American countries attempted to attract foreign immigrants to come and settle down. Such policies enjoyed considerable success as millions of European immigrants relocated to Latin America. Brazil, in particular, especially in southern and southeastern regions, witnessed immigrant from, Italy, Germany, France, Poland, and Hungary, and many other European countries. Indeed, from 1820 to 1947, 4.77 million people immigrated to Brazil, many of who settled in the State of Sao Paulo.[59] Likewise, in the old capital of Brazil, Rio de Janeiro, immigrants constituted a large proportion of the city's population. In 1836, the proportion of foreign immigrants in the city's population accounted for 7%. By 1856, however, that proportion had increased to 35%, while, in 1890, it still accounted for around 30%.[60] Some of the immigrant population temporarily resided in smaller towns, engaging in localized commercial activities until such a time that they had earned enough money to migrate to larger cities, often, then, becoming involved in factory construction. Indeed, such entrepreneurial immigrants were among the first manufacturers in Latin America. The other immigrants generally moved directly into

---

[57]Yanjun (2011, p. 5).
[58]Yanjun (2011, p. 7).
[59]Gwynne (1985).
[60]Bradford Burns (1980).

medium and large cities to participate in the range of economic and social enterprises that had already been established. Therefore, not only did the influx of European immigrants increase the urban population in Latin America, it also promoted and facilitated economic prosperity within cities, along with new sources of capital and economic competence.

The Path of Urbanization Within Rural Area

Rural Urbanization was another prominent feature of Brazil's overall urbanization. For one thing, Brazil was a country rich in natural resources. Consequently, various centers of trade were formed around the country, including, for example, the eighteenth century gold trade in Goias and Mato Grosso, the nineteenth century rubber trade in the Amazon region and the twentieth century coffee trade throughout the southeast. Such trade hubs not only attracted new residents and provided additional employment, but also provided an alternative to farming for the local rural populations, which, in turn, enhanced urbanization process in Brazil even further.

Furthermore, since the 1980s, in order to satisfy the needs of industrialization and urbanization, the government increased its efforts to modernize agricultural production in rural areas. The mechanization of farming was realized in rural areas. Low-quality grassland throughout midwestern and northeastern regions, for instance, was transformed into fields of soybeans and corn, which were particularly suitable for the use of large-scale agricultural machinery. Such developments enabled much larger scales of production, higher labor productivity, and higher land output capacities. Meanwhile, economic stagnation and increasing unemployment in southeastern and southern regions gradually encouraged those who had migrated to urban areas to return to the rural areas from where they originated. Nevertheless, few involved themselves in the newly mechanized agricultural production, choosing instead to find employment in rural hotels, tourism resorts, villas, and other recreational activities or rural services.[61]

Today, in the twenty-first century, the global communications was greatly improved, internet developed rapidly, and the e-commerce became one of the fastest growing areas among others. The precise model of urban construction in Brazil shifted from one which emphasized highly densely populated, concentrated urban centers to one which emphasized improved living standards and environmental conservation. Brazilian people, much like Americans before them, could, to an extent, finally avoid permanent city-based office work. This was, instead, replaced by a more liberal mode of work which included the option to work from suburban or rural homes. As a result, large numbers of professionals began migrating back to rural areas without damaging their career prospects. Such developments, to technology and workplace practices, functioned to gradually promote urbanization within rural areas. It was a process of transformation in modernization. In this way,

---

[61]Yanjun (2011, p. 9).

formerly isolated and traditional rural areas were able to catch up with the values and practices of their more open and advanced urban counterparts. One could say that this reflected the most fundamental meaning of urbanization yet.

3.2.3.3 Problems Caused by Urbanization

While Brazil's rapid urbanization accelerated the nation's process of modernization, it also given rise to a range of problems, including severe economic inequalities, housing shortages, and environmental pollution. Such "urban diseases" were not, of course, limited to Brazil, but rather symptomatic of urbanization in general.

As always, a central component to these problems was population explosions within urban regions. Massive migration from rural to urban areas triggered rapid and unprecedented population growth, overwhelming cities' management and public security capacities. Not only did it reduce the quality of urban life in general, such overpopulation is at the root of all other urban problems.

Widespread unemployment and increased rates of poverty followed. Even though economic development in urban areas created many jobs, urban sprawl generated even greater demand than could be met by the new jobs. Similarly, in contemporary China, it has been difficult for migrant workers, who tend to have little formal schooling, work experience, and few professional skills, to find jobs in a modern economy dominated by mass production. Therefore, unemployment levels within urban Brazil were persistently high. Widespread low or even no income led to the emergence of an urban underclass. In addition, the polarization of income distribution has been a perennial problem in Brazil. Concentration of wealth in the hands of a few super-rich has long been the norm in Brazil. The Brazilian society was noted for its hierarchical structure and serious racial discrimination. In fact, Brazil's notorious wealth disparity was known worldwide.

The quality of the environment within urban regions also became a serious cause for concern. As the size and population of cities grew, the local environment became increasing vulnerable to irreparable degradation, both knowingly and unknowingly inflicted. Many Brazilian cities, for instance, witnessed illegal land use on endemic levels, including, in particular, the widespread construction of unregulated, makeshift slums to house the poor. Such slums quickly developed high population densities. Furthermore, the houses were very old and completely lacked necessary infrastructure, including areas to dispose of household waste. Daily life within these slums was just as chaotic with public security, in particular, becoming an intractable problem for relevant authorities.

3.2.4 Urbanization in India: A Slow Process

India, in South Asia, covers an area of **2.98 million** km^2, making it the largest country on the Indian subcontinent and the seventh largest country in the world.

India, with over 1.2 billion people, is the second most populous country in the world next to China. A population survey conducted by the India Census Commission on March 31, 2011, for instance, showed that India's population had already reached 1.21 billion. Furthermore, a 2001 census revealed that 72.22% of the population lived in more than 550,000 villages, while the rest of the population resided in more than 2,000 towns and cities. India, then, both as a developing country and as home to an enormous population, confronted problems similar to those witnessed in China. When planning for the process of urban development, Indian authorities alike, expected rapid urbanization, as well as economic and social modernization. Since the overall level of development in India was not high, however, there was already noticeable polarization between the rich and poor as well as severely underdeveloped infrastructure. Therefore, while India's early urbanization gave rise to some significant changes, there remained a long process ahead.

3.2.4.1 The Course of Urbanization in India

Urbanization in India could be dated back to the period of the Indus Valley Civilization. Historically speaking, Indian cities had traditionally been shaped by three kinds of civilization. These included early Hindu civilizations, medieval Islamic civilizations, and the Christian civilization of the modern era. For a long period of time, however, the vast majority of Indian people lived in rural areas. It was only in the past 100 years that India witnessed a slow process of urbanization.

First, the period most worth reviewing, then, is that of the century between 1901 and 2001. Within just 100 years, India's urban population increased from 25.8 to 285 million, that is, an 11-fold increase. Furthermore, urbanization rates in India have increased significantly since the country achieved independence in 1947. Such a trend is exemplified by the following figures which outline India's changing rate of urbanization: 26.4%, in 1961, 38.2%, in 1971, 46%, in 1981, 39.0% in 1991 and, finally, 31.4% in 2001. These growth rates were much higher than those witnessed in the first 30 years of the twentieth century.

Traditionally speaking, India had generally been regarded as a country with low levels and rates of urbanization. However, from the 1940s onwards, the growth rate of India's urban population accelerated significantly. Nevertheless, even throughout this period, compared to other Eastern countries, as well as most other developing countries, India's population hadn't particularly concentrated within a small number of big cities. "In 2001, for example, India had more than twenty cities each with a population of over one million. Despite these cities, however, India essentially retained an agricultural status, that is, insofar as 70% of the population resided in around six-hundred thousand villages spread across the country. In addition, based on the three industries that contributed to gross national product (GNP), in 2001, India's agriculture only covered 20% of national GNP. This is surprising given that more than 70% of the total population lived in rural areas. In other countries that had reached similar levels of economic development, the urban population tended to be much larger."[62] Compared to other countries, India's level and rates of urbanization were relatively slow.

There are a number of reasons why the urbanization process in India was relatively slow. After India's independence, a range of institutional and structural problems were unresolved. India's extremely large population, and its poor economic foundation meanwhile, only functioned to maintain India's development gap between rural and urban areas. That was similar to the situation in China. For over 50 years since independence, India had been developing a highly modernized, even post-modern landscape based upon finance, science, and technology, industry and culture. India's overall economic growth, however, still lagged behind Asia's other rapidly developing countries. "Statistics in 2002 suggest that India's IT and out-sourcing industries employed 3.2 million people while its manufacturing sector India employed around 6.2 million. The achievements of the Green Revolution benefited only a relatively small number of farmers, crops and a limited number of regions. Unemployment or underemployment were commonplace for rural labors which, at that time, outnumbered the demand of India's growing cities.[63]

A 2001 survey of India's urban population showed that although the overall pace of urban population growth in India remained modest, it had reached a number of significant milestones. For example, from 1981 to 1991, there had been a 36.7% growth rate in the number of cities and towns, thereby indicating a period of very rapid development. By 1991, meanwhile India's urban population accounted for 25.7% of the national total, meaning that a quarter of the population had, by then, moved into cities. This is as an impressive achievement insofar as, in 1941, this figure had been as low as 13.8% (see Table 3.4). Furthermore, by the early twenty-first century, the total urban population reached 280 million, that is to say, nearly 30%. Compared to certain regions within Latin America and North Africa, India's urbanization levels were relatively low. Compared to the some of the countries in many other developing countries and regions, however, it was not lagging behind significantly. According to United Nations statistics, from 1971 to 1981, India's annual urban population growth was 3.78%. Admittedly, this was below average as regards United Nation's predictions concerning a range of other developing countries in the first 5 years of the same period. Nevertheless, it was higher than the estimation of 3.62% initially predicted by the United Nations in terms of Indian urban population growth. In short, India's urban population growth over the past half-century was generally faster than expected.[64]

Large population shifts, from traditional rural areas to urban centers, was an important, if not the most important, factor behind the rapid expansion of major cities. As such, utmost attention ought to be paid to the potential consequences of this phenomenon. By the mid-twenty-first century, that is, by 2050, it is project that India's population will reach 1.6 billion, an increase of nearly 50%. The proportion

---

[62]Wang (2006, pp. 66–67).
[63]Wang (2006, pp. 66–67).
[64]Hu (1985).

Table 3.4 Urbanization statistic (from 1941 to 2001)

Year of census	Population		The proportion of urban population in the total population (%)	Number of towns	The growth rate of the number of cities and towns per ten years (%)
	Total population (million)	Urban population (million)			
1941	320.3	44.2	13.8	2329	–
1951	360.7	62.4	17.3	2924	25.5
1961	438.3	78.9	18	2462	−15.5
1971	548.2	109.1	19.9	2643	7.4
1981	659.1	156.2	23.7	3425	25.6
1991	845.1	217.2	25.7	4689	36.9
2001	1026.6	285.4	27.8	5161	10.1

Data sources Wang (2006)

of this population that will be urbanized, meanwhile, is estimated to be somewhere between 35 and 45%. In other words, the actual figure might be around 40%. Ensuring that such additions to India's overall urban population are relatively evenly distributed and absorbed among a wide range of towns and cities is, indeed, among the most urgent tasks. Relevant statistics demonstrate that, until 2009, India had 20 cities each boasting a population of over one million people, thereby ranking among the world's so-called mega cities. Besides those, there existed another 269 cities with a population of 100,000 people as well as 355 towns with populations of between 50,000 and 100,000. Throughout the same period, the growth of the number of major cities constituted the dominant trend of India's urbanization. The numerical growth of small cities, meanwhile, occurred at a significantly slower rate while the number of small towns, that is to say, with a population of less than 20,000, actually declined, albeit at a gradual rate.

3.2.4.2 The Primary Driving Forces of Urbanization in India

Urbanization in India was principally driven by industrialization, the development of a nationwide market economy, improvements to education and widespread population movements.[65]

The Driving Force of Industrialization

Following India's independence, the ruling authorities immediately had as its primary goal the rapid industrialization for economic development. Throughout the

---

[65]Wang (2006, pp. 66–67).

following decades, India completed the transformation of its economic structure, namely the transition from the small-scale production of consumer goods to a balanced nationwide distribution of light and heavy industry. As a result India was recognized as the tenth industrial power globally. From the perspective of geographical distribution, Indian industry, whether state-owned or private factories, whether new or old businesses, was primarily concentrated in urban areas. Needless to say, population movements, in general, targeted such concentrations of industry, thereby greatly promoting the development and prosperity of urban areas.

The Coordinated Development of India's Urban and Rural Economy

A major driving force of urbanization in India was the promotion and development of agricultural modernization. In terms of politics and economics alike, the agricultural modernization process in India was closely associated with the Green Revolution. The Green Revolution not only contributed greatly in promoting urban and rural market economy but also saw an increase in grain yields. It was the coordinated agro-industrial development that accelerated the trading and other commercial activities within urban and rural regions. For example, in regions where Green Revolution were undergoing, the improvement of agricultural efficiency increased grain yields as well as gave rise to an abundance of surplus labor. The excessive agricultural products were traded to bazaars in towns by those farmers who were less frequently farmed. They earned money from these transitions that provided sources for merchants in towns and cities. As such, investments in the field of agriculture, giving rise to a new breed of consumers receptive to products manufactured by entrepreneurs and workers in towns and cities. It thus functioned to enhance the trading and commercial activities between urban and rural areas. This change was, then, the main driving force behind India's rapid urbanization in the 1960s and 1970s.

Education as a High Priority

Since India's independence, the Indian government has attached great importance to the role of education in the national development. The people of India also traditionally place great emphasis and expectations on their children's education. Surveys and analysis indicated that, once found a job in urban areas, one's standards of living were higher, which was, definitely, based on better education and training received. Nevertheless, people from very poor rural families, besides their inability to finance such relocations, did not aspire to move to urban areas insofar as urban employers generally demanded higher levels of education from their prospective employees. In fact, to find any position that guaranteed better wages than rural employment within a city presented a significant challenge. For some, then, remaining in rural areas was the only feasible alternative. Many, however, wanted to migrate to cities in the hope that their children would have access to better education. After all, the quality of teaching in urban schools was, in general, substantially better than that in rural areas. Students admitted to urban schools, for instance, had greater chances of proceeding to attend university. If a student was admitted to a university, meanwhile, then financing their tuition fees, considerable as they were, generally required their parents to seek well-paid employment in the city. By that token, whether in China or India, most parents worked outside of their hometowns for the sake of their children's education.

Rural to Urban Migration

A number of the factors explored above were responsible for the continued large waves of rural to urban migration that played a major role in overall urban population growth. Prosperous industry and commerce within urban regions absorbed chunks of the rural population sufficiently large so as to fuel a cycle of exponential urban growth.

All in all, urbanization ought to be viewed as a broad developmental process, a agent for a wide range of economic and social and cultural changes, and consequences of those changes. In terms of development, rapid industrialization and increased technical strength came first, thereby improving the efficiency of India's agricultural production. Such improvements gave rise to a large surplus of labor, much of which relocated to cities, leading, in turn, to an increasingly market-based economy. This economic boom had an accumulative effect which ensured the continued provision of further employment opportunities. The concentrated population centers that began to take shape gave rise to further business opportunities as new entrepreneurs sought to supply the needs of consumers and participate in the profitability of city construction and management services. Needless to say, economic activity on this scale continued to attract new generations of rural immigrants, eventually pushing the urbanization process into the areas surrounding major cities and, ultimately, giving rise to the urban layouts recognizable today.

3.2.4.3 Problems with India's Urbanization Process

The Slums

A complete perspective of the urban life in India gives rise to some worrying insights, particularly as regards living conditions. Around 40% of India's rural population and 50% of its urban population, for instance, live below widely accepted minimum living standards. Besides that, around 1% of India's urban population, those at the very lowest level of society, lives in conditions considerably worse than those expected in even the poorest villages. Indeed, modern luxury skyscrapers can often be found in Indian cities built on small areas of land that are surrounded by deprived slums. This is a vivid representation of severe income polarization within Indian cities. Rather than effecting income alone, however, there also exists extreme inequality in the distribution of resources, social services and employment opportunities. Such inequalities have given rise to vicious cycles of inter-generational impoverishment within which members of the lowest income groups are unable to improve their living standards and must face a perpetual struggle to survive. Nevertheless, despite this risk, the rural poor continued to relocate to urban areas, thereby giving rise to urban slums as there simply wasn't enough room to better accommodate the constant influx.

The number of urban slums grew to such a point that the very idea of Indian cities, in terms of their international reputation, became synonymous with that of slums. "Housing located within commutable distance from the workplace was highly limited while land costs were high in general. Such factors had profound effects on the cost of rent, thereby forcing tens of millions of low-level employees and their families into slums across India. Needless to say, the conditions within such areas were characterized by a lack of basic facilities including water supply, electricity, toilets and bathrooms. Nevertheless, the number of residents combined to slums increased at a much faster rate than improvements to the physical infrastructure of urban areas. Therefore, they essentially became a dominant feature of many urban areas. Studies have shown that, by 1990, in India's largest four cities, that is to say, Mumbai (formerly Bombay), Calcutta, Delhi and Chennai (formerly Madras), the population living in slums was as high as 42, 40, 38 and 39% respectively. Furthermore, a 2000 study showed that the population of large cities living in slums was as high as 32 million".[66]

The existence of slums in the heart of cities is, of course, a common problem and side effect of urbanization faced by many developing countries. It functions as a major and intractable obstacle for further urban planning and development, not to mention as a potential threat to social stability. As a result, the Indian authorities have taken a range of measures to deal with this issue and to prevent any further expansion of slums. For example, one initiative intended to help the poor residents of slums find employment within close proximity to their homes. Another aimed at finding and offering affordable housing to such residents, often located at periphery of the city. Such initiatives implied the long term goal of improving the foundations and construction of slum areas. Unfortunately, the measurable effects of these initiatives were somewhat limited.

Inadequate Transportation and Infrastructure in Municipalities

The public transportation systems of all major Indian cities were seriously over-loaded and unable to meet the needs of passengers during each daily rush hour. A combination of chronic underdevelopment to the transportation system and exponential population growth effectively paralyzed all methods of transportation within India's cities. Great numbers of migrants had settled in the outer suburbs

---

[66]Wang (2006, pp. 68–69).

while the lion's share of economic activity remained concentrated in the city center. Such population distributions only worsened the burden on urban transportation systems. In Delhi, for example, the number of passengers traveling by bus increased by 175% in the last 10 years whereas the number of operational buses increased by just 90%. All in all, the underdevelopment of public transportation, old and narrow roads, passenger overloading, and ineffective planning and management gave rise to severe problems.

An analysis of the resources needed to support urban resources, compared with the resources available and the needs of 280 million urban residents led experts to estimate that, even by the standards of India's lowest level towns and cities, India's urban areas could facilitate no more than 55% of its existing urban population, that was, around 66 million. The tragedy of population overload and over-urbanization, therefore, raised concerns about the future prospects of urbanization in India. According to some forecasts, for instance, in the next 10 years alone, 150 million new apartments will be in demand. Supposing that the land and construction costs of each apartment was 22,000 Indian Rupee (Re), 3.3 trillion rupees would be required to apartment additions to the urban population. Given India's urban housing shortage and the high cost of construction, not to mention land speculation, a satisfactory solution to this problem is unlikely to be forthcoming.

As regards the nation's water supply, assuming even minimal water demands per person, 18.75 billion gallons would be required to meet the needs of all urban residents. On water supply alone, excluding investment in large-scale water-related infrastructure, at least 27 million rupees would be spent each day. According to these figures, in order to make up for urban water shortages, 100 billion rupees would be required for current expenditures.[67]

Energy Resources and Environmental Concerns

Energy supply was an equally important issue for urban planners. As an increasing number of residents gradually moved into cities, the reliance of urban areas on coal and imported oil products would grow. That is to say, an exponential growth of the demand for oil was anticipated even in the near future. According to a recent study on energy consumption in Mumbai (which was 1% of the per capita fuel consumption in the United States), by 2010, the total energy needs of urban residents would require at least 1.7 billion ton of coal equivalents each year.

Partly as a result of this high energy consumption, environmental pollution in towns and cities in India became a particularly serious problem. Most residents, for instance, had to survive in poor sanitary conditions. That, along with the high cost of pollution control equipment, made it impossible both to reduce poverty and control the levels of pollution. Studies made by the Central Public Health Engineering Research Institute of India, across nine different cities, found that in

---

[67]Hu (1985).

some urban areas, pollution had reached almost unprecedented levels. It, therefore, seemed inevitable that even India's prized beaches, rivers, and lakes would, eventually, become highly contaminated by raw sewage. Fresh air, meanwhile, would be contaminated with carbon dioxide, carbon monoxide, sulfur dioxide and other atmospheric pollutants. Environmental degradation would, then, become the most serious problem of urbanization in India in the future.

3.2.4.4   The Future of Urbanization in India

From a historical perspective, especially since modern times, Asia has been a continent inflicted by low levels of urbanization relative to global standards. Nevertheless, this situation is rapidly changing. It is well documented that the most populous countries in Asia, such as China, India, Bangladesh, Pakistan, and Indonesia, are undergoing a process of large-scale urban construction and rural-to-urban population movements, both of which have recently begun to occur at an accelerated pace. This is particularly true in China and India; in particular, due to their strengthening economies, their market commercialization and the large-scale relocation of their agricultural population. What's more, experts have repeatedly predicted that, within the next 50 years, the urbanization rates of China and India will rise from current levels of 30% to somewhat beyond 50%. In fact, China has already reached this level while India remains, for now, somewhat behind. Regardless of this difference, however, both countries are already committed to the decision to vigorously pursue further urbanization. As urbanization continues to accelerate, rural and urban areas alike will, inevitably, face a range of problems and challenges. The scale of these problems and the size of populations involved necessitates that understanding, facing and dealing with such challenges is a topic of utmost importance.

The majority of India's population is, at present, confined to rural areas, that is, insofar as only around one third of them reside in urban areas. To achieve the abovementioned goal of an urban population of over 50% of the total, a great deal more rural-to-urban migration must yet unfold. A number of issues and obstacles hinder the fulfillment of this task. India must, for instance, further enhance the principle driving force of urbanization, that is to say, the industrialization and modernization of agriculture. Likewise, the levels of investment into education, and related infrastructure, ought to be increased so as to improve the technological capability of the population in general which would, in turn, ensure, even accelerate, future industrial and technological development. At the same time, India should also increase investment in the construction of infrastructure within urban regions as well as take meaningful action to resolve the problems of urban slums. Only when the prospect of life within cities becomes an attractive, after all, will rural populations be sufficiently motivated to undergo such a transition. It is also important for India to reform a range of traditional features of its culture including, in particular, the notion of social castes, traditional, yet outdated, farming methods and, finally, the entrenched belief that the rural poor must remain invariably attached to whatever small amount of land they own. Far from being attainable in the short-term, such goals require long-term planning, intensive investment and determination on the part of the Indian authorities. Needless to say, the promotion of India's urbanization process will give rise to numerous social problems. The ultimate success of this process depends upon the capacity to measure, predict and cope with these problems. The maintenance of social stability is, after all, a perquisite of successful urbanization.

References

Bradford Burns, E. (1980). *A history of Brazil* (p. 242). New York: Columbia University Press.
Chen, L. (1999). Urban regeneration strategy in Taiwan. *Taiwan's Land and Finance Quarterly, 36*(4).
Cheng, Y. (1984). The pace and level of urbanization in the Soviet Union. *Urban Problem, 3*.
Duran, R. J. (2009). Legitimized oppression, Mexican American experiences with police gang enforcement. *Journal of Contemporary Ethnography, 38*(2).
Engels. (1957). The current condition of British working class. In *The complete works of Marx and Engels* (Vol. II). People's Publishing House.
Feng, H. (2011). *Research on the drive of abandoned land (Ph.D. thesis)*. Zhejiang University.
Gao, Q. (2002). Model of Japanese cities and rural and agricultural development. *World Agriculture, 7*.
Gwynne, R. V. (1985). *Industrialization and urbanization in Latin America* (p. 144). Johns Hopkins University Press.
Hao, S. (2007). Historical investigation in Japan's industrialization, urbanization and the evolution of agricultural land system. *Japanese Studies, 1*.
Hu, C. (1985). Urbanization in India. *Population and Economy, 2*, 57–62.
Huang, G. (2010). On development of the ideology of mercantile colonialism in the 17th century. *Journal of Jiangsu Second Normal University, 10*.
Huang, S., & Xie, D. (2010). The historic progressiveness and economic analysis of the 'Movement of Enclosures'. *Contemporary Finance and Economics, 12*.
Hobsbawm. (2001). *The extraordinary little—Revolt, rebellion and jazz* (X. Wang, Trans., p. 67). Xinhua Publishing House.
Ji, X. (2002). Analysis and evaluation on urbanization in the Soviet Union. *European and Central Asian Studies*, No. 3, 2002.
Ji, X. (2004). Urbanization and revelation in Britain. *Journal of East-China University of Science and Technology, 2* (Social Science Edition).
Katz, M. B. (2008). Why do not American cities burn very often? *Journal of Urban History, 34*(2), 190.
Li, G. (2003). Urban disease in Britain and its renovation—On British urbanization model. *Journal of Hangzhou Normal University, 6*.
Li, J. (2006). The development modes of seaside industrial zone in Kashima, Japan—Some implications in the development plan of petrochemical zone at Daya Bay in Huizhou. In *2006 Annual Conference of China Urban Planning Council*.
Li, E. (2008a). Path and trend of urban development in South Korea. In B. Zheng (Ed.), *Pioneering research on theory and practice of urban development* (p. 244). Social Sciences Academic Press.
Li, E. (2008b). Path and trend of urban development in South Korea. In B. Zai (Ed.), *Front-line study on theory and practice of urban development*. Social Sciences Academic Press.

Li, L., & Zhong, B. (2007). Experience, lessons and revelation/inspiration in Japan's urbanization. *Japanese Studies, 3.*

Mei, X. (2001). Exploration on the British environmental problems in the 19th century. *Journal of Liaoning Normal University, 23* (Social Science Edition).

Owen. (1981). *Anthology of Owen* (X. Ke, Trans., Vol. 1, p. 196). The Commercial Press.

Qian, B., & Liu, J. (1999). *Globe perspective: The disorientation of modernization* (p. 129). Zhejiang People's Publishing House.

Shen, Y. (2001). On the sources of labour in 'The Movement of Enclosures' and Industrial Revolution in UK. *Journal of Zhe Jiang University, 1* (Social Science Edition).

Sheng, J. (2010). Experience and defect of urbanization in Taiwan. *Taiwan Research Quarterly, 5.*

Sheng, J., & Hu, Y. (2009). *Urbanization and economic development in Taiwan* (p. 93). Jiuzhou Press.

Sun, B., Bai, Y., & Ma, X. (2010). The evolution of urbanization in Japan and its implications. *Economic Review, 12.*

Wang, S. (1990). History, current condition and characteristics of urbanization in the Soviet Union's. *Human Geography, 1.*

Wang, X. (2000a). The meditation on urbanization abroad. *Journal of Hebei Normal University, 4* (Philosophy and Social Sciences Edition).

Wang, X. (2000b). *The history of American cities*. China Social Sciences Press.

Wang, H. (2006). The causes of the slow urbanization process in India. In *The Fourth China Modernization Research Forum Proceedings*, October 29, 2011. http://www.ecmaya.com/article/sort06/sort025/info-28639.html.

Waymer. (2009). Walking in fear: An autoethnographic account of media framing of inner-city crime. *Journal of Communication Inquiry, 33*(2), 181.

Xing, J. (2011). *Analysis on the urbanization in the United States (Master's thesis)*. Jilin University.

Yanjun. (2011). The model and process of population urbanization in Brazil. *Ph.D. Dissertation*. East China Normal University.

Ye, W. (1990). The economic plan of Taiwan. In X. Gao & C. Li (Eds.), *Taiwan's economy for 40 years* (p. 50). Taipei: World Publishing Co. Company.

Yu, P. (2007). Balancing rural and urban development in Japan. *Macroeconomic Management, 9.*

Zhao, X. (2008). The core power of Britain's urbanization—The Industrial Revolution and industrialization. *Lanzhou Academic Journal, 2.*

Chapter 4
Seven Approaches to Urbanization in China

From the middle and late 1990s to the twenty-first century, urbanization in China has undergone a period of rapid development. The concentration of investment and industry in urban areas, not to mention the development of public utilities has directly promoted rapid economic growth in China. It has also functioned to cause population mobility, in particular from the countryside to cities, and population circulation between the countryside and cities, so large in scale and so intensive in amount as never seen before in human history. According to the economists Joseph Stiglitz China's urbanization and high-tech development in the U.S. would be the two major themes that would profoundly influence human development in the twenty-first century.[1] However, up until now, few theoretical studies or thorough analysis have been done on China's urbanization model and its global impacts. There is, for the most part, a lack of applicable theoretical generalizations and few comprehensive paradigms that can be used in the case of China's urbanization. Although scholastic circles in China have attempted to categorize urbanization by advancing notions such as the small-town model, the medium-city model, the big-city model, and the city-cluster model,[2] their efforts have primarily been limited to simple size division. In the other words, exploration into the unique path of urbanization in China has, thus far, been insufficient. The precise features of China's urbanization remain unclear as does the question as to whether or not China's urbanization follows a different pattern to that of other countries.

Comparing China's experience with international norms, this study proposes the notion of the "pushing model", that is the model of pushing ahead with urbanization, attempting to investigate, from different perspectives, the operating mechanisms, and modes through which urbanization in China has been realized. The pushing model generalizes the features of urbanization and the urbanization process in China. It was believed that the most prominent features of China's urbanization included being led by the government, planning on a large scale, and

---

[1]Quoted from Wu et al. (2003).
[2]Fei (1984a), Li (2004).

© Social Sciences Academic Press 2020
Q. Li, *China's Development under a Differential Urbanization Model*,
Research Series on the Chinese Dream and China's Development Path,
https://doi.org/10.1007/978-981-13-9451-5_4

implementing holistically all over the country. The concept of the "pushing model", frequently used in this book, must be thoroughly distinguished from the approach taken by European and American countries.[3]

4.1 The Particularized Process of Pushing Ahead with Urbanization in China

China's urbanization took a unique path as it was built on very different conditions and foundations from that of other countries. Its particularities occurred mainly because of the pushing model, in another word, the operation mode and the processes and mechanisms through which China's urbanization proceeded. These particularities can be analyzed from the following two perspectives: the dynamic mechanisms and the spatial patterns.

First, the dynamic mechanisms should be discussed in detail. There exist three types of underlying dynamics of urbanization in all countries in the world. These are the dynamics of government, of the market and of civil-society itself. The theoretical logic of these three dynamics conforms to the triad of social forces developed by Habermas, Cohan, and Arato, based, originally, on Gramsci's theory.[4] As the space is limited, this book won't extend the discussion of these underlying theories.

But what are the three dynamics of urbanization? The governmental dynamic refers to government initiatives to adjust and control urban development through administrative measures and policies intended to push forward urbanization. The market dynamic depicts the functions of market mechanisms in urbanization, where resources are allocated and distributed and supply and demand are adjusted through market forces to promote the upgrading of industries. Finally, the civil-society dynamic means that urbanization can be propelled by society itself, where every member has a motivation to improve their own living standards, change their lifestyle, embrace civilization and celebrate a more civilized city. In many countries, the civil-society dynamic presents in such a way that members of society participate in the city planning and construction through NGOs, associations and community organizations. The three dynamics are not isolated, but rather they overlap with each other in intricate ways. For instance, the basic principle of social mobility is that the labor force always flows from low-wage or low-price-labor areas to higher ones. This is, in itself, actually a result of the cross-effect of market dynamic and civil-society dynamic.

---

[3]The concept of urbanization in European and American countries usually refers to population shift to cities, while in China, city and town urbanization is more often used, since urbanization happened outside cities too, covering counties(lower than city level)and designated towns which are also important channels to absorb rural population.

[4]Please refer to: Habermas (1999), (2003), Arato and Cohen (2002), Gramsci (1971).

Throughout the urbanization of different countries, two dynamics prevailed throughout history, that is to say, the market dynamic and the government dynamic. It is, however, these dynamics from which the differences between the dynamic mechanisms of China's urbanization and those of Europe and America can be clarified.

The market-driven mechanism has had profound impacts upon the urbanization process around the world. Urbanization in Europe and America has undergone a change from an earlier concentration of population and industry in cities to a later de-concentration and dispersion. Although quite complicated, their development all shared a common background, that is to say, a strong market environment. For example, the dynamics of urbanization in the UK involved the development of domestic social productivity. Ever since the industrial revolution changed the industrial structure, small cities quickly developed into big cities. Furthermore, a well developed transportation network facilitated urban expansion, suburbanization and the formation of city clusters. The U.S. demonstrated another typical case of market-oriented urbanization. Large population migration to urban areas initiated city sprawl, remarkable suburbanization and, finally, city belts, composed of metropolitan areas, came into being. Previous studies on urbanization models, no matter whether they dealt with the bow-shaped model, with the central business district (CBD) as the core at the initial stage of industrialization, or the multiple nuclei model at the suburbanization stage, have all been based on the Land Rent Theory. This lends itself to the fact that the market economy was the dominant factor that influenced the urbanization process in Western countries.

Nevertheless, it is government driven mechanisms that, without doubt, account for the critical features of China's model of pushing ahead with urbanization and its dynamic mechanisms. The Chinese pattern can, then, be distinguished from Western ones. Government-driven mechanisms meant that the Chinese authorities, that is, Party and government organs at all levels, from central to local had complete power to approve of and decide the establishment of cities and towns, urban planning, construction site selection, land use, changes to land function, planning permission, construction engineering permission, infrastructure construction, and the demolition and reconstruction of old cities. This feature was most prominent during the fast-growth period of China's urbanization since the 1990s. The construction of large-scale development zones, the setting-up of new cities and extensive old city renewal were all handled directly by the government, as were the related funds and investment. Market-based reforms to China's economic system meant that attempts were made to establish a basis for non-governmental resource allocation, but its overall influence on urbanization was incomparable with that of government direction. Government and market factors do, however, overlook the dynamic mechanism of civil-society in urbanization. There have always existed bottom-up and top-down forces in China. It is the top-down force that is generally overwhelming. A well-known case of urbanization driven by civil-society, however, is that of Longgang Town in Wenzhou City.[5] This case involved an urbanization process that was self-funded, primarily by farmers, in the 1980s. It was, then, driven by civil society who strived to obtain final approval from the government. This example shows that government permission remains a vital link, for any proposal without government approval was of no consequence.

The particularity of the pushing model of China's urbanization consisted not only in the various dynamics at work, but also in its spatial model. The spatial model of urbanization in all countries can be classified into four types: the internal restructuring model, the continuous development model, the leap-forward development model, and the local in situ development model. The internal restructuring model aims at replacing the function of urban land and rearranging the spatial layout within the built-up areas of cities in order to improve the level of urbanization. The continuous development model intends to expand the city space based on existing urban areas and through differential land rent rates determined by market factors. The leap-forward development model, meanwhile, aims for relatively independent urbanization in rural areas away from major cities. As these areas normally lack the basic elements for urbanization, an external push is often required. Finally, the local in situ development model aims for in situ urbanization in villages and towns, primarily through a process of self-development. The ultimate aim is to upgrade industry, increase agricultural incomes and improve living standards, in another word, to have an urbanized production and life in the countryside Needless to say, however, the four models are never exclusive. Instead, at the lateral level, they often occur during the same period and interrelate with each other closely. For instance, internal restructuring is often accompanied with continuous development or leap-forward development, just like the outward relocation of industrial zones will form new urban areas and old city renewal will facilitate the development of new residential areas in the suburbs. New cities and new zones are often built in rural towns that enjoy better infrastructure, thereby demonstrating a combination of leap-forward development and local in situ development. However,

---

[5]The Longgang town was approved to set up in October 1983. Before its establishment, industries in its periphery developed to some extent. Ever since its set-up, several measures were taken by the town government to resolve the problem of insufficient fund for development, among which one policy was that, by paying a certain amount of utility fee, farmers would be granted the right to use a piece of land for their house-building, and a self-support Hukou (a temporary household registration to recognize their urban household status without offering the same planned provision/supply as assigned to city residents). Under this policy, many get-rich-first farmers flooded into Longgang town and started large-scale construction. By 1987, Longgang town had took an initial shape of a town. Media described it as the "overnight city". In 1994, its population reached to 130,000, with a gross output value of industry and agriculture of 50 million RMB. Longgang town had developed from the first "farmer city" into an industrial city. In 2010, it realized a GNP of 13.31 billion RMB and a gross industrial output value of 30.07 billion RMB. After the merger of some counties and towns in 2011, Longgang had a population of 500,000 people. For further information, please refer to http://www.cnlg.gov.cn/, the e-government website of Longgang Town.

at the vertical level, the prevailing spatial model that characterizes different urbanization stages could be different. Any study of urban evolution indicates that, since the 1950s, the prevailing model of European and American countries was the continuous deployment model, featuring city sprawl. This model demonstrated sharp contrast to the internal restructuring model to revive city centers ever since the 1980s.[6]

Although the four abovementioned spatial models characterize the urbanization process in all counties, the dominant pattern and pushing features of China's urbanization are remarkably different from those of the United States and European countries. China's urbanization is now in an expansion phase, due to rapid development, while the United States and Europe are at the continuous development model, involving, as it does, urban sprawl. Urbanization in China is also more prone to embracing the leap-forward development model. The sudden and rapid construction of development zones and new districts and towns has become an important method of pushing urbanization. This could be described as a development model with particular Chinese characteristics. More than that, according to the spatial characteristics of urbanization, not only does the market play the role of the main force behind urbanization in the United States and Europe, but citizens also, in their role as landowners, have the right to decide whether or not to accept and participate in such development. Urbanization throughout Western countries, therefore, allows for a degree of independence, which is reflected in the fragmentation of urban space. China's urbanization is, however, driven by strong governmental forces and features patterns of rapid and large-scale holistic development, whether it be through internal restructuring or a leap forward style of development.

Integrating the perspectives of dynamic mechanisms and spatial patterns, this section will compare the pushing model of urbanization in China with that of American and European countries. The findings will be summarized through the three following aspects (see Table 4.1).

First, in China, the entire process of pushing ahead with urbanization is government-led. Urbanization in Europe and the United States is, however, driven mainly by economic development, or to say, population concentration and industrial development exert an effect on urban system. However, things are different in China. National strategies play a decisive role in the urbanization process in all cities and regions. Since the founding of People's Republic of China, urbanization in China has been dominated by government forces. From 1949 to 1957, under the urban development policy of "Focusing on the Construction of Key Projects and Making Steady Progress", cities, in the mainland, witnessed rapid development driven by the construction of key projects. From 1966 to 1976, under the strategy of "Preparations for War and Natural Disasters and for the People", the construction of third-tier cities reached its climax. Since 1977, with the deepening of reform and opening up, urbanization in coastal areas, driven by special economic zones, open

---

[6]Tang (1997).

Table 4.1 A comparison of urbanization models in China and in Europe and the America

	Europe and America	China
The guiding force	Economic-development guided Urban system development mainly depends on population concentration and industrial development	Guided by the government; Urbanization is part of the national strategy. The establishment of urban system and urban development model are with a strong administrative features
Land system	Private ownership; urbanization process is fragmented	Public ownership; urbanization is processed in a holistic, large-scale, and rapid way
Pushing model	Bottom-up oriented; Urbanization is a spontaneous action when economy developed to a certain level, with adequate participation of social forces	Top-down oriented Due to insufficient development of social forces, it does not have the conditions for a spontaneous urbanization

cities, and economic development zones, has proceeded rapidly.[7] Since the reform and opening up, government-led features have become more prominent as China adopts urbanization into all aspects of its national strategies. In the urban system, cities have been established on a large scale, with the number of cities increasing from 289 to 666, from 1984 to 1996, while the number of towns has increased from 2786 to 17998 during the same period.[8] Moreover, most of the new large, medium and small cities have strong political characteristics, as their economic centers often merged with political centers.[9] As far as an overall approach towards urbanization is considered, almost every district now follows a development strategy of accelerating urbanization, that is, in accordance with the national goal of raising the level of urbanization since the mid to late 1990's.[10] Although a variety of models of urbanization have been tried in China, all urban development policies were actually deployed by the government. These policies were supported, at every turn, meanwhile, by forceful measures in the implementation process, such as population control and household registration. Even in situ rural urbanization was pushed ahead by government, albeit, at the grass-roots level. Some examples of this include the township governments in Sunan and the activities of local governments throughout the Pearl River Delta Model. Additionally, the policy towards building a new socialist countryside, deployed by the central government in 2005, was yet another approach directed at bringing urban civilization into rural areas.

It is also worth noting that land is state and collectively owned in China. Land in the United States and Europe, however, is mostly private property, such that

---

[7]Gu and Zhu (1993).
[8]Lu (2007).
[9]Gu et al. (2004).
[10]Lu (2007).

urbanization is generally influenced by fluctuating land values. It is the market that works. In addition, the desires and preferences of individual landowners played an important role in promoting or restricting the urbanization of Western countries. This is another reason behind the fragmentation of the urbanization processes. In contrast, the land law in China stipulates that land is of national and collective ownership. Whether it is the outward expansion of urban space, the construction of development zones or the construction of new zones and new cities, owing to the public ownership of land, the government is able to implement large-scale land acquisition, demolition and unified planning for national investment through the construction of large projects. Thus, urbanization in China had been pushed ahead holistically. Liang Shuming pointed out, in his analysis on the differences between Eastern and Western social structures, that Western societies, such as in Britain and the United States, are often based on individualism, while Chinese society is based on holistic collectivism and nationalism.[11] Lefebvre has also proposed, in his study on spatial politics, that, out of the capitalist characteristic of private property, space in the production process is fragmented.[12] Since China's reform and opening up, with the rise of Shenzhen, the construction of Shanghai Pudong New Area, the development of Tianjin Binhai New Area and the planning of Nansha Town, the development of new urban areas and towns, a key part of urbanization, has proceeded at a speed and scale never before seen in the history of the world.

Another key factor is that insufficiently developed social forces in China can't independently provide the factors required to promote spontaneous urbanization. In Western countries, however, urbanization is often a spontaneous process that occurs at a certain level of economic development and as a result of the bottom-up actions of active citizens. As far as the status quo of urbanization in China is concerned, in most of the cases under study, although the public generally agrees with the government-led model of urbanization, there are, in fact, dissentients in quite a few cases. Even violent conflicts and protests are not unheard of. With regard to the practice of spontaneous urbanization, meanwhile, there are few successful stories. Such grassroots urbanization not only relies on strengthening the self-consciousness of the public, but also on certain conditions as regards the objective environment. These conditions include the reform of the land property system, the construction of social organizations and the improvement of market mechanisms.

It is clear, therefore, that the political system, economic structure, and level of development all have an impact on urbanization patterns. Overall, the comparison of urbanization models in China and other countries reveal that the former is prominently characterized by government direction, large-area-based planning and holistic implementation. This displays a sharp contrast with the urbanization process in the United States and Europe. Thus, this study advances the concept of the "pushing model" of urbanization to summarize the features and China's urbanization process.

---

[11]Liang (2003, pp. 72–81).

[12]Lefebvre (2002, pp. 19–30), Bao (2003).

4.2 Review: Research into the Pushing Model
of Urbanization in China

Some studies have been made by domestic scholars on the pushing model of China's urbanization. This section will include a brief discussion of this model, focusing on an analysis of its dynamic mechanisms and spatial pattern.

In most of the studies of the dynamic mechanisms of urbanization, scholars often determined their generalizations and interpretations from two perspectives. These were the top-down perspectives and the bottom-up perspectives.[13] The top-down model includes direct state investment in urban construction, the leading role of large enterprises, key projects and the outward expansion of large and middle-size cities.[14] The bottom-up model, meanwhile, includes the development of township enterprises, family businesses, professional market development, and rural economic development.[15] In addition, there is also an external drive model, including foreign investment, foreign trade stimulation, and travel incentives.[16] Although such a model takes advantage of outside forces to stimulate local economic development, it is often combined with specific policies. Therefore, it also displays top-down features to a certain degree. Some scholars, meanwhile, suggest that China's urbanization is characterized by a new developmental stage involving the joint promotion of the government and market forces[17] (see Table 4.2).

Studies conducted by domestic scholars on the spatial patterns of urbanization usually classify the characteristics of spatial evolution in China's urbanization into two major types: the external expansion type and the internal restructuring type. Nevertheless, a unified view has not yet been formed as to further detailed classification.[18] In their research design, most scholars stressed the importance of dynamic mechanisms in explaining the characteristics of the spatial mode. Many of these studies are, however, either too macroscopic, only discussing the differences between external expansion and inner reconstruction, the two major types of dynamic mechanism as regards the spatial mode of urbanization, or are too microscopic, only analyzing the dynamic mechanisms of local areas or of a particular spatial mode.[19] All in all, the conducted researches lack a comprehensive and systematic analysis of all of the multiple approaches of pushing ahead with urbanization (see Table 4.3).

---

[13]Zhang (1990), Gu et al. (2004, 2008).

[14]Qi and Xia (1985).

[15]Fei (1984a), Liu (1987, 1999).

[16]Gu et al. (2004, 2008), Xue and Yang (1995).

[17]Ning (1998), Chen et al. (2004).

[18]Zhang (2001), Fang et al. (2009), Xiong (2009), Liu (2011).

[19]Zhou and Meng (1998), Ding (2005), Geng (1999), Yang (2004).

Table 4.2 Relevant researches on the dynamic mechanism of China's urbanization

	Subject of research	Dynamic mechanism
Zhang (1983)	Small town	"Top-down": government invest and establish small industrial towns "Bottom-up": the exchange of surplus agricultural products generated by rich rural areas to promote urban development
	Small town	Township enterprises: Sunan model
Qi and Xia (1985)	Urbanization	The construction of large state-owned enterprises and key project, The influence of economic development and diffusion of the potential by original cities Rural economic development The introduction of foreign capital
Liu (1987)	Wenzhou	Family business and professional markets Large population, scarce arable land
Xue and Yang (1995)	Pearl River Delta	Foreign investment
	The new phase of urbanization	government enterprise individual
Liu (1999)	Bottom-up urbanization	Sunan model:community-government-led rural urbanization Wenzhou model: family industry and professional market-driven urbanization Pearl River Delta pattern: urbanization driven by export-oriented economy Jiaodong model: urbanization driven by village merger and restructuring Liuliping model: urbanization in rural area, from top-down model to bottom-up pattern
Chen et al. (2004)	Urbanization since 1996	Government and market jointly driven New industries driven International trade driven
Gu et al. (2004, 2008)	Urbanization	"Top-down" model: administrative guidance, key projects driven, big cities diffusion driven "Bottom up": Sunan model, Wenzhou model External drive model: foreign-investment-led model, foreign trade stimulation and travel incentives

Source Information extrapolated from relevant documents

Table 4.3 Relevant researches on the spatial pattern of China's urbanization

	Object of study	Spatial patterns
Zhang (2001)	Changes in urban spatial structures in China in the 1990s	Expansion of the built-up urban area: ssuburbanization Urban internal space recombination: CBD, residential community transfer, industrial relocation, unit compound's disappearance
Fang et al. (2009)	Evolution of city forms in the period of rapid urbanization	Expansion, exogenous: Suburbanization Internal restructuring: CBD, urban renewal, industrial zones, new urban areas, outlying residential areas, urban village, new towns
Xiong (2009)	Evolution of city forms in China since the 1990s	Exogenous growth: gradual model, leap-forward model Endogenous growth
Liu (2011)	Urban space expansion mode from the perspective of urban function transformation	The return of urban functions and the rise of Central Business District Urban renewal and the "New World" of the old city Land replacement in central area and standing-up of "dwelling city" in suburbs The big event in national strategies and new development areas Cross region capital centralizing and booming of development zones Integration of Regional Economy and development of city clusters Spontaneous urbanization and the sprawl of "urban-village" Town industrialization and the breeding of "village" factories" Leisure-combined convention and "holiday resort" on collective land Spatial limitations of economic development and the development of ecologically vulnerable regions

Source Information extrapolated from relevant documents

4.3   Multi-models of Pushing Ahead with China's Urbanization

Due to the particular dynamics and methods of pushing ahead with China's urbanization, it is of great importance to comprehensively understand the process by studying, combining with the guiding forces, the operational mechanisms, processes and methods that have been used. In accordance with the dynamic

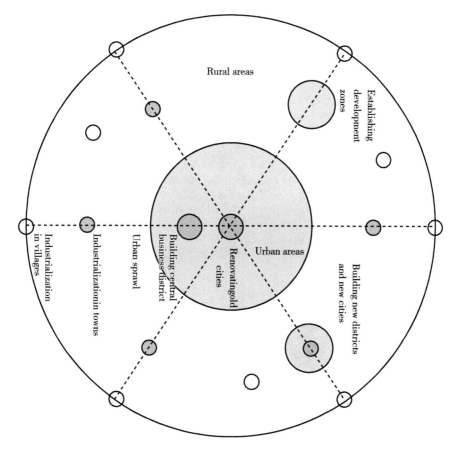

Fig. 4.1 The space pattern of china's urbanization with multi-approaches

mechanisms and spatial pattern of urbanization in China, this study summaries the pushing models, or the models of pushing ahead with urbanization in China, into seven categories. These include the establishment of development zones, the development of new districts and towns, urban sprawl, urban renewal, the construction of central business zones, township industrialization and village industrialization. From the perspective of guiding forces, the seven pushing models of urbanization cover many levels of administrative subjects, from central to local authorities, that are, national, provincial, municipal, regional, county, town and village level administrative bodies. From the perspective of space, meanwhile, these models cover both urban and rural spatial development (see Fig. 4.1).

In Fig. 4.1, the author uses concentric circles to depict the entire urban and rural space. The inner circle represents the city and the outer circle represents rural area. In the central urban area, there is the old city area and the new CBD, while the city sprawls and extends outwards to form an urban expansion area. In the rural area there is located a large number of towns and villages, development zones, new districts which generally constitute the areas selected for new cities. New districts and cities are usually developed using a basis of existing villages and towns. The seven pushing models mentioned in this book, which are the most prominent and frequently occurring models in the process of urbanization, are determined from the actual practice of urbanization in China thus far. On a practical level, these models can be combined and overlapped with each other. For instance, the renewal of the old town can be combined with the development of the central business district. The pushing model of urbanization in the majority regions is not single, meanwhile, but rather often an integration of different models. A general analysis will be made on the driving mechanisms, spatial characteristics, status quo and existing problems in the seven models as follows (See Table 4.4).

4.3.1 The Establishment of Development Zones

The establishment of the development zones is listed as the first pushing model of urbanization in China. It is, after all, the most representative of government-led urbanization, that is, insofar as development zones are government-supported and policy-guided development models that integrate resources from all parties. The model reflects an immense impetus for further economic and social development through administrative resources and government planning. Through development zones, industrial and population concentration can be completed in a relatively short period, thereby leading to massive leaps in the growth of the population and the geographical space of urban areas, not to mention the extensive restructuring of industry. The system of categorizing development zones is, however, rather complex. According to administrative grades, they can be divided into national development zones and local development zones. Local development zones, meanwhile, can be further divided into provincial and municipal level development zones. In line with functional division, national development zones can also be divided into, among others, national economic and technological development zones, high-tech industry development zones, bonded zones, border economic cooperation zones and export processing zones. At the same time, provincial development zones can be divided into economic development zones, industrial incubator parks, industrial parks and industrial incubator, and industrial parks.

From a historical perspective, China's earliest development zones can be traced back to the establishment of the special economic zones at the beginning of the reform and opening up. The zones have since experienced four stages of development. The first of these was the initial start-up stage (1985–1991), followed by the rapid development stage (1992– 1998), the stable development stage (1999–2002) and the scientific development stage (2003–2012). The establishment of development zones has been one of the main carriers of urban space expansion. According to 2005 statistics, before the reorganization of zones, there were 6866 development zones with a planning area of over 38,600 km^2, that is to say, greater

Table 4.4 A comparison of multiple models of pushing ahead with urbanization in China

		The establishment of development zones	The establishment of new districts and towns	Urban expansion	Urban renewal	The establishment of CBDs	Town industrialization	Village industrialization
Dynamic mechanism	The guiding force	The state council, provincial and municipal governments	The state council, municipal government	Municipal governments	Municipal government and government at district level	Municipal governments	Governments at municipal, county, and village level	A unity of village committee and village elites
	The mode of operation	Government-led, market operation, enterprise participation	Government-led, enterprise participation	Government-led, market operation, enterprise participation	Government-led, enterprise participation	Government-led, market operation, enterprise participation	Government guidance, enterprise participation	Village cadres led, the village collective economic development; government promoted, the villagers participation
	Land supply	Central government allocation, and other large-scale agricultural land requisition	Large-scale requisition of rural land	Requisition of rural land	Urban land	Urban land, requisition of agricultural land	Rural collective land	Rural collective land
	Approaches	"Top down"	"Top down"	Top-down and bottom-up combined	"Top down"	"Top down"	Bottom-up and top-down combined	Top-down and bottom-up
Spatial pattern	Occurrence location	Outskirts of the city, suburbs	Outskirts of the city, suburbs	City outskirts	Within the city	Inner city, within new town or the new development zone	Township and village	Village
	Growth	Leap-forward development, continuous development	Leap-forward development, continuous development	Continuous development	Internal restructuring	Internal restructuring, continuous development, Leap-forward development and local development.	In situ development	In situ development
	Scale features	Entirety	Entirety	Entirety, fragment	Entirety	Entirety	Entirety, fragment	Entirety, fragment

than the total built-up area in urban China thus far.[20] In terms of the scale of established zones, the scale of the development zones in Tianjin, Beijing, Shenzhen, Zhuhai, and Pudong was over 20 km^2 in each case. The new urban area in Dalian and Binhai New Area, in Tianjin, grew on the basis of development zones and eventually reached a scale equivalent to a medium-sized city. In fact, the Pudong New Area in Shanghai was over 50 km^2, equivalent, that is, to the size of a large city.[21]

Crucially, the establishment of development zones has its own internal logic of development, in which strict governmental control plays a key role. This logic consists of four key stages. The first of these is the activation stage. At this stage, administrative policies, industrial planning, demonstration effects and regional competition function as internal impetuses. Secondly, there is the resource organization stage, with the full involvement of financial allocations, corporate financing, project financing and social capital. Thirdly, follows the resource revitalization stage. At this stage, land concentration, labor reservoir, cost advantages and local monopolies are all indispensable. Fourth, is the feedback stage, within which the government, the administration committees of the development zones, enterprises, developers, farmers, residents, communities and society at large are all important sources of feedback. If zones' development follows these logical stages, they can achieve a degree of smooth and coordinated operation. Otherwise, their operation may become disorderly, generating a range of economic limitations and social constraints.

The economic limitations of development zones can include monotonous modes of economic growth, overdependence on international economic cycles, wasted land resources, similar models and the spatial misplacement in resource allocation. The social constraints of development zones, meanwhile, no less worthy of attention, include the formation of a leap-forward, unstable, mandatory, artificial, subjective and externally driven process of urbanization. This may be accompanied by the destruction of original social relationships, the degrading of traditional ways of life and the loss of existing social support systems in the community. Such issues can be compounded by the absence of social organizations and social forces in the formulation of public policy. What's more, some of the specialized industrial parks and large-scale enterprises and projects depend on the circular flow of migrant laborers. Such laborers are taken advantage of throughout their most dynamic years, but shunned when they reach a certain age. At this point, they are often forced back to the rural areas. Project, parks and zones such as these avoid the massive costs of building urban service systems and shun the costs of labor welfare and social security systems, passing the buck of social responsibility back to society instead.

---

[20]Zhou et al. (2006).

[21]Xiong et al. (2010).

In recent years, however, the situation has changed to some extent. Some industrial parks have, for instance, proposed the concept of "Interaction between Industry and City", that is, to establish towns, secure homing and urban service facilities around the park.

4.3.2 The Establishment of New Districts and Towns

The establishment of new districts and new towns is listed as the second pushing model, because, in China, this process must pass very strict administrative reviews and approval. In most countries, the definition of a city is fundamentally based on population, namely when the population within a region reaches a certain figure (usually above 1000–2000 in most countries). In China, however, there exists a series of complex standards for establishing cities and towns, including passing relevant reviews and gaining the approval of the Ministry of Civil Affairs and the State Council. Therefore, the establishment of new districts and towns is typical of government-led urbanization. In other words, the government directly promotes the concentration of population and resources in a given area through the re-planning and restructuring of population, land, industry, transport and other infrastructural factors. New districts and towns were usually located within the radius of big cities and generally had some kind of advantage as regards resources. As a result, they could quickly become an important part of the overall urban system, promoting urban economic agglomeration and sharing some of the functions of a city center.

The establishment of new districts and towns was often guided by an extensive planning process. It is, then, important to consider what impacts this highly centralized process might have on society and under what conditions it is appropriate to adopt such a strategy. Satisfactorily answering this question requires considering ecological, economic and social factors.

Ecological factors mainly include the size and density of the population. After all, within China's urban organizational system, the standards, as regards the size of the population, for establishing cities, counties, and townships are different. Moreover, China's administrative grades of city, town, and county directly refer to the allocation of resources and the corresponding administrative treatment packages. Therefore, these standards are likely to become incentives for local authorities to set up cities, towns and counties, even inducing false urbanization and the excessive loss of farmland. Another important ecological factor is spatial location, that is, whether or not a new district is within the radius of an existing city center and how it may, through alterations, acquire some kind of geographical advantage. These are all important aspects for the assessment of the spatial locations of new districts. Economic factors mainly include the type of economy and economic activities within a particular urban area. As part of this picture, the proportion of agricultural and non-agricultural industry and laborers are important factors to be considered in establishing new cities, towns and counties. One significant issue is how to transform a rural registered population into a non-rural population, that is, how to make them into full urban citizens. More than a simple job conversion, this also involves other system-level issues, such as land, household registration, social security and the like. What's more, new districts must determine how to actualize industrial upgrading and transformation, requiring not only the support of infrastructure, but also the formation of an agglomeration economy. This process can only be realized through market forces, that is, rather than by industrial planning.

Social factors refer mainly to the urban lifestyle and living environment. The indicator of social factors is often used to assess the degree of urbanization, although a range of complicated social dimensions must be taken into consideration. For one thing, floating urban populations may maintain aspects of their original rural lifestyle and values, while some rural areas may quickly develop many of the characteristics of an urban society. While newly established urban districts may provide relatively complete living facilities, it is the daily living practices in a city that are at the core of lasting and meaningful urbanization.

4.3.3 Urban Expansion

Urban expansion, the most common and traditional method of urbanization, is a process of constant outward expansion of urban areas, generally accompanied by population growth. Most urbanization in the history of global urban growth has followed this approach. It is in the Western countries that urbanization first occurred, followed by suburbanization and exurbanization from the 1950s to the 1970s. Together, these processes facilitated the expansion of cities into their surrounding areas. On the surface, China's approach to urbanization is similar to that of the West, yet China's urban expansion also has its own distinct characteristics due to the differences in land ownership policies. Public ownership of land in China makes rapid urbanization possible on a far greater scale. At present, the total number of urban planning projects in China is the largest in the world, being unprecedented in all of human history.

Urban expansion is a spatial form of urbanization, including elements of both compact development and urban sprawl. The former occurs when the development of urban space has been effectively controlled and a high density of urban construction has been achieved. The latter refers to a more disordered and blind process of urban expansion that spreads outwards in an unchecked manner. Although those areas covered by urban sprawl do exhibit some of the spatial characteristics of a city, they generate problems such as the extensive use of land conservation, the inadequate supply of industry and public service facilities and the imbalance of intraregional development. These are just some of the issues that may result from such a lack of overall planning. Therefore, how to control disordered urban sprawl is an issue of great concern to all countries in the world. Many countries have made significant steps towards addressing this issue. One such example is the London Green Belt included in the post-war planning of Greater London. Another is the delineation of the Urban Growth Boundary (UGB) in the Portland Metropolitan

Area in the United States. At any rate, appropriate urban boundaries should be analyzed and determined by combining the development phase of a city and the cities particular approach of urbanization.

At the same time, one of the prominent issues in the current process of China's urban expansion is that the rate of land urbanization is actually outpacing the rate of population urbanization. From 2000 to 2009, there was, statistically, a 45.9% increase to the urban population in China. Nevertheless, during the same period, the built-up urban area in China increased by 78.52%. This discrepancy has resulted in a number of serious problems, including decentralized and low-density development, massive waste of agricultural resources and high rates of energy consumption.[22] In the outline of the 12th Five-Year Plan, the central government proposed "reasonably determining the boundaries of urban development" to improve the efficiency of land use as well as to facilitate compact and intensive development. In addition, the process of urban expansion is also accompanied by a series of social problems, including the distinction between "big property ownership" and "small property ownership".[23] Other problems include compensation and re-employment for rural citizens who lose land, uncontrolled urban expansion caused by disordered land development and the absence of management on the fringes of urban areas. All of these urgent problems, and more, must be solved in the process of urban expansion in contemporary China.

4.3.4 Urban Renewal

The transformation of old urban areas, otherwise known as urban renewal, refers to the renewal and reconstruction of old districts, generally those located in the center of a city and with a high economic value, with a view to improving the urban environment and modernizing urban functions. As a result of the state-ownership of urban land, such city reconstruction is, in China, managed by the government in all respects. This includes the development of policies, planning and the relocation and compensation of those citizens affected by urban renewal. In China, this process is usually characterized by both large-scale and rapid action. On the one hand, it is driven by the urgent need to resolve a range of historic problems, including dilapidated housing. On the other hand, it is an inevitable result of the "urban management" concept of local governments. Especially when the intervention of the market force of real estate developers is taken into consideration, this type of reconstruction gradually forms a combined model of government guidance and market operation.

---

[22]National Bureau of Statistics of People's Republic of China (2011).

[23]The big property ownership refers to the right to a house property with two certificates (House Ownership Certificate and Certificate for State-owned Land Use Permit), meaning the property can be transcted in market. While the small property ownership refers to the right to a house property built on collective owned rural land and can only transact within the collective group.

In this process of urban renewal, however, driven, as it often is, by the blind pursuit of "modernization", "image projects" and "economic benefits", some local governments were responsible for large-scale demolition and reconstruction of old buildings. As a result, the unique cultural characteristics of many urban regions disappeared rapidly, thereby resulting in the recent phenomenon that all cities are similar in style. At the same time, a range of social problems were caused by demolishing old buildings and constructing new ones, including the dispute in demolition, and the splitting up of old social and communal networks in old urban communities.

To solve the abovementioned problems of urban renewal, a variety of approaches have been explored and tested in China.

As regards traditional and historical architecture with a particular style and heritage, from his study of the Beijing Shichahai Plan in the late 1970s, Professor Wu Liangyong proposed a theory of "organic updating". This theory advocated a small-scale and gradual approach to transformation by following the existing and organic urban fabric. In this way, the protection of historical architecture could be achieved.[24]

For those buildings constructed after the founding of the People's Republic of China, in 1949, of a poor quality, an uncoordinated style and a lack of any kind of heritage value, renewal should be made on the basis of maintaining the urban landscape and features, increasing the plot ratio, enhancing the load capacity of the urban population and attaching special attention to the principles of social justice.

In recent years, a model of developing surrounding areas through "large site" protection has been adopted in the regions with a rich cultural heritage, thereby providing a new channel for urban renewal. Take the renovation of the Daming Palace Ruins Park in Xi'an as an example. The demolition of the 3.5 million square meters of shantytowns around this site not only enabled the smooth implementation of subsequent site protection and exhibition, but also relieved, through land replacement and housing transformation, the contradictions between large site protection and the scarcity of urban land resources. An organic combination of relic protection and urban development was, therefore, achieved.

4.3.5 The Establishment of CBDs

The establishment of Central Business Districts (CBDs) is a unique way of achieving rapid urbanization in China. CBDs in China are usually established in conjunction with urban renewal or simply built anew in the center of new districts and development zones. At any rate, the establishment of CBDs in China has a range of unique characteristics, quite distinct from models of urban renewal and the establishment of new districts and development zones. The concept of the CBD (the

---

[24]Wu (1989).

central business district) was put forward by the American sociologist Burgess in his study on the Urban Structure of Chicago.[25] He believes that CBDs are the core areas of the five concentric circles in an urban structure and the overall economic hubs of their respective cities. As the functional kernel of a modern city, the CBD is located at the center of the flow economy, where all kinds of people, logistics, information, and capital are aggregated and distributed.

Though models of CBD development outside China can be divided into government-led models and market-oriented models, both essentially evolve from the market. It is through the market, after all, that the prototype of a modern service industry cluster is formed. After their initial development, however, CBDs are often further guided and promoted by the government. The development of CBDs in China is, however, due to China's economic system, completely government-led, including an extensive process of pre-planning. According to statistics provided by the Ministry of Construction, by the end of 2002, 36 Chinese cities, each with more than 200,000 people, were planning to build their own CBDs, of which eight cities, including Beijing, Shanghai, Guangzhou, Shenzhen, had already started the process of development and construction.[26] Though the development and management models of each CBD are not the same, and the involvement and the organizational functions of enterprises display a tendency of increasing in strength, the government is still the decisive force. Nevertheless, the fate of all CBDs, even those established under the guidance of administrative means, will be ultimately decided by market forces. Blind construction, then, might be likely to trigger unintended and disastrous consequences.

The main problem currently facing the CBD boom in China is the blind development of CBDs, far exceeding current levels of urban development, done simply in order to enhance the image of a city and demonstrate the good performance of the government. This strategy all too often results in an unhealthy dissipation of land and financial resources among other things. Besides, though large in number, the new CBDs are built regardless of necessary process of its formation. The planned scales of these new CBDs are often beyond their host cities' economic capabilities, leading to the problem of oversupply. Moreover, a range of additional problems emerge from this kind of single development model, among other things, the poor systematic planning and the implementation deviating from planning. Therefore, the development of CBDs should always be carried out according to local conditions and within the limits of local abilities.

---

[25]Parker (1987, pp. 48–62).
[26]Chen (2003).

4.3.6 Industrialization in Towns

Urbanization does not necessarily proceed in a centralized way. The in situ urbanization of rural areas is a good example of urbanization taking a decentralized form. The in situ urbanization of rural areas is a process by which the urban form appears in rural areas. Due to good employment opportunities in industry and commerce or well-organized social services and living environments, a large number of non-agricultural workers may gradually gather in some rural areas. This relocation will generate something of an urban morphology in those areas in many respects, including population density, land use, architectural design and overall layout. The dynamics for rural in situ urbanization may come from the introduction of external technology, capital, and industry or from the spontaneous economic development within a given rural area. According to different spatial levels, rural in situ urbanization in China can be divided into two types, township industrialization and village industrialization.

As far as the first model is concerned, industrialization within towns generally starts inside towns. As early as the 1980s, the sociologist Fei Xiaotong first proposed the "Small Towns Model", which he thought could discourage excessive population growth in cities. Alternatively, it was described as a "reservoir" to store up population while preventing excessive population concentration in large cities.[27] At any rate, the development of small towns in China can be roughly divided into three stages. The first stage, lasting from 1978 to 1993, witnessed small towns developing under strong government leadership that had put a premium on "the development of small towns". The second stage, was from 1993 to 1999. In this period, the "Small Town Strategy" became central to the government effort to boost the rural economy and social development and to address "the three agricultural issues".[28] Therefore, rural industrialization, represented by township enterprises, underwent a period of rapid development. The Pearl River Delta and Yangtze River Delta regions illustrate this well. Since 2000, especially as the policy of "Building a New Countryside" was proposed in 2005, the third stage emerged, thereby introducing a development model of in situ urbanization for rural areas. Take the rural areas in the Hebei Province as an example. In this case, in situ urbanization was largely a result of rural industrialization, essentially different from the export-oriented development model and the direct introduction of modern industry in cities. It bore the many of the characteristics of a spontaneous and bottom-up rural developmental process. Moreover, the in situ spatial urbanization in the rural areas of the Hebei Province avoided, as intended, the excessive population concentration of large cities. Nevertheless, it also generated a variety of problems, such as reduced agricultural development, damage to traditional rural society and customs, the depletion of resources and increased environmental pollution. In contrast, the development of Yunfu City in Guangdong Province was different. It developed

---

[27]Fei (1984b).
[28]"The issues of agriculture, rural development and rural residents".

spontaneously and independently based on local conditions. To put it more precisely, the Yunfu model broke through the administrative restrictions in terms of overall planning and constituted a prototype for future functional zones. In particular, the Yunfu model included different development strategies according to different regional characteristics and the establishment of a, "Complete Communities", comprised of public spaces, community service systems, social management, infrastructure and a strong sense of community culture, on rural grass-root level. In fact, this approach actually lent itself to a new development model of rural in situ urbanization, which was top-down, insofar as it was initially launched by the government, and bottom-up, insofar as it was largely participated in by the population at large. This approach was inspired by such slogans as "Conspiring Together, Constructing Together, Managing Together, and Sharing Together". Overall, this study concludes that industrialization in towns should combine the government's reasonable guidance with the independent development of a local economy. Besides, the industrialization of towns should not be at the expense of destroying the original agricultural foundations of said towns. At the same time, the development of the rural community and society should be highlighted just as much as economical development.

4.3.7 Industrialization in Villages

Throughout the process of in situ urbanization in rural areas, there is a pattern worthy of consideration, namely, the village industrialization based on the collective economy of villages themselves. Although this process need not necessarily bring about the spatial features of cities, village industrialization still consists of all of the essential features of urbanization. The urbanization of rural life is, after all, substantially promoted by the development of non-agricultural industry. As a general concept, village and town industrialization often overlaps somewhat. The primary reason as to why village industrialization is analyzed as a separate model is simply that the development of village industry occurs within the geographical space of villages. Compared with towns, meanwhile, villages are generally lacking factors of intensive management. Villages, for instance, are, incontrovertibly, the place where resources and opportunities are most scarce. Therefore, the industrialization of villages often requires a certain dynamic, the likes of which generally comes from one of two main sources, namely, either an endogenous dynamic or an exogenous dynamic.

Endogenous dynamic have some similarities with civil-society dynamic in general. Village industrialization driven by an endogenous dynamic can be successful, for instance, when local elites take the lead in propelling the process forward. For one thing, these village elites usually have strong organizational skills and a high prestige among the local population. Their management pattern, meanwhile, is often integrated with the grassroots government of a village. Under their guidance, a set of mechanisms for stimulating the vitality of the villagers can be established. There are many successful examples of such village industrialization driven by endogenous dynamic in China. These include the Huaxi Village in Jiangyin city and Liuzhuang village in Xinxiang City. In the author's research on rural areas surrounding Beijing, a prominent case of urbanization is the Hancun River Town. It followed a path of developing a collective village economy, creating, as it did, a model dominated by the construction industry and co-promoted by a multitude of secondary industries. A large part of the profits gained from these enterprises, meanwhile, were utilized for further rural construction and development. Upscale communities were also constructed, thereby providing high-quality villas for most residents. The rise of the Hanjian Group not only made possible the great-leap-forward of the Hancun River Town, but also benefited the surrounding villages. The planning for Hancun River Central Town included attempts to incorporate surrounding villages in its future development strategy. In this way, the economy of the villages could shift from agriculture to the secondary and tertiary industries and residents could start to enjoy modern living standards while participating in a modern production system. The model of Hancun River Town, that is, one of combining local elites, as regards their role of organization, with enterprises, their financial investment in home village, sets a good example for other rural areas. Nevertheless, there remain a range of factors that still require further consideration, such as the emergence of leaders, the selection of successors, the perfecting of systems, the holding of democratic and fair elections and the sustainability of key enterprises. If these problems cannot be satisfactorily resolved and some executable development plan cannot be offered, then it will remain difficult to apply this model to other regions. In addition, problems such as the scattered layout of enterprises, which is common during the process of rural industrialization, still exist. Active guidance is, therefore, still required from the planning sector and village urbanization should be combined with urbanization in rural areas, so that a comprehensive transformation of the rural industrial and spatial structure may be achieved.

There are also many kinds of exogenous dynamic for village industrialization. For example, the fact that many Chinese citizens, who have spent time overseas, may return home to invest in their villages is one kind of common dynamic. However, an approach more and more commonly adopted is, village industrialization promoted by the government at all levels and the exchange for countryside housing land. In accordance with the precondition that 1.8 billion mu of arable land will not be built over, the land resources at grassroots levels are relatively limited. As such, making good use of rural housing land can expand economic development in many ways. Therefore, the idea of urbanization through the exchange for countryside housing land is popular in many regions. While there were many examples of village industrialization driven by exogenous dynamic in the past, recently a variety of endogenous momentum have taken over. In the actual implementation process, the government generally plans in advance and invites local farmers, by means of village demolition and mergers, to "go upstairs" (move into tall buildings and built "new rural communities". This approach to urbanization can be effective, yet the exchange for rural housing land should be combined with a number of additional strategies. These include the promotion of industrial development in rural areas, increased opportunities for the employment of farmers and provisions for appropriate land compensation. Such measures, together with a good village planning, may enable farmers to live modern and civilized lives and bring untold benefits to rural communities. If not handled properly, however, such a strategy will bring a range of problems, such as forcing farmers to change their original way of life without any kind of guarantees to promote the development of village industrialization nor ameliorate local living conditions in any sustainable or long-term way.

The Table 4.4 outlines the features of the seven pushing models of urbanization in China, with a particular focus on the seven aspects of dynamic mechanism and spatial pattern. All content was gathered from the data and case studies at the author's disposal.

4.4   An Analysis on the Advantages and Disadvantages of China's Models of Pushing Ahead with Urbanization

Judging from the abovementioned pushing models, the present urbanization system in China has a number of advantages and disadvantages.

For one thing, China's urbanization model has evolved from its unique political and economic system and, as such, displays a great deal of institutional innovation. For example, the pushing model of establishing development zones and special development zones created significant opportunities from governmental policies and regulations alone, never mind the basic factors of production, including energy resources, human resources and market factors. Powerful policy resource can, therefore, fully demonstrates the advantages of a government-led model and highlight the advantages of China's strong management resources. At the same time, the innovation of the models of pushing ahead with urbanization in China further reflects the characteristic of flexibility, which has been ubiquitous in the Chinese system ever since the reform and opening up. As for China, a country with vast land and a huge population, as well as massive regional differences, the flexibility of policy and developmental systems are capable of supplying more opportunities for urbanization in more regions, especially, that is, when current market conditions are often inadequate and underdeveloped. This feature, then, although not without its problems, has the effect of a net over-all promotion to urbanization nationwide.

One of the main advantages of the government-led urbanization approach is that it can concentrate a huge amount of capital, human and material resources, as well as a wide range of other resources, to achieve the development goals of urbanization in a relatively short time. This structural framework possesses a range of advantages, particularly in the early phases of urban development. Nevertheless, this approach may not give rise to long term and sustainable development, as often becomes increasingly evident as the urbanization process continues. Therefore, throughout the process of urbanization, basic economic laws should be respected and measures should be taken that are best suited to local conditions. Urbanization, after all, mainly originates from economic and social development in urban and rural areas and success is often dependent upon its own internal operating laws. Accordingly, the formulation of proper targets and strategies for urbanization should be based on the conditions of such urbanization elements as industry, land, natural resources and population. An organic and suitable target and strategy of urbanization should be followed, far from the phenomenon of urbanization for the sake of urbanization or the simple pursuit of a particular urbanization rate.

Since China's reform and opening up, over the last three decades, the market economy has attained a considerable degree of development. Thus, the market should be allowed to play a greater role in the process of urbanization, while the government should largely play the role of legislation, planning, management, and monitoring. It should be the market that functions to allocate factors throughout the process of urban development. At present, the Chinese Government is basically the primary force when it comes to managing cities and operating the urban development process. In comparison, market forces do not perform a full role. What is called "development by-means-of-market-mechanisms" refers to, actually, such a process of urban transformation and development, in which, various economic elements involve, among them, the government makes plans and proposes requests, while the actual operation is implemented by a variety of economic entities. Even the operating funds provided by the government should generally take the form of the government purchasing public services (through bidding, directional entrusting, and invitations to bid, the government entrusts their public service tasks to social forces and enterprises). The author of this study has found that the direct operation of the government in "demolition", due to the intervention of political power, usually decreases the compensation provided to residents and harms the interests of local people, thereby triggering conflicts and mass incidents. Conversely, the standards of compensation for demolition offered by market operators is always much higher than that provided by the direct intervention of the government. This proves that the operation of the market has its own rationality and, in some cases, renders it easier to form reasonable market prices, including the means of protecting the interests of local people.

It is necessary to allow, to a greater extent, a variety of social forces to participate in the process of urbanization. The current situation, however, is marred by the lack of participation of social forces in the process of urbanization. These social forces include various groups composed of urban and rural residents, any groups composed of laborers and employees, social organizations, community organizations and residents in general. Nevertheless, thus far, the vast majority of China's urbanization has been government-led, driven almost entirely by government planning, mobilization and operations, while most urban and rural residents are usually just passive observers. Of course, the top-down approach to urbanization has been a characteristic of urbanization in China up to now. However, the huge energy in the bottom-up model cannot be ignored or neglected. More power should be delegated to rural and urban residents, thereby creating more channels for development. For example, the inhabitants of a community or residential area could be invited to participate in planning, so that they may pursue urbanization according to their needs of life and housing. Only in this way can the phenomenon of "passive urbanization", which, all too often, infringes the interests of urban and rural residents, be restrained.

An economic system based on state-owned land and collective ownership enables China to implement urbanization rapidly and on a large-scale, but the problems of idle and wasted land that result from this are considerable. Therefore, more attention should be paid to the following two factors. Firstly, there should be more scientific planning directed into the urbanization process. This will give rise to urban spaces with a more reasonable layout and include further provisions for the protection of the ecological environment and basic farmland requirements. With the rapid progress of urbanization, the available land resources are diminishing at an alarming rate. At present, the per capita area of farmland is less than half of the average level around the world. A lot of fertile land is occupied and the ecological environment faces a serious threat as a result. The formulation of future urbanization strategies should, therefore, be based on main-functional zone divisions in China, delineating the forbidden and restricted zones for construction, so as to protect ecological environment, safeguard the food safety and balance the relationship between urban development and resource utilization. Secondly, the efficiency of land use should be improved drastically. One of the fundamental features of urbanization is the intensive socio-economic benefits generated by high-density urban areas. These benefits are put at risk from "over-suburbanization" and an excessively scattered pattern of urban development, especially when China is taken into consideration, that is, a nation of a large population with relatively little arable land. Urban planners should, therefore, adopt a pattern of extensive land use and increase the utilization efficiency of land to safeguard the sustainable development of urbanization in China.

Urbanization is simultaneously accompanied by great changes to social structures. With the daily advance of urbanization, land, housing, resources and wealth have all been re-allocated among different groups and social classes. This upheaval invariably results in social conflicts in terms of interests and the increasingly prominent social contradictions. Ostensibly, urbanization brings with it an increase in the number of houses and a greater spread of huge architectural complexes. Nevertheless, deeper problems can be found in the changing relationships between different interest groups and, indeed, individual people. In recent years, with the onset of rapid urbanization, the price of urban housing has soared. Accordingly, a huge "social gap" between those who own urban properties and those who do not has emerged. Therefore, the promotion of urbanization must take equity and justice into consideration, because every detail of urban planning involves different benefits to different interest groups. This is an important and urgent issue to be studied and resolved. At its core is the question as to how to innovate the mechanisms for public participation and how to promote positive interaction between the government and the public, so as to realize a high degree of fairness and justice in urban growth and to bridge the social differentiation that accompanies rapid development.

Generally speaking, there are huge differences between the urbanization models in China and those in European and American countries. According to the dynamic mechanisms and spatial patterns of urbanization, China's approach to pushing ahead with urbanization can be summarized into seven models. These include the establishment of development zones, the establishment of new zones and towns, urban expansion, urban renewal, the establishment of the central business districts, town industrialization and, finally, village industrialization. Analysis has also been made separately of the dynamic mechanisms, spatial characteristics, status quo and the range of existing problems. This study believes that the government-led urbanization model fully demonstrates the innovation and flexibility of China's institutional system. Nevertheless, it must be said that basic economic laws should be respected and measures should be suited to local conditions. Furthermore, the market should be allowed to perform more effective functions, allowing, to a much greater degree, various social forces to participate in the development process. A process of scientific planning and rational land distribution and utility should be adopted in order to improve the efficiency of land use. Expectedly, the mechanisms for social force participation should be innovated, so as to promote a benign interaction between the government and the public.

References

Arato, A., & Cohen, J. (2002). Civil society and social theory. In D. Zhenglai & J.C. Alexander (Eds.), *State and civil society: A perspective of social theory research.* Beijing:Central Compilation & Translation Press.

Bao, Y. (2003). *Modernity and the production of space.* Shanghai Education Press.

Chen, W. (2003). Empirical study on CBD development in Chinese big and medium cities. *Urban Planning,* Vol. 12.

Chen, B., Hao, S., & Yang, X. (2004). Dynamic mechanism of China's rapid urbanization. *Geographical Journal,* Vol. 6.

Ding, C. (2005). Economic dynamic mechanism for concentric-circles-like urban spatial expansion. *Urban Planning,* Vol. 4.

Fang, G., Wang, Y., & Yao, S. (2009). Study on City form and its dynamic mechanism in the period of rapid urbanization. *Human Geography,* Vol. 2.

Fei, X. (1984a). *Small towns, big issues.* Nanjing: Jiangsu People's Press.

Fei, X. (1984b). *Small towns, big problems.* Jiangsu People's Publishing House.

Geng, H. (1999). On impetus mechanism for renewal of urban centers in China. *Urban Planning Forum,* Vol. 3.

Gramsci, A. (1971). *Selections from the prison note-books* (Hoare, Q., & Nowell Smith, G, Trans.), (Ed.). New York:International Publishers.

Gu, C. et al. (2004). *Chinese urban geography.* Commercial Press.

Gu, C. et al. (2008). *Chinese urbanization: Pattern, process, mechanism.* Science Press.

Gu, S., & Zhu, N. (1993). Urbanization in China: The regional differences and regional development model. *China Population Science,* Vol. 1.

Habermas, J. (1999). *Strukturwandel der Offentlichkeit* (W. Cao et al., Trans.). Shanghai: Academia Press.

Habermas J. (2003). *Between facts and norms: Contribution to a discourse theory of law and democracy* (S. Tong, Trans.). Shanghai: SDX Joint Publishing Company.

Lefebvre. (2002). *Space: Social product and use-value. from Cultural pattern and social theory of space.* In: Compiled by Z. Xia & Z. Wang. Mingwen Publishing House, pp. 19–30.

Li, Q. (2004). *Migrant workers and social stratification in China* (pp. 334–348). Beijing: Social Science Academic Press.

Liang, S. (2003). *The essence of Chinese culture.* Shanghai Century Publishing Group, pp. 72–81.

Liu, H. (1987). An analysis on the characteristics of urbanization in Wenzhou and prediction for its development level. *Urban Planning Review,* Vol. 2.

Liu, C. (1999). *Institutional arrangement and innovation for/in china's urbanization.* Wuhan University Press.

Liu, X. (2011). Study on spatial expansion mode of China's urbanization . *Guangdong Social Science,* Vol. 5.

Lu, D. (2007). China's urbanization process and spatial expansion. *Urban Planning Forum.* Vol. 4.

National Bureau of Statistics of People's Republic of China (Ed.). (2011). *China statistical yearbook 2011.* China Statistics Press.

Ning, Y. (1998). The new urbanization process-A discussion on the dynamic mechanism and characteristics of Chinese urbanization in the 1990s. *Geographical Journal,* Vol. 5.

Parker (1987). *Urban sociology.* (J. Song, et al., Trans.). Huaxia Press, pp. 48–62.

Qi, K., Xia, Z. (1985). Urbanization and urban systems. *Architectural Journal,* Vol. 1.

Tang, Z. (1997). Descriptions and explanations of urban spatial structure: a review of research developments. *Urban Planning Review,* Vol. 6.

Wu, L. (1989). The approach of the renovation of residential area in Beijing old city—An exploration on the organic renewal of urban cellular and 'new courtyard'. *Architecture Journal,* Vol. 7.

Wu, L., Wu, W., & Wu, T. (2003). The world and China's tendency of urbanization and the urbanization in Jiangshu Province. *Science and Technology Review,* Vol. 9.

Xiong, G. (2009). Changes in the evolutionary dynamic of city form in yangtze river delta since the 1990s. *Huazhong Architecture,* Vol. 2.

Xiong, G., Yang, D., & Yu, J. (2010). A basic review of urban form evolution in China since the 1990s. *Huazhong Architecture,* Vol. 4.

Xue, F., & Yang, C. (1995). Urbanization under the influence of foreign investment–A case study of the pearl river delta. *Urban Planning Review,* Vol. 6.

Yang, D. (2004). *From development zone to new town: Phenomenon, texture and path—A case study of Tianjin TEDA. (Ph.D. thesis).* Tsinghua University.

Zhang, T. (1983). Discussion on the dynamism of urbanization. *Urban Planning Review,* Vol. 5.

Zhang, T. (1990). Discussion on the dynamism of urbanization. *Urban Planning Review,* Vol. 5.

Zhang, T. (2001). Chnages in the structure of China's urban space and its dynamic mechanism in the 1990 s. *Urban Planning,* Vol. 7.

Zhou, Y., & Meng, Y. (1998). The suburbanization trend of China' s metropolitans. *Urban Planning Forum,* Vol. 3.

Zhou, Y. et al. (2006). Who should be responsible for land going out-of-control. *Urban Planning Review,* Vol. 11.

Chapter 5
The Establishment of Development Zones

Urbanization is a type of social engineering that turns rural agricultural populations into registered urban populations. It is the universal law or trend of social development. In 1949, there were only 132 cities in China and the urbanization level was only 10.6%. After 60 years, urbanization in China witnessed a period of rapid development. By the end of 2009, a total of 655 cities were officially designated in 31 different provinces, autonomous regions, and municipalities. The level of urbanization reached 46.59%, with an urban population of 621.86 million. That is to say, China had entered into a historical stage of accelerated urbanization. The *"China Urban Development Report", volume 1, 2009*, noted that China entered into a period of accelerated urbanization, such that it was estimated that, by 2020, 50% of the population would live in urban areas and, by 2050, this figure would rise to 75% of the population living in cities.[1]

An important dynamic mechanism in the urbanization process is the establishment of development zones. Through the establishment of such zones, industrial and population concentration could be completed relatively quickly throughout many Chinese cities, thereby achieving a leap-forward growth of urban space and population, as well as industrial restructuring.[2] The process of population shift, primarily from rural to urban areas, was characterized by abundant connotation, including both the urbanization of household registration and lifestyles, the in situ urbanization and centralized urbanization through demolition and migration. Among them, however, the establishment of development zones is one of the most characteristic models of pushing ahead with urbanization in China. Indeed, these development zones are platforms for practice from a broad "big government" perspective. It is, therefore, a vivid portrayal of government participation in economic and social development and construction, reflecting the great impetus of

---

[1]China Association of Mayors: "China Urban Development Report". Xinhua Newsnet: http://www.China.com.cn/aboutchina/data/07cs/node_7039769.htm.
[2]Wang et al. (2004).

© Social Sciences Academic Press 2020
Q. Li, *China's Development under a Differential Urbanization Model*,
Research Series on the Chinese Dream and China's Development Path,
https://doi.org/10.1007/978-981-13-9451-5_5

administrative resources for economic and social development at a local level. This chapter will specifically explore the model of establishing development zones.

5.1   The Origin and History of Development Zones

The idea of development zones originated in Europe yet came to full fruition in China. Since the Freeport of Leghorn, in Genoa gulf, Italy was established in 1547,[3] a variety of similar zones have been founded across the globe, including, among others, free trade zones, bonded areas, export processing zones and science and technology industrial parks. Development zones are generally a government-based and policy-guided carrier, utilizing all available resources to engage in specified industries, with benefits distributed to all involved parties. Development zones are one of the models for pushing ahead with urbanization with Chinese characteristics, which, needless to say, has contributed to China's economic and social development on a massive scale. The huge boosts to social and economic development provided by development zones, primarily as a result of huge administrative resources and government planning, reflect the high efficiency and superiority of the socialist system. Development zones are, in essence, a carefully planned and subjectively determined model for driving forward social and economic development. The zones, therefore, enjoy artificial and programming characteristics, which, on the one hand, determine the numerous advantages of development zones, also gives rise to the inherent defects of the model. Such defects include the subjectivity of planning and uncertainty in the implementation of policy. While development zones vigorously promote China's economic and social development, they also expose considerable problems, such as the intensive occupation of fertile farmland, stiff transitions of lifestyle, lack of economic and social returns to local communities and soft restraints on resources and profit distribution. These issues, on the one hand, expose the deficiencies in the zone model, while also providing direction for its further improvement.

5.1.1   Background for Establishing Development Zones

Generally speaking, scholars believe that China's model of development zones can be traced back to the beginning of the economic reform and opening up. The Special Economic Zone (SEZ) established at that point was the first development zone in the broader sense of the concept. It was in 1981 that the State Council approved the establishment of economic and technological development zones in

---

[3]Wang (2009).

China's open coastal cities. China's development zones were set up in an extremely complex domestic and international background. They were both a product of their age, as well as an inevitable requirement of history.

5.1.1.1   International Background

The international context in which development zones were established can be divided into three parts. The first of these is a perceived variation in the theme of global affairs. Deng Xiaoping believed that the theme of the world had changed, such that peace and development had substituted war and peace to become the defining characteristic of global interactions. Accordingly, China itself should also focus mainly on economic construction and social development. Secondly, there were changes to the international capital market. After a long post-war boom, the Western capitalist world had accumulated a solid basis of industrial and financial capital. The profit-driven nature of capital had since forced capital to flow into something of a low-cost "depression". The raw materials, labor, and development prospects of China, therefore, were very attractive. Thirdly, there was a massive international transfer of industry. With the unfolding of the scientific and techno-logical revolution, Western countries were experiencing an adjustment to their industrial structure, retaining and developing high-tech industries, while transfer-ring labor-intensive industries to developing countries.[4] These three factors con-stituted the external background for the establishment of development zones in China.

5.1.1.2   Domestic Background

Specifically, there are five aspects in terms of the national background to the establishment of development zones. The first of these emerged from an ideological foundation. During this period, the idea of "emancipating the mind", "seeking truth from facts" and the primacy of "economic construction" all became gradually pervasive. As a result, the economic reform and opening up became part of the national will, thereby laying the ideological foundation for the establishment of development zones. Secondly, there was the role of the Special Administration Region (SAR) system. The successful development of the SAR system functioned as a promising pilot and precondition for further development zones. Thirdly, the shortage of funds played a pivotal role. At this time, China had just emerged from the "Cultural Revolution" and the economy was on the brink of collapse. The state was desperately short of domestic capital and had severely diminished reserves of foreign currency. Development zones, however, offered a potential solution insofar as they were an important organizational form for raising funds for construction, as

---

[4]Lei (2009).

well as a vehicle for further economic construction. Fourthly, technological backwardness played its own role in the emergence of development zones. In 1980, China's overall technological level was poor, especially in terms of the high-tech industries, heavy industry and industry for people's livelihood. Nevertheless, development zones is a beneficial attempt and good institutional arrangement for the introduction and absorption of advanced foreign technology. Fifthly, China was in the grip of a significant labor surplus. With the introduction of the household contract responsibility system in rural areas, the rural labor force had been greatly liberated. Substantially speaking, along with productivity growth, the problem of surplus labor had, therefore, emerged. This trend led, inevitably, to low labor costs. The employment-intensive development zones became an important and promising solution to attract a large number of these rural laborers. In fact, the process of labor absorption is, in essence the urbanization process itself.

5.1.2   History

The history of development zones in China is both a portrayal of China's reform and opening policy and an important part of the policy itself. Immediately after the establishment of development zones, they demonstrated tremendous productivity and became a driving force, effectively promoting the rapid development of China's economy and society. The zones themselves underwent four distinct periods of historical development, including the initial start-up period, a high-speed development phase, a period of stable development and, finally a phase of scientific development (see Fig. 5.1).

5.1.2.1   The Initial Start-up Period (1985–1991)

From 1984 to 1988, the State Council approved of the establishment of 14 state-level development zones in twelve open coastal cities. In the initial stage, the central government did not give direct financial support to the zones, but rather provided them with policy and decision-making power, thereby encouraging them to move ahead. Firstly, the development zones developed from scratch, facing, as they did, poor foundations and a chronic lack of funds. At the same time, foreign investors had only just entered into the Chinese market. As such, these investors were still inclined to monitor the situation rather than commit capital of their own.

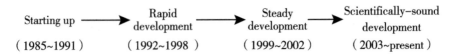

Fig. 5.1 The history of development zone in China

"In 1991, the fourteen development zones achieved a gross industrial output value of 14.594 billion yuan, tax revenue of 790 million yuan, exports of 1.14 billion US dollars and contracted foreign investment of 814 million US dollars. The actual utilization of foreign investment was, however, 361 million US dollars. By the end of 1991, meanwhile, the cumulative use of foreign capital had grown to reach 1.374 billion US dollars."[5] At this stage, each zone made bold explorations and innovations. They gradually formed a model of funding infrastructure, established and improved their management systems and legal frameworks and established the principles for development, that were, stress should be put on industrial development, attracting foreign investment, and an export-oriented approach of development, at the same time, committing, wholeheartedly, to the development of a high-tech industry. Together, these factors laid a solid basis of human resources, capital, policies and regulations for the future development.

5.1.2.2 The Period of High-Speed Development (1992–1998)

In 1992, Deng Xiaoping delivered a number of speeches during an inspection tour of the South. Amongst other things, the state had decided to deepen and widen the opening up strategy, to include the area from the coast to regions along the Yangtze River, Yellow River, and Pearl River as well as those bordering cities and inland provincial capitals. This policy triggered a nationwide wave of new development zones. "In 1998, the first batch of fourteen state-level development zones achieved, in total, an gross industrial output value of 186.909 billion yuan, tax revenue of 13.116 billion yuan and actual foreign investment of 3.252 billion US dollars. These figures represented a 6.2 fold (at constant prices), an 8.9 fold (at constant prices) and an eightfold increase, respectively, compared to 1991 figures. All in all, the average annual growth rate reached 32.5, 388, and 36.9%, respectively."[6] The technological standards of the projects introduced into the development zones also improved significantly, thereby directly boosting China's industrial modernization. As a result, development zones became the biggest magnet for foreign investment in China, and an important economic growth pole of surrounding cities. Needless to say, this approach was regarded as a successful model of economic development, leading to a nation-wide wave of developing zones, as provinces, cities and counties all established their own development zones. After 1993, the state began to rectify the zone rush, initially seeking to curb this trend. Nevertheless, after the state's decision to allow the central and western provinces, municipalities, and autonomous regions to select and recommend, among regional zones, the successful zones for application to become national development zones, there was, once again,

---

[5]Wuxi (2011).
[6]Wuxi (2011).

a new round of zone rush.[7] Whilst all of this unfolded, during this period, the number of national development zones increased from the initial 14–32.[8]

A Period of Stable Development (1999–2000)

To curb and control the zone fever, mechanisms for the promotion and knock-out of development zones were initially established. When China implemented the strategy of developing its under-developed western provinces, the state gradually established a number of additional state-level development zones in capital cities throughout the Midwest provinces. Consequently, the number of zones and industrial parks enjoying preferential policies increased to 53. From then, development zones entered into a period of stable development and the functions of these zones became increasingly comprehensive. This differed from the initial simple and extensive development zones, and had a variety of functions extended to urban communities with residential, service and other functions. The fierce external competition of the zones quickly challenged the original model of zone development and required further in-depth development and a 'second round start-up'. In 1999, on the fifteenth anniversary symposium celebrating the establishment of development zones, Vice Premier Wu Yi systematically expounded the development orientation of this 'second round start-up'. 'Firstly, the goal was to optimize the industrial structure and continuously raise the level of the open economy. Secondly, the state intended to unswervingly follow the road of intensional development. Thirdly, the new direction involved allowing the activities of the development zones to set a model and radiate outwards in full play, so as to promote development outside of the zones, especially in the Midwest regions. Fourth, establish and improve the socialist market economic system.'[9]

5.1.2.3 A Period of Scientific Development (2003–2013)

While zones generated huge economic benefits, they also exposed huge problems, of which the most serious was the violation of land rights. 'In 2003, there were, all together, 6015 development zones of a variety of different types. The planned area for various development zones, meanwhile, was 36,000 km², that is, more than the country's total area of construction land in existing cities and towns. Among thousands of development zones, those approved by the State Council only accounted for 6%, whereas those approved by provincial government accounted for 26.6%, and those development zones approved by authorities below the provincial

---

[7]Lei (2009).

[8]National Economic and Technological Development Zone, http://baike.baidu.com/view/887968.htm.

[9]Guo (2011).

level accounted for 67.4%. Meanwhile, in the development zones and industrial parks, land was often used without the proper authority or approval. Therefore, the problem of the illegal possession and trading of land was rather serious, resulting in a large amount of idle land and a large number of farmers losing their livelihoods. According to statistics, 43% of the land in development zones went unused.'[10] 'In 2003, the State Council issued a series of documents such as "An Emergency Notice of the Moratorium on the Approval of Various Development Zones", "A Notice on Straightening Out Various Development Zones and Strengthening the Management of Construction Land", and "Cleaning Up and Rectifying Existing Specific Standards for Various Development Zones and Policy Limits", intending to rectify the land market, stop the approval of the establishment of new development zones and prohibiting the expansion of the original development zones. There were originally 6015 development zones. From among this figure, 3763 zones were then revoked, 178,000 cases of violations of land law were found, 127,000 cases were investigated and prosecuted and 124,000 cases were closed. Forfeitures and penalties added up to 1.22 billion yuan and an area of 5878.4 ha of land was recovered.' The problems that had been caused by the unchecked expansion of development zones, for the most part, eased considerably.

The direction of the new period of scientific development throughout the development zones, meanwhile, was to develop a recycling economy, build an ecological civilization and create a model eco-industrial park. This approach emphasized the advantages of industrial clustering in concentrated zones, the potential of technological innovation and the benefits of an investment environment. It aimed to speed up the transformation of economic development patterns, improve ability in scientific and technological innovation and build eco-industrial parks through four key projects.

A. The first was the development of low-carbon industries. To be more specific, a plan was outlined to develop low-carbon industrial pattern, that was, to develop four major and competitive leading industries, including the electronic information industry, the food and beverage industry, the manufacturing of machinery and the bio-pharmacy industry. Likewise, low-carbon goals were applied to four new industries, that is, the manufacturing of motor vehicles and parts, the new energy and materials industry, the outsourcing of services and creative industries and the modern logistics industry.

B. The second was the development of ecological industry. Part of this project involved making improvements to the eco-industrial chains, that was, establishing inter-industrial coupling and intra-industrial closed loop of recycling. At the same time, there was scope for setting up exchanging channels for industrial materials and wastes between the major industrial sectors. It should also be

---

[10]"Comparative Analysis on Rectification of National Development Zones", *Information for Deciders Magazine*. Vol. 15, 2004.

ensured, that material metabolism, water metabolism, and unimpeded energy flow can all be achieved. Finally, efforts could be made to enhance the exchange of information and technology between manufacturing and service sectors, as well as ensure the efficient utilization of technology and information.

C. The third was the improvement to the process of infrastructure construction and the use of clean energy sources.

Finally, it was the advocacy that people switch to a low carbon lifestyle. At the same time, through planning and implementation, the most advanced environmental monitoring and integrated information platform should be set up across the country, thereby playing a leading role in nationwide environmental protection.

5.2 The Types and Spatial Layout of Development Zones

Classifying and ranking the specific type of a given development zones is a complex process. According to the administrative ranks, each one can be classified as a national-level development zone or a local-level development zone. The latter type can be further classified into provincial-level development zones or city-level development zones. According to their functions, each development zone can also be classified into, amongst others, economical and technological development zones, new and high-tech development zones, bonded zones, border economic cooperation zones and export processing zones.

5.2.1 National Economic and Technological Development Zones

5.2.1.1 The Basic Concept

Economic and technological development zone is the most prominent type of development zones. National level economic and technological development zones in China are, and remain, important sources of economic growth and constituent parts of those Chinese regions that open to foreigners. Economic and technological development zone is a limited area designated in open cities, where government plays a dominant role in infrastructure construction and makes it an international-standard platform. In this area, the utmost efforts are made to attract and use foreign investments and to create a highly modern and technological industrial model, thereby giving rise to a core region from which local and neighboring regions could also develop foreign trade and industrial clusters of their own.

Fig. 5.2 The distribution of national level economic and technological development zones. *Source* China Development Zone Association Website. http://www.cadz.org.cn/kfq/index.jsp?id=561

5.2.1.2   The Current Condition

The national level economic and technological development zones generally make up a great proportion of the GDP in cities, contributing significantly to central and local exchequers. They account for far more than average levels of national GDP growth and much higher than average levels of total contracted foreign capital. Economic and technological development zones, therefore, develop rapidly across China, creating a highly competitive nationwide trend. Up until May 2011, for instance, the number of economic and technological development zones approved by the Stated Council had increased to 127 (Fig. 5.2).

5.2.2   National Level High-Tech Industrial Development Zones

5.2.2.1   The Basic Concept

The establishment of these high-tech industrial development zones is meant to create a favorable environment for the growth of high-tech industries, primarily through tax reliefs and preferential policies relevant to high-tech manufacturing. It is, at the same time, hoped to foster comparable agglomerative advantages to

Fig. 5.3 The distribution of national-level hi-tech industrial development zones. *Source* China Development Zone Association Website. http://www.earthtree.cadz.org.cn/kfq/index.jsp?id\x3d624

industrial clusters and, through the agglomeration of talents, technology and capital, to speed up the industrialization of the latest scientific achievements.

5.2.2.2   Current Condition

With different focuses, high-tech industrial development zones emphasize new technologies, while economical and technological development zones emphasize the development of the economy and enhancing GDP. Indeed, since the state approved the Torch Program in 1988, high-tech industrial development zones have developed rapidly and, up until now, there have been 67 such zones constructed nationwide (Fig. 5.3).

5.2.3   National Bonded Areas

5.2.3.1   The Basic Concept

Approved by the State Council for development, bonded areas, where international business and tax protection businesses are located, are similar to the free trade zones popular in other countries. In bonded areas, foreign businesses are free to undertake

Fig. 5.4 The distribution of national level trade zones. *Source* China Association of Development Zones website: org.cn/kfq/index.jsp?id\x3d562

international trade, as well as develop their processing and exporting activities. Bonded areas are significant for promoting the hard power of trade in the areas where they are but, at the same time, also strengthen the power, influence and radiation of these areas. They function as junctions at which the Chinese and world economy can integrate.

5.2.3.2   The Current Condition

At present, fifteen ports, including Tianjin Port, Dalian Port, Qingdao Port, Zhang Jiagang, Shanghai Waigaoqiao, Ningbo, Fuzhou, Xiamen Xiangyu, Shantou, Shenzhen (Futian, Sha Tau Kok, Yantian), Guangzhou, Zhuhai and Haikou, among others, are in operation. They have become the new economic focus and city card of their respective port cities. See Fig. 5.4.

5.2.4   National Level Border Economic Cooperation Zones

5.2.4.1   The Basic Concept

The development of economic cooperation across the border of two countries is an important measure for promoting economic development and enhancing good

Fig. 5.5 The distribution of national level border economic cooperation zones. *Source* China Association of Development Zones website: http://www.cads.org.cn/kfq/index.jsp?id=563

neighborliness and international cooperation. It can also function as a national strategy for safeguarding the economic and social development of border areas. As such, in the border areas of open cities, it is necessary to establish certain areas within which to maintain appropriate levels of trade and exports so as to develop economic ties with neighboring countries, even those located overseas, and to facilitate the processing and exporting of domestic products.

5.2.4.2 The Current Condition

From 1992 until now, the State Council has approved of a total of fourteen border economic cooperation zones, including those located at Heihe, Hunchun, Manzhouli, Dandong, Yining, Tacheng, Bole, Pingxiang, Dongxing, Ruili, Wanding, Hekou, Erenhot and Suifenhe, among others. The overall economies of these border zones, which have good-neighborly relationship, have since developed well and the areas themselves have become models for mutually beneficial cooperation and good-neighborly relationships (see Fig. 5.5).

5.2.5   National Level Export Processing Zones

5.2.5.1   The Basic Concept

State-level export processing zones provide good business environments for enterprises so as to promote foreign trade. It is an important state measure to promote the development of processing trade, standardize the management of processing trade and centralize the otherwise scattered distribution of the processing trade. It is not an independent entity, but rather a zone, often relatively small-scaled, that is established within existing development zones to conduct export processing related experiments.

5.2.5.2   The Current Condition

In April 2000, the State Council began to establish export processing zones that were supervised and administrated by the relevant customs authorities. The earliest such experimental export processing zones are distributed amongst 60 separate sites (see Fig. 5.6).

Fig. 5.6 Distribution of national level export processing zones. *Source* China Association of Development Zones website: http://www.cads.org.cn/kfq/index.jsp?id=563

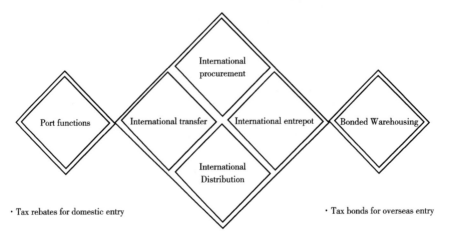

Fig. 5.7 Functions of bonded logistics park. *Source* Bonded Logistics Park: http://baike.baidu. com/view/344445.htm

5.2.6 Other State-Level Development Zones

5.2.6.1 National Tourist Resorts

National tourist resorts, contrary to expectations, actually operate mainly for the reception of foreign tourists. These resorts exist within definite areas and are suitable for centralized supply of supporting tourist facilities, usually rich in tourism resources, with convenient traffic and good foundations for opening to the outside world.[11] Since 1992, China has established twelve national tourist resorts, including Dalian Golden Pebble Beach, Sheshan in Shanghai, Taihu Lake in Wuxi, Taihu Lake in Suzhou, Hangzhou Zhijiang, the Wuyi Mountain, Meizhou Island, the Shilaoren in Qingdao, Guangzhou South Lake, Beihai Silver Beach, Sanya Yalong Bay and finally, Kunming Dianchi Lake.

5.2.6.2 Bonded Logistics Parks

Bonded logistics parks are specific areas where certain deals are conducted and items are purchased, distributed, delivered, exhibited, and transited. All of this is conducted under a policy of tax rebates for domestic goods that enter the park and tax bonds for foreign goods (see Fig. 5.7). Currently, there exists Tianjin Bonded Logistics Park, Zhangjiagang Bonded Logistics Park, Ningbo Bonded Logistics Park, Xiamen Xiangyu Bonded Logistics Park, Qingdao Bonded Logistics Park and Shenzhen Yantian Bonded Logistics Park.

---

[11]National Tourist Resort. http://baike.baidu.com/view/4450172.htm.

5.2.6.3 Sino-Russian Trade Zones, Cross-strait Science and Technology Industrial Parks and Taiwanese Investment Zones

Sino-Russian trade zones included the Manzhouli Sino-Russian Frontier Trade Zone and the Dongning-Poltavka Trade Zone. The cross-strait science and technology industrial parks include Shenyang Cross-strait Science and Technology Industrial Park and the Cross-strait Science and Technology Industrial Park in Nanjing. The Taiwanese Investment Zones include the Fuzhou yuanhong Investment Zone, the Xinglin Taiwanese Investment Zone, the Fuzhou Taiwanese Investment Zone and the Jimei Taiwanese Investment Zone.

5.2.7 Provincial Development Zones

Provincial development zones include economic development zones, industrial parks, industrial incubator parks, and industrial incubator and industrial parks, usually named after the region that they're located in. The number of development zones in economically developed areas is usually greater than the number in underdeveloped central and western provinces. Comparing the number of provincial development zones in Shanghai, Jiangsu with Xinjiang and other regions in central and west provinces, it is not difficult to find that the number of development zones in cities along rivers and coastlines is also significantly higher than that in other provinces. In the coastal provinces such as Jiangsu, almost every county has an economic development zone (see Table 5.1), while in less developed provinces, each city generally has only one development zone (see Table 5.2).

Table 5.1 The provincial development zones in Jiangsu province

Baixia Hi-tech Industrial Park, Nanjing	Pukou Economic Development Zone, Nanjing	Gaochun Economic Development Zone, Jiangsu	Nanjing Chemical Industrial Park
Qixia Economic Development Zone, Nanjing	Liuhe Economic Development Zone, Nanjing	Yuhua Economic Development Zone, Nanjing	Binjiang Economic Development Zone, Jiangning, Nanjing
Lishui Economic Development Zone, Jiangsu	Liyuan High-tech Industries Park, Wuxi, Jiangsu	Wuxi Economic Development Zone, Jiangsu	Huishan Economic Development Zone, Wuxi, Jiangsu
Xishan Economic Development Zone, Jiangsu	Shuofang Industrial Park, Wuxi, Jiangsu	Lingang Economic Development Zone, Jiangyin, Jiangsu	Yixing Pottory Industrial Park, Jiangsu
Yixing Economic Development Zone, Jiangsu	Xuzhou Industrial Park, Jiangsu	Pizhou Economic Development Zone, Jiangsu	Xinyi Economic Development Zone, Jiangsu

(continued)

Table 5.1 (continued)

Tongshan Economic Development Zone, Jiangsu	Suining Economic Development Zone, Jiangsu	Fengxian Economic Development Zone, Jiangsu	Zhonglou Economic Development Zone, Changzhou, Jiangsu
Tianning Economic Development Zone, changzhou, Jiangsu	Qishuyan Economic Development Zone, changzhou, Jiangsu	Xinbei Industries Park, Changzhou Jiangsu	Wujing High-tech Industries Park, Jiangsu
Wujing Economic Development Zone, Jiangsu	Liyang Economic Development Zone, Jiangsu	Hushuguan Economic Development Zone, Suzhou Jiangsu	Jintan Economic Development Zone, Jiangsu
Wuzhong Economic Development Zone, Jiangsu	Fenhu Economic Development Zone, Wujiang, Jiangsu	Xiangcheng Economic Development Zone, Jiangsu	Huaqiao Economic Development Zone, Kunshan, Jiangsu
Changsu Southeast Economic Development Zone, Jiangsu	Zhangjiagang Economic Development Zone, Jiangsu	Chongchuan Economic Development Zone, Nantong, Jiangsu	Gangzha Economic Development Zone, Nantong, Jiangsu
Haimen Economic Development Zone, Jiangsu	Haimen Industrial Park, Jiangsu	Qidong Economic Development Zone, Jiangsu	Tongzhou Economic Development Zone, Jiangsu
Rugao Economic Development Zone, Jiangsu	Rudong Economic Development Zone, Jiangsu	Haian Economic Development Zone, Jiangsu	Lianyungang High-tech Industrial Park, Jiangsu
Lianyungang Economic Development Zone, Jiangsu	Haizhou Economic Development Zone, Jiangsu	Ganyu Economic Development Zone, Jiangsu	Guanyun Economic Development Zone, Jiangsu
Donghai Economic Development Zone, Jiangsu	Lianyungang Chemical Industry Park, Jiangsu	Huaian Economic Development Zone, Jiangsu	Chuzhou Economic Development Zone, Jiangsu
Huaiyin Economic Development Zone, Jiangsu	Jinhu Economic Development Zone, Jiangsu	Xuyi Economic Development Zone, Jiangsu	Hongze Economic Development Zone, Jiangsu
Lianshui Economic Development Zone, Jiangsu	Tinghu Economic Development Zone, Jiangsu	Yandu Economic Development Zone, Jiangsu	Dongtai Economic Development Zone, Jiangsu
Dafeng Economic Development Zone, Jiangsu	Sheyang Economic Development Zone, Jiangsu	Funing Economic Development Zone, Jiangsu	Binghai Economic Development Zone, Jiangsu
Xiangshui Economic Development Zone, Jiangsu	Jianhu Economic Development Zone, Jiangsu	Weiyang Economic Development Zone, yangzhou Jiangsu	Hanjiang Economic Development Zone, yangzhou Jiangsu
Yizheng Economic Development Zone, Jiangsu	Jiangdu Economic Development Zone, Jiangsu	Gaoyou Economic Development Zone, Jiangsu	Jurong Economic Development Zone, Jiangsu
Yangzhong Economic Development Zone, Jiangsu	Danyang Economic Development Zone, Jiangsu	Dantu Economic Development Zone, Jiangsu	Runzhou Industrial Park, Zhengjiang, Jiangsu

(continued)

Table 5.1   (continued)

Jingkou Industrial Park, Zhengjiang, Jiangsu	Baoying Economic Development Zone, Jiangsu	Haining Industrial Park, Zhengjiang, Jiangsu	Taizhou Economic Development Zone, Jiangsu
Gaogong Hi-tech Development Zone, Taizhou, Jiangsu	Jingjiang Economic Development Zone, Jiangsu	Jinjiang- Jiangyin Industrial Park, Jiangsu	Taixing Economic Development Zone, Jiangsu
Jiangyan Economic Development Zone, Jiangsu	Xinghua Economic Development Zone, Jiangsu	Suqian Economic Development Zone, Jiangsu	Sucheng Economic Development Zone, Jiangsu
Suyu Economic Development Zone, Jiangsu	Shuyang Economic Development Zone, Jiangsu	Sihong Economic Development Zone, Jiangsu	Siyang Economic Development Zone, Jiangsu
Peixian Economic Development Zone, Jiangsu	Yangzhou Chemical Industry Park, Jiangsu		

Source China Association of Development Zones website: http://www.cads.org.cn/kfq/sjkfq_sh.jsp?ID=701&Itemid=564

Table 5.2   Provincial development zones in Xinjiang Uygur autonomous region

Shuimogou Industrial Park, Urumchi	Toutunhe Industrial Park, Urumchi	Huocheng Economic Development Zone, Xinjiang	Miquan Industrial Park, Xinjiang
Shanshan Chemical Industry Park, Xinjiang	Turpan Economic Development Zone, Xinjiang	Shihezi Industrial Park, Xinjiang	

Source Data extrapolated from China Association of Development Zones website

5.3   The Model of Governance in Development Zones

5.3.1   The Basic Concept and Characteristics of the Model of Governance in Development Zones

5.3.1.1   Basic Concept of the Model of Governance in Development Zones

The model of governance is a very important issue in the daily operation of development zones. Some scholars believe that a model is an intuitive and simple description of the internal and external mechanisms of objective things. It is a simplified form of theory that provides the overall framework of objective matters. The governance in development zones is characterized by interaction and cooperation between the government forces, market forces and social forces at work in

Fig. 5.8 The model of governance in development zones

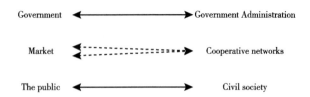

these zones.[12] The model of governance in development zones is both an external manifestation of the governance of zones, and, of course, the main driving force of further zone development itself. Essentially, the model of governance is actually evolved throughout the promotion of zone development so far and is, therefore, a combination of the effective systems, institutions and operational mechanisms. The model reflects the combined effect of government forces, market forces and social forces. The core of the model is the demarcation of roles and the division of power between government forces (generally in the form of the Administration Committee of the Development Zone), market forces and social forces, demonstrated, in particular, by the cooperative network between them (Fig. 5.8).[13]

5.3.1.2   Characteristics of the Model of Governance in Development Zones

An ideal governance model should be one of "good governance". "Good governance" as an ideal model of zone governance should have, in turn, at least two core features. The first of these is the involvement of multiple participants. The governance and management of the development zones has never depended on the unilateral actions of one party, but rather the pluralistic interactions between the government, enterprises and communities. Excluding any such party, or ignoring its voice, will inevitably lead to extremely serious consequences. For example, if the wishes of those who reside in the community were ignored in the process of land acquisition and compensation, and an agreement was reached only between enterprise managers and the carders responsible for rural collective affairs, it would inevitably trigger a backlash from the excluded residents. Some respond by petition,[14] others resort to extreme or desperate forms of protest such as self-immolations,[15] and some carry out violent attacks, such as the bombing of government buildings.[16] All such eventualities would result in huge economic and

---

[12]Wang (2009).

[13]Wang (2009).

[14]"Chinese People's Livelihood Hotline: Successful Petition for the Demolition in Lingang Economic Development Zone in Linyi City Is Given Instructions by the Central Government", January 11, 2011, http://wwwsdbfzm.com/Article/ShowArticle.asp.ArticleID\x3d688.

[15]"Farmer Li Wei Burn Herself to Prevent/Stop the Demolition in Changchun Economic Development Zone, Severely Injured", http://www.tt1890.com/ttdaily/13758.htm.

[16]"Fuzhou, Jiangxi bombings", http://www.huanqiu.com/zhuanti/china/jxbzh/.

social costs, largely offsetting the economic and social progress achieved through development zones. Secondly, equal coordination and interaction is required throughout the governance process. It is necessary, as numerous parties involved, to define their status and the precise form of participation afforded to them throughout proceedings. The ideal model of zone governance involves a kind of equal coordination and interaction, with ample consideration afforded to the interests of all parties concerned and a constant striving to find the points of intersection between their interests. This requires that the model of development zone governance be flexible rather than rigid, democratic rather than pressuring, open rather than closed.

5.3.2   Classification of Zone Governance Models

Many scholars have conducted valuable research into the different models of development zone governance. In her "Research on Management System in Development Zones", Lei Xia insists that government-enterprise relationships constitute the main basis of classification. She categorizes the different models of zone governance into government-led, enterprise-led and a government-enterprise mixed management model.[17] The government-led model refers to the government's direct or indirect management of development zones and, according to the power of the Administration Committee of the Development Zone (henceforth the ACDZ), it can be divided into a government managed model or a quasi-government managed model. The zone governance model in China mainly depends on the relationship between the local government and the relevant ACDZ. Different relationships will produce corresponding differences in governance models, so the governance model in China's development zones is, on the whole, a dynamic concept.

In an article titled "A Study on the Innovation in Zone Administrative Systems", Sun Hongjian argues that the relationship between the government and the ACDZ is an important foundation for classifying different models of governance. The zone governance system in China has undergone a process of change. As early as the development zones were established, they were identified as new industrial areas under the jurisdiction of the direct leadership of local governments, which generally enjoyed preferential policies. However, with the gradual development of the zones, their functions expanded gradually, from single industrial function to multiple functions and, as a result, the Administration Committees of Development Zones (ACDZs), with their quasi-governmental nature and independent administrative functions, appeared.[18] He categorized zone governance models into three types of system: a system-combined model, a system-separated model and a transitional system model.

---

[17]Lei (2009).
[18]Sun (2009).

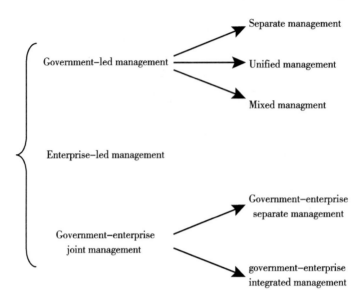

Fig. 5.9 Classification of development zone governance models

Nevertheless, this study advocates that a better classification lies in an organic combination of the two abovementioned kinds of categorizations (see Fig. 5.9). Sun's focus on the relationship between the Administration Committee of Development Zones, under the leadership of the government, and the local government, should actually be included in the context of Lei's "government-led" model. Therefore, the category of a government-led model can be further divided into three further subcategories, those are, the system-combined model, the system-separated model and the transitional system model. The enterprise-led and government-enterprise mixed governance models are juxtaposed with the government-led model with the latter of the former two being further divisible into two categories: the government-enterprise separated model and the government-enterprise combined model.

5.3.2.1   The Government-Led Model

The government-led model treats the Administration Committees of Development Zones as quasi-governmental organizations in accordance with their functions. Under this governance model, either the ACDZ or the local government has direct or indirect power over the planning, guidance and management of the economic, political, social, and cultural affairs related to a given development zone. According to the relationship between the ACDZ and the local government, zone governance models can be classified into three sub-types, which are the separated, combined, and mixed governance models.

The Separated Governance Model

The core feature of this governance model is the separation and isolation of the local government and the Administration Committee of Development Zones (ACDZ). The development zone is more like a self-governed organization, often known as a "state within a state" or a "government within a government". The ACDZ conducts independent leadership and planning and bears all corresponding responsibilities. It enjoys independent, discretionary and administrative power over party, administrative, economic, social and cultural affairs. The "quasi-special administrative zone" nature of some development zones has led to a lot of controversy. The advantages of this model are easily recognizable. With such discretionary powers, development zones could prioritize their own professional operation, special treatment, and industrial clustering. All of this could be favorable to developing special industries and exerting greater influences and radiation throughout surrounding regions. Nevertheless, disadvantages of this approach are also obvious. The policies and planning implemented by ACDZs may not always achieve a satisfactory level of harmony with the local government's policies. Needless to say, such harmony, as external environment, is an important part of the development of these zones. Any such incompatible features of its management and, administrative power could give rise to shackles and obstacles that are preventative of sustainable development. For example, Suzhou Industrial Park belongs to the abovementioned separated type. The Park Administration Committee is an agency that, assigned by Suzhou Municipal People's Government, independently exercises administrative power on behalf of the municipal government. Because of its unique background, the "block-based" management system is the most thoroughly implemented and is currently one of the most successful management systems in operation.[19]

The Combined Governance Model

The key point of the combined model is that the Administration Committee of Development Zones (ACDZ) is actually equivalent to the local government. That is to say, the ACDZ is, in essence, the first-level of government, under which the administrative authorities of the development zone and those of the local government are effectively united. The organization form is actually "one team, two titles" model.[20] The chief official of the ACDZ is also the head of the local government. For example, Suzhou High-Tech Industrial Park had, in the beginning, a typical separated type of development zone governance. According to the principle of "small government, big society", with a "block-based" management system, Administration Committee of the High-Tech Zone was an agency dispatched by the Suzhou Municipal Government and its power had been bestowed from the

---

[19]Wang (2009).

[20]Fan Ning: "How to Prevent the Return of Old System after the Expansion of Development Zones —A Reflection on the Adjustment of Suzhou Zones".

municipal authorities. The High-Tech Zone was, therefore, relatively independent from the local government's administrative division. It operated independently and had the power to decide its own affairs, human resources and finances. The Administration Committee of the High-Tech Zone consisted of one office and fourteen bureaus which were both streamlined and efficient. Nevertheless, adjustments were made to the urban administrative divisions in Suzhou, in September 2002. At this point Suzhou New District merged with Huqiu District, resulting in an expansion of its area to 258 km². Huqiu District Government and the Administration Committee of the High-Tech Zone also adopt the "one team, two titles" model of zone governance. As such, the Suzhou High-Tech Development Zone is both a development zone and an administrative borough, thereby making it typically representative of the combined type.[21]

The Mixed Governance Model

In the mixed governance model, the relationship between the Administration Committee of Development Zones (ACDZ) and the local government has both the characteristics of the separated type, on the one hand, and the combined type, on the other hand. For example, Kunshan Development Zone originally had a separated type of governance, until, that is, a recent change of personnel. The Party Secretary of the Kunshan Municipal Committee and the Mayor of Kunshan City served concurrently as the Secretary of the Development Zone Working Committee and the Director of the ACDZ. This, therefore, involved a mixed state of separation and integration, as well as a state of transition.[22]

5.3.2.2 The Enterprise-Led Governance Model

The enterprise-led model, also known as the non-administration-committee management system, does not actually allow enterprises to independently manage all of the affairs within a development zone. Instead, under this system, an independent economic and trade corporation is established to organize all of the economic activities within the development zone. The economic and trade corporation effectively replaces the government's role in economic management as an independent legal person. Nevertheless, some of the other functions of management, such as personnel, taxation, industry and commerce, environmental protection and cultural affairs are still exercised by other government departments (see Fig. 5.10). For example, the Shanghai Caohejing New Technology Development Zone possessed a typical enterprise-led governance model. In 1988, this zone was further approved as a national high-tech park. By 1990, the Development Corporation of

---

[21]Wang (2009).
[22]Wang (2009).

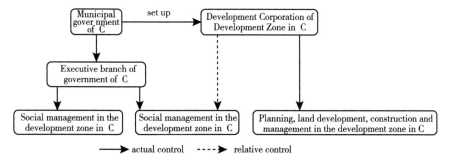

Fig. 5.10 Enterprise-led governance structure. *Source* Lei (2009)

Caohejing High-Tech Park had also received approval, by the Shanghai Municipal People's Congress, to co-ordinate all economic affairs within the park, including infrastructure, fund-raising, real estate management, attracting investment and foreign capital, introducing technology, starting-up new enterprises, general trading, and further real estate development.

5.3.2.3 The Mixed Governance Model

This is an intermediate model occupying a position somewhere between the government-led and the enterprise-led models. Some scholars, in accordance with the relationship between the Administration Committee of Development Zones (ACDZ) and the Development Corporation of Development Zones, divide this model into two separate sub-models. These are the government-enterprise separated model and the government-enterprise integrated model.

5.4 The Strategic Functions of the Development Zones

Development zones, as a manifestation of national strategy and the state will, have great strategic functions in the economic, social, political, and cultural realms. In other words, they are a strong impetus to the progress of the whole country. Among all the qualities of zone, those attributes such as programming, human factor and external drive dovetail well China's national conditions. As an important model of urbanization, development zones in terms of the economy, regularly release the potential of the social economy and promote the industrial upgrading. In terms of society, on the other hand, they promote urbanization, cultivate farming society and increase the range of public services. In terms of politics, meanwhile, they improve the special administrative region (SAR) system, highlight the benefits of the Chinese model of development and promote exchange across the Taiwan Straits. Finally, from a cultural point of view, they cultivate an innovative mercantile culture.

5.4.1   The Economic Functions of Development Zones

5.4.1.1   The Contribution of Development Zones to the National Economy

Development zones, as a specific setting for technical and economic development, effectively promote massive economic development in China and, overtime, became one of the key growth poles of economic development, reflected (see Table 5.3) as one of the country's main economic indicators. In 2010, for instance, the major economic indicators of NETDZs (the National Economic and Technical Development Zones) were much higher than national averages. In 2010, China's GDP grew by 10.3%, yet the growth rate for national economic and technological development zones was 25.67% for the same year. The GDP growth rate of development zones in the east is 25%, 30% in central regions and 23% in the west, all of which are far higher than the national economic growth rate of 10%. Economic growth rates of development zones are also generally far higher than local average growth rates. Needless to say, this enhanced economic potential is an important cause of the nationwide wave of new development zones.

5.4.1.2   Increasing Fiscal and Tax Revenues

The vigorous promotion of national economic development zones inevitably brings huge benefits to national fiscal revenues and tax revenues. As far as finance is concerned, in 2010, national fiscal revenues grew by 21.3%, while the growth rate of the national economic development zones was 37.58%. Among them, the GDP growth rate of the development zones in the east was 36%, 47% in central regions and 59% in the west. As for taxation, in 2010, national tax revenues grew by 22.74%, but those from national economic development zones grew by 29.37%. Among them, the eastern zones grew by 30%, the central zones grew by 33% and the western zones grew by 15.7%. Development zones also enjoy policy advantage, as regards to fiscal revenue and, especially, tax revenues, and various advantages brought about by industrial clustering (see Table 5.3).

5.4.1.3   International Trade

The establishment of development zones also effectively promotes levels of international trade. Correspondingly, development zones generally become the front runners in international trade, enjoying a range of advantages including considerable economies of scale and first-mover advantages. As for exports, in 2010, the national export growth rate was 17.9%, while that witnessed in development zones was 28.1%. To be more specific, eastern areas witnessed growth of 26.7%, central areas witnessed growth of 55.2% and western areas witnessed growth of 40.0%.

Table 5.3 Major economic indicators in national economic and technical development zones (NETDZs) in 2010

Economic indicators	Nation wide		90NETDZs			47 Eastern NETDZs		
	Year 2010	YoY (%)	Year 2010	Year 2009	YoY (%)	Year 2010	Year 2009	YoY (%)
Local GDP	397,983	10.30	26,849.13	21,364.43	25.67	19,137.54	15,304.12	25.05
Among them: industrial added value			18,660.5	15,185.21	22.89	12,937.5	10,716.19	20.73
Among them: tertiary industry added value			6404.93	5087.53	25.89	4958.64	3940.88	25.83
Total industrial output value	70,772	30.40	77,541.52	61,660.16	5.76	57,880.25	4413.89	24.7
Fiscal revenue	83,080	21.30	5627.07	4089.93	37.58	425,014	3182.46	33.55
Among them: local general budget revenue			1961.77	1654.67	18.56	1441.01	1253.77	14.93
Tax revenue	77,390	22.6	4650.3	3594.55	29.37	3636.35	2793.8	30.16
Among them: foreign-invested enterprises			2636.96	2120.15	24.38	2254.91	1816.17	24.16
Total exports (0.1 billion $)	1541.49	17.90	2536.3	1979.96	28.1	2348.79	1853.49	26.72
Among them: high-tech product exports (0.1 billion $)			1643.76	1356.25	21.2	1557.17	1283.36	21.34
Total imports ($ 0.1 billion)	1410.7	25.60	2430.12	1765.4	37.65	2228.8	1634.11	36.39
Among them: high-tech product imports			1272.14	890.38	42.88	1186.06	850.95	39.38
Foreign investment ($ 0.1 billion)	1057.35	17.44	305.85	255.76	19.59	242.92	201.6	20.5
Over-years accumulated contractual foreign investment (US $ billion)			3913.18	3386.21	15.56	324.24	2934.65	11.23
Accumulated over the years the amount of foreign capital actually utilized ($ 0.1 billion)			2371.95	1993.49	18.98	191,781	1672.91	14.64
Investment in fixed assets (0.1 billion RMB) (this year)			12,870.4	10,222.69	25.9	8085.8	6641.66	21.74
Among them: high-tech product exports (US $0.1 billion)			70.66	31.81	122.14	15.42	7.62	102.33

(continued)

Table 5.3 (continued)

Economic indicators	Nation wide		90NETDZs			47 Eastern NETDZs		
	Year 2010	YoY (%)	Year 2010	Year 2009	YoY (%)	Year 2010	Year 2009	YoY (%)
Actually utilized the amount of foreign capital (US $0.1 billion)	1057.35	17.44	46.8	35.15	33.17	16.13	19.02	−15.17
Over the years accumulated contractual foreign investment (US$0.1 billion)			373.88	30.13	23.75	275.06	149.43	84.08
Accumulated over the years actually utilized the amount of foreign capital (US$0.1 billion)			350.44	232.97	50.42	13.71	87.61	18.37
Investment in fixed assets (0.1 billion RMB) (this year)			2732.4	1924.79	41.96	2052.2	1656.24	23.91
The number of newly approved enterprises			534	4617	15.85	7312	7041	3.85
Among them: foreign-invested enterprises			205	158	29.75	77	108	−2.7
Accumulate over the years developed land (km²)			396.57	319.79	24.01	316.46	289.26	9.4
Zone employed personnel by the end of the year (0.1 million)			164.36	148.38	10.77	121.49	112.79	7.71
The number of newly approved enterprises			40,794	32,344	26.13	28,133	20,686	36
Among them: foreign-invested enterprises			225	2075	6.27	1923	1809	3
Developed land accumulated over years (km²)			2392.94	211,134	13.34	1679.91	1502.29	11.8
Zone employed personnel by the end of the year (0.1 million)			898.23	818.48	9.74	612.38	557.3	9.88
Local GDP	397,983	10.30	4756.39	3664	29.79	2955.21	2395.51	23.36
Among them: industrial added value			3635.31	2853.67	27.9	2087.7	1615.34	29.24
Among them: tertiary industry added value			835.51	585.58	42.68	610.78	51.07	8.86
Total industrial output value (0.1 billion RMB)	707,772	30.40	12,962.96	10,087.21	28.51	6698.3	5159.06	29.84

(continued)

Table 5.3 (continued)

Economic indicators	Nation wide		90NETDZs			47 Eastern NETDZs		
	Year 2010	YoY (%)	Year 2010	Year 2009	YoY (%)	Year 2010	Year 2009	YoY (%)
Fiscal revenue (0.1 billion RMB)	83,080	21.30	767.94	523.74	46.63	608.98	383.73	58.7
Among them: local general budget revenue			298.59	22.18	33.79	222.17	177.72	25.01
Tax revenue (0.1 billion RMB	77,390	22.64	655.22	490.68	33.53	35.73	310.06	15.7
Among them: foreign-invested enterprises ($ 0.1billion)			325.58	213.16	52.74	56.47	90.81	−37.2
Total exports ($ 0.1 billion)	1541.49	17.90	107.3	69.22	55.02	80.24	57.25	40.15
Among them: high-tech product exports (US $0.1 billion)			74.74	3.36	117.53	11.85	38.53	−69.25
Total imports (US$0.1 billion)	1410.7	25.60	120	73.82	62.57	81.3	57.47	41.49

Source China Association of Development Zones website: http://www.cadz.org.cn/Content.jsp?ItemID=1570&ContentID=99806

The growth rate of development zones, then, is far higher than national averages. Secondly, as for imports, in 2010, the national growth rate was 25.6%, of which eastern areas witnessed 36.39%, central areas witnessed 62.57% and western areas witnessed 41.49% (see Table 5.3).

5.4.1.4 Economies of Scale

Industrial cluster and economies of scale reflect the development zone's influence, degree of radiation and driving effect over the development of an entire region. It is a kind of intangible capital or soft power which depends on both the public relations and management style of a development zone. For one thing, scale effects can attract more enterprises to relocate to the zone, thereby bringing in more capital and technology whilst also effectively sharing the costs of production. The introduction of new enterprises may also promote a degree of healthy competition in the region. For example, Zhan Shuifang discussed industrial cluster and economies of scale in Shanghai in her thesis "The Institutional Thickness in Shanghai's Development Zones and the Construction of a World-Class Industrial Base". In it, she analyzed deeply the scattered, dotted, blocked and regional industry cluster models and reached the conclusion that industrial cluster and economies of scale exert far-reaching influences on industrial restructuring and layout, space restructuring and the prospects for constructing a world-class industrial base.[23]

5.4.1.5 Industrial Upgrading

Industrial restructuring is an important and pressing issue to be confronted by China's economy. For a long time, China's development zones made great efforts in the field of OEM (original equipment manufacturing) and processing (processing with given materials, samples and components and compensation trades), raw material supply, contracted manufacturing and other services. These fields are now, however, at the low end of the global industrial chain with low profits and high levels of dependency on foreign markets. Development zones, meanwhile, do not have their own intellectual property rights or their own core technology, nor do they have their own brand identity or marketing channels and they lack systems of standards and have no voice. Development zones are of great significance for the absorption of advance foreign technology, building national brands and competing for a voice in the global economy. In the category of development zones, high-tech industrial development zones are among the most important class. One of their main responsibilities is to develop advance technology and hold the high end of the international industrial chain.

---

[23]Zhan (2004).

5.4.1.6 Strategic Industry

Strategic resources and strategic industries are a core guarantee of national strength, which directly relates to the survival, security and economic autonomy of China. These strategic resources include rare metals, steel, high-tech materials, new energy resources, heavy equipment manufacturing, advance communications, such as triple play (tri-networks integration) and cloud computing. It is, therefore, necessary to open corresponding international development zones to develop strategic resources and strengthen the vital strategic industries. As such, currently, many development zones lock their focus on these strategic industries. For example, Yantai Development Zone focuses on the field of new materials, optical materials and rare earth fluorescent materials.[24] Hangzhou Economic Development Zone focuses on new energy-use vehicles and new Internet of things (IoT). Zengcheng Zone emphasizes cloud computing and cloud storage, Internet of things (IoT), new energy resources and new materials. All of these development zones have made significant progress in the specified fields and more. In addition, Baotou Rare Earth High-Tech Industrial Development Zone is the only state-level development zone operating under a rare-earth strategy. All of this is to say that development zones play a major role in the development of strategic resources and the overall strategic industry.

5.4.2 Social Functions

The economic functions of development zones are obvious enough, yet the social function of development zones attracts more and more concern from academics and the government alike. Development zones, as a leading model for urbanization with Chinese characteristics, are a strong impetus to China's urbanization process and an important part of promoting the overall planning of urban and rural development. Meanwhile they have made important and unique contributions to the innovation of management systems, the reinforcement of social construction and the nurturing of civil society.

5.4.2.1 Promoting Urbanization

The promotion of urbanization in China by development zones includes four dimensions. These are regional urbanization, population urbanization, lifestyle urbanization and ideological urbanization. As urbanization is an internal and multi-staged process of development, it is largely endogenous in nature. While

---

[24]"Yantai Development Zone Fostering Strategic Emerging Products to Create One-hundred-billion Entity", http://tv.people.com.cn/GB/150716/156856/158298/14825091html.

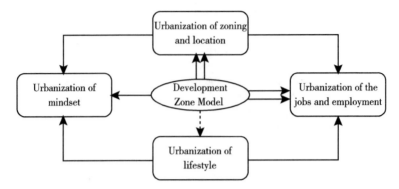

Fig. 5.11 The inherent logic of zone model in promoting China's urbanization

urbanization process in China is exogenous, with external forces playing a major role. Therefore, China's urbanization has formed a complete loop, incorporating geographical location, population employment, lifestyle and ideology. In China's urbanization, the logical starting-point is the reform and opening up. China actively leant from the experiences of development zones abroad. These experiences led the relevant authorities to set up specific areas as development zones in the coastal cities along the Yangtze River (taking into account higher urban land prices, the development zones were mostly confined to suburban or rural areas). After the establishment of development zones, the surrounding population was encouraged to work in the zones and, as a result, gain significantly improved incomes. Farmers were, therefore, economically integrated into the city through employment. Among them some successful high-tech and high-income families also moved near the zones and became urban residents. In this process, farmers and their families were influenced by the urban lifestyle and ideology, and, gradually citizenized. These, all together, constitute the inherent logic of the promotion of urbanization by development zones (see Fig. 5.11).

The author believes that the role of development zones in the four stages or aspects of the urbanization process are functionally different. For one thing, as many development zones emerge in what were previously suburban or rural areas, and, form new urban areas, they powerfully strengthen the process of local urbanization. These development zones also play a huge role in population urbanization since they absorb large quantities of surplus rural laborers (who participate in construction, processing, logistics and so on). Nevertheless, development zones have a relatively weak influence when it comes to promoting the urbanization of lifestyle and ideologies. The *"People's Daily"* published a range of commentaries related to this topic including: "Urbanization Is Urbanization of People, not the Land" and "A 'Great Leap Forward' Emerges in Urbanization, Land Urbanization is Faster than the Urbanization of the Population, the Impulse of Managing the City Goes beyond the Laws of Economic Development". These headlines point out a common problem with urbanization in China, that land

Four dimensions of urbanization	Functional assessment of the Development Zone Model
Urbanization of zoning and location	Strong (==========➤)
Urbanization of jobs and employment	Strong (==========➤)
Urbanization of lifestyle	Weak (- - - - - - - - - - - ➤)
Urbanization of mindset	Medium (————————➤)

Fig. 5.12 Assessment on the four dimensions of urbanization and the role of development zones

urbanization is faster than the population citizenization.[25] Therefore, in terms of the urbanization of public ideology and promoting the urban way of life, the role of development zones is relatively weak (see Fig. 5.12).

5.4.2.2 Promoting the Overall Planning of Urban and Rural Development

Urbanization joins country sides and cities. It is a process of transforming once backward rural areas into modern towns. It is also an important systematic setting to promote the overall planning of urban and rural development. Development zones are usually allocated to rural or suburban areas, the likes of which could be classified as the countryside. Through the development of industry in these zones, the local residents have access to a more stable and higher income than farming would provide. At the same time, local government revenues increase significantly as well, thereby providing capital for bridges, roads and other infrastructural construction. Besides, real estate projects, the financial industry and various services also develop in and around these zones. Such a process often, subsequently, leads to the prosperity and development of the surrounding rural areas. The development zones, then, became an important systematic innovation, albeit with Chinese characteristics, in promoting the overall planning of urban and rural development.

5.4.2.3 The Innovation of Management System

The innovation of social management systems in China is a longstanding, ongoing and dynamic process, rather than something new. Indeed, the socialist market economic system itself represents a radical innovation of social management systems. Furthermore, since the reform and opening up, the setting-up of various additional systems, each of which with Chinese characteristics, represents further

---

[25]"Urbanization is an urbanization of people not the land". *Peoples Daily*. Feb. 14, 2011. Reprinted by Xinhua Net. http://news.xinhuanet.com/2011-02/14/c_121072956.htm.

innovations of social systems and social management systems based on the particular national circumstances of modern day China. The Administration Committees of Development Zones, as well as the Development Corporation of Development Zones, are also effective and efficient models of management systems that have been innovated in this way. Subsequent success in development zones has demonstrated that the market and the government can, indeed, share and cooperate effectively in handling a range of development issues. Yet, it remains clear that development zones still require further innovation from the perspective of the law. Until now, laws of national-level development zones has not yet been enacted. Instead, only the "Tentative Regulations of Development Zones" is in practice, so the complete and permanent legislation of development zones is sure to be a dominant trend of future development.[26]

5.4.2.4 Promoting Social Development

Urbanization is a process of converting backward rural environments into advanced cities. The backwardness and advancement mentioned here mainly refer to that of physical infrastructure and the ideology or mindsets of the local population. Urbanization, then, should mean both investment in infrastructure and influence over the cultural ideology of citizens. In the end, the process aims to gradually prepare an agricultural population for a more modern way of life and thinking. With the advancement of urbanization, it has been witnessed that, perhaps wrongly, all rural areas are being forced to become urbanized towns. Indeed, this kind of "in situ urbanization" is another very effective method of urbanization. Such development does, of course, enable farmers to enjoy basic urban living standards, including cultural and recreational facilities, that is, through the construction of infrastructure, a process often called "public service equalization".[27] Development zones, with their good economic returns and high fiscal revenues, in other words, with abundant resources, are key players as regards investing in science, education, culture and other public services.

5.4.2.5 Cultivating a Civic Society

It is the material or 'hard' objective of urbanization for development zones to promote the construction of social infrastructure. It is, meanwhile, something of an intangible or 'soft' objective to cultivate a civic society. Migrant farmers were the first social group in Chinese society to make new contact with urban culture and become newly urbanized to some extent. They were the farmers from surrounding areas that moved to work in the new development zones. As the development zones

---

[26]Sun (2009).
[27]Liu (2010), Yang (2010).

expanded geographically and enhanced their economic strength, they gradually formed a comprehensive urban community, eventually giving rise to cities. The surrounding farmers, meanwhile, experienced the whole process and, consequently, became the first group of new urban citizens. Not only did their new urban citizenship extend to their work and home life, but also it equipped them with efficient, open, fair and rational mindsets that affected their ways of doing things, their ways of thinking and their civility in general.

5.4.3   Political Functions

A range of economic and social functions are two latent functions of development zones. Nevertheless, these development zones have had, since their inception, clear political function as well. This is reflected in the way in which they maintain and emphasize the socialist system, albeit with Chinese characteristics, and how they promote the peaceful reunification of China.

5.4.3.1   Developing the SAR System

The development zones located in countries other than China naturally come into being when the levels of economy and trade develop to a certain extent. Development zones in China, however, are an exogenously planned product of government intentions. Therefore, they can be further characterized as an institutional innovation with Chinese characteristics. The source of this innovation came from the SAR (Special Administrative Region) system. To be more specific, in 1979, the four coastal cities of Shenzhen, Xiamen, Zhuhai and Shantou become the first cities approved for the establishment of development zones, although a range of other coastal cities and cities along the major rivers followed afterwards. From 1984 to 1988, the State Council approved of establishing a further fourteen state-level development zones in twelve coastal opening cities. Therefore, figuratively speaking, the development zones were like "SARs in SARs". They could be seen as a result of the natural development and extension of the SAR system and a means of verifying the success of this system, and the superiority of the socialist system in general.

5.4.3.2   Highlighting the Chinese Model

China's development zones offer an important growth pole for the economic development mode with Chinese characteristics. For one thing, the growth of GDP and fiscal and tax revenues within these zones is much higher than the national averages. Therefore, the discussion of development zones is an indispensable step in trying to understand the overall economic development model of China. Indeed, the popularity of studying the "China model" at all is, in itself, an important manifestation of the global impact of the socialist system with Chinese characteristics. Any successes of the development zones will, then, inevitably become a championed part of the Chinese model. This will, in turn, be an important instrument for China to extend a greater influence and degree of radiation force over the world stage.

5.4.3.3   Promoting Cross-strait Economic Exchange

The development zones have played a huge role in cross-strait economic exchanges. Due to a range of reasons, economic and trade exchanges between the two sides of the Taiwan Straits often face a variety of obstacles, including political risks, institutional disagreements and regulatory disharmony. Opening up a special Taiwan Zone, however, can creatively solve those problems. So far, the mainland has opened up cross-strait science and technology industrial parks and Taiwanese investment zones, as well as other forms of development zones, to this effect. The former includes Shenyang Cross-strait Technology Industrial Park and Nanjing Cross-strait Science and Technology Industrial park; the latter includes Fuzhou yuanhong Investment Zone, Xinglin Taiwanese Investment Zone, Fuzhou Taiwanese Investment Zone and Jimei Taiwanese Investment Zone. This greatly facilitated economic and trade based exchanges between the two sides and, in the process, eased political tensions.

5.5   The Logic in Pushing Ahead with Urbanization by Development Zones

Development zones are one of the main models of pushing ahead with urbanization with Chinese characteristics. It is, therefore, necessary to make an enquiry into the inherent logic of the process. To this end, the model of development zones, in accordance with their overall operational loops, can be divided into four phases. The first of these is the start-up phase, the second is the resource organization phase, the third is the continuous operation phase and the fourth is the phase of returns. The phase of returns, meanwhile, has far reaching effects on the previous three phases. After all, a sound interest distribution structure is bound to promote the sound operation of the zones. Once long-term imbalances in benefit distribution occur, this could constitute an obstacle to zone development, generating economic limitations and social constraints, damaging and blocking the sustainable development and progress of scientific development (see Fig. 5.13).

5.5.1   The Start-up Phase

The start-up phase is the birth stage of the development zones. Generally, four factors will lead to the establishment of a zone. These include administrative

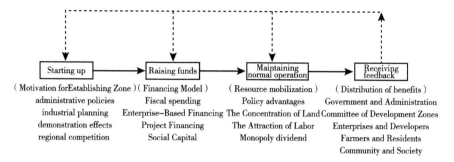

Fig. 5.13 The logic in promoting urbanization by development zones

policies, industrial planning, demonstration effects and regional competition. All of these factors are intrinsic motivations to facilitating the establishment of development zones. In other words, the will of the state, preferential policies, effective demonstrations and competition will, all together, drive the government, at all levels, to set up various types of development zones.

5.5.1.1   Government Policy

Government policy is the foremost factor responsible for zone establishment. The establishment and development of all zones in China is the result of strong government support. In fact, not one development zone was separable from government policy. The development zones themselves enjoyed preferential policies and special incentives from the government, embodied by such things as taxation, personnel, grading, land allocation and human resource affairs.[28] Together, these formed a "resource basin" that provided development zones with strong competitiveness and vitality.

5.5.1.2   Industrial Planning

Industrial planning was also an important motivation. Throughout the 1980s-1990, development zones generally consisted in the lower-end of the global industry chain, primarily engaged with primary industry, OEM (original equipment manufacturing), processing (processing with given materials, samples and components) and compensation trades. They, therefore, became the preferred destinations to which developed countries would transfer their low-end industries. In order to carry out industrial restructuring and seize the high-end of the international industrial

---

[28]"The Temporary Management Methods of Loan Interest-subsidy to the Infrastructure Projects in National Economic and Technical Development Zones in Central west Areas". China Association of Development Zones website: http://www.cadz.org.cn/Content.jsp?ItemID\x3d1602&ContentID \x3d78714.

chain, The National High-tech Industrial Development Plan—the Torch Program—was implemented in August 1988. To establish high-tech industrial development zones and open high-tech innovation service centers were both explicitly included as important parts of the Torch Plan. Since 1991, the State Council has approved the establishment of a total of 53 national high-tech industrial development zones.[29]

5.5.1.3   Demonstration Effect

As far as the "nationwide wave of developing zones" across the country, especially in the 1990s and early twenty-first century, is concerned, the positive demonstration provided by matured zones was an important motivation for applying for the establishment of further zones nationwide. The process of reform and opening up with Chinese characteristics itself was a process of continuously learning form advanced models, foregoing and fore-testing, as well as constant exploration into more effective models. Therefore, the demonstration effect of typically successful industrial parks should not be underestimated. That said, the overzealous construction of such zones across the country also led to many problems, including land concentration and vicious competition.

5.5.1.4   Regional Competition

Since total economic, social and policy resources are definite, the establishment of development zones often entailed necessarily the decline of the economic status of the surrounding area, despite, that is, the possibility of win-win development. Consequently, zones were established one after another across the country in order to maximize said policy, economic and social resources, thereby leading to an inevitable degree of competition among regions. Benign competition in the market can, of course, lead to the more effective flow of resources, but vicious competition and the inefficient use of social and policy resources is more likely to occur when development zones have not yet highly matured. Therefore, research into the orderly competition and balanced development of zones remains high on the agenda.[30]

5.5.2   The Organization of Resource

The major task of development zones in this phase is to raise funds and prepare resources, namely the issue of the financing model. In terms of the financing model,

---

[29]National Economic and Technological Development Zone. http://baike.baidu.com/view/887968.htm.com/view/887968.htm.

[30]"The Orderly Competition and Coordinated Development in Development Zones". China High-Tech Industry Herald. March 11, 2005.

many effective attempts and explorations have been made as regards development zones. Sources of funding may be financial allocations, but can also be industrial capital from enterprises or estate capital, as well as social capital.

5.5.2.1 Fiscal Spending

Fiscal spending is an important source of capital for development zones, especially at the beginning of a project, when government support is most acutely needed. Obviously, while it is by no means the only source of funding, the government plays a critical role in the early stages of any development zone construction. How the government allocates its matching funds reflects the strength of the support it is capable of providing, the areas it deems worthy of such support, and where different projects lie on its priority ranking. Fiscal spending, however, does not account for the bulk of capital investment in development zone construction. A much more common practice is providing loan guarantees for enterprises. For those development zones that are functioning properly, government funding accounts for a relatively small share of it total capital, while the private sector and other social organizations contribute a much greater share.[31]

5.5.2.2 Corporate Financing

Enterprise capital was, in general, the main capital of development zones. Enterprise financing refers to any financial intermediation with enterprises as the mainstay. The objective of the government fund may be to ensure the overall and sustainable operation of the zones, but the purpose of enterprise financing is based on minimizing costs and maximizing profits. Enterprise financing usually takes the form of internal financing (internal capital accumulation), lease financing (leasing equipment to other companies to obtain capital), mortgage and pledge-financing (to mortgage fixed assets or land use rights to obtain capital), government-guaranteed loans, equity financing (selling more shares) and the issuance of corporate bonds.[32]

5.5.2.3 Project Financing

Project financing refers to financing that is guaranteed by bright market prospects, operational performance and capital flows of the project itself. In other words, project financing does not demand any guarantees of the investor's credit or tangible assets. There are, meanwhile, two main types of project financing. Firstly, the franchise model which involves an enterprise authorizing, for a fee, a secondary

---

[31]Fang (2009).
[32]Fang (2009).

party to operate such resources as certain patented trademarks, labels and business models. Secondly, the public-private-partnership (PPP) model[33] which involves the government and private enterprises working together as regards investment and construction. Generally speaking, the government will provide supporting conditions. Projects with high sunk-costs, high levels of investment and slow rates of completion are suitable for this model, commonly used, as it is, in the field of infrastructure construction (including roads, bridges, tunnels and electrical supply).

5.5.2.4 Social Capital

Social capital refers to the capital accumulated from civil society in general, including the personal funds of residents, a variety of public welfare funds, privately offered funds and even sources of idle funds. Currently, it is a general practice of national development zones to seek all kinds of social capital for investment into project development and subsequent operation. For example, Beijing Economic Development Zone introduced social capital as early as in 2003.[34] Likewise, in 2006, Lianyungang Economic Development Zone introduced social capital for the construction of infrastructure. In 2011, Wuhan Development Zone created a "capital zone," in which the introduction and emphasis of social capital was prioritized.[35]

5.5.3 Resources Mobilization and Deployment

The third phase in the operational logic of development zones is the continuous operation phase, also referred to as a phase of resource mobilization and deployment. It is a phase in which development zones maintain normal operations, play a leading role in industry and generate huge economic and social benefits, that is to say, the intended normal state for the zones. Advantageous policies and land resources, competitive labor supply and monopoly dividends are all crucial factors.

---

[33]"The Interim Measures to Encourage Social Capital to Invest and Operate Infrastructure Projects in Beijing Economic and Technological Development Zone". http://www.most.gov.cn/tjcw/tczcwj/200708/t20070813_52377.htm.

[34]"An Introduction to the First Group of Projects that Using Social Funds in Infrastructure Construction and Energy in Beijing Economic and Technological Development Zone". http://www.bda.gov.cn/cms/qt/9038.htm.

[35]"Lianyungang Economic and Technological Development Zone Introducing social Capital in Infrastructure Construction". http://www.fdi.gov.cn/pub/FDI/gjjjjkfq/kfqdt/t20060402_13278.htm.

5.5.3.1   The Concentration of Land

The concentration and relatively low price of land is an important factor to guarantee the continuous operation of the zones. Due to unstable economic environments, unclear prospects and uncertain political policies, few enterprises desired to enter development zones throughout their initial periods, that is, unless there were tremendous incentives to do so. The relatively low price of land was, however, one such key attraction. The reason for the relative concentration and low price of land was, primarily, that the value produced on that piece of was already low before the construction of development zones. Consequently, there was the theoretical possible, at least, of continued low prices for those enterprises that elected to move into development zones throughout their early stages. The concentration and low price of land, although criticized by many scholars, played an important and undeniable role in maintaining a competitive advantage for development zones and leading, in turn, to their sustainable growth.

5.5.3.2   Favorable Labor Condition

Favorable labor condition is another important factor in maintaining the competitive advantage and sustainable development of the development zones. Favorable labor condition obtains when the development zone is highly attractive to residents from surrounding areas both in terms of labor demands and wage offers. In general, the average incomes within cities and development zones are higher than their agricultural counterparts. Consequently, a steady flow of surplus rural labor would enter zone factories seeking stable employment. At this stage, because of the huge labor reserves, wages were, in fact, only slightly higher than agricultural incomes. Part of the problem was that, with the depletion of the labor pool, agriculture began to exhibit an increasing importance and the prices of agricultural products began to rise. As ever, the game of supply and demand was to gain a new balance. This trend, however, threatened the sustainability of development zones because, if the marginal income in cities and zones was lower than agricultural incomes, there would be a shortage of much needed migrant workers (see Fig. 5.14).

5.5.3.3   Cost Advantages

As in Fig. 5.14, labor cost is an important advantage of the development zones. Whether employed in cities or occupied by farming at home, the marginal incomes of farmers and migrant workers was decreasing. When the marginal incomes of migrant workers are higher than that of farmers, more farmers choose to go to cities or zones for employment. As more and more farmers enter cities to work, the supply of agricultural products will be reduced and the price of agricultural products, including meat, poultry, eggs and milk, will rise. Consequently, the marginal incomes of farmers will, once again, exceed that of migrant workers. After this

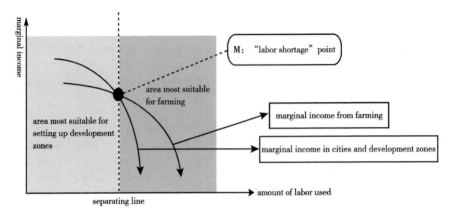

Fig. 5.14 The attraction of labor and cost advantages of development zones

transition point, a shortage of migrant workers will gradually develop. The zone just before the transition line is, however, the optimal area for development zones, in which they have the advantage of wages and costs, and that will support the sustainable development of the zones. In addition, the cost advantages of development zones include policy support, loans, their regional location and propaganda. All of these factors can reduce transaction costs for enterprises operating in the zones.

5.5.3.4   Local Monopolies

As high-bracket taxpayers, generators of substantial financial revenue, industry-intensive areas, where talented people cluster and representatives of the government's image, development zones enjoyed, overtly or latently, superior resources and the advantage of monopolizing their surrounding areas. These development zones gathered all the local resources, such as finance, materials and knowledge, to one place, and were, after all, important economic enterprises for the government to develop and protect. Usually, a single development zone is set up in a region. Once it was set, it will monopolize all surrounding resources in order to promote its development. Specifically, this monopoly will include administrative, policy, industrial and market monopolies. The administrative monopoly, for instance, include the vigorous support provided by the government to the development zone within the limit of laws and regulations. Policy monopoly, meanwhile, include the financing, investment and infrastructural advantages afforded to development zones. Likewise, industrial and market monopoly generally involve the allocation of newly-emerging strategic industries to development zones, such that their regional monopoly is substantially strengthened further.

5.5.4   Returns

In the phase of returns, the most important issue for development zones is the distribution of benefits. It is a crucial phase that will have significant impacts on the previous three phases. If uneven distribution occurs, due to problems in distribution, this could form obstacles that may hinder the sound operation and sustainable development of the development zone. As such, the distribution of benefits must take into account all sides, including the government, enterprises, residents and communities. Once imbalances are permitted to take hold, comparative inferiority, namely, cask effect, will be produced. Any disadvantages will cause great economic limitations and social constraints. In particular, then, there are four relationships to be carefully considered when it comes to benefit distribution.

5.5.4.1   Government and the Administration Committee of Development Zone

The success in economy of a well-run development zone is very beneficial for the local government as well as the zone's administration committee. It plays a enormous role in generating tax and fiscal revenues, policy returns, positive demonstration effects, political prospects and enhancing the city image. Likewise, through operating the development zones, the hard power of the local economy and the soft power of the investment environment are both enhanced. At the same time, the administrative and service income of the administration committee will also increase, which is conducive, in turn, to further investment in municipal construction and management. The government and the administration committee are both responsible for the dynamic monitoring and management of any problems that may emerge in development zones. They should, then, both ensure a degree of sustainable development and problem solving efficacy.

5.5.4.2   Enterprises and Developers

Developers and enterprises will inevitably see abundant and sustained returns in addition to industrial and commercial prosperity. The participation of developers in the construction of real estate and infrastructure would enable them to recover costs besides their regular profits. Enterprises, as the major participants of development zones, also enjoy sustained profit margins and high-quality public services that is, as the government's stressed open area. All in all, then, enterprises will benefit from a high-quality pro-business environment, supporting preferential policies, excellent infrastructure, free brand propaganda and good public relations. A healthy-functioning development zone is supposed to have a positive externalities or "spillover effects" that is highly favorable for enterprise.

5.5.4.3 Farmers and Residents

Development zones, too, have an externalities or spillover effects on local and nearby farmers. Firstly, the development zones would provide jobs and wages to local people. Secondly, enterprises in the development zones should provide farmers with a variety of long and short-term security and welfare. Thirdly, while the prosperity of the development zone brings jobs to the farmers, in turn, it will also hasten an industrial chain for an entire service industry. Transportation, hotels, travelling, food and drink, clothing and other industries will all develop around the zone. Fourthly, the existence of development zones may change some flexible and literate farmers' minds and inspire them to start their own business. Fifthly, development zones are the very place where farmers can be citizenized. In short, development zones promote the progress of farmers as regards money, property, social relations, lifestyle, ideology and other aspects.

5.5.4.4 Community and Society

A healthy functioning development zone must also pay returns to the local community, not simply take resources. In other words, there should be a benign interactive relationship between the zone and the nearby communities. Nevertheless, throughout much of their existence, the main focus of development zones has been economic concerns, with little attention paid to their relationships with surrounding communities or society at large. This problem has much to do with the social responsibility of corporations and enterprises, which usually believe that paying tax is their primary contribution to society. As such, they believe, that there is no need to contribution any more. Needless to say, this is a misunderstanding. It is, after all, the responsibility of development zones to promote the prosperity and development of the surrounding areas alongside their own development. They should, for instance, increase their infrastructural input, including, amongst others, roads, parks, schools and fitness facilities in nearby communities. In terms of industry, meanwhile, they should promote the development of a range of services that are relevant to their constituent enterprises, such as hotels, apartments, restaurants and others. Together, these measures should promote the development of the entire region. At the same time, there is also a profound need for the promotion of community culture, both of which may provide a sense of security and harmony.

The phase of returns focuses on the relationships of interest distribution around the zone. At the core of this is an emphasis on promoting the positive externalities or "spillover effects" of the zone, encouraging its further co-development with local communities and residents. As the benefit return stage is a core stage, improper dealings could constitute an obstacle to the sustainable development of the zone. Development zones, then, should not only obtain government support, but also build appeal to local residents and communities, not only contribute to the economy, but also to society (see Table 5.4).

Table 5.4 The returns and externality system of development zones

Parties	The returns and externality system of development zones
1. Government and Administrative Committee of Development Zone	Fiscal and tax revenue, management fees, municipal construction, the government's image, investment environment, soft power
2. Enterprises and Developers	Good infrastructure, preferential policies, unified propaganda for their brands
3. Farmers and Residents	Currency income, property and social relations, lifestyle, Citizenization of ideology
4. Society and Community	Industry chain expansion, community safety and harmony, infrastructure share, social responsibility

5.6 The Economic Limitations and Social Constraints of the Development Zone Model

Although the idea of the development zone originated from abroad, the complete development zone model was conceived of in China and features unique Chinese characteristics. One such feature is that development zones, in China, not only bear a range of economic functions, but also function as an important model of urbanization. As is shown in Fig. 5.15, the advancing logic of the zone model consists of a closed-loop with four sections, namely the start-up phase, the resource organization phase, the continuous operation phase and the phase of returns. The implied logic is that a model for a prosperous and sustainable development zone must integrate these four sections and progress in a carefully coordinated manner. But in the actual operation of the zones, as opposed to the theory behind them, such logic is often disobeyed, especially, that is, as economic development and efficiency are emphasized at the cost of neglecting social returns and social justice. At any rate, advancing development zones in accordance with the abovementioned biased logic will inevitably bring about two sorts of problems, namely economic limitations and social constraints. Indeed, these are the very difficulties that the current development zone model in China has encountered. The deep-seated causes of

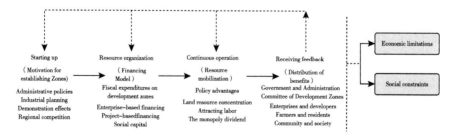

Fig. 5.15 The development pattern, economic limitations and social constraints of Chinese development zones

these difficulties are problems that occurred throughout the four sections of the advancing logic, especially in the phase of returns. Economic limitations and social constraints are major obstacles for the continuous development of the zones, thus, priority is given to it in the discussion of this chapter (see Fig. 5.15).

5.6.1   Economic Limitations

5.6.1.1   A Monotonous Economic Growth Model

Development zones were originally conceived of as a collection of advanced factors of production intended to foster new economic growth industry and new industrial strategy.[36] Therefore, each development zone has a particular growth pattern. Usually, development zones allocate most of their resource to a few domains such as OEM (original equipment manufacturing), trade or developing new materials and energy sources. Overall, the major growth pattern of the zones consists in secondary industry, especially high-tech industry and equipment manufacturing. This pattern did, however, lead to a monotonous model of economic growth, including underdeveloped supporting industries, and low degrees of risk resistance. Therefore, it was necessary to further promote the development of tertiary industries, such as, amongst others, tourism, trade, finance, accommodation, catering and cultural industries. Together, these industries could achieve a more differential industrial zone.

5.6.1.2   Low Levels of International Risk Resistance

It was mentioned at the beginning of the chapter that the two important preconditions of establishing development zones are attracting advanced technology from foreign countries and obtaining foreign investment. Indeed, there is nothing wrong with the idea of attracting advanced foreign technology, but the goal of attracting foreign funds should be judged dialectically. In the economic boom years, foreign funds contributed significantly to domestic investment and consumption, thereby stipulating the growth of GDP. Nevertheless, this trend risks leading to an increasing dependence, of domestic development zones, upon foreign capital. This could, in turn, lead to situations in which multiple zones may compete for foreign funds by, for instance, lowering prices. That kind of compitition once happened between two zones. As such an over reliance on foreign funds tends to damage the security and stability of zone funding chain. Furthermore, if an international financial crisis occurs, it will inevitably impact the zones in serious ways.

---

[36]Wang et al. (2004).

5.6.1.3 The "Quasi Enclosure Movement" Wastes Land Resources and Restraints Future Development

Since the mid-1980s, due to the government's enthusiastic pursuit of political achievements and increasing GDP, not to mention the way in which development zones had lifted the economy, the enthusiasm to establish additional development zones has been rigorously pursued. Development zones have become an important channel for interest groups or individuals to enclose land. In 2003 a total of 6015 zones of all types were established. As such, the planning area of the various zones reached 36,000 km^2, more than the total area of the construction land in existing cities and towns throughout China. Among them, only 6% of the land was actually approved by the central government, while the land for development zones that received approval from below the provincial level authorities accounted for 67.4%. Nevertheless, according to relevant statistics, 43% of the land within development zones is left unused.[37] In 2003, the State Council investigated 127,000 land lawsuits, settled 124,000, imposed fines of 1.22 billion yuan and took back 5878.4 ha of land.[38] In 2011, however, these kinds of problems reappeared.[39] Such land related problems have repeatedly constrained the future development of development zones.

5.6.1.4 Competition and Difficulties Due to Monotonous Models of Development Zones

Competition among zones is positive to a certain extent and often functions to improve the efficiency of resource allocation and usage, realizing, in the meantime, their maximum value. However, the competition between the zones in China has often exceeded the limits of necessity, thereby falling into competitive difficulties,[40] that is to say, a cycle of vicious competition. Therefore, the more of this sort of competition, the lower the rate of development. Such competition has no limits, lacks a unified platform and is bound, in the end, to be harmful to all sides. Unfortunately, at present, there are many such cases of this unchecked competition. In order to attract foreign investment, development zones compete to lower their prices and constantly break the bottom lines of land and taxation policy. The result

---

[37]Bao (2002).

[38]"A Comparative Analysis on the Rectification of National Development Zones". Information for Deciders Magazine. Vol. 15, 2004.

[39]"The Resurgence of Illegal Occupation of Land by Some Zones". January 11, 2011, http://finance.sina.com.cn/g/20110111/06519231950.html.

[40]"The Orderly Competition and Coordinated Development of Zones". "China High-Tech Industry Herald". March 11, 2005.

is that land prices get lower, tax revenues continuously decrease and, in some zones, drastic measures, such as a policy of exempting corporate income tax for the first ten years and cutting 50% of corporate income tax for the second ten years, are taken.[41]

5.6.1.5   The Spatial Misplacement in Resource Allocation in Development Zones

An effective allocation of resources could bring greater benefits to a development zone. Yet, in the actual process of zone resource allocation, many resources are not allocated efficiently, primarily due to planning, policy and other reasons. This phenomenon is has been referred to as "spatial misplacement".[42] For example, in the Nanjing state-level development zone, this sort of spatial disconnection has become a normal state. Firstly, there is a breakage in the allocation of the internal functions of the zone, mainly a spatial misplacement of employment, housing and assorted service functions. Those who worked in the developments zones generally did not go shopping or see doctors and receive an education there. Secondly, there is a mismatch between the functions of the development zones and universities. Newly built university towns and the development of zones are, in general, mutually separated and isolated. Nevertheless, obviously, the planning of development zones must take into account the region in which the zone is to be established. Any such planning should be conducted in the context of larger environmental considerations.

5.6.2   Social Constraints

The economic limitations of development zones, some of the more obvious problems, can generally be objectively described and studied through data analysis and site visits. Social constraints, however, are more of a potential process, which require more in-depth excavation and research to uncover. In this sense, the problem of social constraints concerning the zones is more far-reaching and fundamental. It should not, then, be taken for granted that the development of the zones will proceed smoothly once economic limitations alone have been overcome. In fact, if the more far-reaching and fundamental social contradictions and constraints are left unaddressed, then a development zone is not necessarily sustainable. In particular, the Chinese model of development zones has the following social constraints.

---

[41]"The Orderly Competition and Coordinated Development of Zones". "China High-Tech Industry Herald". March 11, 2005.
[42]Wang (2008).

5.6.2.1 A Leap-Forward and Unstable Urbanization Process

As a model to promote urbanization, development zones in China have their own features. It is common practice that a particular area will be designated as a development zone and the residents in the area will be transformed into urban citizens concurrently. In practice, however, it is a leap-forward[43] as well as unstable process of urbanization. In 1994, Fengqiao Town was incorporated into Suzhou New District. Consequently, its size was enlarged from 16 to 52 km^2 and its population increased from 21,400 to 73,900.[44] This leap-forward and unstable urbanization process is prone to exert a series of far-reaching social impacts. Firstly, it can lead to the changes in social property relationships, that is to say, improvements to old-age and medical social-security systems. Some residents received resettlement or demolition cash awarded to them for the loss of their old property. Secondly, it led to changes in social relationships. To begin with, the residents in the surrounding areas were all farmers, but, now, these same residents can be grouped into urban and rural categories. Finally, it leads to the change in social psychology. For one thing, these changes can cause an increase to people's sense of inequality.

5.6.2.2 A Mandatory, Artificial, Subjective and Externally Driven Process of Urbanization

The urbanization process driven by development zones in China was effectively mandatory. Behind many development zones, then, are the conflicts that erupted as a result of demolitions and resettlement. Some commentators even exaggerate that "the demolition is the principal contradiction of Chinese society".[45] Such statements require, of course, further discussion, but they unveil the problem of demolition. Urbanization in China has, in twenty years, progressed as much as urbanization in the West has progressed since the Industrial Revolution. Western urbanization may have been a natural process of development, yet China's urbanization is undoubtedly a process of human planning. It is urbanization with Chinese characteristics, primarily those of being driven by external forces. The major external force, meanwhile, consists in the will, planning and executive power of central and local governments. The subjective, externally driven and mandatory quality of urbanization led to the rapid development of Chinese urbanization and produced as well a lot of problems in the process. Conflicts regarding demolition, disagreements between officials and civilians, tension between the police and the public, civil and commercial conflicts and conflicts between private citizens all erupted during this period.

---

[43]Wang et al. (2004).
[44]Wang et al. (2004).
[45]Zhang (2011).

5.6.2.3 The Destruction of Original Social Relationships, Ways of Living and the Existing Social Support System of the Community

Rural communities in China can be best understood as societies of acquaintances. The interactions between people are not isolated events, such as they are in cities of strangers, but rather a balance achieved through regular and close interaction. There are, then, a range of overt and covert principles for people to follow and, indeed, which constitute the basis upon which deep social relationships and networks of emotional support have formed, due, in no small part, to the long-term exchanges that have been shaped in accordance with said principles. Within any given rural community, the residents enjoy extensive contact and interaction over a long period of time, much like extended relatives. In the face of frustration in daily life, they could find, within their community, abundant advice, support and psychological comfort. Together, these factors comprise an extremely durable and comprehensive system of social support, the likes of which "money cannot buy", that is to say, is immeasurable in terms of economic value. As these original communities became development zones, the original communal relations also changed, particularly as residents were relocated to high-rise buildings because of demolition. Generally speaking, financial and economic motivations began to take center stage. At the same time, it became very difficult and costly to maintain the original methods of communication. As a result, the social relation and support systems that previously characterized rural communities were degraded and destroyed. Instead, people's lives become strange, rational, intense, busy and anxious. Such huge social and psychological costs are undoubtedly one of the great losses in the process of urbanization. Only those people directly involved can feel the loss, which is both immeasurable and irreplaceable, especially in terms of financial compensation.

5.6.2.4 The Absence of Social Organizations and Social Forces in the Formulation of Public Policy

The overall development of social organizations throughout China is, so far, still at a low level. Besides, there are no clearly defined mechanisms and channels for the participation of social forces,[46] a problem also reflected in the administration and operation systems of the development zones. The development zones in China usually follow an administration based governance structure, influenced strongly by government governance. The governing institute of each development zone is the "Administration Committee of Development Zone (ACDZ)", with little or no social organizations or forces exerting any influence over it. The current decision-making mechanism of the development zones in China is shown in Fig. 5.16. The Working Committee of Development Zone of the CPC is the superior or mother department

---

[46]Wang (2009).

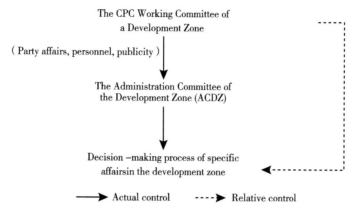

Fig. 5.16 Decision-making mechanisms of the zone model

of ACDZ, it instructs and makes decisions on specific matters for the zone through ACDZ. Furthermore, it can directly make decisions in terms of party, personnel, culture and propaganda affairs. There exists a huge problem here, that is, as the process lacks the participation of citizens in all decision-making mechanisms, let alone the participation of larger social organizations and forces. When making specific policies, the relevant authorities within the development zones seldom use the mechanism of listening to public opinion or having a public discussion.[47] Such decision-making mechanisms pay little attention to mass concerns, thereby resulting in some unscientific decisions that totally lack the understanding and support of the local population. This problem will inevitably influence the environmental foundation and sustainability of the development zone.

5.6.2.5   A Monopoly on Public Property Supply and an Inadequate Supply of Public Services

Unitary public decision-making mechanism will inevitably leads to the monopoly of public property supply. For public services, the ideal pattern should be the rational allocation of limited public resources through competition and the equal participation of multiple subjects. The current supply mechanism is dominated by the government and the Administration Committee of Development Zone, who take specific funds from fiscal and tax revenues to buy and supply public property. This uniform pattern of public property supply does, however, mean that government bureaucracy, corruption and inefficiency might become commonplace, because the supervision mechanisms for a monopoly of supply were, and remain, weak and there were huge vested interests behind the mechanisms. For public property, there

---

[47]Wang (2009).

are very mature procedures in other countries. The government may, for example, pay for the services by appealing to the emphasis of cost-to-income ratios of private enterprises. These enterprises may then compete for the supply right of such services and, therefore, supply the most satisfactory service at the lowest possible cost. This process is also known as "the marketization of public services." Supply monopoly is, however, a major driver of the insufficient supply of public services. In the development zones, a common problem is, indeed, the weak supply of public services. Economic interests are the top priority in the zones and most of their employees are very young. These employees do not enjoy any public services and are excluded from urban communities. The burden will, then, eventually be passed on to rural communities in which the employees used to live.

5.6.2.6 The Material Weakness of the Zone Performance Evaluation System

The main political goal of local governments has long since been to increase the area's GDP since the reform and open up. It was not until the twenty-first century, that such ideas such as developing GDP in a sustainable or "green" way were even put forward. It is undeniable, meanwhile, that the current performance evaluation system of development zones is still dominated by GDP, overemphasizing economic development indicators and neglecting social development and livelihood indicators.[48] The author's of this study believe, however, that a concept of "Comprehensive Assessment of GDP" should be advocated in the case of society in general and the construction of development zones in particular. As is shown in Fig. 5.17, Comprehensive Assessment of GDP is equal to GDP minus economic limitations, social constraints and environmental costs. Economic limitation refers to losses and decrease caused in the process of economic development. Social constraints refer to the necessary funds required for investment in social development, that is to say, social costs. Environmental costs are the amounts of financial compensation required to offset environmental pollution. With this in mind, a comprehensive assessment of GDP should be adopted as a core indicator of zone performance.

5.6.2.7 Inequity in Resource Allocation and Its Adverse Consequences

In the phase of returns, that is, the one in which benefits are distributed, failure to meet the demands of fairness or justice can lead to economic limitations and social constraints. Social constraints usually come in the form of social inequality. There

---

[48]Wang (2009).

$$\begin{array}{c}\text{A Comprehensive}\\\text{Assessment of GDP}\end{array} = \text{GDP} - \begin{array}{c}\text{Economic}\\\text{Limitations}\end{array} - \begin{array}{c}\text{Social}\\\text{Constraints}\end{array} - \begin{array}{c}\text{Environmental}\\\text{Costs}\end{array}$$

Fig. 5.17 A comprehensive assessment of GDP

exists, meanwhile, two particular emphasis and two neglects in terms of the interest distribution and resource allocation in current development zone models. The "two emphases" refers to the emphasis on the government and the administration committees of development zones, and the emphasis on enterprises and developers, particularly in the form of fiscal revenue, tax revenue and profits. The "two neglects", meanwhile, refer to the neglect of farmers and residents, not to mention the neglect of the community and society at large. Development zones bring with them huge economic profits, but they often fail to offer returns to farmers, communities and society. That, subsequently, will produce serious social inequality. The sharp contrast between the sustainable development and prosperity of the zones and the unilateral resource outputs of the surrounding communities may trigger a strong sense of social injustice among farmers and local residents, demonstrated by the frequent occurrence of mass incidents and individual incidents of self-harm, all in the name of protecting their interests.[49] These protests are mainly over wages, labor and social security, land acquisition and demolition. They will inevitably give rise to a range of social constraints relevant to the development of zones.

5.6.2.8   The Dilemma of Rationality: Omnipotent Humans or Human Weakness

Weber, Simmel and other sociologists generally believe that modernization is a process of rationalization, which increases efficiency and output, but sacrifices the possibility of personal freedom and resistance. An individual, much like a standardized part of a giant rational machine, once worn out will be replaced by another part of the same specifications, thus becoming insignificant and vulnerable in the face of the whole. There is, however, a debate concerning this rational dilemma, that is to say, whether modernity makes humans almighty or weak. Development zones, as rational artifacts, are also faced with the same dilemma. Supporters of the former view believe that modernity has greatly changed people's daily life, especially modern transportation, communications, networking and other "tools", all of which enable human beings to transport freely to different places and present on different occasions, which gives rise to the illusion that human beings can do everything. Modernity, then, seems to have, if anything, made human agents more powerful. Nevertheless, behind this seeming omnipotence, the weakness of humanity, in the face of modernity, are readily apparent. Individuals are constantly

---

[49]Nanchang Reported: Mass Incidents and Organized Attacks to Development Zones. http://news.qq.com/a/20070720/002605.htm.

constrained by the man-made objects or artifacts that surround them, moved, in turn, away from the natural state of things. The individual must now live surrounded by created rationality, etiquette, culture, institutions, rules, cities and networks. Rather than using these things as mere tools, the individual has become a project image of these things.

In short, the development zone model is a major product of China's reform and opening up. It has become a powerful growth pole of China's economy, as well as an important and critical component for China's economic takeoff. It is an important institutional innovation representing the Chinese model. Since their establishment, the development zones in China have demonstrated a tremendous capacity to create huge economic wealth, great contributions to GDP and have greatly promoted China's urbanization. They have great strategic functions in the economy, society and politics, and their historical achievements and contemporary vitality are incomparable with any other institutions. Dialectically speaking, the development zones have, indeed, been responsible for brilliant economic achievements, but, at the same time, there exist economic limitations and social constraints as well. These may yet prove to be barriers for the future in-depth development of these zones. While allowing zones to play their economic and social functions, social administrators should also attempt to solve the existing problems of economic limitations and social constraints of the zones, so as to promote their sustainable and scientific development.

References

Bao, K. (2002). *HINA's development area: An institutional study and design.* People's Publishing House.

Fang, Z. (2009). A comparative analysis of the financing model in development zones. *Financial Supervision, 18.*

Guo, W. (2011). Right time for zones to make the second round of start up. May 12, 2011. *China Environment News.*

Lei, X. (2009). *Research on management system in development zones.* Ph.D. Thesis, Shandong University.

Liu, G. (2010). *Research on the equalization of basic public service in China.* Master Thesis, Henan University.

Sun, H. (2009). *Study on the innovation in zone administrative system.* Master Thesis, Jilin University.

Wang, X. (2008). A study on the mismatching of space allocation and use in development zone in China—A case study of Nanjing national development zones. *Urban Studies, 2.*

Wang, Y.H. (2009). *Research on the governance model of development zones.* Master Thesis, Suzhou University.

Wang, H., Yuan, Z., & Hou, A. (2004). A research on development zones in urbanization. *Areal Research and Development, 2.*

Wuxi, M. (2011). *Economic benefit evaluation on land usage based on DEA—A case study of Taizhou economic development zone.* Master's Degree Thesis, Zhejiang University of Technology.

Yang, Z. (2010). *Research on township government function of public service in the context of the equalization of urban and rural basic public service*. Master Thesis. Changchun University of Technology, 2010.

Zhan, S. (2004). *The institutional thickness in Shanghai development zones and the construction of world-class industrial base*. Master Thesis. Central-East Normal University.

Zhang, Y. (2011). Institutional survey shows: Demolition contradiction become the top social contradiction in China. *People's Daily,* June 23, 2011.

Chapter 6
Developing New Urban Areas

The development of new urban areas is a model of urbanization promoted from the top down under the guidance of macro-targets issued by the government and dictated by urban planning guidelines. Since the 1990s, China had been facing the population and environmental pressures that often accompanied the development of big cities. As a result, urban planners looked, with increasing attention, towards the development of new urban areas. As part of this drive, the earliest plans to develop new urban areas were approved in Guangzhou, Shanghai, and Beijing successively. Afterwards, many other big cities in China also initiated such processes. Based on previous experiences, there were two main models of urban development in China. On the one hand, there was the market-oriented model, in which private property developers played a dominant role, while governments were restricted to a supplementary role. This model often saw the development of new residential areas, thereby only releasing the population pressure in big cities whilst generally failing to address many of the problems caused by a lack of public services or facilities and failing to upgrade cities or to extend city-functions. On the other hand, there was the government-dominated model, in which governments were responsible for attracting investments while private property developers were involved in the actual development of new urban areas. However, these models often lacked strong industrial support, thereby giving rise to the overdevelopment of real estate, the waste of land resources and even environmental pollution. A question must, therefore, be asked as to how to build new urban areas which will meet the requirements of urban zoning, urban functioning, intensive utilization and the fair distribution of resources. This chapter will discuss, from the perspective of specific cases of urban planning, the necessities for the development of new urban areas.

© Social Sciences Academic Press 2020
Q. Li, *China's Development under a Differential Urbanization Model*,
Research Series on the Chinese Dream and China's Development Path,
https://doi.org/10.1007/978-981-13-9451-5_6

185

6.1   New Urban Area Development and Urbanization

The development of new urban areas, which facilitated the concentration of population and resources, primarily through the government-led re-planning of population, land, industry, transportation, and infrastructures, was a process of urbanization. New urban areas were usually located within the radius of big cities. Some urban resources were, therefore, available to them and they could function as an important link in the development of urban system. It also meant that they could promote the economic agglomeration and shoulder some of the urban functions throughout the region. The questions to be addressed include the issue of whether or not this planning-dominated development of new urban areas could be an effective model of promoting urbanization? Furthermore, what social influences or results may it bring about? What are the particular conditions under which this urban development model should be adopted? All such questions can be discussed through a comparative analysis on the definition of a city.

A city contains three basic factors, namely ecological, economic and social factors.

6.1.1   Ecological Factors

Ecological factors refer to the size and density of the population.[1] The concentration and dispersion of the population is invariably based on certain economic and social conditions. Wirth L. believes that the size, density, and heterogeneity of an urban population determines the way of urban life there.[2] How does the population converge in cities? McGee, T. G analyzed the trends which characterized the mobility of the American population and believed that economy and transportation were the major inducements for population mobility.[3] Economic factors may be the driving force for population mobility, yet transportation makes such movements possible. Researchers into the dual economy theory also pointed out that the expansion of the industrial sector attracts labor from the agricultural sector. Even when the urban unemployment rate is high, the population will still continue to migrate from rural areas to cities due to their anticipation of higher urban incomes.[4] Besides such economic factors, the attractiveness of urban living standards, as well as a range of personal reasons might also lead to the flow of population into cities.

---

[1]Paddison (2009, p. 32).
[2]He (2003, p. 65).
[3]He (2003, pp. 7–11).
[4]Xin (1998).

6.1.1.1 The Conditions and Features of Population Migration

The economic variables that influence population migration include relative incomes, employment conditions in the labor market and a range of other push-pull factors.[5] As for voluntary migration, incomes after migrating are usually relatively higher than before. In fact, the total number of migrants is very sensitive to overall income gaps. It is not only the income gap between where the population moved to and the where the population came from that counts, but also the income gap that would endure between migrating and staying in one's hometown. All in all, the average income of the intended destinations of economic migrants is a bigger influence in determining the total number of migrants.[6] The employment conditions mainly refer to the state of the labor market, such as the rate of employment or unemployment, salary or expected salary. Alternatively, other factors referred primarily to the distribution of land and human capital in the place where the migrants came from.

In a complete system of an urban hierarchy, in both developed and developing countries, population migration generally has the feature of moving in staggered phases. That is to say, the population often migrates, firstly, from rural areas to small cities, and, then, from small cities to big cities.[7] That said, urban growth is not necessarily the result of the migration of rural populations into cities. With the increase of base urban populations, the natural growth of these population centers plays a more and more important role.[8]

6.1.1.2 Conditions and Features of Population Migration in Newly Developed Urban Areas

Is the process of population concentration within newly developing urban areas influenced by the same push-pull factors mentioned above? In China, in new urban developments, population concentration was controlled by administrative measures or by means of planning that often involved placing previously rural areas under urban administration. In this case, levels of economic development, transportation and other personal factors were not, in fact, the primary reasons behind population migration. Therefore, it is necessary to analyze the differences in the prevalent attitudes, wills and behaviors of the migrants that constituted the population concentrations achieved through administrative measures. After the completion of such a migration to a new urban area, the impacts of implementing an urban development plan, on population migration from both within and outside the relevant area, needs to be analyzed from the perspective of other urban factors.

---

[5]Mills (2003, p. 335). Other conditions mentioned here will be explained in detail in later analysis.
[6]Mills (2003, pp. 335–336).
[7]Mills (2003, p. 334).
[8]Mills (2003, p. 329).

The development of a new urban area is usually accompanied by a process of land concentration, often the result of the requisition of farming land and homesteads from farmers and the subsequent use of this land for other purposes. During the process of land requisition, direct land compensation also brings about changes to relative incomes. The distribution and the results of this distribution are both important factors to explain why and how a given population concentration is realized.

There is another factor that is important to the overall development of a urban area, that is to say, its spatial location. Whether a new urban area is within the radius of a big city or whether any other alterations make it an advantageous location are equally important factors in measuring the feasibility of its spatial location. Only when the position of a new urban area, as regards a relative hierarchy of urban areas, is determined, can relevant economic and industrial planning be properly made, based, as they often are, on the flow of resources and information between cities. Specific economic and industrial planning also exerts specific requirements upon the population. The type of population which concentrates and disperses in a new urban area is directly linked to the demands of implementing an industrial plan.

In the development of a new urban area, a new population concentration often materializes in a short period of time as a result of relevant urban planning. For one thing, the incoming population usually shares the same social and economic background and concentrates in a given location within the city. There is a lack of variety in the population in terms of occupations, skills, interests, and hobbies. That is to say, the population may, at first, fail to meet the urban demand of population heterogeneity, that is, an indispensable factor in forming the urban way of life. It is, after all, very difficult for a population with similar social and economic backgrounds to form various microcosms and cultural diversity, which might as well reject the acceptance of other cultures from the outside world.

In an ideal model, when the accumulation of resources reaches a certain level, along with, presumably, the development of a city's economy, such resources will begin to move outwards as urban functions differentiate, widening gradually the influence of the city and, thus, stimulating the city's growth, even giving rise to a city circle (with the city as the center and several satellite cities positioned around it). During that process, both politics and the market will play an important role. Through administrative forces, a rapid concentration of resources may be realized within a short period of time, thereby promoting rapid economic growth. However, this process equally requires the vigor of the economy. In other words, enterprises, which constitute the main market participants, should be able to make profits, individuals should be able to have rising incomes and social welfare, distributed amongst the whole of society should be improved. Nevertheless, the fact is not always as perfect as the ideal. Standards are stipulated in the urban organizational system in China that the strategy which underpins the development of cities, counties, towns, and villages should be based primarily on population size. The grade of cities and towns, as stipulated by the urban organizational system, determines the administrative level of a city and what resources shall be distributed to them. Thus, such standards often function as incentives for local governments, who desire additional resources or higher administrative positions, to set up or enlarge cities and towns or upgrade their administrative levels, especially when land usage has a direct link with the allocation or reallocation of huge benefits. Therefore, the process is characterized by a range of problems relating to fraudulent urbanization, which often gives rise to, amongst other things, the loss of farmland.

6.1.2 Economic Factors

Economic factors mainly refer to the type of economy and various economic activities conducted within an urban area.[9]

Indeed, the close link between the level of urbanization and the level of economic development has long since been observed. The potential resources and population of a country or region, at a certain period of development, can provide support to cities with a diverse range of functions and scales. The combination of products and services provided in such cities, as well as the major economic activities related to them, have a considerable influence on their levels of urbanization level. Hence in every country and region, at different stages of development, certain types of urban areas may develop faster than others.[10] That is to say, the correlations between urbanization, the concentration of population and economic activities are very complicated.

6.1.2.1 The Urbanization Process and Economic Activities

In the early stages of industrialization, those economic activities which required access to natural resources tended to be scattered in their distribution, while other kinds of production were generally concentrated within big cities, which provided accesses to experienced labors with different skills, markets that were, to an extent, developed and new technologies and knowledge. It was in big cities that the diversification and the agglomeration of the economy really took place.[11] Meanwhile, early public policies were also more favorable to central cities, providing more resources to the realization of the industrialization and modernization of the country. This important strategic choice, made by developing countries in the early stages of development, is also responsible for the contemporary problems that accompany the development of mega-cities or super-cities. To be more specific, the concentration of resources in just a few big cities caused population explosion and all kinds of related social problems.

---

[9]Paddison (2009, p. 32).
[10]Mills (2003, p. 465).
[11]Mills (2003, p. 465).

As fewer and fewer constraints are applied to the resources required for the process of urbanization, medium-sized cities and second-tier cities start to grow, influenced by a range of factors. Cities whose primarily functions which somehow serve the development of their more central counterparts start to develop. One of the reasons for this is that production activities are easy to copy and expanded. The nature of urban economic agglomeration has, therefore, been changed. It has nothing to do with the scale of a city anymore, but rather is linked to the specific localized economy.[12] This phenomenon, that is the gradual agglomeration of enterprises and commercial entities, is also common in the economic development of urban areas.

The agglomeration economy generally involves the relative concentration of different types of enterprises in a certain area which will result in the agglomeration effect. It may attract a huge population influx, thereby increasing the population density and further enhancing the agglomeration of the economy and its subsequent agglomeration effect. As this economic agglomeration unfolds in a variety of locations throughout a city, the functions of different locations become more distinctive and the population starts to shift accordingly. This division of working place and residential areas promotes, in turn, the further expansion of cities.

With the growth of central cities and the increases to population density, the price of land generally starts to rise. Labor costs also rise primarily due to changes to the relationships of supply and demand as well as the influence of social and political factors. Some enterprises cannot, therefore, maintain high profit margins and start to move to the peripheral areas or second-tier cities. The central cities then gradually expand outwards, or second-tier cities develop rapidly. At any rate, as part of this process, the changes in the skill sets and education of the local labor force can also influence the concentration or dispersion of the population within the city they are in.

In fact, the educational level of the local population and, in particular, their ability to use modern technology can have a profound impact on the population concentration within a city. At the beginning of economic development, the levels of population concentration tend to rise alongside improvements to education. When the educational opportunities available to the labor force continuously increase, it has an obvious influence on the dispersion of the population within a city.[13] Judging from this, urban concentration in China is still at a relatively early stage, that is, insofar as educational levels remain prone to stimulating and shaping population.

The overall relationship between urbanization and urban concentration is very complicated. Relevant research has shown that affluent and populous nations generally have more evenly distributed populations and economic activities are less likely to be concentrated within a limited number of central mega-cities.[14] The

---

[12]Mills (2003, p. 466).
[13]Mills (2003, p. 464).
[14]Mills (2003, p. 464).

urbanization in developing countries seems to possess different characteristics, however. Economic activities tend to be increasingly concentrated within just a few mega-cities. China has shown some characteristics similar to this pattern, but there are also new trends. Guangzhou, for example, is one of the Chinese cities in which urbanization has proceeded relatively rapidly. In recent years, following extensive upgrades to industry, some labor-intensive manufacturing and processing enterprises, previously based in Guangzhou, started to relocate to inland cities. This trend is further supported by the distribution of the nation's so-called floating population. In recent years, some central cities started to transfer labor and resource intensive enterprises to peripheral areas as part of adjustments to their overall industrial structure. From the perspective of urbanization, it is a process of expanding the influence of central cities to the peripheries through spreading resources, forming city clusters and expanding urban areas. While this process may move part of the population to the peripheries, in the case of Beijing, some people choose to stay in the City by cutting the cost of living or lowering living quality, waiting for opportunities to rise, to materialize. Likewise, because of its special resources and preferential policy position, Beijing will remain an attractive destination for populations migrating from rural areas and other cities.

6.1.2.2 The Economic Conditions Required for the Development of New Urban Areas

According to normal patterns of urban planning, new urban areas should be developed as part of existing urban economic systems and hold some relevant economic functions. The original economic activities in the new urban area, meanwhile—goods or services—are its basis for entering into the system of urban hierarchy to begin with. For example, such an area may have a service function relevant within its region, or the capacity to improve agricultural production, agricultural infrastructure or agricultural policies. It may even create new demands for local products or services and, thus, expand the scope of production or service coverage, creating more jobs in the process. In a word, an important part of the development of new urban areas is to realize industrial upgrading and to facilitate the transfer or substitution of industry in order to realize a wholesale transformation of agriculture, industry, and services. Industrial transformation requires not only supporting infrastructure, but, more importantly, it requires an "agglomerative economy". However, the process cannot be completed through industrial planning alone, it needs to be realized within the market itself and it also needs supporting policies and improvements to public investment.

6.1.3 Social Factors

Social factors refer to the social character of a city, mainly the living environment and the various ways of living within that city. Such social factors, meanwhile, are often used to evaluate levels of urbanization.[15] Nevertheless, social character can be relatively complicated, especially insofar as the floating population within a city may keep their own way of living as well as their own cultural values, while many rural areas may, paradoxically, have a social character resembling that of city.

Generally speaking, the development of new urban area gives rise to a systematic urban social environment, including schools, medical institutions, parks, cinemas and major improvement to transportation networks as well as public facilities. However, it is the demands of daily life that are at the core of the issue. As far as urban development in China is concerned, besides improving infrastructure, issues of employment and social security for the general population needs to be addressed, after the concentration of population. In accordance with these requirements, as part of current urban planning, a social planning is included besides ordinary concerns such as land-based spatial and material planning, affording a degree of attention to social factors as employment, social security and development.

6.2 A Case Study: New Urban Area Development in PG District

There are many cases of new urban areas being developed in China. In the actual processes of development, the roles played by governments, private enterprises and the public differ considerably. In some cases, the government plays central role while enterprises participate at the peripheries, while, in other cases this relationship is reversed. Alternatively, the public may be the major player, or, perhaps, the power of all three parties may be somewhat balanced. Needless to say, such dynamic relationships give rise to the question as to which combination can best promote the development of new urban areas. To answer this question, cities themselves, as well as their surrounding environments, ought to be analyzed. The precise pattern of the development of new urban areas in the PG district took all stakeholders into consideration. What's more, the public participated to some degree in the actual implementation of urban plans. As such, this is a meaningful case for detailed analysis.

---

[15]Paddison (2009, p. 33).

6.2.1 Reasons for the Development of New Urban Areas, Parties Involved and Problems Encountered

Generally speaking, China's cities are under huge pressure for further development. On one hand, they need to provide better public services and social security. On the other hand, each city is faced with fierce competition from its surrounding cities. At the same time, the general public has come to expect improvements to their living standards and quality of life for individuals and their families. Even the administrators of urban areas are subject to immense pressure for promotions. While facing all of the above-mentioned problems, it becomes especially important for the relative underdevelopment of the PG district, compared with its competitors in the surrounding areas, to render a new urban development project.

6.2.1.1 A Goal of Romantic Urban Development

In the northeast of the central city B, the PG district covers an area of 1075 km^2, with mountainous regions making up two-thirds of its total area. With a population of 420,000, of which 75% are farmers, it is, in many ways, a typical rural community. When central city B embraced a policy of "turning counties into districts", the then PG County made great efforts to finally became a district of city B. Its administrative rank was upgraded to prefecture-level and the individual administrators enjoyed promotional posts. However, by 2010, PG's economic development hadn't made much progress. Since it became a district of city B, it had been subject to significant pressure to achieve the levels of urbanization enjoyed by surrounding urban districts. This pressure was increased by the demands of administrative officers, at a range of different levels, and the public itself.

The current level of development in PG was deficient in a number of ways. For one thing, its agricultural industry was relatively underdeveloped and the financial revenue of the district remained low. Unfortunately, this limited its capacity for infrastructural development and social security provisions, whilst also affecting the incomes of local residents. From the public at large to all manner of administrative officials, everyone in the PG district aspired for development and construction. Such entrenched desires for further development are, in fact, quite common across China.

In 2006, City B started compiling *"The Overall Plan for New Urban Areas in the Outskirts"*. Officials of the PG district in charge of planning repeatedly reported on their zoning plans and authorized professional institutions undertake some planning, but the layout, scale and concept of the overall plans still came from government officials. Actually, most of the plans originated from an overseas investigative tour. After visiting a small hilly town abroad, the district official who was responsible for the area's planning proposed selecting an area in the shallow hills along the expressway between the PG district and City B. This was to be the pilot zone for the "first shallow-hill town". This idea was not, however, based on the analysis of PG's position in the urban hierarchy nor any of its strengths and resources. It referred instead to a romantic goal for the areas development. The aim was to create an unprecedented, modernized suburban model that could give rise to a new type of urban landscape in City B. On top of this, local officials wanted to use the project to promote the PG distract to all those passing through the district on the expressway.[16] This goal carried many good wishes, yet its implementation would be responsible for numerous conflicts of interest between the different parties involved.

6.2.1.2   Governments, Enterprises, and Individuals in New Urban Area Development

When local governments faced pressure for improving local economic and social environments, the relevant officials could only achieve promotions following positive appraisals as regards their political achievements. One such priority was economic growth. Towards this end, local governments introduced a variety of preferential policies and promoted a range of projects, especially the "land finance" project implemented in recent years. However, whether it was attracting investment or constructing different kinds of projects, the core issue was always land. The current land system allows local governments to make an actual transfer of the ownership or change of land usage within a legal framework.

As mentioned above, the new urban development project implemented by the PG district government was both romantic and ambitious. To make this project a reality, the main task was to reach an agreement among different governmental divisions, get approval from the government at a higher level and obtain support in terms of land reserve funds. However, due to the different responsibilities and positions of different governmental divisions, not to mention their vague understanding of the new urban development project, an agreement wasn't reached until a series of formal and informal meetings and discussion had concluded. To further push forward the project, the PG district government invited professional research and planning institutions to make a research report verifying the technical feasibility of the project.

The PG district government entrusted the task of project implementation to the town where the project was located. As such, the town government compiled an overall *Master Plan* for *the Town*, accompanied by a detailed *Land Regulatory Plan*, which allotted urban development land quotas to several villages within the project site. The details of which were directly linked to the adjustment of land uses of those villages and various land-related interests. Following the announcement, at the town-level people's congress, that the PG district would host the development of a new urban area, there were a series of wide-ranging discussions. As part of this process, the local authorities discussed the plans with a variety of influential local

---

[16]Source: Log of PG district.

people, including former government officials, successful entrepreneurs and any-body else who could help enlist the support of local people.

It is worth mentioning that the town government was also responsible for land requisition, housing demolition and disposition, compensation, general manage-ment and other specific tasks. The criteria for any final plan, therefore, was not only whether the scheme is reasonable or not but which scheme received more support from local residents and could be implemented most efficiently. Nevertheless, the final scheme didn't consider villages where the organizational capacity was weak and there were greater conflicts of interests, despite, that is, the geographical and topographical advantages often held by such villages.

In a similar way, the successful development of new urban areas also required extensive coordination between different levels of government, not to mention broad regional support from the proposed location. For the most part, the goal of the government, that is, to promote the development of new urban areas, was genuine, and, to some extent, sometimes shaped by idealism. Whether a good will alone, however, could bring about the expected results or not, depended on actual practice and operational concerns.

All the while, the aim of enterprises, including those involved the project, was to generate profits. Unfortunately, this aim conflicted with a range of the individual interests at play. As in a government-dominated construction and development, the relationship between government and enterprises was, therefore, rather complicated and subtle. Enterprises, intent upon accumulating profits, would try to influence the local government by some means, such as lobbying. The government, meanwhile, would offer all range of preferential policies in a bid to attract investments from enterprises. Through this complexity, in some cases at least, the government, enterprises and some individuals even formed a "developmental alliances" with a view to promoting urban development.[17]

PG district government had indeed been in communication with some enter-prises ever since the initial designing stage of the development project. For example, some enterprises were actively involved in contributing to the design of housing, roads, and service facilities. Generally speaking, additional businesses would subsequently become involved as construction proceeded, particularly in terms of land utilization and development. In the case of the PG district, however, enterprises were not involved in land requisition and development because, in this case, the greatest concentration of land belonged to the government's land reserve plan. Therefore, enterprises were, for the most part, not on the opposite side of local residents. To the contrary, they actually became useful service providers insofar as they had actively participated in the development of the new urban area.

Nevertheless, individuals still faced hard decisions during the development process. Development was not always achieved on Pareto Optimality. In most cases, the interests of only some of the individuals involved would be furthered by the process of development, while others might bear disproportionate costs of

---

[17]Logan and Molotch (1987).

development, or even lose their existing interests. People in different social positions and economic status would face different development opportunities and risks. Good development in theory was not always destined to bring good development in practice. One of the only certainties was that individuals persevered to protect their own interests and battled for their place in the distribution of interests.

During the design and discussion phases of PG's development, most people paid attention to the project primarily out of consideration of their own interests. Some individuals had direct dialogues with the local governments, in one way or another, to express their opinions and expectations regarding the development project. During project planning, the PG district government and town government invited a range of village administrators and ordinary villagers for field visits and listened to the opinion they offered. The town government even conducted a questionnaire survey to collect opinions and comments in a more systematic way. Anyhow, this process allowed only limited involvement of the public, that is, on a feedback basis only. Neither were they involved in the decision-making itself nor the actual development process.

Individuals were, as specified by the government's official statement, intended to be the beneficiaries of the new urban development. In the process of urban planning, PG authorities verified the existing land and houses of each individual and family that would be influenced by the project. If land was requisitioned and houses were demolished, each household would be entitled to compensation in the form of two apartments in the new urban area. To the extent their new home exceeds the old one in monetary value, each household would be able to keep the difference as net gain in cash from the transaction. At the same time, households could earn at least a basic income to support themselves by renting one apartment out. Since many families had, in fact, already left the village, such that their houses or homesteads were idle, once the project was implemented, these families could benefit from some additional income and the wider problem of idle land would be reduced. According to relevant policies, those whose houses which were demolished would be included in urban pension schemes.[18] Nevertheless, it remained an open question as to whether or not individuals would accept these proposals. When the new urban area development plan was still in the discussion and design stage, some villagers, including village authorities (such as retired officials or CPC party members) visited the town government and talked to project leaders in the hope that their villages could be incorporated. The town government did, indeed, receive many members of these village committees and listened keenly to their expectations concerning the development of the new urban area. Given the prevailing view that "development brings wealth and non-development leads to poverty and backwardness", everybody wanted to be included in the development scheme. At the same time, it was well received, at all levels, that the plans for development spoke nothing of changing the prevailing values or pastoral identity of the area.

---

[18]Source: Log of PG district.

6.2.1.3 Issue of Land During New Urban Area Development

The issue of land was vital in the development of new urban areas. Indeed, land, as well as the methods of redistributing obtained interests, was central to the interests of different groups involved in the redevelopment process. An important cause of nationwide conflicts, related to land requisition, was the unfairness in the process of redistribution process. Land requisition of the PG district was part of the urban land reserve scheme, which also provided the funding for compensation in return for said land requisition. There were, however, great differences between the government-dominated land reserve scheme and developer-dominated land requisition. The government-dominated land requisition had been influenced by a sense of ideological reasonability and was, therefore, more easily accepted by the public who generally regarded it as part of an overall aim to serve the good of the nation. That is to say, it was widely expected that the role of the government would include a strong emphasis on serving the public interest. Nevertheless, in the case of developer-dominated land requisition, the role of the government was hard to narrow down, especially when local authorities adopted a range of preferential policies intended to attract investment. In such instances, the public often believed that the government was on the side of developers, or even acting to further their own interests. Indeed, since governments were directly involved in land requisition, it was very difficult for them to stay neutral. That said, in the case of the PG district, the government was approached land requisition reasonably, such that the process was completed smoothly in the context of top-down "developmentalism". Of course, there were also many other reasons behind the smooth process. These included the effective coordination of different levels of government and sufficient inclusion of local residents. Another important factor was the relatively high level of compensation allocated to residents based on an agreement on the method of payment, thereby giving rise to almost universal assent. However, there were still a range of other issues that required solutions, including reemployment and social security, particularly pertinent after the loss of land.

6.2.2 Position and Functions of the New Urban Area in an Overall Urban System

6.2.2.1 Geographic Location and Transportation

The new urban area was located in a basin-like shallow hilly area, around 4 km away from the center of the PG district, surrounded by a bend of the expressway that linked the PG district and the central city B, as well as a nearby mountain range. The gradient and altitude of the terrain varied sporadically and it was covered with dense vegetation with high mountains in the background. All in all, this gave rise to an agreeable natural environment. The new urban area, located, as it was, next to the expressway, benefited from convenient transportation links. It even had the capacity to become a hub of the express railway line passing through the district. Needless to say, such a huge flow of passengers and goods would bring untold benefits.

6.2.2.2 Economic Status

The site for the new urban area was a traditional agricultural community, with farmers composing around 50% of the total population. As part of the development plan, the new urban area was designed as a part of the PG district as well as a tourist center located in the east of the central city B. In recent years, the PG district had already started to integrate agriculture with tourism. As the natural and cultural landscape in the district were notably attractive, it even got the nickname "little Beidaihe".

6.2.3 The Demographic Character of and Resident's Attitude to New Urban Area

The farming population in village X, where the new urban area was to be located, numbered at approximately 6000, while the number of people actually living there was around 10,000. Before the development started, a questionnaire was distributed to all families in the village in order to collect basic information regarding each household and their attitude towards the development project. In all, 2314 house-holds filled in the questionnaires. Nevertheless, several samples were excluded on account of their containing incomplete data and the final number of effective samples changed throughout the process of analysis according to the answers.

6.2.3.1 Occupations and Skills of the Population

89.5% of the respondents (2070 people) lived in this region and only 5.6% (129) had left. 36.3% (834) of those who lived in the region were engaged in farming, 4.0% (93) were unemployed and 13.0% (301) did not enter into the labor market at all or had left the labor market. Most of the migrant residents were farmers facing a transition to non-farming way of life, to which they still required significant adaptation. What jobs they could hope to do in the future, meanwhile, depended a great deal on their educational background and occupational skills. At the same time, 44.9% (1038) of the respondents had completed junior high school, 26.9% (621) had received primary or below primary school educations and 24.2% (562) had received a senior high school education or above senior high school level.

As 71.8% of the population was educated to a level below junior high school standards, some additional training or education would be required to prepare them for work and life in a new urban area.

There were, however, members of 53.9% (1248) of the households, among the respondents, engaged in non-agricultural jobs. The non-farming median income, meanwhile, was above RMB 10,000. A rough comparison of the medians of income from farming and animal breeding with the non-agricultural sectors indicated that the income from non-agricultural sectors was, indeed, the highest. Generally speaking, households with members engaged in non-agricultural jobs would also find it easier to adapt to urban life.

6.2.3.2 Employment Intentions

According to the survey, 74.4% (1721) of the respondents wanted to take a non-agricultural job in the new urban area and 44.6% (1032) wanted to get a job related to enterprise. The percentage of those who wanted to be self-employed or do sanitation work in communities, meanwhile, was relatively low. Crucially, 73.8% (1708) of the respondents also hoped that the government would provide pre-job training free of charge. Generally speaking, during the process of population migration, migrants had to undergo a transition from the informal sector to the formal sector. While they usually hoped to get a job in the formal sector, for a higher income, most of them would find it hard. It could take an indeterminate length of time working in the informal sector to accumulate any valuable work experience, obtain any skills or get any kind of training before shifting to the formal sector, otherwise they might have to continue working in the informal sector. The process of government-dominated urbanization and population migration was, therefore, characterized by the expectations of migrants on government arrangements and great difficulties in making the shift from the informal sector to the formal one.

6.2.3.3 Resident's Attitudes Towards the Development of New Urban Areas

Most of the respondents agreed to promote rural economic growth through urban development (77.6%) and accepted the proposals relating to land requisition (76.8%). After migration, they would become residents of an urban area, rather than the countryside, such that land would no longer be the focus of both their economic and social life. Previous social and economic relations would, therefore, need to be reorganized accordingly. How migrants received the process would have great impacts on their concept of and attitude to later life.

Educational Level and Attitude Towards the Development of New Urban
Areas

Education level was an important factor in determining an individual's attitude.
Through an analysis of the educational levels of residents and their attitudes
towards the project (as shown in Table 6.1), it is possible to see significant
chi-square test differences.

Through logistic regression tests, we can further understand the differences in the
attitudes towards the development of new urban areas among those with different
educational levels. Take the illiterate group as a comparison group, below a 0.05
probability level, the regression coefficient of the "senior middle school level"
group and the "college and above group" is significant. In terms of the odds ratio,
the "senior middle school level" group is 1.749 times that of the "illiterate group",
while the "college and above" group is 2.677 times the "illiterate group" (see
Table 6.2). All of this is to say, those who are illiterate generally hold a negative
attitude towards the development of new urban areas, but those who belong to the
"senior middle school" level and have a "college and above" educational background are generally more positive towards new urban area development.

These findings give rise to the question as to why there are such differences in
attitudes towards the development of new urban areas among those with different
educational backgrounds. Based on a detailed analysis of the living conditions and
occupation types of those with college and above educational levels (living condition here refers to whether they live locally to their birthplace or leave for work or
business elsewhere), it has been found that 29% of people with college and above
educational backgrounds live outside of their local areas and only 0.6% of this

Table 6.1 Interactive analysis on the connection between educational level and attitude towards
new urban area development

| | | Whether agree to the requisition of land for new urban area development | | Total |
		No	Yes	
Educational level	Illiterate	44	166	210
	Primary school level	59	323	382
	Junior high school level	178	813	991
	Senior high school (Technical school) level	55	363	418
	College and above	10	101	111
Total		346	1766	2112

Chi-square test

Significance level of difference (two-layer test)	Statistical value	Degree of freedom	
	12.829 2112	4	0.012

Table 6.2 The statistical test for logistic regression equation of educational level and attitude towards new urban area development

Model summary							
Regression step 1	−2 log maximum likelihood 1870.263		Cox and Snell coefficient of determination 0.06		Nagelkerke coefficient of determination 0.11		
Variables in regression equation							
		Regression coefficient	Standard error	Wald value	Degree of freedom	Significance	Odds ratio
Review step 1	Education level			12.540	4	0.014	
	Primary school level	0.372	0.221	2.841	1	0.092	1.451
	Junior high school level	0.191	0.189	1.026	1	0.311	1.211
	Senior middle school level (Technical school)	0.559	0.223	6.295	1	0.012	1.749
	College and above	0.985	0.372	6.994	1	0.008	2.677
	Constant	1.328	0.170	61.320	1	0.000	3.773

group live within their local areas and are engaged in agricultural labor. People educated to a college, or higher level no longer, then, take the land as the center of their daily life, but rather tend to move much closer to the urban way of life. As such, they are more willing to show support for the development of new urban areas. On the contrary, the majority of the illiterate group (99.1%) live close to the area in which they were born. Around 31% of them, meanwhile, are engaged in agricultural labor, whereas the other 59.3% are absent from the labor market (such as recipients of pensions, the unemployed, or those occupied by domestic housework).

The correlation between educational levels and attitudes towards the development of new urban areas is, therefore, in line with alternative research conclusions. That is to say, higher educational levels or better vocational skills generate higher migration rates and better financial opportunities for those who migrate.

Employment Rate and Intention

One's vocation reflects, in many ways, one's social and economic status and one's ability to adapt to change in general. Through an interactive analysis (see Table 6.3), it is possible to see that vocation will influence attitudes towards the development of new urban areas and a chi-square test can generate significant results.

Table 6.3 Interaction analysis on vocation and attitude towards new urban area development

		Whether land requisition for new urban area development is acceptable		Total
		No	Yes	
Employment	Personnel absent in the labor market (with pension, unemployed, or doing housework)	97	493	590
	Farmers	159	633	792
	Individual practitioners	23	115	138
	Personnel in production, merchandize and service fields	26	203	229
	Entrepreneur, managers, skilled personnel	14	151	165
Total		319	1595	1914

Taking one's vocation as a standard for social stratification, it is possible to make measurements as regards three particular aspects: economic resources, organizational resources, and human resources. Those who have all the three resources are in the upper stratum. They live a secure life and are more able to adapt to change. On the contrary, those who depend on the land, with just one source of income, will be more vulnerable to social change. This vulnerability will be reflected, in turn, in their attitude towards the development of new urban areas. Through a logistic regression analysis, it can be found that, if enterprise owners, management and technical personnel are taken as a comparison group, it is below a 0.05 level of significance, while the regression coefficient of those who are absent from the labor market, agricultural laborers and the self-employed are significantly negative (see Table 6.4). This means that these three types of people are relatively reluctant to give up their land for the development of new urban areas.

Land, Livestock Breeding, Non-agricultural Labor and Attitudes Towards New Urban Area Development

There are three main sources of income in a family, land income, livestock breeding income, and income from non-agricultural labor. The requisition of land mainly alters land income and the development of the livestock breeding industry. If any family members are engaged in non-agricultural labor, then the family income will be more differential and less vulnerable to changes of land use.

Table 6.4 Logistic regression equation test on vocation and attitudes towards new urban area development

Model summary

Regression step 1		−2 log maximum likelihood 1703.914		Cox and Snell coefficient of determination 0.011			Nagelkerke coefficient of determination 0.018	

Variables in regression equation

		Regression coefficient	Standard error	Wald value	Degree of freedom	Significance	Odds ratio
Review step 1	Occupation			18.556	2	0.001	
	Personnel not in labor market	−0.752	0.301	6.263	1	0.012	0.471
	Farmers	−0.997	0.293	11.561	1	0.001	0.369
	Individual practitioners	−0.769	0.361	4.539	1	0.033	0.464
	Personnel in production, merchandize, services	−0.323	0.348	0.860	1	0.354	0.724
	Constant	2.378	0.279	72.465	1	0.000	10.786

Of all the surveyed households, 92.7% (2145) have their own homesteads and the median area of the homesteads is 0.4 mu.[19] In terms of land allocation, 62.5% (1448) of the surveyed households have farmland for living and the median farmland for living is 1.4 mu per household. The average median income from farmland of this sort was 666 yuan in 2007 and 657 yuan in 2008. The number of those who had contracted collective land, meanwhile, remained relatively small, at only 13.6% (315). The median of the contracted land area was found to be 9.8 mu and the average income of contracted collective land was 857 yuan in 2007 and 727 yuan in 2008. There tends to be little leasing or subleasing in the local areas, generally less than 1%.

Only a few families reared livestock in the local area, accounting for 6.3% of the respondents (146). Livestock breeding income was, however, relatively high, with a median income of 7000 yuan in 2007 and 10,000 yuan in 2008. Livestock breeding income, therefore, accounted for a larger proportion of overall household incomes. But it is extremely difficult to maintain livestock breeding after the construction of new town areas.

One or more members of 53.9% (1248) of the respondent's households undertook some kind of non-agricultural work. The median income of non-agricultural work, meanwhile, was over 10,000 yuan. By rough comparison, we can see that this kind of non-agricultural income is, indeed, the highest among all other incomes.

A logistic analysis was also made as regards whether the contracting of land by a family alters their attitudes towards the development of new urban areas. This analysis found that the odds of families, who do not contract land, agreeing to the requisition of land, for the purposes of new urban development, are 1.455 times higher than those of families who have contracted land (see Table 6.5). When further analyzing the relationship between the area of the contracted land and the attitude towards the development of new urban areas, it can be found that there is no significant effect on attitudes by increasing the volume of the contracted land by one mu. After dividing the contracted land into four sub-groups, through a contingency (table) analysis, the data shows that the different sub-groups of the broader contracted land group are not correlated to attitudes towards the development of new urban areas. That is to say, the difference of attitude is mainly reflected in whether a family holds contracted land or not, that is, rather than the area of contracted land they hold. Whether a family has subsistence farmland also has a similar correlation with their attitudes.

The contingency table analysis also shows that livestock breeding in a family is correlated with their attitudes towards the development of new urban areas. Further analysis, by logistic regression, shows that the odds of families who are not engaged in livestock breeding agreeing with the requisition of farm land for urban development is 1.673 times higher than families who are engaged in livestock breeding

---

[19]A unit of area (= 0.0667 ha).

Table 6.5 Logistic regression equation test on family contracting land and attitude towards new urban area development

Model summary							
Regression step 1		−2 log maximum likelihood 1894.046		Cox and Snell coefficient of determination 0.003		Nagelkerke coefficient of determination 0.004	
Variables in regression equation							
		Regression coefficient	Standard error	Wald value	Degree of freedom	Significance	Odds ratio
Regression step 1	Whether contracting land	0.375	0.155	5.847	1	0.016	1.455
	Constant	1.305	0.141	85.735	1	0	3.687

Table 6.6 Logistic regression equation test on family breeding livestock and attitude towards new urban area development

Model summary						
Regression step 1	−2 log maximum likelihood 1894.210		Cox and Snell coefficient of determination 0.003		Nagelkerke coefficient of determination 0.005	
Variables in regression equation						
	Regression coefficient		Standard error	Wald value	Degree of freedom	Significance	Odds ratio
Regression step 1	Whether breeding livestock	0.515	0.206	6.232	1	0.013	1.673
	Constant	1.146	0.197	33.913	1	0	3.147

(see Table 6.6). In other words, families engaged in livestock breeding are more likely to disagree with the requisition of farmland for new urban development.

Earning from non-agricultural labor is an important component of aggregate family income. Besides, the median of non-agricultural incomes is higher than any other income group. Yet it remains an open question as to whether or not engagement in non-agricultural occupations alters attitudes towards urban development. Indeed, the contingency table analysis shows that there is a correlation between non-agricultural labor and attitudes towards new urban area development. Further analysis shows that a family engaged in non-agricultural labor is 1.443 times more likely to approve of the idea of urban development than families not engaged in non-agricultural labor (see Table 6.7).

Table 6.7 Logistic regression equation test on non-agricultural labor and attitudes towards new urban area development

Model summary							
Regression step 1	−2 log maximum likelihood 1857.611	Cox and Snell coefficient of determination 0.005				Nagelkerke coefficient of determination 0.008	

Variables in regression equation							
		Regression coefficient	Standard error	Wald value	Degree of freedom	Significance	Odds ratio
Regression step 1	Whether non-agricultural labor	0.366	0.118	9.571	1	0.002	1.443
	Constant	1.429	0.085	281.81	1	0	4.175

Income and Attitude Towards New Urban Area Development

The above analysis is intended to understand attitudes towards the development of new urban areas and how they are subject to the structure of family income. Further analysis is, however, required on the correlation between specific family incomes and family behavior. The total income of a household includes land income, livestock breeding income and non-agricultural income. Different families have different income structures, yet, regardless of the income structure, the result will eventually be reflected in their level of savings. Through the contingency table analysis, it was found that the amount of money each household has saved can alter their attitudes towards the development of new urban areas. Population migration studies show, meanwhile, that the poorer people are, the more reluctant they tend to be to migrate (Table 6.8).

In short, this survey finds that most people find acceptable the idea of having their land requisitioned for developing new urban areas and have high expectations about the outcome. On such a premise, attention also ought to be paid to the fact that disadvantaged families and individuals may be impacted negatively by, or at least may not benefit from, the development process. They are often unable to adapt to the great changes brought about by these projects, especially in terms of

Table 6.8 Logistic regression equation test on family saving income and attitude towards new urban area development (Unit: per cent)

		Whether agree to the requisition of land for new urban area development		Total
		No	Yes	
Saving income	Below 3000 yuan	224	1073	1297
		17.3	82.7	100
	3000–5000 yuan	10	90	109
		9.2	90.8	100
	5000–10000 yuan	14	126	140
		10	90	100
	Above 10000 yuan	14	131	145
		9.7	90.3	100
	Total	262	1429	1691
		15.5	84.5	100

Chi square test

	Statistical value	Degree of freedom	Significance
Pearson chi square valid sample	13.454	3	0.004
	1691		

education, income structure, and lifestyle. At the same time, they also lack the ability to deal with risks. Therefore, special attention should be paid to such groups throughout the construction process.

There is, in general, however, an impression that future life in urban areas will be significantly improved. That is to say, respondents generally believed that, after the development of new urban areas, basic social facilities will be greatly changed and social living conditions will be improved. These expectations include incomes, job opportunities, social security and a range of other factors. These expectations notwithstanding, are beautiful, the questions as to how social living conditions can be improved remain. During the course of the investigation, only the option of employment intentions is set for the respondents. Among all the respondents, 94.8% of people express willingness to engage in non-agricultural work in the new urban areas. But as to the question "what kind of job do you want to take in the new urban area", 69.7% respondents, currently living in the area, elected to find a job in enterprises in the new urban area, while 18.9% selected the community service sector in the new town and 17.9% intended to do business instead. Likewise, the respondents who live outside of the area are similar in terms of employment intentions. Such problems must be addressed during the process of new urban area development. After the requisition of land and migration, besides direct economic compensation, it is also necessary to consider how to maintain and improve the living standards of immigrants and, of course, how to replace the immigrants. Direct economic compensation alone is, of course, unable to solve the poverty and other social problems caused by migration. Instead, it is also necessary to make developmental investments or establish some kind of social safety valves.

The previous analysis has shown that the more differential the family income and the more independent the family is from their land, then the more likely it becomes for them to have positive attitudes towards the development of new urban areas. In fact, in many ways, present life has been gradually moving in the direction of urbanization and many are already experiencing the urban way of life. Indeed, this is one of the strongest bases for promoting the development of new urban areas. Nevertheless, at the same time, one aspect should be noted. An important premise for facilitating agreement with the development of new urban areas may yet prove to be psychological expectations, namely that the new urban area will bring about benefits in all aspects of life; good for individuals and families alike. This psychological appeal is also reflected in the choice of employment intentions, with many hoping to find a job related to enterprises in the new urban area. Whether or not these psychological expectations can actually be realized after the development of the new urban area is an entirely different matter. The possibility of psychological disappointments remains a significant risk. The psychological expectations of the migrating population may, meanwhile, influence the actual process and results of population migration.

6.2.4 Social Factors in the New Urban Areas

An important issue faced by newly developed urban areas is how to facilitate the transformation of an agricultural population into a non-agricultural one. This is not, meanwhile, simply reflected by a change of vocation, but rather a systematic transformation of land usage, household registration, social security and a range of other factors.

6.2.4.1 Household Registration

Among all the respondents, those registered to urban areas accounted for 11.8% (272), while agricultural residents accounted for 82.5% (1910). The two fundamentally different types of registered households will, meanwhile, express different attitudes towards the requisition of land. Through the contingency table analysis, the coefficient of association is significant. It is found by further logistic analysis that the odds of non-agricultural households agreeing to the requisition of land are 1.772 times higher than those of agricultural households (see Table 6.9).

Household registration is, then, an important systematic factor as regards the process of urbanization. Crucially, household registration is directly related to land and social security and places restrictions upon resources and identity for those seeking a new urban life after having migrated from a rural area. The development of new urban areas has expropriated all local agricultural land and uniformly replaced rural homesteads. According to relevant laws, regulations and policies of land compensation, the household registration status of those farmers who face land requisition ought to be changed in order to establish for them the relevant social security systems. During the process of issuing land compensation, an important issue is how to convert such compensation into an effectively managed pension

Table 6.9 Logistic regression equation test on types of household registration and attitude towards new urban area development

Model summary							
Regression step 1	−2 log maximum likelihood 1837.291	Cox and Snell coefficient of determination 0.004			Nagelkerke coefficient of determination 0.007		
Variables in regression equation							
		Regression coefficient	Standard error	Wald value	Degree of freedom	Significance	Odds ratio
Regression step 1	Type of household registration 1	0.572	0.213	7.238	1	0.007	1.772
	Constant	1.579	0.062	642.62	1	0	4.849

fund. However, the change of household registration alone does not necessitate the actual urbanization of migrants. Rossi, for instance, believes that the concentration of people and the development of an urban landscape is only one limited aspect of overall urbanization. Far more important are the cultural values of the city. If there is only a concentration of population, without any changes to concepts and culture, then the urbanization can only be described as illusory.[20] The urbanization of lifestyle is, then, an important concern when studying the urbanization of China in recent years.

6.2.4.2   Social Insurance and Security

Social insurance is an essential component of social safety, which can provide basic living security for individuals throughout the transformation process. As far as the respondents are concerned, most registered agricultural residents participate in cooperative programs of rural medical care (94.3%), among which 23.8% participated in a pension's insurance program. The number of people covered by unemployment and maternity insurance were, however, very low. Social insurance requires, therefore, more investment as the process of new urban development unfolds.

After the requisition of land, the livelihoods of residents must be transformed from the agricultural to the non-agricultural. What's more, the residents in question must face the loss, or partial loss of the social relationships and security, once enjoyed, that was based upon their ownership of land. In rural areas, for instance, land ownership is an important means of supporting the elderly. The responsibility of caring for the elderly can also be transferred on to the next generation along with the transfer of the land in question. Furthermore, throughout the process of shared labor required to cultivate land, various social relationships are established, practiced and reinforced. After the requisition of land, the joint enterprise of a family unity may face significant reductions. The way that a family may attempt to support its elderly member may also alter, which will also be a challenge for community and social provision making for the aged. Previous studies have already discovered a significant social consequence of land requisition and the social mobility of farmers. As a result of this process, networks of family support have disappeared while it has become increasingly difficult to establish community pension systems.

6.2.4.3   Infrastructure Construction

A great deal of planning generally goes into providing infrastructure for new urban developments. Residents have, therefore, high expectations as regards this process. More than 70% of people believe that their quality of life will be enhanced by urban

---

[20]Yefu (2002).

development. Most of these expectations are directed towards level of incomes, job opportunities, living conditions, infrastructure (water, electricity, and gas), public transportation, healthcare, entertainment facilities, education, social security, neighborhood relationships. As part of this, in excess of 85% of people support the construction of infrastructure within new urban areas, including roads, hospitals, cinemas, libraries, gymnasiums and activity centers. Indeed, infrastructure in new urban areas will face significant improvements, but this will coexist with great discrepancies in the level of incomes, job opportunities and social security for different individuals and groups. During and after the development of new urban areas, it shall remain unknown precisely how many and what kind of job opportunities will be provided, what kind of investment shall be made and by how much individual incomes will increase. At present few respondents report having ever engaged with public-space leisure and entertainment facilities. More than 87% of the respondents, for instance, have not ever been to a cinema, karaoke TV, bar, or recreation center. Few of them, meanwhile, regularly take part in playing cards, chess or other similar activities (76.6% of them never participate). Likewise, relatively few people participate in sports activities and reading (26.2 and 18.7% respectively). Most leisure activities are carried out with the family, such as watching TV and listening to the radio (77.5%). Future trends, therefore, depend greatly upon whether or not public-space activities will become more available and popular following the development of new urban areas.

As far as the new urban area development within PG district is concerned, both the government and individuals have strong incentives to actively promote the urban development process. Likewise, both have invested huge quantities of manpower, material resources, expectations and even emotion in the process. But for a new urban area built in a traditional agricultural community, the difficulties it encounter can never be solved by the construction of infrastructure alone. What's more important is to endow the new urban area with full vitality. On the one hand, the new urban area should be able to find a place in the city's production or service system, maintain its continuous operation, provide more employment opportunities and solve the issue of employment for a population which has just lost its land. On the other hand, the new urban area has to face, adapt to and overcome a new urban way of life.

So far, the demolition and reconstruction of the new urban project have been completely successful. The job, thereafter, is to facilitate the relocation of the original residents into new houses which have been chosen in accordance with the plan for a new urban life. That is a new start point. At that point, the residents would have changed their style of dwelling, while their employment and corresponding way of life may yet not have altered. When undergoing this process of social mobility, farmers have to face this transformation gradually. The status quo involves such residents living a centralized life like other urban residents while still actually maintaining something of a rural lifestyle. Such a transitional period may exert great pressure on the urban environment, healthcare and other services. The direct transition from rural to urban living conditions also leads to the breakdown of social relations, especially in intergenerational family relationships. This breakdown will give rise to many challenges including compromised networks of family support and limited means of caring for elderly family members. Yet, the development of new urban areas continues to advance. More research is, then, necessary, particularly as regards the process, specific systems and policy designs required during the urban development process. Only in this way, can a real and smooth transition from rural to urban life be achieved.

6.3   Problems and Countermeasures

There is still a degree of uncertainty surrounding the precise conditions that are most favorable for the development of new urban areas. The above comparative analysis, of the basic factors that constitute cities, attempted to shed light upon when such development may be feasible. Part of the problem is that, during the process of urbanization, many factors exert a complex influence on the overall process, which is, itself, contingent on the support of society, the economy and technological development. At present, the development of new urban areas in China is driven by the government, primarily through resource allocation and policy adjustment. But the real vitality of a city also depends on market or economic factors. Without these, a new urban area may become depressed or transformed into a dwelling centralized countryside. In the process of developing new urban areas, the core issue to be faced is whether or not government directed action really can tally with the natural process of urban development. Meanwhile, tackling issues such as poverty and inequality should not be ignored throughout the process of urbanization.

6.3.1   Government and Market

Generally speaking, governments at all levels are driven towards the development of the area under their jurisdiction. The tax-sharing system fixed the mode and the proportion of benefit distribution between the central government and local governments. In other words, the opportunistic space in the budget system for the local governments was eliminated. The system altered the relationships between the central government and local governments while considerably shaping the behavior of local governments.[21] In order to gain more tax revenue, a common practice of local governments is that of land financing. Large-scaled construction has, therefore, become one of the most effective and direct ways for local authorities to gain

---

[21]Feizhou (2006).

more income out of the budget system. As such, it can be said that local governments have beneficial strong motivation for pushing forward the urbanization process.

This has, however, created a situation in which local governments must compete for a dominant position. After conducting the process of land requisition itself, local governments must attract enterprises to move into the area and undertake development and construction projects on said land. From this point, local authorities can increase their revenues via taxation paid by enterprises and their well-paid employees. Therefore, cities often compete by offering more preferential policies in a bid to attract more investable resources. In the urban development process of western countries, the most influential factor in the competition among cities is the market factor. But in China, the government plays a more important role in the process of competition, primarily due to the impact of various systematic factors, such as the land system. The main advantage of resources owned by local governments, far more important than the investment attracted by preferential policies, is any financial support filtering down from the upper levels of government, perhaps even the central government. In practice, this often means not only the direct allocation of government funds, but also a range of other preferential terms.

Nevertheless, even if the urbanization process is promoted by the government, it should not violate the logic of urban development or that of market development. Any government-led push of the urbanization process should be implemented within the grade of a city and its existing economic system. The government may well go ahead with infrastructure construction, thereby providing a huge base for further development and construction. But whether or not a city can build upon this base and support an extensive exchange of people and goods in the urban space system is another matter. Securing a position in the overall urban system, in this way, depends on the resources of a city and the support of its leading economic agents, such as businesses and services.

What's more, an important procedural factor, which cannot be ignored in the process of stimulating new urban development by government or market forces, is that cities and towns should only be set up with the administrative approval stipulated by China's urban organizational system. This restriction can function to make market forces slightly passive throughout the promotion of new urban development. This is because such market forces can only really function within the limits recognized by government. That is to say, market forces are not completely independent. As far as the development of a city is concerned, this restriction can limit the impetus for the bottom-up development. Take Longgang town in Wenzhou city as an example. Longgang had first been equipped with urban standards of infrastructure in the middle of 1980s. Nevertheless, it was not recognized as a town in terms of any kind of administrative approval, so subsequent development was highly limited. On the contrary, some cities, which don't actually meet many of the practical requirements of city development, are subject to the centralization of land and population, simply through the adjustment of administrative divisions and other administrative means. This often results in the waste of urban resources, perhaps even the destruction of the urban environment. There is, then, much to be done as regards ensuring a good match between government and market forces within existing procedures of administrative approval. Adjustments are required in terms of system and policy, that is, in order to respect the will of the public and to prevent the low-density expansion or sprawl of cities.

6.3.2   Inequality and Poverty in Urban Development

The level of resistance to risk and crisis, as well as the capacity to gain benefits, throughout the process of urbanization, vary for different groups of the population. Facing the same process of development, different groups have to face an unequal playing field, due, in part, to the constraints of their own position (such as lower educational levels, a lack of labor skills and a lack of capital).

When the government participates in the process of urbanization, it may become embedded with market forces, thereby forming something of a growth coalition that can drive forward urban development. In this process, vulnerable groups may, however, become urban "refugees" suffering from poverty. This is especially the case throughout the process of implementing land values. In order to pursue differential rates of land rent, the government might place affordable housing and replacement housing in areas with a lower land value. More often than not, these areas will be far away from the city center and play host to much fewer opportunities for development. As a result, not only are the residents of these areas largely excluded from the development process, but also they may be forced to pay a higher cost of living and be isolated from other advantageous resources.

Similar problems could be found in the design of the PG project. All replacement houses were placed intensively within a district of the new urban area. According to the plan, the new urban area was to be divided into three residential areas, including replacement residential areas, commercialized residential areas and low-density residential areas. The three residential areas, meanwhile, will be inhabited by different groups of the population. The replacement residential area, for instance, was intended to accommodate the original rural residents. Previous surveys have, however, have shown that some of the original rural residents no longer lived in the local area, so there would be a supply of vacant houses to attract immigrants. The price of the houses in commercialized residential areas would be higher than the replacement residential areas and the price of houses in the low-density residential areas would be even higher. Simple divisions can be used, then, to form different types of residential areas, but it is not beneficial for people from different classes to live together.

Throughout the development of new urban areas in Columbia, America urban design involved the construction of different types of residential housing within single districts. As a result, people from different classes and with different levels of income could buy suitable houses in a variety of residential areas around the new urban area. Consequently, people in different residential areas could all enjoy the same standard of public facilities and services and can support the operation of these facilities and services, thereby creating a rich public space. As a result, the development of impoverished and disordered areas with inadequate public service could be avoided. Nevertheless, in the planning and design of new urban areas in China, for the sake of convenience and the maximization of interests, replacement houses were generally concentrated within the same district. This concentration resulted in the spatial separation of local people and immigrants, as well as the separation of the rich and poor.

6.3.3 Land Requisition, Migration and Benefit Redistribution

An unavoidable issue of new urban development is the matter of land requisition and migration, as well as the contradictions and conflicts which result. Needless to say, a range of relevant regulations and policies have been developed by the central and local government concerning how to convert rural land into construction land, how to compensate farmers and how to arrange migration and resettlement. Scholars have also discussed the issue repeatedly, yet, in reality, conflicts remain commonplace. PG area went through such a process of land requisition on two occasions. The first land requisition, initiated in 2006, was for the construction of roads. The second, initiated in 2009, was for the development of new urban areas. The first requisition triggered large-scale incidents. Villagers blocked the traffic, besieged the staff on construction sites, and organized a four-month long collective petition. The second was relatively smooth and received positive support from collective organizations and villagers. There were many reasons responsible for the different responses to the two requisitions. For one thing, the government, in the second instance, changed their working method during the process of land requisition. There was more cooperation with local people, especially, in some matters, local community leaders, and more control over the timing and means of disseminating information. The most important factor, however, was the redistribution of land interests.

When collectively owned rural land was converted into urban construction land, there were good prospects for appreciation. How to reallocate the appreciated value of the land was an issue at the core of the controversy surrounding land requisition. In accordance with the provisions of the "Law of the People's Republic of China on Land Administration," rural land owners should be compensated according to a multiple of agricultural production value. After requisition, the agricultural products should be compensated for on the basis of an assessment of their potential value. Likewise, the resettlement of the residents also comes with a range of specific provisions. With the improvement of the economy, different regions adjusted and continuously improved the standards of compensation by combining a range of market factors. However, there remained considerable room of benefits following land development. It is, then, critical to assess how best to reallocate the benefits, especially during the rapid urbanization process and when facing a shortage of land for urban construction. At the same time, it is also very important to consider how to ensure a fair allocation of the overall benefits gained from the development of the whole area. In other words, it is important to consider whom the process of urban development actually being carried out for and who will benefit from it? Due to their limited education and skill-set, it is difficult for immigrants to be involved in the development process, that is, after the land requisition itself, or to become the primary recipients of the benefits accumulated throughout the development process. That is also the source of conflicts. As such, both the employment of migrants and their resettlement have to be solved simultaneously.

Accordingly, throughout recent years, local governments have explored reforms as regards land requisition and resettlement and gathered some experiences. The core idea is to make clear the issue of land and the related benefits. The land ticket system adopted by Chengdu City, for instance, clarified the rights of farmers as regards the land in question. By methods such as this, the land can be transacted in stipulated area and the interests of farmers are safeguarded. The land and the employment problems are thus solved, to an extent, in a flexible way. During the process of reconstructing an urban village in Guangzhou City, the rights of farmers, regarding, in particular, the disposal of land, were clarified and, subsequently, performed very well. In the process of land requisition, the interests of farmers were guaranteed and some families and individuals were allocated benefits from the land. All in all, there are many similar experiences, although PG area didn't clarify the rights of farmers throughout the land requisition and compensation process. Nevertheless, the overall compensation standard was very high, which means farmers could enjoy at least part of the benefits resulting from the increased value of the local land. At the same time, the new urban development, including its design and planning meet the expected interests of local people. The fact that the local community expects benefits from the development is an important foundation for the smooth implementation of the development of new urban areas.

There remain many issues in the process of new urban area development. A rather significant one is to gain people's recognition of the city. It should be made clear that it is for whom this new urban area is built, who will take over the task of construction, whether or not the local residents will be able to participate in the urban development process and whether they can become the main force behind future development It must, then, be the case that the local residents will be able to benefit from this development process such that they will come to recognize its legitimacy. In the planning and design stage of the PG project, the local government consulted with residents on some issues, such as the types of residential housing and public service facilities. Nevertheless, it remains difficult for local residents to be involved in the overall planning and design process, including the future status of the new urban area, its relation with the old town and what's the main objects of construction and development. All of the goals and expectations regarding development were designed and planned by the government. One important thing that should be noted is that local residents all hoped that new urban area development would promote the development of the local economy and society.

These issues highlight the difficulty of facing the various kinds of problem encountered throughout the urbanization process and trying to maximize the level of social equity that results. Urbanization is a process that everyone is involved in. During this process it is necessary to provide more systematic security in order to protect vulnerable groups. All in all no matter what kind of urbanization it is and how it is promoted, the key is that the livelihoods of residents should be secured and a common goal of development and common prosperity should be pursued.

References

Feizhou, Z. (2006). The ten years of tax-sharing system: System and its influence. *Chinese Social Science, 6.*

He, C. (2003). *Urban sociology: Theory and view.* Sun Yat-Sen University Press.

Logan, J. R., Molotch, H. L. (1987). *Urban fortunes: The political economy of place.* Berkeley and Los Angeles: University of California Press.

Mills, E. (2003). *Handbook of regional and urban economics* (Vol. 2) (H. Shouyi et al., Trans.). Economic Science Press.

Paddison, R. (2009). *Handbook of urban studies* (A. Guo et al., Trans.). Truth & Wisdom Press, Shanghai People's Publishing House.

Xin, Y. (1998). Dual economy theory and labor transfer theory—On China's labor transfer. *Population and Economics, 2.*

Yefu, Z. (2002). *Urban sociology* (p. 107). China City Press.

Chapter 7
The Urban Expansion Model

Urbanization is traditionally driven by spatial expansion, which, essentially, entails the constant outwards expansion of urban areas, typically accompanied by population growth within these areas. Indeed, this approach is followed by most countries throughout their own individual processes of urbanization. Urbanization, which was first witnessed in the West, was followed by processes of—suburbanization and ex-urbanization, that is to say, the expansion of cities into their surrounding areas, throughout the 1950s and 1970s.

In a similar fashion, urban expansion was also the primary driving force behind urbanization in China. This was typified by the single-center expansion model of urbanization that was initially adopted in Beijing and subsequently implemented across China. To be more specific, urban development in Chinese cities generally followed the pattern of rings of expansion radiating outwards from an original old city area. China and the West were, meanwhile, ostensibly similar, that is, insofar as each of them underwent a process of urban expansion. Beneath this fundamental similarity, however, there actually existed great differences. For one thing, urban expansion in China bore its own distinctive features due, in large part, to different systems of land ownership. Most importantly, the public ownership of land in China meant that large-scale rapid urbanization was possible. Indeed, the total number of individual urban development projects in China was the largest in the world and remains the largest ever undertaken in human history. Furthermore, in contrast to the urbanization process in western countries, China's urban expansion can be classified as a government-led model of urban expansion. Informative though they are, these differences give rise to a range of pertinent questions. How, for instance, can urban expansion in China be explained in more precise terms? How did such a model of government-led development become possible? What were the basic features of this model? The following chapter will attempt to answer these questions.

Urban expansion was a spatial form of urbanization that included processes of both compact and extended development. The former involved the development of urban spaces in an effectively controlled and comparatively intensive way. The

© Social Sciences Academic Press 2020   219
Q. Li, *China's Development under a Differential Urbanization Model*,
Research Series on the Chinese Dream and China's Development Path,
https://doi.org/10.1007/978-981-13-9451-5_7

latter, however, involved urban expansion without any carefully planned order or aim, thereby leading to widespread urban sprawl. Although such extended urban areas did have many of the spatial features of cities, including, not least, the extensive use of land, the supply of industry and public service facilities were both inadequate, whilst intra-regional levels of development were greatly imbalanced. In fact, developing methods of controlling disordered urban spread became an issue of great concern for all countries undergoing this process. Many countries explored solutions in this field, such as the Greater London "Green Belt" implemented after the Second World War and the urban growth boundary (UGB) delimitations in Portland in the US. In a similar way, great progress was made in China through planning, policy and legislative restrictions on disordered urban development. Nevertheless on the whole, blind city expansion was still common and lacked coordinated effective control.

Two problems are especially pronounced in China's urban expansion. Firstly, land urbanization increased at a faster rate than population urbanization. According to the Statistics Yearbook, China's urban population increased by 26%, from 2000 to 2009, while built-up urban areas increased by 41% in the same period. Notably decentralized and low-density development such as this came hand in hand with the waste of agricultural resources and the high consumption of energy. As a result of this, the central government's twelfth five-year plan proposed to determine properly the boundaries of urban development so as to improve the efficiency of land usage and develop cities in a more compact and intensive pattern.

Secondly, urban expansion was accompanied by a range of social issues, most of which simultaneously exemplified significant spatial and stratum differentiation. Along with the progress of urbanization and the deepening of urban housing reforms, uneven development became more evident. It was noteworthy that, at least in the next twenty to thirty years, social spatial differentiation within city areas is set to surpass the overall urban-rural differentiation and regional differentiation and, therefore, become one of the major long-term problems besetting urban development.

All in all, this chapter reviews relevant theories of urban expansion, analyses the urban regiming method by which government was able to lead urban development and points out the characteristics and problems of the government-led model of China's urban expansion.

7.1   The Government-Led Urban Expansion Model

As the urbanization process driven by economic growth accelerated in China, the model of a government-led urban expansion process gradually formed. In this model, the government, influenced by the above-mentioned political and economic mechanisms of urban expansion, played a key and leading role in promoting urban growth, regulating social distribution, making urban plans, and controlling urban expansion. Nevertheless, this model was not followed in exactly the same key, but rather with a degree of diversity. It exhibited differences in economic geography, that is, between coastal and inland areas, resource endowment, political and economic mechanisms, such as the interaction between government and local enterprises and general management capabilities. Nevertheless, in most of the various government-led development models, the following phenomenon were easily observable.

7.1.1   Large-Scale, High Speed and Significant Regional Differences

Three decades after the inception of China's reform and opening up policy, the country witnessed the rapid, large-scale growth of the built-up areas within its cities. The overall urbanized area increased from 7438 km^2, in 1981, to 38,107.3 km^2, in 2009, that is to say, a total increase of 5.12 times (see Fig. 7.1). Although urban areas expanded rapidly, the precise expansion speeds of different cities demonstrated significant variation. From 1973 to 2007, for instance, the built-up area within the boundaries of Haikou city increased 23.42 times, an increase of 100 km^2, while the built-up areas of Fangchenggang city, Zhengzhou city, and Ningbo city only increased somewhat more than fivefold. The smallest overall change was witnessed in Qiqihar city which grew only by a factor 1.21 in the period from 1989 to 2008. The average annual increase in area of seven major cities, Beijing, Shanghai, Shenzhen, Nanjing, Guangzhou, Zhengzhou, and Chengdu rose by over ten square kilometers each year. From among them, Beijing had the largest the annual average expansion area of around 26.69 km^2 each year

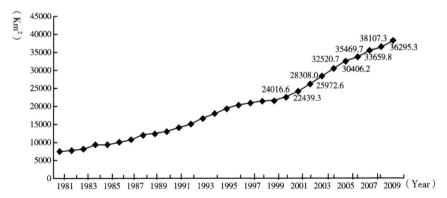

Fig. 7.1 The built-up urban areas in China (1981–2009). *Source* China Development Report 2010. China Statistical Yearbook 2004–2009

for more than thirty years. On the other hand, the average annual expansion of eleven other cities, Rikaze, Karamay, Wuwei, Yichang, Qiqihar, Nanchong, Lasa, Lijiang, Xiangtan, Xining, and Bengbu, increased by less than one square kilometer each year, with Rikaze, in particular, only growing by 0.25 km^2 annually.[1]

7.1.2 Rapid Increase and Large Proportions of Residential and Industrial Land

According to data released by the National Bureau of Statistics, residential land and industrial land accounted for a larger proportion of urban construction land as far as the changes in the constitution of urban construction land from 2004 to 2009 was concerned. In 2004, residential land accounted for 31.61% and industrial land accounted for 21.79%. In 2009, residential land declined to 31.13%, while the proportion of industrial land rose to 22.27%.

In general, the proportion of both industrial land and residential land was comparatively large whilst industrial land usage tended to increase faster than residential land usage (see Fig. 7.2). In 2009, for instance, the overall area of residential land usage in China accounted for 45.80% of the total whereas that of industrial land usage accounted for 42.30%. In 2010, the proportion of residential land dropped marginally to 44.80%, while industrial land actually rose to 42.70%. Furthermore, until 2011, the overall proportion of residential land continued to decline to 35.40%, while industrial land continued to rise to 52.10%. Consequently, industrial land usage actually exceeded the scale of residential land usage for the first time.[2]

What's mentioned above exposes two of the main causes for the increase of land usage for urban construction projects under the model of government-led urban expansion. The first of these was the rapid development of real estate. The second, meanwhile, was the rapid development of industry, aided, in particular, by policies favoring the promotion of investment. As such, it can be easily understood that the government's efforts to contain excessive real estate development, accompanied by relevant policy adjustments, resulted in a decline in the proportion of land used for residential purposes as well as a relative increase in the proportion of land used for industrial purposes.

---

[1]China Development Research Foundation (2010, p. 59).

[2]"Industrial Land Supply Surpassed Residential Land for the First Time, Significantly in the Second and Third Tier Cities". Xinhua net, July 29, 2011. http://newsxinhuaiiet.com/house/2011-07/29/c_121745427.htm.

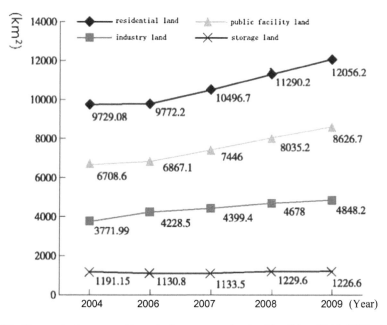

Fig. 7.2 Changes in the composition of urban construction land in China (2004–2009). *Source* National Bureau of Statistics of the People's Republic of China

7.1.3   Larger Proportion of Infrastructure and Low-Income Housing Construction in Local Government Debt

It was reported by the National Audit Office of the People's Republic of China in 2010 that local governments in China first accumulated debt in 1979. Following from that, all provincial governments (including cities under separate state planning), 90.05% of municipal governments and 86.54% of county governments were in debt by 1996. By the end of 2010, meanwhile, except for the 54 county governments that were without debt, the overall debt of the provincial, municipal and county governments totaled 10.717491 trillion yuan. Out of this total, the figure for which government bodies were liable for repayment reached 6.710951 trillion yuan (62.62%), the figure guaranteed by government bodies reached 2.336974 trillion yuan (21.80%) and the figure for which government bodies have to some extent obligation to render salvage reached 1.669566 trillion yuan (15.58%).[3] According to another related study, local government debt, in total, accounted for about 20–30% of GDP. The need for financing, which resulted from the capital expenditure in the construction of infrastructure and affordable

---

[3]"Report on the Audit Work of Central Budget Implementation in 2010 and Other Financial Revenue and Expenditure". National Audit Office of the People's Republic of China, June 27, 2011.

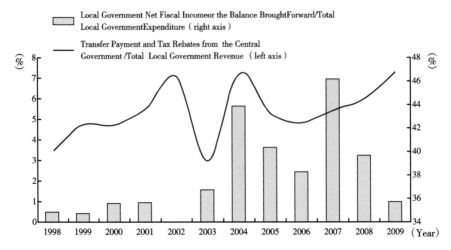

Fig. 7.3 Payment transfer, tax refund from the central government and financial surplus of local governments. *Source* Cao and Wang (2011)

housing, resulted in such debt expansion.[4] Furthermore, it was particularly note-worthy that, in recent years, especially from 2003 to 2009, the proportion of payment transfers and tax returns by the central government have both risen. Furthermore, the proportion of the total financial surplus of local governments after revenue and expenditure balanced out, or the balance brought forward, in the total local governmental expenditure, kept rising (see Fig. 7.3).[5] "Under the current financial system, public service and infrastructure construction by municipal governments actually lacked stable and sufficient funding. The tax system stipulated, meanwhile, that all taxes, such as revenue from land sales, taxes upon land, real-estate development and the construction industry as well as any other taxes related to land, were mainly at the disposal of municipal governments. Consequently, local governments had an incentive to occupy as much land as possible in the name of urbanization. The foundation and financing of local government financing *platforms, which* became increasingly popular in recent years, to a great extent, depend on the land ownership by local government and its scale.[6]

---

[4]Cao and Wang (2011).
[5]Cao and Wang (2011)
[6]China Development Research Foundation (2010, pp. 74–75).

7.1.4   Capability and Differentiation in Urban Renewal and Development

Among the coastal cities of China, some expanded while following a comparatively well-ordered pattern, but the expansion of others lacked control, thereby resulting in social-spatial polarization. The root of this was that some municipal governments had a much greater capacity for the renewal and development of urban areas. On one hand, this was often due to the different abilities of various local governments to obtain and manage their financing. On the other hand, this also resulted from the choice of spacing strategy that was adopted when cities were first planned. To be more specific, once an impoverished area had begun to form on a large scale, the cost of any subsequent renovation would be extremely high.[7] Under the existing political and economic mechanisms within cities, urban governments exerted considerable power over resource allocation and were responsible for the formulation and implementation of urban development strategies, programs, and policies. The competence and capacity of municipal governments to govern, therefore, was an indispensable factor as regards the success of urban development and transformation.

For municipal governments, urban development was not only a prerequisite for further economic growth, but also a factor that fit into their private interests. Regardless of whether their city was located in an economically or geographically advantageous location, local authorities all wanted to meet certain needs through the promotion of urban construction, thereby compelling them all to raise funds, often by borrowing money and selling land. To fulfill the primary task of urban development–urban growth, a wide-range of measures were used, including vigorously attracting investment, reducing the price of industrial land, providing preferential taxation policies and promoting the expansion of urban space, and intensified the continuous expansion of industrial land. Furthermore, while maintaining their regular expenditures, a system of land finance was formed by promoting the development of real estate. Debt borrowing through the financing platform of local governments was also adopted in order to make up the shortfall in funding from the construction of infrastructure and affordable housing. This in turn, further increased the land for urban construction and intensified the continuous expansion of residential land. Under the guidance of local governments, then, whether compelled to borrow money or raise funds by selling land, as regards both industrial and residential land, spatial change was characterized by rapid, large-scale expansion. However, in terms of social differentiation, the low price of industrial land and tax incentives restricted social expenditure and investment in public service, thereby intensifying the differentiation in social distribution. At the same time, although the development of residential land did increase the income potential of land, it also raised housing prices, which further entrenched the

---

[7]Rithmire (2010).

emerging social differences within urban areas and, ultimately, made it more difficult for local governments to positively transform urban landscapes. As one point of view, this process of urban expansion made possible to use such factors as the growth of green belt land and the degree of differentiation to indicate the overall ability of the government to enact urban transformation and the differentiated styles of urban expansion this would have resulted in.

The author's survey conducted in Huludao city, for example, analyzed, from the existing statistical data, the development of green land in the city, finding that it could be divided into three general stages. The first stage was characterized by steady growth from 1989 to 1995. Both the green coverage ratio and the designated public green areas slowly increased. The second phase was, however, characterized by rapid growth from 1996 to 2002. During that period, the green coverage ratio, the area of green coverage and the public green areas as well as the amount of green area per capita all increased rapidly. The third stage was characterized by a period of stagnation from 2003 to 2010. To be more specific, the growth of green areas stagnated while the scale and speed of urban expansion otherwise increased. This led to a considerable decline in the amount of green area per capita (see Fig. 7.4). In the end, the percentage of green coverage reduced sharply to around the level witnessed in 1999 (see Fig. 7.5). Moreover, the allocation of further green resources skewed towards the development of the green belt areas in closed neighborhoods of working units and public green spaces while the proportion of residential green spaces shrunk significantly. The abovementioned statistical classification of the built-up green land in Huludao city specifies that there were 1166.66 ha of green area constituting a green buffer or environmental protection area around the city. All in all, this accounted for 41% of the total green area, whereas the 29.50 ha of green area in scenic spots accounted for 1% of the total green area, the 595.46 ha of

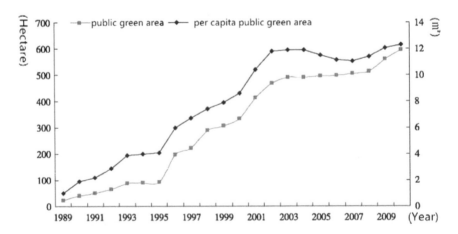

Fig. 7.4 The change of public green areas and the per capita public green area in Huludao city for 21 years (1898–2010). *Source* Statistics of indexes in previous years from landscaping management offices in Huludao city, 2010

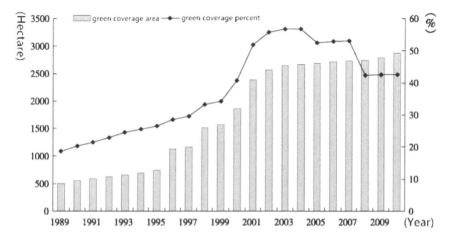

Fig. 7.5 The change of urban green coverage and the percentage of green coverage in Huludao city for 21 years (1989–2010). *Source* Statistics of indexes in previous years from landscaping management offices in Huludao city, 2010

public green area accounted for 21% of the total green area and the 240.92 ha of residential green area accounted for 8%. The 651.24 ha of the green belt area in working units, meanwhile, accounted for 23% whilst the 122.68 ha of green area as a buffer to production accounted for 4% and the 71.45 ha of tree crowns shadowing areas accounted for 2%. The development of green land in Huludao city was rather uneven. The proportion of public green land and the green land area in working units were both rather large, the latter as much as three times greater than residential green land (Fig. 7.6).

7.2 Understanding Urban Expansion: Growth, Differentiation and Sprawl

7.2.1 Urban Growth

To interpret China's urban growth, the first factor to confront is the extent to which it can be explained by existing theories of urbanization. John Friedman, for instance, argued that what happened in China could not be fitted neatly into the narrative of any grand theory. Whether that be the narrative of modernization or globalization, urbanization or national integration. That is because Chinese cities, in all instances, root deeply in her history and culture, and China is not just another country but a civilization deserves to be understood on its own terms.[8] Indeed, such

---

[8]Friedman (2005).

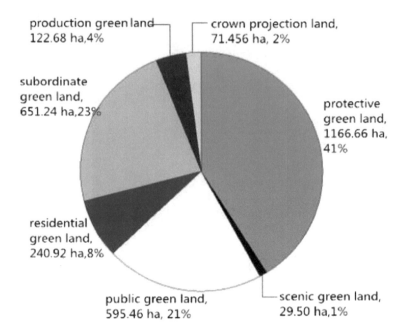

production green land
122.68 ha,4%

crown projection land,
71.456 ha, 2%

subordinate
green land,
651.24 ha,23%

protective
green land,
1166.66 ha,
41%

residential
green land,
240.92 ha,8%

public green land,
595.46 ha, 21%

scenic green land,
29.50 ha,1%

Fig. 7.6 The distribution of green land resource in Huludao city. *Source* Landscape management offices in Huludao city, 2010

a view constitutes a potentially informative challenge to existing theories that nods towards an historical perspective. To embrace such a dynamic and original approach may, after all, prove to be prudent in dealing with the case of urban growth in China. John Logan believed, however, that even if no single theory could explain everything, then, at the very least, a combination of different theories may, instead, provide a feasible alternative. In other words, a study of the urban development process in China was important not only in and for itself, but also insofar as it may give rise to original insights that are applicable to the rest of the world.[9] This chapter is to approach urban growth in China firstly from the point of view of those existing theories regarding the urbanization process in developing countries. Nevertheless, special attention should also be paid to the particularities of China's transformation from a planned economy to a market economy.

There are six main rival theories which explore urban growth in China. These include the Theory of Modernization, the Theory of Independent Development and the World System Theory, the Neo-Marxist Urban Theory, the Glurbanization Theory, the Market Transition Theory and the Theory of the

---

[9]Logan (2008).

Developmental State.[10] According to Logan's opinion, none of the six theories could effectively and solely explain urban growth and urbanization in China, but each theory may contribute partially to an overall explanation. The six theories, meanwhile, are basically divisible into two categories. The first emphasizes the importance of the external environment. This category abovementioned includes the former four theories, all of which are keen to stress that China's urbanization was a part of the worldwide capitalist industrial system. Consequently, it was involved in the process of industry transfer and the changing international order that accompanied globalization. The second category looked to internal logic in order to explain the distinctive urban development in China. This category included the latter two theories, both of which emphasized the dissimilarity of China, as compared with other countries, as well as the role of state and, finally, the so-called post-socialism market transition.

On the one hand, although national policy, regional economic growth and a variety of historical and geographical factors had a considerable impact, foreign investment played a role of utmost importance in the regional urbanization of China. In addition, a great deal of documental evidence indicates that after China became a member of the WTO, the volume of foreign trade and direct investment significantly promoted urban expansion in China. Many Chinese cities engaged in the competition over the global flow of capital, thereby becoming a part of the global network of cities. Beijing, for instance, intended to become a world city, therefore indicating that external forces were playing an increasingly important role in the process of urban development throughout China.

On the other hand, the role and power of the state in the urban development process cannot be underestimated. Local governments initially led the way as regards drawing in early investment and pioneering urban development. These early measures considerably promoted economic growth and brought about great changes to Chinese cities. There were, nevertheless, at the same time, a range of negative consequences. Cases of urban land use violation in China increased rapidly in recent years while the number and scale of a variety of development zones increased rapidly. In fact, the area of construction planned within development zones actually exceeded the total area of land allocated for construction nationwide. Under the urban development model led by local governments, land use violations and planning failures were commonplace.[11] Furthermore, large-scale urban development, led by local governments, exacerbated tensions in the relationship between the state and the society at large. For example, conflicts related to the demolition of urban housing and the relocation of residents were frequent and generally caused a degree of antagonism and instability in society. At the same time, land became the center of local politics.[12] Those cities which lacked long-term development

---

[10]Translated Logan's words in *Urban China in Transition* by the author besides the added new Marxist urban theory and the global urban theory. Whether the translation of "developmental state" is acceptable is open to discussion.

[11]Li and Yang (2006).

[12]Hsing (2010).

strategies, suitable planning, policy continuity, capital accumulation and improvements to the built-up environment witnessed rising land prices and increasing difficulty as regards the subsequent reconstruction and transformation of the built up environment.[13] For example, because of the high cost of rebuilding, urban villages were often selectively forgotten in the process of urban expansion.[14] Many studies subsequently focused on the economic drive and entrepreneurial behavior of local governments. Searches conducted around such key phrases as "tax distribution system", "land finance" and the "development model of GDPism", generate a lot of literature, which, to a certain extent, exhibits the behavior of local governments during the urban expansion process.

As far as the impacts of urban growth were concerned, the main factor was from an external perspective, capital and, from an internal perspective, power. As to the capital, David Harvey's capital accumulation and cycle theory laid the foundation of political economics for the built environment of cities. It specified that urban space, as part of the accumulation of capital, actually participated in the capital cycle.[15] Castells' collective consumption theory, meanwhile, regarded the city as the "conflict and focus between capital accumulation and society allocation, and between state control and the public autonomy."[16] Furthermore, the "Global city" theory, proposed by Saskia Sassen, pointed out that in the course of global capital flows, cities formed a global network and that the global flow of capital, therefore, had a tremendous impact on the reorganization and transition of urban space.[17] The abovementioned theories are, however, based on western democracy and the political economy of free capitalism. They cannot, therefore, be applied directly to studies about China. However, the basic logic of capital operation remains explanatory, at least to a certain degree.

Harvey Molotch's growth machine theory, on the other hand, asserted that there was a growth coalition which benefited from promoting growth in the perspective of the driving force of city growth. The formation of the growth coalition became the political and economic dynamics in urban growth.[18] On the other hand, the regime politics theory, proposed by Clarence N. Stone, suggested that governmental institutions were subject to public control to some extent. The economy, meanwhile, was primarily, although not exclusively, guided by privately controlled investment decisions. Therefore, the overall "regime" was an arrangement or division of urban power and capital.[19] Interestingly, the regime politics theory, compared to growth machine theory, paid more attention to the interaction between power and capital at a system level. It had a certain explanatory power, particularly,

---

[13]Rithmire (2010).

[14]Li (2009).

[15]Harvey (1985).

[16]Castells (2013). Quoted from Cai and He (2004).

[17]Sassen (2001).

[18]Molotch (1976).

[19]Stone (1993).

that is, concerning the analysis of the political and economic factors at play as part of urban growth in China at present. When the political and economical causes responsible for China's urban growth were analyzed, the relationship between power and capital, which formed during the transition from a planned economy to a market economy, should not be neglected. Before the reform and opening up, the state had enjoyed full systematic power to be yielded in response to any emerging crisis since modern times. This was referred to as a "totalistic state" by Tang Tsou.[20] In such a totalistic system, the first reforms that started in China involved delegating power to economic enterprises and to lower level governments. In this way, the systematic power of the totalistic state was gradually decentralized. During the transition to a market economy, capital and power were closely connected and played an increasingly important role in the allocation of resources, a process which was generalized by Victor Nee as "politicized capitalism". He pointed out that there were consistently close political affiliations between the government and corporations, whilst the decisions of the latter remained subject to modification by the former.[21]

To sum up, there were two primary factors affecting the growth of Chinese cities. One was the flow of capital whilst the other was the coalitions and regimes driving urban growth. Together these factors explained urban expansion in China to a large extent. Urban growth in China could be viewed from either the perspective of the state, the market and social relations or from the perspective of the relationship between power and capital. In both cases, however, the government, as either an important participant of an overall coalition towards growth or a leader of urban regime, not only possessed the dynamics for urban growth, but also could allocate resources on a larger scale so as to lead urban development and urban expansion, on a large scale and at a high speed.

7.2.2 The Differentiation of Social Space

It should be noted that social differentiation increased along with urban growth. Firstly, economic growth attracted a large number of immigrants to urban areas. But, under the household registration system, the new immigrants were not eligible for permanent residence. Many migrants were, therefore, essentially temporary laborers, perhaps best described as semi-urban residents.[22] Despite this, since the economic reform and opening up, rural-urban migration was, indeed, the main driving force of urban expansion in China.[23] As part of this, however, the household registration system and population movement, driven by large-scale

---

[20]Zou (1994).
[21]Nee and Opper (2007).
[22]Bai (2008).
[23]Park (2008).

urbanization, exacerbated the social-spatial differentiation within urban areas. Urbanization accelerated the birth of many new communities, most of which were roughly divisible into four types. These included new communities of commodity houses, cross management communities in rural-urban fringe zones, concentrated residential areas of immigrates and, finally, mixed communities.[24] The differentiation of social space in urban area thus grew increasingly polarized accordingly.[25]

Secondly, it should not be ignored that, in the process of urbanization, the combination of governmental power and market forces also contributed to the differentiation of social space.[26] The government had a great deal of power and was responsible for almost all of the public services. In other words, the government was, to a great extent, the only provider of public services.[27] Throughout the process of urban growth, and subsequent differentiation, power and capital not only played a key role in the allocation of basic resources, but were also profoundly reflected by the differentiation of social space that followed. Firstly, massive inequalities resulted from the differences of primary distribution received by those within public owned systems and those who were not. For example, in addition to higher wages, employees in state-owned enterprises had much more stable and comprehensive welfare. Having, a monopoly of industry and production enabled state-owned enterprises to maintain large profits. Furthermore, barriers within the labor market led to unequal opportunities, such that these excessive profits were only converted into personal incomes for those fortunate enough to be employed within appointed industries.[28] Secondly, the changes in employment structure brought about by industrial restructuring, technological progress and other changes led to a rising unemployment rate. Thirdly, the small and medium labor-intensive enterprises faced the pressure of rising production cost and falling profit margins, which, in the end, further exacerbate unemployment rates. Over time, these problems obviously led to and broadened social space differentiation. From the perspective of redistribution, local government policies to promote urban growth were often based on tax discounts and tax returns. As a result, the financial pressure on local governments was relatively heavy, such that expenditure on public services and social welfare tended to decline, at least at the local level. In addition, a larger proportion of local government expenditure was allocated to investment in infrastructure and construction, neither of which directly improved the serious imbalances as regards redistribution. "Excessive capital intervention" was also prominent.[29] That is to say, from the perspective of economic growth and social distribution, urban economic growth ultimately led to an increase to the volume of

---

[24]Li (2009).
[25]Gu (2002).
[26]Shen (2007).
[27]Saich (2008).
[28]Lu (2010, p. 8).
[29]Lu (2011).

urban construction, but, at the same time, something of a restraint upon social distribution. The growth of local government's social expenditure, meanwhile, remained relatively slow whilst unequal distribution continued to be clearly embodied in urban space differentiation and imbalanced spatial development. Some researches indicated that the reasons for the new urban poverty in China was mainly an employment structure dominated by low-income positions, limited access to public services and opportunities, high deposit rate and low levels of education, all of which, in turn, exacerbated the differentiation of social space.[30]

In short, in addition to the institutional factors encountered throughout the developmental process, the direct and significant impacts, upon patterns of urban social differentiation, of particular economic structures and social distributions clearly deserve recognition.

7.2.3 The Sprawl of Cities

As described above, urban growth and social differentiation are generally inter-twined together, thereby promoting the further differentiating expansion of urban spaces. Moreover, it is noteworthy that this type of differentiating expansion also gives rise to urban sprawl, that is, urban expansion characterized by a considerable degree of outward growth.

Theoretically, whether or not development was characterized by urban sprawl depended, to a large extent, on technology, lifestyle, land ownership, administrative governance and a range of more specific factors. For example, the use of cars, the expectation for the way of life of urban middle class, the scale and extent of the development of residential land and the availability of housing reforms and financial support. All of these factors, amongst others, provide a general and basic explanation to the urban sprawl in China. However, it deserved noticing that the sprawl of Chinese cities was also highly correlated to its growth pattern. To be more precise, urban sprawl in China generally accompanied a growth model driven by investment. Such investment often led to the large-scale expansion of industrial land, as well as land for infrastructure construction, but with a low overall efficiency of land use.[31] The large-scale expansion of residential land, despite high housing vacancy rates, was also commonplace.[32] What also worth noticing was urban sprawl had a profound influence on the degree of social differentiation in urban areas. The growth of urban fringe areas, as a direct result of urban sprawl, was accompanied by the emergence and expansion of so-called "urban villages" and poor residential areas. That is to say, rapid growth brought with it the intensification of social differentiation. In fact, the case of the United States was even clearer in

---

[30]Gu (2002).
[31]Jiang et al. (2007).
[32]Zhu and Cheng (2010), Tang (2010).

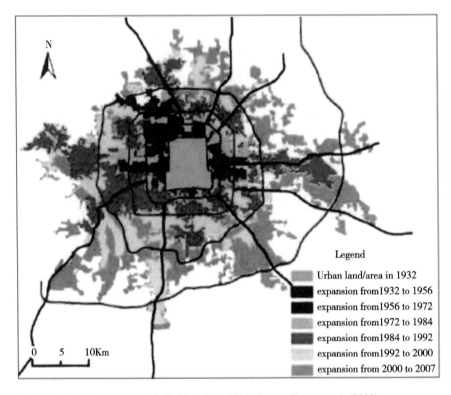

N

Legend

Urban land/area in 1932
expansion from 1932 to 1956
expansion from 1956 to 1972
expansion from 1972 to 1984
expansion from 1984 to 1992
expansion from 1992 to 2000
expansion from 2000 to 2007

0   5   10Km

Fig. 7.7 Map of urban sprawl in Beijing since 1932. *Source* Kuang et al. (2009)

this regard. According to a recent study of six American cities, social differentiation was more often found in sprawling areas.[33]

As for China, Beijing functions as an informative example. According to current geo-spatial indices (see Fig. 7.7), the rapid expansion of Beijing has occurred twice since 1932. To be more specific, Beijing underwent large-scale growth from 1984 to 1992 and from 2000 to 2007.[34] The urban sprawl pattern of Beijing could be characterized as disjointed and sporadic development of newly added non-agricultural construction land. Construction and development tended to proceed in a fragmented and irregular fashion, lacking both good planning and effective controls. This gave rise to noticeable trends of discontinuous development, characterized, primarily, by large, sprawling development belts and sudden, uncontrolled leap forwards in particular directions. In a word, the style of expansion was not reasonably or carefully planned. Such newly added non-farming construction land was also distinguished by low levels of building density and volume. Furthermore, the population density and the economic output were both lower than

---

[33]Lee (2011).

[34]Kuang et al. (2009).

those that resulted from the original use of the land, thereby indicating an unusually low efficiency of expansion. A high concentration of farmland and open space was taken during urban sprawl. This adversely affected the burden of traffic and cast significant negative impacts on agriculture, the environment, and urban life.[35] Professor Wu Liangyong analyzed these problems from the perspective of space and urban planning. The cause was found to be two-fold, including, on the one hand, a single centered urban spatial model and, on the other hand, the fact that the development of the outskirts of the city was far behind that of downtown areas.[36] The concentric circle theory could explain and describe the urbanization process and spatial socialization in Beijing, but in addition to some similarities, however, there were also big differences between contemporary Beijing and Chicago at that time. The city of Beijing was structured by circles. Outwards expansion or sprawling, meanwhile, was generally accompanied by the fragmentation of the governance process.[37] Visibly, then, the reasons for the urban sprawl of Beijing, besides general growth and technical factors, included uneven urban development, social differentiation, and the emergence and expansion of poor residential areas.

Overall, urban space reconstruction in China was, on the one hand, a process of the poor moving outward. Urban villages and poor communities where large-scale flow population shifted towards and gathered emerged in suburbanization. On the other hand, it was a process of the rich moving inward. It was characterized by the gentrification of the inner city, involving the inward movement of the rich and upper middle class towards the centre of the city. Indeed, studies focusing on this subject identified two main features of social differentiation inside Chinese cities: First, the non-permanent residents (nonregistered urban residents) lived on the fringe or outskirts of cities. Second, the differentiation of educational attainment was the premier of spatial differentiation, which was, in large part, due to the occupational stratification under the units system prevailed before the economic reform.[38] By comprehensive analysis, we believed that under the existing political and economic conditions of urban expansion in China, urban growth is to be characterized by social-spatial differentiation that, in turn, accelerates the process of further urban sprawl.

In short, throughout the process of urbanization, development alone had its limitations. The concept of scientific development, proposed at the third plenary session of the sixteenth conference of the Chinese Communist Party in 2003 aimed at preventing blind expansion and uneven development to avoid the negative effects of development. In terms of urban growth, the West had adopted the concept of "managing city" in the 1970s. In China, this type of managing city also boomed for a while. The management city refers to the introduction of market mechanisms to cities in such a way to treat cities as a development machine. The result of this style

---

[35]Jiang et al. (2007).

[36]Wu (2005).

[37]Jiang et al. (2007).

[38]White et al. (2008).

of management city was that urban development was over commercialized and land prices remained high. Although the government acquired a lot of land revenue in this way, people were unable to afford their housing because of high prices. In order to prevent the local municipal governments from making money through the sale of land and to control any potential financial crises, in the recent years, the central government issued a series of corrective policies. These were intended to strengthen the local government's basic function of serving the people and allowing them to enjoy a good and prosperous life. Urban expansion in China was a very complex process in terms of social differentiation. It involved compensation for landless peasants, the management of urban villages formed by disordered urban sprawl and the management of urban-rural fringe areas, as well as many other issues. On the one hand, it was related to the rapid population inflow directed into cities. On the other hand, it was related to the urban planning and housing systems. It was not the issue of space the core of urban development, but rather the issue of social development.

7.3   The Political and Economic Mechanisms of Urban Expansion

If the discussion was not to go any further beyond the analysis of the aforementioned urban growth, social differentiation, urban sprawl and their relationships, then it would avoid touching the essence of Chinese urban sprawl. Just as important is a perspective of urban mechanisms that emphasizes the interaction between government and enterprises. This can provide a theoretical base for the study of urban expansion through the relationship between power and capital.

Although the political and economic mechanisms formed by local government and enterprises in the urban development were of considerable flexibility, they demonstrated wide variations between different cities. In general, the market transformation brought about economic growth, changed the order of social organizations and reshaped the relationship between the state and the market. From the perspective of urban mechanisms, the urban political and economic mechanisms lurked behind the visible differences in China determine, to a large extent, the precise pattern of government-led urban expansion. On the face of it, government intervention gradually withdrew from the market, but, all the while, retained strong political connections throughout the state-owned section of economy, while remaining relatively weak as regards the private economy.[39] Indeed, it was necessary for a party, in a totalitarian society, to strengthen its control over the economy which had relatively weak political ties, in order to achieve leadership over economic development, no matter whether motivated by ideological reasons, legitimate concerns or actual socio-economic demands. For this reason, such

---

[39]Nee and Opper (2010).

political and economic mechanisms, behind urban development, became the basic premise of the government-led developmental model. To be more specific, government-led economic development manifested itself mainly through four particular aspects.

A. **Finance**

Daily corporate operations often relied, to a large extent, on state-dominated financial systems. Throughout much of the urban growth period, small and medium enterprises lacked well connected networks of social relationship with the power inside the financial systems, thereby rendering them hardly able to obtain vital loans. Obtaining such loans depended not only on the supporting policies of the state, but also on corresponding local policies, systematical circumstances, and social networks. At a local level, for instance, the government could easily interfere in the credit decisions of financial institutions. In fact, they could even directly appoint and recommend executive staff in banks according to their own interests and needs.[40]

B. **The Structure of Corporate Governance**

The "Company Law of the People's Republic of China" was adopted by the Chinese government in 1994 in the hope to govern corporate affairs and establish organizational standards on the basis of the western experiences and existing models.[41] These reforms were intended to replace the traditional state-socialist governance structure, primarily governed by the party and government, with the western governance structure. As in the West, the management staff themselves constituted the most significant force in the management of a company.[42] The change in corporate governance structure avoided the re-occurrence of enterprise performing social functions and relieved them from heavy labor costs such that they could focus on market factors. However, the transition of the working unit system was, in the end, not as thorough as expected. Despite some changes, the ideology, concepts, systems and organization of the working unit system remained in a large number of state-owned enterprises. Though the political status of employees underwent a fundamental change, the control and supervision over enterprises by the party and state was not significantly loosened. Most of the board members in state-owned enterprises owned a party membership and came from a political background. Even a number of foreign-funded enterprises and non-state-owned small and medium enterprises set up party groups and party committees one after another. Within a large number of public enterprises and private companies, whether under strong or weak state control, management personnel usually had good connection with the party and government. The difference lied in the fact that company executives from different areas had different links with the party and

---

[40]Park and Sehrt (2001).
[41]Guthrie (1999), Hayek (1945).
[42]Wong et al. (2004).

government. Those companies in coastal areas, for instance, generally had weaker links than their inland counterparts. Private companies, meanwhile, also possessed comparatively looser links than their public competitors.[43] In recent years, with the implementation and promotion of the "Go Global" strategy, the extent to which Chinese enterprises could seek overseas development was significantly enhanced. This, in turn, facilitated the modernization of overseas M&A (mergers and acquisitions) as well as the transformation of corporate governance. In Chinese companies that have undergone modern transformation of their corporate governance structure, senior managers, many of who having government connections of one kind or another, play a crucial role. This laid the institutional foundation for the government's decisive role in corporate governance and for a new operational model.

C. Resource Allocation

With the establishment of the market economy, the penetration of power into the economy differentiated in pace with the deepening of market segmentation and specialization. In general, control over the market was strengthened in two ways. Firstly, was to distinguish between factor markets, commodity markets and capital markets, before adopting different control strategies for these different sectors. Secondly, was to strengthen the social environment within which the market was embedded. The vast majority of large and medium state-owned enterprises belonged, primarily, to the resource factor markets. For example, among the producers of the bulk commodities in the raw material market, including the oil, metallurgical, chemical, steel and electricity industries, state-owned capital gave rise to a solid monopoly. Indeed, this state-owned sector controlled pricing, set industry standards and further enhanced its total monopoly policy, or at least, the formation of a clearly dominant industrial force.[44] According to the "Factor Endowment Theory" and the "Comparative Advantage Theory," the difference of the comparative advantages of the Chinese economy across different regions was enormous. Given such comparative advantages, not to mention the formation of industrial monopolies, the prevailing existing systems and of vested interests were continuously strengthened. This was, to a certain extent, not conducive to full market competition. The conditions favoring small and medium enterprises, for instance, would gradually deteriorate whilst comparative regional differences would increase. At the same time, it would further increase the thirst of capital for political power.

---

[43]Nee and Opper (2007).
[44]Lu (2010, p. 23).

D. The Operating Environments

The operation environment referred specifically to the external conditions of the existing political and social environment that affected the economic actions of enterprises. These include the conditions for handling a variety of administrative licenses that were necessary in starting a business. Likewise, businesses were required to go through a large number of checks and approvals whilst also being subject to supervision and evaluation throughout the actual operation process. Equally important was corporate social responsibility, and enterprises' ability to reach a variety of other mandatory targets set by the government. They were also required to negotiate specific conditions for attracting investment and ensure local public security as well as production safety. Such external conditions imposed restrictions on corporate development by subjecting them to stringent requirements and unreasonably high standards. If enterprises wanted to survive, they were forced to rely on the operation of existing power systems. Political roles, for instance bestowed many such restrictions on economic activities, resulting in rent-seeking and rent-setting behavior of the government.[45] To a certain extent, the government's responsibility was indirectly passed on to enterprises.

In short, through such political and economic mechanisms, municipal governments were capable to effectively and comprehensively promote urban development. In the early years of urban development, government-led urban expansion model contributed significantly to the improvement of urban landscapes and infrastructure. However, as development continued, the drawbacks of this model were gradually exposed. An especially serious problem was, as mentioned above, the fact that land urbanization proceeded faster than population urbanization, generating social tension and leading to urban sprawl. Of course, different cities have different conditions and situations as regards the four aspects mentioned above. Different policies were adopted and actions taken to address them. The political and economic relationship between government and enterprises in different cities also varied considerably. Some cities had a strong capacity for attracting capital while maintaining a certain degree of social expenditures and making the primary distribution and re-distribution fairer. Some cities, however, lacked this advantage. In particular, they went without both the ability to bring about a fairer society through regulation and to control the expansion of urban space whilst promoting urban development and urban growth, that, however, usually resulted in urban sprawl.

---

[45]Krueger (1974).

7.4 Conclusions

The difference between China's urban expansion model and the model in European countries consists in the leading role and pushing function of the Chinese government throughout promoting the process of urban expansion. Under the strong influence of such a government-led growth coalition or urban political and economic mechanisms, cities in China underwent an earth-shaking degree of change in a very short time. The amount of urban construction expanded dramatically whilst suburbanization, social spatial differentiation, urban sprawl gradually followed and were intertwined intricately. The government-led development model, on the one hand, witnessed large-scale and rapid urban expansion, rapid increases to the area of residential and industrial land and, finally, rapid increases to local governments' investment and credit for urban expansion. On the other hand, it brought about a range of social problems and the unbalanced distribution of social resources, thereby giving rise to inefficient urban sprawl and expansion. The origin of such a government-led urban expansion model was mainly due to a set of urban mechanisms formed gradually while promoting economic development and the market transformation. These mechanisms allowed the city government to guide urban economic growth primarily by leading finance, corporate governance, resource allocation and, finally, altering the overall operating environment. These measures made it possible for further large-scale and rapid urban growth. Taking everything into consideration, we should continue to adjust the current political and economic mechanisms to promote sustainable and inclusive urban development, change the current government-led development model and explore a new approach that is able to achieve a balance between the urban economy and social development.

References

Bai, N. (2008). Urbanization and rural labour migration (Chap. 3). In *Social change in China 1975–2008*. Social Sciences Academic Press.

Cai, H., & He, Y. (2004). *Collective consumption and social inequality—A perspective of contemporary capitalism urban society*. Academic Research (The first period).

Cao, M., & Wang, L. (2011, February). The structural risks of debt financing by local government and proposals for its reform. *China Bond*.

Castells, M. (2013). Theory and ideology in urban sociology. In C. Pickvance (Ed.), *Urban sociology: Critical essays* (p. 75). London, Tavistock.

China Development Research Foundation. (2010). *China development report 2010*. People's Publishing House.

Friedman, J. (2005). *China's urban transition*. Minneapolis: University of Minnesota Press.

Gu, C. (2002). Social polarization and segregation in Beijing. In *The New Chinese city: Globalization and market reform*. Blackwell.

Guthrie, D. (1999). *Dragon in a three—Piece suit*. Princeton: Princeton University Press.

Harvey, D. (1985). *Urbanization of capital: Studies in the history and theory of capitalist urbanization*. Johns Hopkins University Press.

Hayek, F. A. (1945). The use of knowledge in society. *American Economic Review, 35*, 519–530.

Hsing, Y.-t. (2010). Land and urban politics. In *The great transformation: Politics of land and property in China*. Oxford University Press.

Jiang, F., Liu, S., & Yuan, H. (2007). Measuring urban sprawl in Beijing with geo-spatial indices. *Journal of Geographical Sciences*.

Krueger, A. (1974). The political economy of the rent seeking society. *American Economic Review, 64*, 291–303.

Kuang, W., Shao, Q., Liu, J., & Sun, C. (2009). Analysis on features and mechanism of land use and spatial expansion in the main city of Beijing since 1932. *Geo-information Science*, 4.

Lee, S. (2011). Metropolitan growth patterns and socio-economic disparity in six US metropolitan areas 1970–2000. *International Journal of Urban and Regional Research, 35*(5), 988–1011.

Li, Q. (2009). *Study on major social issues and solutions in Chinese urbanization process*. Economic Science Press.

Li, Q., & Yang, K. (2006). *Urban sprawl*. China Machine Press.

Logan, J. (2008). *Urban China in transition*. Blackwell.

Lu, M. (2010). Analysis on the causation of high income in monopoly industries. *People's Tribune*.

Lu, M. (2011, November). Guard the perverted hand. *Finance, 305*.

Molotch, H. (1976). The city as a growth machine: Towards a political economy of place. *American Journal of Sociology, 82*, 309–332.

Nee, V., & Opper, S. (2007). On politicized capitalism. In V. Nee & R. Swedberg (Eds.), *On capitalism* (pp. 93–127). Stanford: Stanford University Press.

Nee, V., & Opper, S. (2010). Political capital in a market economy. *Social Forces*.

Park, A. (2008). Rural urban inequality in China (Chap. 2). In S. Yusuf & T. Saich (Eds.), *China urbanizes: Consequence, strategies, and policies*. Washington DC: World Bank.

Park, A., & Sehrt, K. (2001). Tests of financial intermediation and banking reform in China. *Journal of Comparative Economics, 29*, 608–644.

Rithmire, M. E. (2010). *Closed neighbourhoods in open cities: The politics of socio-spatial change in urban China*. Paper for the Annual Meeting of the American Political Science Association. Washington DC: APSA.

Saich, T. (2008). The changing role of urban government (Chap. 8). In S. Yusuf & T. Saich (Eds.), *China urbanizes: Consequence, strategies, and policies*. Washington DC: World Bank.

Sassen, S. (2001). *The global city: New York, London, Tokyo*. Princeton University Press.

Shen, Y. (2007). *Market, classes and society: Critical issues on sociology of transformation*. Social Sciences Academic Press.

Stone, C. (1993). Urban regimes and the capacity to govern: A political economy approach. *Journal of Urban Affairs, 15*(1), 1–28.

Tang, X. (2010). *China's housing vacancy is "Systemic Vacancy"* (21st Century Economic Report), August 18, 2010.

White, M. J., Wu, F., & Chen, Y. P. V. (2008). Urbanization, institutional change, and sociospatial inequality in China, 1990–2001. In J. Blackwell (Ed.), *Urban China in transition*.

Wong, S. M. L., Opper, S., & Hu, R. (2004). Shareholding structure, depoliticization and enterprise performance: Lessons from China's listed companies. *Economics of Translation, 12*, 29–66.

Wu, L. (2005). The edge of city and regional planning—The case of Beijing. *Architectural Journal*, 6.

Zhu, X., & Cheng, D. (2010). The political economics of vacant housing. *Southern Weekend*, November 3, 2010.

Zou, D. (1994). *Chinese politics in twentieth century*. Oxford University Press.

Chapter 8
The Old Town Renewal Model in China

In the later 1980s, China entered a period of rapid urbanization, the main feature of which was the massive movement of rural laborers into urban areas and their subsequent engagement in industries other than agriculture. Coincided with this process, on the one hand, a large amount of land, formerly used for agricultural purposes, was adapted for urban construction purposes. On the other hand, land within the existing boundaries of city areas was regenerated and utilized in order to meet the needs of substantial new urban development. For the most part, this land (old town area), located within the original urban boundaries, occupied what became the center of China's new developing cities. The economic value of these plots was, as a result of their prominent locations, substantial. Such values functioned as a significant incentive for local governments to comprehensively redevelop old town areas. The large-scale residential and commercial transformations to these areas that resulted did, to an extent, solve some of the challenges presented by the rural population inflow. Nevertheless, as a result of their blind pursuit of economic efficiency and modernization, some local authorities championed the large-scale demolition of old town areas. Consequently, many of the traditional, often unique, cultural characteristics of Chinese cities were lost. Such features were instead replaced by uniform patterns and styles of construction, thereby giving rise to innumerable cities that were fundamentally similar in layout and appearance. At the same time, this large-scale transformation, conducted, as it was, within a short time, caused a range of social problems.

© Social Sciences Academic Press 2020
Q. Li, *China's Development under a Differential Urbanization Model*,
Research Series on the Chinese Dream and China's Development Path,
https://doi.org/10.1007/978-981-13-9451-5_8

8.1   Concept and the Current Condition of the Development

8.1.1   Concepts

The phrase "old town" present throughout this chapter is being used mainly to refer to the area of the original city that existed before the onset of rapid urbanization in the 1990s. This includes the areas that were newly built in order to meet the needs of developing industry and housing from 1949 to 1990 as well as the historical areas of the city that predated 1949. Beijing's first 25 historical conservation sites, established in 1990, are typical of this category. Likewise, "old town renewal", another key word throughout this chapter, refers to the redevelopment of "old town areas" more precisely, historical areas of cities, a process more commonly referred to in the 1990s in China, as the "reform of the old town".[1]

The transformation of the oldest parts of cities has been an ongoing process. Since the founding of the People's Republic of China, the vast majority of Chinese cities was gradually developed with a particular emphasis in and around the old town area (for example, the transformation of Beijing since 1949). Most cities, for instance, gradually expanded outwardly from the old town area such that these areas were ultimately surrounded by more recent developments. Since China's reform and opening-up urban centers had, on the one hand, generally been equipped with modern and convenient accommodation, health, education, and transportation facilities. The land values of these areas subsequently soared, thereby creating an incentive for the continued investment of real estate developers. On the other hand, people living within the old town area were, to a certain degree, willing to pursue modernization and improve their overall living conditions. Such factors put great pressure on the need to renew and develop old town areas throughout China's rapid urbanization process since the 1990s.

In addition, due to the fact that all urban land in China was publicly owned, old town renewal was inevitably left to the government to lead and manage. At all stages the Government played a central role regarding the policy, planning as well as the demolition of and compensation for renewal. Such urban renewal, led, as it was by the government, tended to be on a large scale and at a rapid rate. For one thing, a large amount of dangerous and substandard housing needed to be renovated in a very short time such that the living conditions of residents could be improved. For another, it was an inevitable result of the "land finance" model of the local governments in China. That is to say, revenue from urban land development was among the main sources of income for local governments. When market-driven real estate developers involved themselves in the old town renewal process, the intricate and subtly changing relationship between local governments and real estate developers led to a developmental method that was both government-led and

---

[1]"Reform of the old city" has been widely used in 1990s, and it is replaced by the term "urban renewal".

market operated. Crucially, urban construction, as a particularly shining growth point of local economies, became one of the most important indicators of a local government's limited-term performance. Taking all of these factors into consideration, the "transformation" of old town areas was inevitably to be characterized by its large-scale and rapid speed, pushing over and "making" fake street.[2]

By the end of 2011, the State Council had announced 118 national-level cities of historical and cultural importance. These included super cities as well as a range of other large and medium-sized cities like Beijing, Tianjin, Shanghai, Guangzhou, Chongqing, Nanjing, Xi'an etc., which, overall, accounted for 40% of the prefecture-level cities in China. On the one hand, these cities were afforded a degree of national protection. On the other hand, throughout the process of China's urbanization, the industrial development of these cities, as well as their ability to absorb an incoming population flow, played a crucial role in promoting a highly differential strategy of urbanization.

8.2 The Current Condition of the "Old Town" Area

8.2.1 The Aging of Buildings in the Old Town Area

Historical buildings and streets comprised a great deal of old town centers throughout the vast majority of cities in China. Whilst most of these buildings were prized for their age, a shortage of maintenance and funding meant that most of them were damaged, decayed and suffering from leaking roofs. According to a 2003 survey of the Shichahai area in Beijing, conducted by the Departments of Sociology and Architecture of Tsinghua University (hereinafter referred to as the "2003 Survey"), grade four and five[3] housing, constructed to relatively poor standards, accounted for approximately 10% of the total buildings. The whole areas were, however, primarily dominated by grade three houses, which accounted for approximately 46% of the total. The substandard quality of many of these buildings necessitated the renovations in old town areas.

8.2.2 High Population Density and Poor Living Conditions

Due to various historical reasons, up to dozens of families often lived in one old building (a quadrangle or siheyuan). Needless to say, this meant that the density of the population in these areas was rather high. Since most of the old buildings in the

---

[2]Study on *Major Social Issues and Solutions in Chinese Urbanization Process*. Economic Science Press, 2009, p. 47.

[3]Housing in China are divided into six grades according to their structures.

old town of Beijing were quadrangles, there, the popularity of unauthorized residential buildings gave rise to overcrowded tenement courtyards. Such a high population density meant that old city areas were often overcrowded and subject to poor living environments.

8.2.3   Serious Problems with Infrastructure

As well as a high population density and poor living conditions, the old areas of cities also suffered from underdeveloped infrastructure. The reconstruction of basic services, such as gas and electricity supply, was limited primarily due to substandard roads and insufficient funding. Likewise, sewage management, fire protection, and waste disposal were also among other severely neglected issues.

8.2.4   Empty Nesters and Population Aging

Given the poor infrastructure, high population densities and unsatisfactory factors, the residents of old town areas were, unsurprisingly, often from low-income, as well as, aging, groups of the population. According to the abovementioned 2003 survey, among the 774 people surveyed in the Shichahai area, the average age of residents was 41.96 years old. Furthermore, the proportion of young people (aged 18–35) was significantly lower than any other age group. Part of the reason for this is that crowded and dilapidated living conditions often forced young people into leaving these areas as soon as they reached working age and requirements. Similarly, in the Bai Mixiejie and Yandaixiejie areas, the proportion of the population aged 65 years or above was 20 and 16% respectively, that is to say, significantly higher than the average age throughout Beijing.[4] Aging is manifest there.

At the same time, as demonstrated by the 2003 survey, as well as practically any survey of most other areas throughout China, those living in the old town were generally poorly educated. To some extent, this exacerbated the marginalization of these people whilst also making the problem of addressing their interests and social security significantly harder.

---

[4]Study on *Major Social Issues and Solutions in Chinese Urbanization Process*. Economic Science Press, 2009, pp. 49–51.

8.2.5   Housing Property Rights

Citizen's rights to property, especially in regards to residential housing also attracted much attention throughout the renewal of some cities. After the founding of the People's Republic of China, residential properties within cities was once nationalized. Meanwhile, the Urban Housing Management Bureau, as well as other public agencies, was established in order to be responsible for the routine maintenance and distribution of the public (nationalized) housing. Although the Housing Management Bureau historically played a positive role, limited funding and ambiguous property rights led to some serious difficulties, especially since the period of reform and opening up, that is, following the introduction of market-economy. In Beijing, for instance, residential properties within the old town area were divisible into four categories. Firstly, there was privately owned houses, houses owned by working units, rented privately-owned-houses and, finally, directly managed public houses.[5]

8.3   The Previous Approaches to Old Town Renewal

8.3.1   The Renovation of Dilapidated Houses

A dilapidated houses renovation scheme was initially promoted by the government in order to improve the quality of old houses, as well as the living conditions of residents, in old town areas. Prior to the 1990s, such government-driven renovation projects did make some improvements to the dilapidated houses, and did benefit residents there. Nevertheless, owing to the huge funds required for widespread renovation, not to mention the limited financial resource of local governments, as well as the fact that the widespread construction of residential housing, across the country, had just commenced, such schemes did not go as far as intended.

8.3.2   The Impetus of Real Estate

Throughout and since the 1990s, however, as real estate development in China accelerated substantially, renovation efforts gradually extended to include dilapidated and old houses within old town areas. Nevertheless, the aim of the scheme also shifted from a focus on improving the living conditions of residents to a focus on enhancing the economic value of real estate. Those real estate developers, who were pursuing economic interests and profits, gradually cornered the entire old town renewal industry, which, in turn, became a major profitable point for said

---

[5]The public houses built by local or municipal governments.

developers. The involvement of real estate enterprises dramatically increased the scale and speed of the urban renewal process. At the same time, old town renewal was conducted simply by demolishing old buildings and constructing new and high ones. The *People's Daily*, for instance, reported, on September 23, 2005, that 161 million m^2 of housing was dismantled throughout urban areas in 2003 alone. This represented an increase of 34.2% on a year-on-year basis and, even more significantly, this meant it took 41.3% of the total area utilized for the construction of new commodity housing (around 390 million m^2). China, then, was the world's largest construction site, building 1600–2000 million m^2, that is more than the annual total built-up areas in developed countries, of housing annually.[6]

Old town renewal in this fashion, conducted by real estate enterprises, unsurprisingly, turned out to be a fully market-driven process by which land and property in old town areas was regarded purely as a market commodity to be utilized for financial profit. This process did still, to some extent, improve the infrastructure and living conditions of old town areas and even create some commercial areas with unique styles, often matching the old towns original style, such as Xintiandi in Shanghai and Qianmen in Beijing. The main purpose of this urban renewal remained, however, the pursuit of private financial interests. As a result, it inevitably led to various conflicts of interest, not least the blind destruction of uniquely styled old town areas and numerous conflicts regarding the relocation of existing residents.

8.3.3 Old Town Renewal Promoted by Important Social Events

A number of large-scale old town renewal projects occurred due to important events, both domestically and internationally. Such projects include the construction of new roads in old town area, the improvement of the natural environment and the conservation of cultural relics and heritage sites. Large-scale renovations of old town areas sort did, to an extent, change such areas for the better, thereby improving the living environment and quality of life for local residents. The 2008 Beijing Olympic Games and 2010 Shanghai World Expo typified this process. In preparation of the Olympic Games, for instance, in 2003, Beijing benefited from a project intended to protect cultural relics. In order to secure such a humanistic legacy of the Olympic Games, local authorities, over five consecutive years, invested 600 million yuan in cultural and environmental preservation and conversation projects. Likewise, in preparation of the World Expo, Shanghai launched a series of targeted renovation projects. These include the "toilet renovation project"

---

[6]"Pain and Pity: Large-scaled Reconstruction of Old City". *People's Daily*, September 23, 2005.

in the old lanes of the Luwan district, the "kitchen renovation project" throughout the Jinan District, finally, the "lane renovation project" throughout the Xuhui and Hongkou Districts.

8.4 Problems with the Process of Old Town Renewal

8.4.1 The Loss of Unique Features and Distinctive Cultures of Cities

The so-called "unique features of cities" has become something of a buzzword phrase, frequently used in the mass-media throughout recent years. As the term suggests, it mainly refers to the unique cultural and architectural features of individual cities that have formed and evolved throughout certain periods of history. It is these features that are often used in distinguishing one city from another. They are interpreted as reflecting both the development of each city's unique civilization and representing each city's cultural heritage. As one commentator noted that, "Every city had its own particular personality, which was so strong and full of individualized character".[7]

As mentioned before, however, since the 1990s, the older areas of some cities underwent tremendous and rapid changes. A large number of buildings, including many houses and historic sites, built using local and traditional styles, disappeared rapidly. The original layout of the city, meanwhile, was generally replaced by one better suited for modern transportation. As this process continued to accelerate, commercial forces took an even stronger hold, such that the renewal of old town areas evolved into full-scale commercial real estate development. Consequently, a great range of irreplaceable cultural relics, of great value, were damaged throughout old town areas. Throughout this period, traditional buildings lining the streets of many cities were generally earmarked for demolition, in particular, by the presence of a distinctive white circle painted upon them. Demolition, it seemed, was a first and a necessary step of urban construction and renewal throughout China. Indeed, this phenomenon was commonplace, including such examples as the renovation of Yujia Lane in the Moon Lake district of Ningbo City, the renovation of Dajipian area in the Xuannan district of Beijing, the renovation of Financial Street in Beijing, the renovation of Xianyukou area in Beijing and, finally, the renovation of the East Yuhe district on Dianmen Street in Beijing. As expected, however, the blind pursuit of economic interests inflicted catastrophic damage upon the distinctive cultural features of those areas. Insofar as something like the so-called western model of urbanization was relentlessly followed, whilst little or no attention was afforded to locating, preserving or excavating cultural and historical, a great number of heritage sites were reduced to nondescript construction sites. In the end, hundreds of

---

[7]Mumford (2005).

renowned historical and cultural cities effectively became identical. In response to the disappearance of traditional lanes and courtyards in Beijing, the French magazine *Le Figaro* reported: "Now it seems that nothing can stop the culture suicide, Beijing is changing its own great culture into mediocrity."[8]

The loss of the unique feature of culturally rich cities was a problem confined not only to the southeast of China. This problem also plagued the urbanization process throughout some inland cities and even some areas specific to particular ethnic groups. For example, the urban construction of Lhasa city in recent years witnessed an unprecedented period of rapid development, such that size of the main city areas doubled twice in just a few years. Unfortunately, the traditional cultural features of the city were generally neglected in the process. Its new architectural layout simply copied the style that had been followed by any number of other inland cities. The problem reached a point at which the number of high-rise buildings degraded the culturally significant traditional landscape around the Potala Palace in Lhasa city. This issue even aroused the attention of UNESCO, that is, insofar as the World Heritage Convention expressed concerns over the rapid urban construction of the Lhasa area, even asking the local government to submit periodic inspection reports from 2004 onwards. As urbanization accelerated and spread outwards, the construction process in small towns and villages also developed in the same way. Developing a new countryside meant, in practice, building a great number of new villages, thereby resulting in the same widespread demolition and reconstruction that had been witnessed in old town areas.

8.4.2 Building Brands Through Imitation Classics and Fake Antiques

On the one hand, massive urban demolitions and construction was rapidly destroying the traditional landscape of cities. On the other hand, as more people became critical of this development, and a number of cultural and creative industries continues to grow, more and more provisions for traditional architecture and other pertinent cultural features were included by local authorities within their urban development strategies and became a criterion job performance evaluation of local authorities. Some city planners were, for instance, determined to "construct" special cultural features while in office, while others were preoccupied with shaping an urban cultural landscape more generally. For the most part, however, some of them neglected the interests of the people, some neglected the national traditions and some, the independent innovation, that is, in all but the most superficial and similar attempts to "construct and "mold" cultural features.

In fact, the tasks of ensuring the preservation and enhancement of the unique culture of urban areas and ensuring the rapid physical expansion of urban areas

---

[8]Shan (2005).

were worlds apart. Physical expansion was concrete, simply required continuous construction efforts which could be implemented by institutions at all levels as they issued the relevant tasks and directives. The enhancement of urban cultural could not, however, follow such a simple path. The unique cultures of urban areas had, after all, accumulated as part of piecemeal process. The unique features were a result of long-term protection and careful nurturing. Therefore, it was effectively impossible to artificially manufacture such culture variety in just a few years. The attempt to "make" elegant cultural tastes and rich cultural heritages, as part of a unique overall cultural landscape, was bound to fail. Indeed, such an attempt seemed oblivious to the fact that such heritage was a shared public good, cultivated over a long historical period and nurtured by successive generations.

As evidence of prior urban development, traditional architecture and historic blocks and streets reflected the then prevailing economic, scientific and cultural characteristics of the city. As a reflection of history, these features cannot be faked. Despite their importance, however, the demolition of genuine heritage sites, generally followed by the manufacture of fake replacements was commonplace. A large number of streets which imitated the style of the Ming, Qing and Han Dynasties, for instance, emerged. Numerous historic blocks and buildings, each with unique characteristics, meanwhile, were gradually replaced by fake antiques. As economic concerns and the records of governance were generally prioritized by policy makers, genuine historical building were, on occasion, intentionally replaced with fake reconstructions, that is insofar as the maintenance of traditional architecture was time and labor intensive. The value of the original historic architectures was thus, from their point of view at least, undermined. As a result, news concerning successive ribbon-cutting events of historic replicas was forthcoming on almost a daily basis. On the other hand, a great deal of authentic historical architectures was being bulldozed on a daily basis. The local authorities in some other cities did save the original architecture, but then relocated local residents such that these sites could be transformed into tourist facilities. Whilst the physical sites remained, the unique cultural practices that had permeated almost every aspect of daily life was now altogether absent. On the contrary such practices were replaced by mere performances that imitated ancient activities for commercial reasons. This was, in fact, however, simply another sort of counterfeiting—one which disclosed a both cultural ignorance and regression. Both the physical and cultural replicas constructed as a result of this blind process were neither conductive to the protection of nor conducive to further urbanization.

8.4.3 The Social Problems Caused by Old Town Renewal

As mentioned above, in the early 1990s, the residents of old town areas were encouraged to move back to these areas after they had been redeveloped. During the process of renewal, it was arranged, by the relevant authorities, that these residents would live in temporary lodgings or receive an appropriate compensatory payment by the government or a real estate developer. As the costs of land continued to rise, however, former residents were generally offered monetary compensation, on a one off basis, rather than retaining the option to move back after the renewal process was completed. The residents of old city areas were generally offered a sum determined by an evaluation, conducted by either the government or real-estate developers, of the value of their old properties. In some cases, this approach completely replaced previous approaches that had orientated around providing former residents with new housing or preferential policies for them to move back. As a result, local residents were generally deprived from sharing in the benefits generated by the increase in land values that followed throughout the following few years.

Meanwhile, the financial compensation provided was rarely sufficient for the residents to purchase another house in the same area. On the contrary, most former residents could only afford cheap housing in suburban areas or, if they elected to remain in the area, properties that suffered from considerably worse conditions. Both such outcomes had unfavorable consequences for former residents. The former alternative meant that the closely tied communities to which the residents of old city areas had, over successive generations, become accustomed to were severely disrupted. Gradually these residents were forced away from, or forced to commute great distances to, the jobs, schools and other social and commercial establishments that had comprised their lifelong social networks. The latter alternative, on the other hand, meant that the former residents of old city areas did not actually benefit the renewals. Instead of improving the quality of their life, their living conditions stayed the same or even worsened. In one instance, jokes circulated that if you wanted to hear a genuine Beijing dialect then you ought to go to the suburbs of Beijing.

In addition, real-estate developers and local governments often embarked on short-term, not to mention opaque and behind-the-scenes, strategies as regards old town renewal. The compensation schemes, for instance, often resulted in unfair distributions as those who opted to move early received less compensation, whereas those who opted to move later received more. Issues such as this complicated the old town renewal process. On the one hand, it caused homeowners to delay relocating because they believed that the compensation procedure was still undecided and unreliable. On the other hand, homeowners delayed relocating because they also believed that if they left earlier, then they would receive less compensation compared to those who relocated later. The pursuit of short-term economic interests plagued the old town renewal process such that this phenomenon was a common occurrence across the country.

Such cases in the process of old town renewal usually stored up unstable factors for future social harmony and stability. According to a survey made by "Research Center for Independent Observation and Countermeasure of Social Contradictions and Problems" established under the Office of Calls and Letters of Beijing and other organizations, the contradiction of demolition had become one of the major problems at present development stage in China. It was far more pressing both in depth and breadth. The malignant incidents or even mass incidents due to demolition happened now and then.[9]

8.5   Countermeasures and Suggestions for Improvements to the Old Town Renewal Model

In the process of rapid urbanization, the blind pursuit of economic interests and ignorance about cultural features resulted in the mass demolition of old areas which, in turn, produced a range of substantial social problems. A more suitable approach would have been to treat the old town renewal as a complex, multifaceted systematic process. A more suitable approach would have been to have focused on comprehensively developing the city and its surrounding regions simultaneously whilst affording utmost importance to the interests of the inhabitants (both occupants and owners alike). Likewise, the development of local communities, improvements to infrastructure, the conservation of cultural heritage and the adequate planning and management of urban areas should all have been prioritized in equal measure. Even the prospects for future real-estate development (e.g. on brown-field sites) and the experience of tourists should have been considered. Only when attention was paid to all of these factors, amongst others, could the multifaceted old town renewal process unfold as an element of overall urbanization.

8.5.1   A Focus on People's Livelihoods and the Adoption of Multifaceted Programs

8.5.1.1   Concern About Disadvantaged Groups

As mentioned earlier in this chapter, residents living in the old town areas, on the one hand, significantly older, on average, than the residents of other areas and, on the other hand, had relatively low levels of overall education. The violent transformation of the old town area, that accompanied the process of rapid urbanization, meanwhile, abruptly unseated their traditional way of life. Due to their disadvantage of age and educational level, unsurprisingly, though, these residents struggled to adapt to such a rapid pace of change and, in time, clearly became something of a disadvantaged group. Therefore, the process, as a whole, would have been preferable if, in fact, more attention was paid to the disadvantaged groups, perhaps, for instance, through affirmative action policies directed at retraining, re-employment and suitable pensions for their would-be members.

---

[9]*Beijing Daily*, 2011, 6.

8.5.1.2   Respecting the Will of Residents and Launching Multi-facet Solutions to Tackle Problems

Many of the residents of old town areas, for instance, actually had different preferences as regards provisions for compensation and relocation such that it was hard to reach generally accepted agreements. A number of different policies were, therefore, required to appease these preferences. Different residents, for example, had, depending on their own unique circumstances, different demands in terms of whether and how much financial compensation was demanded and whether they expected to move back to the area as well as where they desired to be relocated, if at all. Therefore, thorough investigations and surveys were required in order to avoid a "one size fits all" approach to compensating former residents. An approach more closely tailored to their needs may well have reduced the difficulty relocating residents prior to the old town renewal process.

8.5.1.3   Reasonable Compensation and Including Residents in the Future Benefits of Increasing Land Values

Initially, compensation schemes generally took the form of one-off initiatives, such as monetary compensation, guarantees related to moving back, or relocated to designated housing areas or housing evaluation. Such schemes successfully contributed to accelerating the old town renewal policy making and facilitating a quick demolition. Nevertheless, compensation compromised of a one-off payment, in particular, was often problematic. Many of the recipients, for example, lacked financial know how and, subsequently, engaged in blind, irrational and short-term consumption practices, which in turn, led to new social problems. Additionally, this one-off payment deprived the residents of their share of the benefits that accumulated as the land on which their former properties were situated steadily increased in value. Old town areas, located, as they are, in a central position, would after all enjoy a range of increasing economic and geographical advantages as part of the urbanization model as a whole. A great deal of the land appreciation that followed the resident's departure was due to government investment in infrastructure and other commercial operations, generally conducted by real-estate developers. Nevertheless, it goes without saying that the value of land in the centermost areas of major cities is intrinsically high and objectively likely to rise. The one-off compensation, received by residents, did nothing to reflect the inevitable process of appreciation that would unfold around their former properties. As such, a fair and equitable policy, which balanced one-off payment and incorporating long-term value changes, would have been a considerable step forward.

8.5.2   The Protection of Historic Buildings in Old Town Areas

8.5.2.1   Organic Renewal

This approach focused mainly on the renovation of those old town areas that contained historic sites, generally of interest from the point of view of heritage, culture and traditional architectural styles. In the renewal process of such historic areas of old towns, the infrastructural development, as well as the overall condition improvement should, based on the relevant laws and regulations, follow a model of organic renewal, involving small-scale, gradual and highly diversified techniques.[10]

The theory of organic renewal, reflecting his study on the planning of the Shechahai area in Beijing, was proposed by professor Wu Liangyong in 1980. According to this theory, residential buildings should be afforded special treatment. Firstly, buildings that have historic value should be, assuming they are not in an excessive state of disrepair, largely kept in their current state. Likewise, repairs should be cautiously made to those buildings that are at least partially well preserved whilst outright renovations should be made to dilapidated buildings. The precise deployment of the abovementioned renewals should be based on the results of investigations and tailored planning, that is, rather than any generic "one size fits all" policy. Secondly, roads within residential area should be reconstructed such that they continued to follow the original layout of prior alleyways and block patterns.[11]

As Shan Jixiang, the then director of the state Bureau of Cultural Relics, commented, "the organic renewal concept enriched existing theories relating to urban conservation and renewal within historically areas. The core of the theory advocated for a process of urban renewal in historic areas that followed the law pertaining to development inherent to historic areas, conformed to the original patterns of historic areas and progressed only at a gradual rate so as to achieve an organic order. This is a scientific approach presenting an attractive alternative to the overall protection of historic sites and the construction of better living environments."[12]

Later on, this theory of organic renewal was repeatedly practiced in the process of protecting famous historical and cultural sites in cities such as Beijing, Suzhou, Nanjing and Jinan. After Mr. Wu Liangyong was awarded the "National Science and Technology Award" in 2012, his organic renewal method received a great deal of acclaim and, consequently, the opportunity to paint a portrait on a much larger canvas and was recognized at a much deeper level.

---

[10]Fang (2000).

[11]Fang (2000).

[12]Shan (2006).

8.5.2.2 Renewal Based on Overall Protection

The greatest value of the old town area, where a large number of historic buildings and neighborhoods are located, was its integrity. Whilst some courtyards and building may have been more valuable than others, the wholeness and integrity of entire blocks was, by far, more important. It was this wholeness and integrity which better reflected the overall traditional styles of urban living environments. With this in mind, focusing on the sole protection of individual isolated buildings, whilst separating them from their historical context, as, indeed, did occur as a consequence of the old town renewal process in some cities, became wholly unsatisfactory.

As such, it was a factor of utmost importance, for the future of urban development, to achieve a degree of mutual coordination between efforts related to the protection and development. Rapid urbanization was, indeed, the overall trend of development in China at the time. Nevertheless, it remained necessary to preserve unique historical and cultural traditions, even if doing so complicated the process of urbanization, such that they may be inherited by future generations. Therefore, the development of urban areas with sites of cultural or historic importance should not focus on building fake old building. Instead, authentically designed buildings should be erected that are in sync with local cultural practices, architectural styles and way of life.

8.5.3 The Modifications Carried Out to Buildings Without Heritage Values in Old Town Areas

As for buildings built after the founding of the People's Republic of China in 1949, most have little heritage value and are generally poorly constructed. These should simply be renovated in a way that would maintain the overall style and framework of the city, and the residential housing capacity of these areas.

During this process of updating and reconstruction, special attention should be paid to the principles of social justice. Widespread increase of housing capacity and the widespread replacement of traditional land usage undoubtedly brought about huge economic benefits. As such, how to balance the interests of all involved parties whilst also ensuring a reasonable distribution of profits to the government, property developers and local residents called for special concern. Similarly, the residents' right to know about and participation in this process, and the protection of the interests of disadvantaged groups also reflected the principles of social justice.

8.6 Other Aspects

Some cities had a rich cultural heritage, including a large range of sites of historical interest. The model of developing these areas, as well as the surrounding regions, which was driven primarily by the need to protect such sites, gave rise to a new approach to urban renewal.

For example, in the reorganization and development of the Daming Palace ruins, in Xi'an city, the demolition of 3.5 million m^2 of shanty town, on the one hand, constituted good preparation for the protection, exhibition and upgrading of the ruins. It also enhanced the image of the city by improving the environment and the construction of infrastructure. On the other hand, through land usage replacement and housing renovation, the contradiction between large site protection and scarce land resources was, to some extent, reduced. Therefore, it improved the efficiency of land use and realized the organic combination of the protection of relics and the development of urban areas.

In fact, the ultimate goal of the discussion of the "old town renewal model" in this chapter was, with a particular emphasis on the protection of traditional urban culture and style, to improve living conditions, encourage an adjustment to current trends of urbanization and advocate an active role for old town renewal in the overall urbanization strategy. Indeed, investigations as to how the renewal model of historic cities could be integrated into the urbanization process and social development have been conducted by scholars from a range of fields.

References

Fang, K. (2000). *The renewal of old city in contemporary Beijing* (p. 194). China Architecture and Building Press.

Mumford, L. (2005). *The city in history—The origin, evolution and prospects* (p. 2). China Architecture and Building Press.

Shan, C. (2005). A discussion from the image of city. *Chinese Cultural Relic News*.

Shan, Q. (2006). On scientific approach and organic order of historic areas in cities—From mass construction of dangerous and dilapidated housing to gradual and organic renewal (Part 2). *Cultural Relic, 3*.

Chapter 9
CBDs Development Model

It has been more than 80 years since the concept of the Central Business District, or CBD, was first put forward by the American sociologist E.W. Burgess. From theory to practice, by integrating the flow of people, goods, capital and information, the idea of the CBD has gradually formed a commercial "commanding heights" of industrial development. The rise of the CBD, meanwhile, is not only a result of the internal needs of a developing service industry, but also an inevitable consequence of the development of urban functional areas. As opposed to the development of CBDs in other countries, which is generally based on the market economy, as well as some planning and guidance, the development of CBDs in China possesses a range of distinctive features, the result of numerous factors, including the political and economic system, as well as history, culture and globalization in general. Among all of these causal factors, the mobilization capacity of the Chinese Government is the most significant. As a result, different from the market-guided and customer-oriented CBDs in other countries, which are usually planned upon building, the building, planning and development of CBDs in China are all unifiedly organized and carried out by government, thereby clearly demonstrating the leading role of Chinese Government in China's urban development. On the one hand, the government-led model has accelerated the development of CBDs in China. Without such intervention, it generally takes decades for CBDs to gradually mature, as indeed they have in major cities around the world. Nevertheless, in the case of China, it only took a decade or less for CBDs to take shape in many first-tier cities. In Beijing, for example, the CBD did not begin to emerge until 2001. Yet by the end of 2008, more than 12,000 enterprises had moved into the functional areas of Beijing's CBD, including 148 Fortune Global 500 enterprises, offering jobs for 180,000 people.[1] On the other hand, the government-led model also brings about a range of unique problems. Compared with the CBDs of other countries, the market, often known as the "invisible hand", plays a much weaker regulatory role in China. The level of CBDs in China depends, instead, highly on the scientificity of gov-

---

[1]Jiangsan et al. (2009).

© Social Sciences Academic Press 2020
Q. Li, *China's Development under a Differential Urbanization Model*,
Research Series on the Chinese Dream and China's Development Path,
https://doi.org/10.1007/978-981-13-9451-5_9

ernmental planning and the effective implementation of this planning. When these two aspects cannot be guaranteed, such as when the planning of a CBD is over ambitious, repetitive construction, the waste of resources and the idleness of land could follow, a dilemma in present-day China.

According to statistics provided by the Ministry of Housing and Urban-Rural Development of the People's Republic of China, 36 cities with populations of more than 200,000 are currently planning and developing their own CBDs.[2] Among them, the development of the CBDs in Beijing and Shanghai has entered a far more mature stage, whereas the development in other cities has faced a range of setbacks, such as the problems witnessed in Zhujiang New Town, Guangzhou city. A number of cities that are entirely unsuited for the establishment of CBDs, meanwhile, continue to blindly pursue such projects, leading, in turn, to the waste of resources and severe financial burdens. At any rate, as a high-end business center and economic hub, reviewing and reflecting upon the development model of CBDs could provide irreplaceable lessons as regards the exploration of urbanization with multiple approaches in China.

The first of four parts of this chapter introduces the typical and distinctive characteristics of the Chinese CBD model, that is, from the perspective of international comparison. In particular, it compares the differences between the spontaneous market-driven CBD model in western countries and the planning-first-market-force-later CBD model in China. The second part introduces and explains the status-quo and persisting features of CBDs in China, with a particular focus on analyzing the impact of government dominance in the development of CBDs. The third part analyzes specifically, with case studies, the feasibility of different levels of cities to establish CBDs. With reference to international standards, as well as the current situation in China, it discusses the requirements for CBD development in China to be successful. Amongst these requirements, industrial orientation and location optimalization are included. It further analyses the two cases of CBD development, in Shanghai and in Guangzhou.

9.1 An Introduction to the CBD Model: General Rules and International Comparison

This part provides, first, a brief review of the connotations, characteristics and evolutionary laws of CBDs from an international perspective and, then, proceeds to analyze the features of CBD construction in China on the basis of international comparison.

---

[2]Chen (2003).

9.1.1   The Definition, Characteristics and Evolutionary Laws of CBDs

9.1.1.1   The Connotation of CBDs: CBDs in a Modern Sense

American sociologist Ernest Watson Burgess put forward, in his study of the social structure of Chicago city, the concentric zone model of urban development and a definition of the central business district (CBD).[3] In his concentric model, the CBD functioned as the core of the five zones and the economic hub of a city. Three attributes were given by Burgess to the CBD, namely the central, historical and stable attributes. With the progression of urbanization all around the world, the definition of the CBD has gradually evolved and extended. In the eighty years from the birth of the concept to the present, the functions of the CBD underwent significant changes. It has developed from a retail-dominated phase (an embryonic stage of the CBD) to a balanced phase of central business and commerce (the growing-up stage of the CBD) and, finally, to a central business-dominated phase (the mature stage of the CBD).[4] The idea of the CBD, in its modern sense, refers to the maturity phase with its main function as a central business hub.

9.1.1.2   The Basic Characteristics of CBDs in a Modern Sense

The CBD, in a modern sense, mainly functions as the commercial and business centre of a city with integrated functions of finance, consultation, trade and services. With its highly integrated flow of people, goods, capital, and information, CBDs are easily recognizable as the economic hub of their respective cities. With the advantage of rich resources, meanwhile, CBDs, of world-class, often attract internationally renowned multinational companies, banks, and financial groups, to set up their headquarters and representative branches there.[5]

Combining a range of studies conducted by other researchers, it is possible to deduce that modern CBDs have a range of typical characteristics. For one thing, CBDs are generally the center of a certain area with convenient transportation links, a dense concentration of buildings and a high rate of employment. They also, typically speaking, play host to a highly concentrated service industry and a concentration of the population in general, not to mention the highest rates of rent and land prices.

---

[3]Robert (1987).
[4]Liu (2007).
[5]Han (2008).

9.1.1.3   The Evolutionary Law of Modern Service Industry
                   Agglomeration in CBD

The industrial structure of a city generally evolves alongside its development. In the post-industrial era, the scale and proportion of the tertiary industry increases considerably, thereby becoming a pillar of the overall national economy. Above all else, it is the increasing size of the tertiary industry that fuels the development of a CBD. This observation is clearly reflected by the fact that the industrial make up of a CBD is primarily composed of the tertiary industry, including financial services, insurance, real estate, commerce and other professional services.

Such a concentration of the modern service industry demonstrates numerous advantages of an agglomeration economy, including the development of excellent infrastructure, prosperous commercial consumption, advanced industrial networks and the presence of professionals from practically all fields. When reviewing the evolution of CBDs in all of the major global cities, it can be seen that such agglomeration is usually spontaneous and driven by market factors. It is generally after the prototype of a clustered, modern and market-driven service industry takes shape that the government takes further measures to promote the service industry and the development of the CBD. Such government intervention will generally be directed towards realizing a rational use of space, optimizing resource allocation and protecting the urban ecology, thereby eventually contributing to a sustainable model of development.[6] Compared to the development of CBDs in other countries, which prioritizes market forces over governmental guidance and coordination, the whole process of CBD development in China can be characterized by the consistently dominant role of government.

9.1.2   The Development Model of CBDs in China:
             An International Comparison

The development of CBDs in the world has undergone more than 80 years of change and progress. The famous CBDs, such as Manhattan in New York, Lombard Street in London and La Defense in France all contribute lessons for the development of CBDs in China. A comparison of the characteristics of CBDs in China and western countries is as follows (Table 9.1).

Table 9.1 summarizes synoptically the differences between CBDs in China and those in other countries. The main reason for these differences, meanwhile, is the leading role of the government when it comes to the development of CBDs in China. The intervention of the government is consistent throughout the whole process of CBD development, from the planning of industry and construction, in the pre-CBD stage, to the specific orders, investments, and regulations in the

---

[6]Jiang et al. (2009).

Table 9.1 Comparison of CBD in China and Western countries

Characteristics	CBD in Western countries	CBD in Chinese cites
Origin	Coastal cities, mainly market-driven	Capital city, coastal cities in the Southeast Government-unifiedly planned
Evolution	Agglomeration, ecologicalization, integration	Mainly commercial, With mixed functions: Beijing, Shanghai, Guangzhou and Shenzhen are inclined to clustering, stressing on mixed-functions
Zone	Division between CBD and commercial center, or even separation	Located in the city center with mixed commercial functions
Coverage area	1.5–3.5 km^2	1–6 km^2
Floorage(for construction)	World-level: 15–25 million square meters Region-level: 5–10 million square meters	Over 10 million square meters
Structure	World-level: multi-core structure Region-level: single-core structure	Mainly single-core structure, some planned to be multi-core (a main center and a minor center, a main center and two minor centers, etc.)
Function	Clustering of headquarters of multinational companies, financial center, production and service industry, stressing on the comprehensive function	Comprehensive function
Characteristics	Agglomeration, accessibility, high density and land price	Similar to those in western countries
Transportation	Dense road network, mainly for buses, with differential forms and ways, three-dimensional transport network	Traffic congestion Lack of diversity
Planning	Planning based on the concrete situation of construction, market-driven	Unified planning, carry out in phases, Start from a high level
Infrastructure	Well-established and still improving	Lagging-behind, increasing effort being made
Government role	Guiding and coordination role	Leading role

Quoted from: Zhangjie. "A Study on the Development Model of CBD in Beijing and Its Strategy". *The Journal of Capital University of Economics and Business,* 2006,1

shaping and further development of the CBD. Regardless of its high efficiency, the government-led model often poses risks as it inevitably contradicts the laws of a market economy. Since CBD development in other countries is spontaneous, market-driven and host to sophisticated industries, there can be a gap between CBD development in China and that witnessed in other countries. One example of this is that the ratio of industrial agglomeration is relatively low in China. The added value of trade volume in regional finance in Shanghai is 1/20th of that in Manhattan, 1/9th of that in Shinjuku, Tokyo, 1/9th of that in the City of London and 1/3rd of that in Singapore.[7]

Moreover, the industrial function of CBDs in China remains in need of improvement. CBDs across the globe, when at a mature stage of development, are usually dominated by a concentration of commercial offices. In China, however, CBDs are dominated by a combination of commercial offices, commerce and the service industry. Among them, the proportion of business functions is quite large while the proportion of commercial offices remains non-significant.

Generally speaking, compared to most mature CBDs abroad, the CBDs in China place more emphasis on the role of government. This emphasis often takes the form of central planning and a range of differential models. Nevertheless, experience of CBD development, at home and abroad, shows that their success depends on the integration and combination of government guidance and effective market mechanisms.

9.2 The Current Condition and Characteristics of CBD Development in China

9.2.1 A Brief Introduction to CBD Development in China

9.2.1.1 The Statistics of the Planning and Building of CBD in Chinese Major Cities

A Survey published by the Ministry of Housing and Rural-Urban Development in 2002 reveals that, by December 2002, among 359 cities with populations of over 200,000 (excluding Taiwan, Hong Kong and Macau), 36 cities have proposed and implemented the development of CBDs. These cities include Beijing, Shanghai, Guangzhou, Shenzhen, Wuxi and a range of others. Overall, those cities with plans, proposed or implemented, for CBD development accounted for 10% of the cities under survey. Among them, eight cities, including Beijing, Shanghai, Guangzhou, and Shenzhen, have already implemented such plans, thereby accounting for 2.2% of the total surveyed.[8]

The distribution of CBDs in the three major metropolitan areas (Beijing–Tianjin–Tangshan, Yangtze River Delta and Pearl River Delta) is obviously more clustered and shows a strong directionality of location. Meanwhile, the level of CBD development in cities with a population of over one million is much higher than it is in cities with populations of less than one million.

As has been mention above, CBD development in China is directed, to a large extent, by the government, that is, in the form of prior planning and the operation of

---

[7]Zhang (2006).
[8]Chen (2003).

multiple models of development. When analyzing CBD development in China, especially as regards the level of government and market involvement, as well as the various kinds of operating mode, it can generally be divided into four sub-categories. The first of these is the government-led type, such as the CBD in Shanghai, under which planning and investment comes from the government. The second kind is the government-guided type, such as the CBD in Beijing, under which the government intervenes by providing policy support. Thirdly, there is the government-authorized type, such as the CBD in Wuhan, under which the government authorizes enterprises to undertake the process of CBD development. Finally, it is possible to observe the market-driven type, such as the CBD in Chengdu,[9] which is mainly driven by enterprise, but remains regulated by the government to a certain extend. In the first three cases, the processes are government-driven, while in the fourth, the government acts as a "referee", exerting its influence on the process. On the whole, the government plays a decisive and leading role in the planning and development of CBDs in China.

9.2.2 The Characteristics of CBD Development in China

As mentioned before, the government plays a dominant role in the development of CBDs in China. This contrasts with the pattern in other countries, where CBDs are naturally formed based on the market economy, albeit often followed by a degree of government regulation and planning. This trend has bestowed a range of distinctive Chinese characteristics upon the development of CBDs. In accordance with a *2009 Annual Report of the Beijing CBD Research Base*, this chapter seeks to summarize the characteristics of CBD development in China.

9.2.2.1 Government Leadership and Planning

Different from the CBDs in other countries, which usually grow spontaneously out of the market economy, with governmental planning and guidance coming later, almost all of the CBDs in the major cities of China are preplanned by the government, which is keen to stress the modern service industry, including financial services and business offices. Fundamentally, this trend is a result of the government's enormous capacity to mobilize resources, not to mention its dominant role in society more generally.

In Beijing, for example, it was in a 1993 "Overall Plan of Beijing" that the municipal government of Beijing first proposed the idea of developing a CBD. In 2000, a special institution responsible for the organization and promotion of CBD development, that is, the Regulatory Committee of the CBD in Beijing, was

---

[9]Zhang (2007).

founded. In 2006, the land for CBD development was enclosed by the Chaoyang District Government in Beijing and, by 2008, the Finance Services Office of Beijing had published documents that specified the development orientation of the CBD, that is to say, as the financial center in the Chaoyang District of Beijing. Today, the CBD in Chaoyang District is dominated by impressive financial institutions and office buildings, which stand in great numbers, thereby representing the fruition of the government's initial planning.

The development of CBDs in other cities throughout China also follows a similar pattern, that is, initial government planning, which specifies the industrial orientation of the CBD, that is the modern service industry, including financial services and business offices, followed by expanded development, generally driven by a range of introduced forces.

There are also a range of reasons accounting for why cities throughout China are keen to develop CBDs of their own.

For one thing, a CBD provides an impressive urban landscape, which coincides the center of a city and planned and constructed through massive government investment. As a result, the appealing landscape of a CBD, including modern office buildings, a beautiful and clean urban environment, especially the impressive skyscrapers that many cities are enthusiastic about investing in such projects, made the CBD a landmark of the city, a shining brand for the image of the city.

Furthermore, CBDs are often rather useful. The successful establishment of a CBD often leads to a range of benefits accumulated from comprehensive urban development, including, amongst other things, upgraded industry and abundant investment as well as increasing rates of employment. As the upland of modern service development, CBDs are generally characterized by high additional value and high technological content. They can raise industrial level, optimize industrial structures, increase employment and provide a place for a bank of talented people, that is, attracting professionals from all around the world. Moreover, the successful establishment of CBDs can serve as a platform for future investment, thus stimulating the entire regional economy.

In summary, CBDs not only provide an impressive urban landscape but also are rather useful. It is, then, clear why local governments, as the dominant agents in urban resource distribution, actively allocate resources in the planning and development of CBD projects.

9.2.2.2 Industrial Layout: Commercial Development with Business Offices as the Secondary Function

As mentioned before, mature CBDs are primarily occupied by a complex range of business functions. On the one hand, CBDs in China used to be dominated by commercial development with business offices as a secondary function. This pattern is largely determined by the present pattern of industrial structure in China, namely that the modern service sector is still at a primary stage of development. On the other hand, local and national authorities generally guide, by means of planning, the development of real estate with a view to stimulating the economy. The real estate developers, meanwhile, driven by profits, often prioritize projects that generate quick returns from investment, such as commodity housing. In many cases, such short-term priorities may contradict the original intention and plan for a CBD.

Again, the CBD in Beijing functions as an informative example. Generally speaking, the development of CBDs in other developed countries takes at least a decade, often multiple decades. In Beijing, however, only five years were required to complete the construction of the core area of its CBD, which covers more than 8 million square meters, among which more than 1 million square meter became commercial areas. As a result of this enormous supply of commercial space, focused in a central area of 4 km², developed in just five years, with 60% taking shape in just two years, commerce developed rapidly, especially the real estate business, in Beijing's CBD. However, such a rapid rate of development also triggered high rates of vacant housing.[10]

In recent years, large high-class commercial centers have been constructed in quick succession throughout Beijing's CBD. These include the Zhonghuan World Trade Center, including 20,000 m² of low-rise commercial area, the Century Fortune Center, of roughly equal size and the China Trade Center, which boasts commercial coverage of 200,000 m². Because of the exclusively high cost of rent encouraged by the business mode of a CBD, such commerce is characterized by high-end and individualized businesses.

Ultimately, that CBDs in China are still dominated by commercial development, with business offices as secondary function, indicates that CBDs in China are still in a primary stage of development.[11]

9.2.2.3 Finance as Top Priority in Industrial Development

As mentioned before, mature CBDs should function primarily as hubs for business offices. Nevertheless, the precise industrial makeup of a mature CBD, as observed internationally, is usually determined by a combination of factors, including history, physical location, resources, culture and the market. For example, the industrial specialty of the CBD in La Defense is tourism, a factor which dominates in its industrial chain accordingly. CBDs in western countries, then, take on a range of forms based, to a large degree, on their individual situations, which often has much to do with spontaneous market factors. CBDs in China are, however, generally planned in advance by the government, using blindly the success of Beijing and Shanghai as models by other cities. Needless to say, this process leads to high levels of homogeneity in the industrial planning of CBDs throughout China. Almost all of the CBDs in China, for instance, focus on the development of the finance industry and take the number of international financial institutes present as a standard for

---

[10]Yu (2010).
[11]Yu (2010).

measuring the level reached by their modern service industry. This, however, present a challenge for the development of CBDs in many second-tier cities, for the number of international financial companies is highly limited and most of them chose to operate in first-tier cities instead. It is, then, no surprise that there are often massive vacancies in CBDs throughout second-tier cities, which took great efforts, in vain, to invest especially to attract international financial enterprises. If these second-tier cities could lower their standards and obtain a more reasonable positioning as regards the development of CBDs, then they may have a greater opportunity to spur regional economies by meeting the increasing demands of domestic businesses.

As the whole country follows the example of Beijing and Shanghai, while Beijing and Shanghai followed western countries, local governments in different regions across China frequently issue policies intended to attract financial institutions. In 2008, the municipal and district governments of Guangzhou city offered around 40 million yuan of incentives and subsidies for any financial institutions which established branches in Zhujiang New Town. Beijing, too, reserved a special fund to provide subsidies for financial enterprises (that is, the Special Fund for the Development of Finance in Chaoyang District). The authorities in Beijing also established financial security zones, established and improved social credit systems and undertook examination and approval procedures on behalf of financial enterprises, while also providing abundant resources and information services. Even more, Beijing provided preferential policies, such as giving residency permits to the executives of financial enterprises and their families, even going so far as to help their children gain admission to kindergartens and primary schools.

However, such homogeneous policies, which sought to attract financial institutions, brought about, to an extent, a vicious cycle of competition between different cities and regions. Quite unexpectedly, then, financial enterprises faced difficulties as regards establishing themselves in one place for they were often motivated to follow preferential policies.

9.2.2.4 Industrial Policy Focusing on Settlement Related Capital Return and Subsidies for Enterprises

Facing the fact that CBDs all over China strived for the development of a modern service industry, local governments cannot do anything but to use favorable policies so as to attract more large and medium international enterprises. Due to the characteristics of urban economic development and the government's leading role in resource allocation, compared to CBDs in other countries, preferential policies in China usually involve subsidies and tax refunds.[12]

Take the CBD of Hexi in Nanjing City for example. Starting in the second half of 2005, an annual figure of 50 million yuan was arranged specially for the

---

[12]Yu (2010).

development of the financial industry in Hexi, which was to last over the course of three years.[13] Utilizing this special fund, the CBD in Hexi witnessed the implementation of a series of policies pertaining to capital return and additional subsidies for enterprises which relocated there. These included a one-time capital subsidy, tax preferences and financial support, and within the boundaries of municipal government's power, reduction in operating fees, subsidies for purchasing or renting houses and subsidies for senior financial executives.

Besides the above-mentioned range of preferential policies, the CBD in Beijing also offered a large-sum subsidy for key enterprises. In January 2009, 10.597194 million yuan of subsidies were given to sixteen major financial institutes, such as General China Life Insurance Company, ABN AMRO Beijing Branch, for expenditure on housing rent.[14]

Needless to say, multinational companies generally choose to locate in cities and regions with favorable policies and relatively developed markets. It is for this fundamental reason that Beijing and Shanghai were able to attract more multinational companies. To raise the level of markets, meanwhile, is a difficult and gradual process. Therefore, it becomes an easier and more widely used option for local governments to use preferential policies, often represented by the offering of repayments and subsidies, in order to attract multinational companies.

9.3 The Feasibility of CBDs in China and a Case Study: From the Perspective of Governmental Administration

Referring to the development of the most preeminent international CBDs, it is evident that their success is closely tied to specific urban economic development more generally, as well as infrastructure and geographical conditions. At present, many cities in China have proposed or started planning the development of CBDs. It is, therefore, important for urban planners in China to consider how to learn from the experience of other countries and how local conditions should be taken into account. Only in this was can correct choices be made in the planning stage, including important issues such as whether or not a CBD should be constructed and how to build a CBD in accordance with local conditions. As mentioned before, most of the proposals for new CBDs are located on the east coast. It is in these areas, meanwhile, that urban CBDs already exist in a relatively better or mature state, especially in the city of Shanghai, that is, the economic center of China. Therefore, this chapter takes the CBD in Shanghai city as a representative of a relatively well-developed CBD. In the meantime, the CBD in Guangzhou, which began its construction in the early 1990, at the same time as Shanghai's, and suffered from a range of problems that typically arise in CBD development, is taken

---

[13]Yu (2010).
[14]Yu (2010).

as a representative of a CBD that has suffered setbacks throughout its development. As already mentioned, the model of Chinese CBD development features a central role for the government. Therefore, stress will be laid on the perspective of governmental administration in the analysis of both cases. The strategy for Shanghai's CBD development was proposed by government and the Guangzhou CBD suffered setbacks, thereby triggering adjustments after the government's reflection on its plan. Discussion on the second case, in this chapter, will focus on the evaluation and analysis of the adjustment process, that is, after the government's initial plan suffered setbacks. This chapter will first carry out an analysis of the feasibility of CBD development in major cities in China. Then, it will analyze the two cases of the Shanghai and Guangzhou CBDs based on a number of papers, such as "A Study on the Economical Structure and of Governmental Administration Model in CBDs - International Experience and Experiment in Lujiazui of Shanghai City",[15] "A Discussion on Improving the CBD Development in China",[16] and "A View on the Planning of Zhujiang New Town".[17]

9.3.1 An Analysis on the Feasibility of CBD Development in Large and Medium-Sized Cities in China

9.3.1.1 Conditions for CBD Development

There is an urgent need to establish which cities in China have the conditions and are ready and eligible for developing new CBDs. Towards answering this question, it can be informative to look at the standards followed by other cities in the world. By doing so, it is possible to observe two conditions for the emergence of new CBDs. To begin with, it is clear that underlying levels of economic development must reach a certain level, that is, a GDP per capita, within a particular region, of around 5000–10,000 dollars. Secondly, the city within which the proposed CBD is to be located must be, undoubtedly, the central city in that region.[18] By these standards, meanwhile, in 2010, there were only four cities in China with a GDP per capita of 10,000 dollars, those were, Beijing, Shanghai, Guangzhou and Shenzhen. There may, then, be concerns that other second-tier, and below, cities are not suitable for CBDs, although some evidence exists to the contrary. As early as the beginning of 1990s, Shanghai had started planning the development of its CBD, yet, at this time, the per capita GDP in Shanghai was only 720 dollars, far below the abovementioned first standard. Despite this apparent drawback, Lujiazui CBD in Shanghai has successfully become the financial center of China. Obviously, then,

---

[15]Han (2008).
[16]He (2006).
[17]Cen (2005).
[18]Jiang (2005).

international experience does not necessarily apply here. One reason is that China has been able to maintain a record of 10% GDP growth for more than 30 years. With such high growth-rates, it comes as little surprise that big cities in China require CBD preparation much earlier than other cities with just average GDP growth. Otherwise there may be higher costs and risks for the future development of CBDs, that is, if central areas within major cities are still occupied by other, less essential, functions. Therefore, the standard of per capita GDP for CBD development in China should be lower than the generally accepted international standard.

The second standard directly determines the regional competitiveness of CBDs and depends, to a large extent, on the macro-regulation of the central government. For instance, the development of a CBD in Shanghai may impede in the development of CBD in the city of Nanjing, while CBD development in the city of Guangzhou and the city of Shenzhen could give rise to apparent geographical competition.

In addition, another issue worthy of attention is the status or level afforded to each CBD. If the city is an international metropolis, then its CBD should be at international level. It also follows that there should be regional level CBDs and national level CBDs. Nevertheless, many of the proposals to develop CBDs that have been raised by second and third-tier cities seem to confuse the concept of a CBD with that of a simple city center.

9.3.1.2 The Function of CBD Development in Large Chinese Cities

It has been a dream for many major cities in China to have world-class CBDs and to become international business and financial centers. Nevertheless, for most inland cities, for now at least, this dream cannot be realized. The number of headquarters of multinational enterprises has always been regarded as an important indicator of an international level CBD. When it comes to the distribution of these headquarters in China, a majority of 70% are located in Shanghai and Beijing, while 10% are located in Guangzhou and Shenzhen, leaving only 20% spread throughout all other cities.[19] As indicated by these statistics, especially when it comes to second-tier, and below, cities, it is unrealistic to expect major CBDs to develop with international business as their main functions. In the meantime, China's increasing economic development brings with it an increasing demand for domestic business offices. If smaller cities, located in the center of their regions, could fully utilize their regional advantages, find a reasonable position for their CBDs and attract domestic business offices on a large scale, then they will undoubtedly promote the shaping and development of regional CBDs.

---

[19]Jiang (2005).

9.3.1.3 Location Selection

Most CBDs, whether in China or other countries, are located within city centers. That is, after all, a reason why CBDs are often confused with mere city centers. A city center is usually characterized just by a large flow of people and a convenient transportation network. It is in the city center that the flow of people, commodities, capital, and information integrate, thus creating something of a "commanding heights" for regional business.

If ever the location allocated to a CBD ignores these factors and is posited at a considerable distance from the city center, then the entire project could be undermined. In the following part, the cases of Shanghai's CBD and Guangzhou's CBD development will be introduced. Coincidentally, both of these were initially constructed at the beginning of the 1990s, in locations that were far removed from their respective city centers. Now, Lujiazui in Shanghai has become China's financial center while Zhujiang New Town in Guangzhou continues to suffer setbacks as regards its development as a CBD. These two cases provide valuable experiences that worth careful reflection. Historically speaking, there has been a huge development gap between the districts of Pudong and Puxi in Shanghai, separated, as they are, by the Huangpu River. As part of developing the Lujiazui CBD, a range of measures were included to develop the Pudong district, thereby breaking the historical division constituted by the Huangpu River and allowing the economic advantages provided by Puxi's prior development to give impetus to the development of Pudong. While the original intentions of this project were well implemented, by contrast, the development of the CBD in Guangzhou suffered a number of setbacks. The future of the Zhujiang New Town project really depended on whether or not its non-central location could be integrated with the existing downtown area. Given the complexity of these cases, further analysis is required.

9.3.2 Mature CBDs: A Case of Lujiazui Financial and Trade Zone in Shanghai[20]

9.3.2.1 The Planning Process

The planning of the Lujiazui Finance and Trade Zone began in the 1990s. "*The Planning for Adjusting Lujiazui as a Central Area*", published in 1991, clearly specified the core position of Lujiazui in the overall planning of Shanghai's future urban development. At that time, China was lacking in experience when it came to developing CBDs and most CBDs, in western countries at least, had been

---

[20]The Case of Lujiazui Financial and Trade Zone is based on Han Kesheng: `A Study on the Economical Structure and of Governmental Administration Model in CBDs - International Experience and Experiment in Lujiazui of Shanghai City' PhD thesis. East China Normal University, 2008.

spontaneously formed via the market system. As such, the designers of the CBD in Shanghai wisely looked to learn from the development of the CBD of La Defense in France, a CBD that was itself driven by governmental planning and guidance. Promoted by two mayors of Shanghai, Zhurongji, and Huangju, China and France reached agreement on the cooperative framework regarding the planning and design of the Lujiazui CBD. In 1992, France officially presented their planning for further international consultation.

In the planning conducted by the French, the whole building area of the Lujiazui CBD was approximately 4 million square meters. This area was composed of the following seven distinct parts. First, provisions were made for 2.65 million square meters of office buildings, 0.3 million square meters of luxurious residences, 0.5 million square meters of hotels and similar facilities, 0.25 million square meters of convention and exhibition centers, 0.12 million square meters of shopping malls, 0.1 million square meters of cultural centers and comprehensive service facilities amounting to 0.03 million square meters.[21] After extensive consultation and international bidding, the planning was officially approved in December 1993. In spite of a lack of experience in constructing CBDs, Shanghai's government had been able to learn from the experience of the French planners, thereby laying a solid foundation for the future development of the Lujiazui CBD.

In the process of actually constructing Lujiazui, a unique development strategy was adopted. This strategy involved trying to implement a high standard planning by making first-class investment. In particular, infrastructure construction was conducted in such a way as to address all infrastructural needs of the CBD comprehensively and at one go. The overall process witnessed a pattern of simultaneous function and morphology development and the implementation of a scattered development strategy, through which independent development zones could work independently. Companies were established by means of void circulation of capital and real circulation of land while the government cooperated extensively with enterprises, all with a view to realizing rolling development. The management system of small government and big society was chosen, which notably improved the efficiency of administration.[22]

9.3.2.2   The Current Condition of the Lujiazui CBD

The Spatial Pattern and Clustering of the Lujiazui CBD

After two-decades of development and construction, an export-oriented, modern and multifunctional CBD started to take shape. It became "a symbol of China's reform and opening-up and the epitome of Shanghai's modernization".[23]

---

[21]Han (2008).

[22]Han (2008).

[23]Han (2008).

Moreover, the Lujiazui Finance and Trade Zone (the central zone of the CBD), alongside the New Shanghai Business Town, the Zhuyuan Commercial and Trade Zone and the Huamu Administration and Culture Zone, where the headquarters of various large domestic enterprises were grouped, formed four spatial clusters that echoed one other. An integrated multi-level industrial eco-chain was thus taken shape. These clusters, please, see Fig. 9.1. At any rate, the development of Shanghai's CBD proved that a mature CBD cannot be formed without market mechanism. From 2000 to 2001, the Lujiazui CBD faced a challenge of vacant properties that came to be known as "empty buildings" (no people during the day) and "black buildings" (no lights during night). As a result, academic circles expressed doubts about the development of the Lujiazui CBD. In order to improve the situation, the government changed part of business zone into a residential area. However, it was totally unexpected that the utilization of buildings in the Lujiazui CBD would reach as much as 95%. The over saturation that followed

Fig. 9.1 The spatial clusters of Lujiazui CBD. *Source* Planning and Construction Department, Shanghai Lujiazui Functional Area Management Committee. Quoted from Han Kesheng. "The Economic Structure and Government Management Model of CBD - International Experience and the Practice of Shanghai Lujiazui."

triggered soaring house prices and high costs for businesses, thus threatening the development of industry and commerce. Therefore, the government further promoted the development of the Zhuyuan Commercial and Trade Zone and the Huamu Administration and Culture Zone. In part, in the short term at least, the government's leading role was efficient, but, on the whole and in the long run, it was the inherent laws of the market that played a more fundamental role. It has, therefore, been demonstrated that when the government's planning follows economic laws, the development of CBDs will be most effective.

The Industrial Chain of Lujiazui CBD

One indication of the success of the Lujiazui CBD was the formation of an industrial chain. After two-decades of planning and construction, Lujiazui CBD had become well-known for its modern buildings, excellent infrastructure, high-quality integration of resources and information, convenient transportation and beautiful environment. Needless to say, as a result, it attracted the presence of numerous international and domestic modern service enterprises. The spatial clustering of its building economy, not to mention the subsequent radiation effect increased day by day, thereby leading to the formation of an industrial chain in the CBD (see Table 9.2).

Table 9.2 The layout of industrial chain in Lujiazui CBD

	Total number	The number of enterprises	The number of tax-paying enterprises	Total revenue (Unit: ten thousand yuan)
Business buildings	136	4517	3352	411,162.23
High-end apartments	220	309	199	34,058.52
New communities	338	556	186	19,234.75
Department stores/shops	156	274	184	9336.11
Industrial zone	27	151	131	3644.38
Government buildings	37	261	141	41,859.96
Schools and hospitals	100	140	83	4445.20
Tourist attractions	9	12	9	571.69
Other buildings	67	66	50	3134.55

Source Planning and Construction Department, Shanghai Lujiazui Functional Area Management Committee. Quoted from Han Kesheng. "The Economic Structure and Government Management Model of CBD - International Experience and the Practice of Shanghai Lujiazui."

Among all of the buildings in the CBD, business buildings account for more than 70%, thereby demonstrating that the industrial chain of the Lujiazui CBD is dominated by business functions and the CBD can be classified as mature accordingly.

9.3.2.3 Problems Faced by the CBD

The Short Chain of the Financial Industry, an Excessive Traditional
Financial Service Sector and Low Added Value

China still lags behind developed countries in financial industry development. Despite its status as an industry leader inside China, the Lujiazui CBD has many of the same shortcomings that plaque other financial centers in the country. The financial industry has a rather limited presence in Lujiazui, dominated by traditional financial institutions such as banks and insurance companies, with very few newer kinds such as trusts, investment companies, and leasing companies. Lujiazui has still a long way to go before becoming a world-class international financial center.

In addition, financial services and products available in the Lujiazui CBD lack diversity. For instance, loans and deposits still constituted the main source of business for banks while creative financial products remain a rarity. These limitations result in a single financial channel in comparison to the CBDs of other developed countries, as well as a relatively low added value to the area's financial industry.

Shortage of Famous Brands and Weak Competitiveness Internationally

In the minds of Chinese people, Shanghai is the financial center of China and the Lujiazui CBD is the financial center of Shanghai. However, with the exception of the Shanghai Pudong Development Bank, the four major national banks of China, as well as a range of other important joint-equity banks, do not operate their headquarters in Shanghai. Although HSBC and Citi Bank, as well as some other foreign banks and financial companies, have launched branches in Shanghai, there are no headquarters of first-class international investment banks and fund companies settled in Shanghai. Relevant statistics reveal that, in the Lujiazui CBD, the number of financial institutions is one-third the number of those in Hong Kong and one-thirtieth of the number in New York. What's more, the total assets owned by the banking industry are just one-fiftieth of those in New York and one-fourteenth of those in Hong Kong. At the same time, the number of professional service institutions is around one-hundredth of that in New York and the number of law institutions is only one-sixth of those present in London. Finally, the number of regional headquarters of multi-national companies is just one-fourteenth of those in

Manhattan, one-seventh of those in the City of London, one-sixth of those in Tokyo and one-seventeenth of those in Hong Kong."[24]

9.3.2.4 Countermeasure: From the Perspective of the Administrative Pattern of Government

As mentioned above, the major difference between the development of CBDs in China and that in other developed countries consists in the government's leading role. Therefore, this chapter focuses on a range of strategies and recommendations as regards the development of Shanghai's CBD from the perspective of government administration. These strategies include, amongst other things, the rationalizing of the government's administration pattern. As a saying goes, "once the key link is grasped, everything falls into place". In a similar way, perhaps, the specific problems of the development of the CBD could be better solved through measures such as these.

First, the administration pattern of the Lujiazui Finance and Trade Zone, as the core area of the CBD, needs to be addressed. On a regional level, the Management Committee of Lujiazui Functional Zone is supposed to have direct administrative jurisdiction over the Lujiazui Finance and Trade Zone. However, recent experiences indicate that it does not have sufficient power. For one thing, the approval of financial institutions in the Lujiazui Finance and Trade Zone is given by the relevant department of the State Council, while the actual planning should be approved by the Shanghai Municipal Government. As such, the administration process, diffused, as it is, throughout a range of different governmental departments, is one of confusion in the Lujiazui Finance and Trade Zone. What's more, those who do have the power to genuinely shape the development process often do not have the energy. After all, powerful as they may be, the State Council and Shanghai's government are unable to concentrate all of their attention to Lujiazui. At the same time, those who have the energy to push for further development often do not have the power, that is, insofar as the government of the Pudong New Area and The Management Committee of Lujiazui Functional Zone, which do indeed invest most of their attention into Lujiazui Finance and Trade Zone, has only a limited range of powers.

With this in mind, it is advisable that the various administrative institutions that exert authority over the Lujiazui Finance and Trade Zone should be integrated and an overall management committee of the Lujiazui Finance and Trade Zone should be established (to integrate with the Management Committee of Lujiazui Functional Zone, by means of the same staff working under the name of two separate institutions). In this way, the various functions of the financial service sector in Shanghai and, in particular, the Pudong New Area could be integrated effectively. The State Council and municipality government should grant the committee the

---

[24]Han (2008).

power of planning, financial examination and approval, not to mention the legislation of financial policy and financial services. These measures will promote the rapid development of an industrial chain with finance at its core.

Secondly, specifically from the perspective of government administration, the development of Shanghai's CBD requires the support of many policies. For instance, it would be aided by the continuous pursuit of special preferential policies from the central government and the innovation of administrative patterns in Shanghai by China's financial regulator. Besides, CBDs themselves should take great effort to implement policies that are likely to attract foreign financial institutions.

The above advice is mostly put forward from the perspective of government administration. Only a well-organized system of governmental administration will, for the part of overall planning at least, lead to the smooth development of a CBD and provide both a favorable environment and policy platform for further market development. Based on these considerations, the Lujiazui CBD could achieve further development through a series of measures such as the optimization of the soft environment as well as that of the hard facilities, the fostering of a new financial industrial chain and the acceleration of optimizing and upgrading the economic structure.

9.4 Lessons to Be Learned About CBD Development in China: The Case of Zhujiang New Town in Guangzhou

9.4.1 Background

The development background of Zhujiang New Town involved the Guangzhou Municipal Government attempting to alleviate the deficit caused by subway construction through the collection of land transfer fees in the process of CBD development. In addition, other contributing factors, as mentioned before, were expectations regarding the extent to which CBDs can stimulate the development of the tertiary industry and realize the anticipated benefits of the intensive concentration of business, commerce, and services. In accordance with the layout of the city of Guangzhou, office buildings were widely scattered, thus making it unlikely to witness any of the advantages of such concentrations. Therefore, it was, in many ways, a good policy to upgrade the city's industry by taking the opportunity to build a CBD that could integrate all of Guangzhou's business office resources. Finally, with the rise of Hong Kong and Shenzhen, the status of Guangzhou, as the central city of the Zhujiang Delta, was on the decline. Under such circumstances, it became an inevitable choice for policy makers to draw foreign investment, promote industrial upgrading, popularize the city brand and accelerate overall urban development through CBD development. It was against such a background that

Guangzhou Municipal Government, after extensive consultation, made the development plan for Zhujiang New Town.

9.4.2 The Location of Zhujiang New Town

The Zhujiang New Town was located in the Tianhe District of Guangzhou City, stretching from Huangpu Avenue in the North to Zhuajiang River in the South, bordered by Guangzhou Avenue in the West and the Huanan Expressway in the East. Meanwhile, it covered a total area of 6.6 km² with a core area of 1 km². The construction area was around 8,450,000 m² with 30% of this area allocated to commercial apartments and 70% allocated to businesses, office buildings and apartments. It was located in the junction of old and new urban areas, divided into the east and west districts. The east district was mainly residential district and the west was primarily a district for businesses and offices.[25]

The location of Zhujiang New Town was actually quite advantageous as it sat in the junction of old and new urban areas, thereby making it something of a central urban area itself. It was also located at the junction of the Zhujiang River and the new town axis, thereby becoming the center of all tourist attractions in Guangzhou.

The original plan involved transforming Zhujiang New Town into the future center of Guangzhou. For one thing, the business and office functions in the west area were earmarked for integration with the existing business and office functions of the central area of Tianhe District in the north. Then, through an overall planning, other functions, such as commerce, culture and diplomacy, would be included in the project. However, thus far, the development of Guangzhou's CBD has not proceeded so well.

9.4.3 Challenges and Responses

9.4.3.1 Challenges

From 1992 to the end of 1999, the accumulative investment in Zhujiang New Town amounted to 4.4263 billion yuan, yet 70% of the Town's area remained undeveloped. The developed area mostly consisted of high-end apartments, the costs of which were easily recovered by real estate developers. Not a single business office building was opened and Guangzhou's CBD had, quite unexpectedly, been hijacked into a high-end residential area.

---

[25]Cen (2005).

9.4.3.2 Reasons for Setbacks

The external factors which contributed to the failure of Zhujiang New Town included the austere economic policy forwarded in 1994 and the economic crisis that followed in 1997. As these factors provide few lessons as regards the development of a CBD, this chapter will not investigate it in any detail. The causation of the setbacks can, however, be summarized as follows.

One major causal factor was the deficiencies of government administration when it came to integrating the business offices of the old city and the new town areas. The oversupply of office buildings in Guangzhou's old city area made it impossible to maintain a strong and concentrated CBD by market demand. The original intention of developing the CBD was to integrate the central business functions of Guangzhou city, but the actual implementation of the plan ran contrary to the original policy. The old city continued to develop business office buildings and the total area of newly-built office buildings far exceeded that achieved in Zhujiang New Town. This led to an oversupply of business office buildings in Guangzhou, which, along with their scattered layout, was entirely contrary to the original plan of integrating the whole city's demand for business offices.

A number of issues relating to land also caused difficulties for the development of Zhujiang New Town. For one thing, some land was reserved by former villages in the newly developed urban area, for another, land was developed into residential apartments by real estate developers, who were driven exclusively by economic interests. During the development of Zhujiang New Town, some land were reserved by villages and turned into "villages in the city", the prices of which were considerably lower than those of the neighboring land. That disrupted the land market severely and weakened the government's capacity of macro-regulation over land values and in the real estate market. In addition, restricted by policy, it became difficult for the reserved land to apply for further construction, hurting the incomes of farmers in the area. The revenue Xi Village, for example, was over 50 million yuan in 1992, yet, by 2004, the number had shrunk to just two million yuan.[26] That resulted in resentment among villagers and elevated the risk of social tension.

Another cause of setbacks was the fact that the development plan of Zhujiang New Town was not strictly followed. In order to recoup the investment quickly, real estate developers gave priority to the development of residential apartments, leading to a much higher percentage of apartments in Zhujiang New Town than the limits set in the original plan. As a result, the land price increased dramatically and the CBD turned into, above all else, a high-end residential area.

In response to these emerging problems, in 2000, the Guangzhou Municipal Government conducted an in-depth review of the planning and status of Zhujiang New Town. In 2002, a resolution titled "Lessons from Misteps in Planning for Zhujiang New Town" ("Lessons" hereinafter) was passed and the previous plan was scrapped.

---

[26]He (2006).

The new plan was not, however, a complete rejection of everything that was in the one it replaced. It was, instead, an adjustment in accordance with the ongoing process of development, which also took the economy, municipal administration, employment, and the environment into consideration. The new version left largely unchanged the scope of the plan and its vision for the place of Zhujiang New Town within that region. In "Lessons," the construction of a twenty-first century CBD in Guangzhou (GCBD21) was reintroduced as a development target for the city, this time as part of the larger strategy of turning Guangzhou into an international city.

The new version of the plan included a number of changes.

First, the adjusted plan was "putting people first". This involved lowering the intensity of development, reducing a area of 1,500,000 m^2 allocated to office buildings and increasing the number of public squares and total area of green land. As a result, the central square of Zhujiang New Town stretched, from north to south, from a major entrance square to an urban green core square, followed by a culture and arts square and, finally, to Haixinsha Citizen's Square. Together, these squares formed the largest city-level public square system in Guangzhou city.

Secondly, adjustments were made to patterns of land development and improvements to public transportation followed. Furthermore, the new plan adopted a general international PUD pattern (planned unit development), which makes unified plans for green areas between buildings to form several beautiful small gardens. In terms of public transportation, three more buses were added to the only bus route into Zhujiang New Town. The name of the area's station, situated on subway line three, was also officially established. The development of public transportation was beneficial for the commute between the old and new city centers, not to mention the integration of superior resources.

Thirdly, supporting facilities in the new CBD were upgraded to a higher standard. For one thing, as part of the new plan, educational and cultural facilities in Zhujiang New Town were strengthened significantly, including the expanding of the area allocated to kindergartens, libraries, elementary schools and hospitals.

Through these adjustments to the plan, Zhujiang New Town became more and more a center of commerce and public life in Guangzhou city. From any apartment or office building in the newly-planned Zhujiang New Town, it took only one hour to reach all corners of Guangzhou city.[27] This extricated Zhujiang New Town from the previously mentioned difficulty presented by its distance from the city's central area.

9.4.4 An Evaluation of the New Plan

According to an interview with experts conducted by the journal *Real Estate Guide* in 2005, the new plan was approved unanimously. In 1993, when China was in a period of economic austerity, land development usually adopted a pattern characterized by extremely high floor area ratios on small plot. Adherence to this old pattern of

---

[27]Li (2005).

development would pose negative impacts on the image of Guangzhou, the area of urban public buildings and urban ecology. Among these issues, the most severe problem, the lack of planning for vegetated areas, proved difficult to rectify.

Experts interviewed by the journal *Real Estate Guide* also pointed out that the adjusted plan was made under the premise of guaranteeing the consistence of planning and the balance of different interest groups. It placed more emphasis on enhancing the quality of the environment and improving supporting facilities, thereby focusing more on the idea of putting people first in the spatial design. There were, in particular, three praiseworthy features of the new plan. The improvement and completion of public facilities was particularly impressive, as was the development of a multi-dimensional transportation system, which provided utmost convenience for residents, reaching, as it could, within one hour, every corner of Guangzhou. Finally, there was much to be said for the newly-designed spatial layout of the city, including the skyline of Zhujiang New Town, along with Tianhe Sports Center in the North and Citic Square, forming what was a rhythmical and wavy overall skyline.[28]

At all stages of the planning process, from the early 1990s to 2003, the government played a leading role in the development of Guangzhou's CBD. In other words, governmental regulation was central to this process of CBD development. Without the macro-regulation provided by government, the process would have been contingent upon real estate developers, and the development of the CBD would have encountered great difficulties. As evidenced by the early setbacks of Zhujiang New Town, the developers gave priority to residential housing, effectively turning Zhujiang New Town into a high-end residential area, just insofar as costs could be recovered quickly. Moreover, as part of the old plan, the location of Zhujiang New Town was isolated from the traditional city center. The future destiny of Zhujiang New Town was, therefore, tied to whether or not a connection could be established with the traditional city center and whether or not the former could capitalize sufficiently on the advantageous location and resource of the latter. These challenges, not to mention their solutions, show how important and necessary scientific planning is to CBD development. The process of such planning, meanwhile, as well as its forceful implementation, depends, primarily, on government leadership. It is these lessons that Zhujiang New Town offer urban planners faced with the task of CBD development.

9.5   The Problems in and Solutions to CBD Development in China

9.5.1   An Analysis of Problems in CBD Development in China

By reviewing the process of CBD development in China, with particular emphasis on CBD development in Shanghai and Guangzhou, some of the unique challenges

---

[28]Li (2005).

of CBD development in China can be clarified. In Chinese society, within which the government plays a leading role, CBD development, even from the earliest stages of planning, can be decisively influenced by the government's behavior. Therefore, rationalizing the government's behavior may be a key step towards the scientific development of CBDs in China. First, the government should seek to improve the quality of their planning and establish a proper system of management in order to guarantee the effective implementation of and prompt adjustment to the plan. Specifically speaking, there are a range of typical problems to be addressed, as explicated below.

9.5.1.1   Misunderstanding of CBDs and Erroneous Positioning for CBD Levels

Nowadays, there are at least two significant misunderstandings when it comes to CBDs in China. For one thing, there is a confusion between CBDs and traditional city centers. It is a common misconception that any city is capable of building its own CBD, while even some districts below the city-level have proposed plans for the development of their own CBDs. The second major issue is a misunderstanding as regards the complexity involved in the development of CBDs. It is widely advocated that CBDs can only be built in international cities, such as Beijing and Shanghai. There is, however, widespread ignorance of the possibility that different CBDs could operate at different levels (international, national, regional level). CBDs at different levels should, of course, be tailored to their corresponding position. That is to say, if a regional CBD cannot realize its own developmental position, but blindly pursing international business institutions, without any regard for domestic demands, it will, after all, only bring about a waste of resources, as it doesn't have the advantage of an extensive impact over other parts of China, and the ability to attract multi-national corporations in the manner of Beijing or Shanghai. All of these misunderstandings and misconceptions have misguided the theoretical research into CBD development, thus damaging the healthy development of CBDs in China.

9.5.1.2   The Disorderly Governmental Behavior

CBDs are often considered the symbol of the economic development of a city. Urban economic development is, meanwhile, one of the most important indicators to evaluate governmental performance. As a result, governments at all levels launched CBD projects in order to enhance their image and have political achievements. Moreover, the CBD plans put forward in some cities have been unrealistic and excessive to the point that existing conditions have been all but excluded from consideration. Plans such as these have triggered a surge in wasted resources and idle land.[29] As was mentioned in the previous chapter, when discussing why major cities in China are so keen on such projects, CBDs do not only provide an impressive urban landscape but also are rather useful. These factors explain why regional governments are obsessed with CBDs. The impressive urban landscape part of the vision, meanwhile, can be easily achieved insofar as governments control the allocation of urban resources. However, whether a CBD is useful or not is directly determined by the basic conditions of a city, such as whether or not it has a strong economy, regional or even international influence, a modern service industry and convenient transportation. Unfortunately, most cities in China simply have not yet reached such a high stage of development.

In the meantime, it also involves the unclear positioning of CBDs. CBDs should be ranked at different levels, including international CBDs, national CBDs and provincial CBDs. The ranking of CBDs, in this way, should be realistic and suitable to regional conditions. However, CBD planning in China has been characterized by grand and unrealistic ambitions, frequently proposing slogans of "building a first-class international CBD". These projects rarely amount to more than unfinished projects and a huge waste of social resources.

9.5.1.3   The Homogenous Pattern of CBD Development and Construction

Internationally, there are two types of CBD development and construction patters. The first of these is the market economy oriented pattern, under which market mechanisms play a leading role while governments only provide a degree of direction through relevant policy making, such as in Manhattan in the U.S. The second is the government-dominated pattern which sees the government controlling every detail of the whole process from planning to completion. The development and construction of CBDs in China always falls under the second kind due to its particular kind of economic system. As mentioned before, then, owing to disorderly governmental behavior, there have been numerous problems throughout the CBD development and construction process.

A homogenous pattern of development also follows from the fact that most CBDs in China were built from scratch as part of a process that was not separated from the development of new urban areas in general. Needless to say, this phenomenon had much to do with the furious urbanization process witnessed in China. By contrast, CBDs in other countries were seldom newly built, most of them instead developed slowly based on the growth of the market. The scale of CBD development in China was, however, totally determined by government planning, thereby posing the risk of planning failures, such as excessive construction of offices, far beyond the genuine needs of businesses in a city as in the planning of

---

[29]Luo and Zhang (2004).

Zhujiang New Town. In fact, it was this very planning that triggered serious setbacks in the development of Zhujiang New Town.

9.5.1.4 Flaws in Planning and Falty Objectives

At present, CBD construction in China generally lacks systematic planning. CBD development should involve all aspects of a city, including, amongst others, industry, infrastructure, transportation, and the physical environment. It is a systematic project that requires coordination and cooperation among different government departments. If each department acts in isolation from the others, then repetitive construction and vicious competition will result. Therefore, macro-regulation from the government, at all levels, is necessary. Such regulation ranges from the coordination of CBD development between regional hubs, such as the coordination between Nanjing and Shanghai in the Long River Delta and Guangzhou and Shenzhen in the Pearl River Delta, to the coordination between districts within a city or different zones within a single CBD. The abovementioned setbacks in the early stages of the Zhujiang New Town project are a clear example of what can go wrong. Both the Old City and the New Town areas concentrated on the construction of business office buildings, thereby exceeding existing demands and wasting resources. Likewise, the CBD in Beijing is controlled by three levels of governments, including the central, municipal and district governments. These three levels of government did not achieve any kind of systematic cooperation, thereby resulting in the functions of the CBD overlapping with those of other central areas. The CBD was, therefore, unable to achieve a specialized and intensified industrial chain, as desired, but witnessing diluted resources and vicious competition.[30]

In the meantime, the objectives of CBD planning in many cities are restricted by the interests of real estate developers. Therefore, the development of CBDs often deviates from the targets specified in the original plan, as was exemplified by the temporary setbacks in the development of Zhujiang New Town. For the first decade of development, little more had been achieved than a high-end residential area.

9.5.1.5 Imperfect System and Weak Management

In their paper "A Study on Problems in China's CBD Development", Luo Yongtai and Zhang Jinjuan pointed out that, in CBD development of many cities, the mechanisms of management have been far from smooth. On the one hand, many CBD administrative organizations were only temporarily responsible for the development process and could not exercise fully their power in management. On the other hand, organizations at different levels all wanted to interfere, resulting in the failure of some CBD projects. Another problem was the land management

---

[30]Luo and Zhang (2004).

system. Though the land should not enter into the market directly, as it belongs to different governmental departments and their land-use right can be transferred, some corporations and enterprises involved in developing CBDs started to attract investment, seek self-supporting facilities and develop their own projects independently. Such ventures often left the development of the overall CBD in a state of disorder.

9.5.1.6 Defects in Industry Development Inside CBDs

Compared to the mature CBDs of other countries, those in China still have a long way to go in terms of industrial development. As mentioned before, the key feature of a mature CBD is marked chiefly by the business office function. But most CBDs in China haven't met that standard so far, as is evidenced by an excess of business branches and commercial apartments. The CBD in Guangzhou, for instance, practically turned into a high-end residential area for a period. From international experience, the proportions for each functional area in a mature CBD should roughly accord to the following. 40–60% should be allocated to office buildings, 20% to commercial facilities and 20% to commercial apartments and the related supporting service facilities.[31]

At the same time, some CBDs in China drifted towards the other extreme, that is, the construction of high-level CBDs regardless of the pre-existing economic conditions. As mentioned in the previous part, many CBDs were only interested in hosting a large financial industry, especially one composed of international financial institutions or companies. As such, domestic financial institutions and low-level business and commercial institutions were often ignored. This approach meant that many CBDs were unable to achieve their desired targets, which, when combined with an unwillingness to accept a more modest vision, resulted in complete failure and wasted resources on an enormous scale. Though the size of a CBD's financial industry is an international indicator of maturity, exclusive emphasis on this factor increases economic risk in a region, especially when a crisis arises in the finance industry. A domino effect will surely follow, thereby threatening the real economy on a large scale. In short, with the exception of the first-tier cities, such as Beijing, Shanghai and Shenzhen, other cities in China, regardless of their considerable ambitions, clearly do not have the conditions required for the development of international financial centers.

In addition, in terms of the spatial distribution of industry, the tendency of clustering and concentration in China's CBDs is not obvious. From international experience, a concentration of industry will give rise to intensive benefits and improve economic efficiency. A spatial pattern characterized by the presence of different industries in different zones is another clear indicator of successful CBD in

---

[31]He (2006).

the international community. Therefore, in terms of adjustments to and upgrading of their industrial structures, CBDs in China still have a long way to go.

9.5.2 Suggestions for CBD Planning in China

Regarding all of the abovementioned problems in the process of CBD development in China, this chapter will put forward some sensible proposals for future consideration.

9.5.2.1 Standardizing Approval Procedures, Understanding CBD' Proper Role in the City, Making Long-Term Planning and Guaranteeing Sufficient Capital

As mentioned before, at present, the development of some CBDs represents expectations that are too ambitious and unrealistic. Therefore, some cities whose conditions are not suitable for the development of CBDs still blindly follow a slogan of "building a world first-class CBD". Yet, as pointed out previously, for most cities in China, it is impractical to develop a CBD dominated by international business functions. The aimless pursuit of attracting more foreign investment has already resulted in a huge waste of resources. For those regional central cities, such as Wuhan and Chongqing, catering for domestic demands for business offices, instead of unrealistically pursuing international business offices, will help shape highly productive regional hubs. The central government should organize expert bodies tasked with strictly evaluating CBD plans in all cities, to prevent the waste of resources and the vacancy of land due to overly ambitious projects. In terms of establishing the feasibility of CBD development in China, there is already a considerable body of research for reference. For instance, the Project of National Natural Science Foundation of China hosted by Southeast University: "A Study on the Index System of the Feasibility of CBD Development in Cities of China" (50,508,043), designed an index system for the feasibility of CBD development for cities in China. This index follows the inherent laws of CBD formation and the nature of urban operation, including 29 basic elements, 6 conditional elements, 3 supporting systems and an integrated composite result. The system can be further divided into four levels, including the overall level, the system level, the condition level and the element level. Through such a multi-level calculation and analysis, which includes space-time identification of weight and threshold values, the system can provide a basic evaluation and dynamic monitoring of the feasibility of CBD development in most Chinese cities.[32]

---

[32]Yang and Wu (2006).

In addition, as mentioned before, there is fierce competition among central cities which share similar locations, such as Guangzhou and Shenzhen, as well as Shanghai and Nanjing. Replacing competition with cooperation will rely on the macro-regulation, guidance and coordination of the central government. Otherwise, repeated construction and wasted resources will surely follow on a large scale.

9.5.2.2   The Reinforcement of the Government's Macro-Regulation with Emphasis on the Rational Layout of Different Functional Zones in CBDs and the Avoidance of Shortsighted Behaviors by Real Estate Developers

The successful experiences of international CBDs show that office buildings usually account for 70–80% of the total area of a CBD. By contrast, in the course of CBD development in China, due to an unclear management system, real estate developers gave priority to development of commercial apartments in order to recover the costs of development as quickly as possible. For instance, the CBD in Zhujiang New Town was almost transformed entirely into a high-end residential area. Therefore, the government's role of reasonable guidance should be further promoted in CBD development in order to coordinate the interests of all parties involved, so as to avoid object deviation in the process.

9.5.2.3   A Comprehensive Consideration of the Integration of Land-Use Efficiency, Transportation and Environment to Promote the Comprehensive Social Welfare Present in CBDs

In the current planning process of CBDs in China, it is common that one consideration will be addressed at the cost of others. This single-minded approach is particularly applicable to issues such as transportation, the environment and building efficiency. The loss of some of the benefits of city development is often demonstrated as a result. These losses include the low intensity of land use and insufficient building height, a construction pattern which ignores the high price of the land being developed. Likewise, environmental costs increase by an urban development pattern which favors clusters of buildings separated by small green areas. Problematically, broken green spaces, such as these, cannot exert any significant ecological merits. Instead, these scattered green spaces, in city areas, simply increase maintenance costs, while also degrading the ecological value of what little green land remains, compared with the value of areas of concentrated green land. At the same time, lacking of a rational balance between employment and housing, the cost of commuting by urban transportation is greatly increased, and accompanied by worsening traffic conditions.

Therefore, the above-mentioned situation requires CBD builders in China to realize and follow the laws of spatial distribution and the features of urban land use under the market mechanisms. Only in this way can they further improve the professional and scientific nature of CBD planning so as to enhance the efficiency of urban land use and promote smoothly China's urbanization.[33]

References

Cen, J. (2005). A view on the planning of Zhujiang New Town. *Guangdong Science and Technology, 8.*

Chen, W. (2003). An empirical research on the development of CBD in big and medium domestic cities. *Urban Planning, 12.*

Ding, C. (2009). Highly concentrated central business district—International experience and evaluation of Chinese urban business district. *Planners, 9.*

Han, K. (2008). A study on the economical structure and of governmental administration model in CBDs—International experience and experiment in Lujiazui of Shanghai City (Ph.D. thesis). East China Normal University.

He, Y. (2006). *A discussion on improving the CBD development in China* (Graduate thesis). Guangxi University.

Jiang, Z. (2005). A debate over central business district (CBD) construction in big Chinese cities. *Urban Planning Overseas, 4.*

Jiang, S., Wang, M., & Zhang, J. (2009). *Path of the modern service industry agglomeration in CBD* (p. 122). Capital University of Economics Press.

Jiangsan, G., Wang, M., & Zhang, J. (2009). *A study on the path of modern service industry clustering in CBD* (p. 122). Capital University of Economics and Business Press.

Li, J. (2005). The Itch of CBD in Pearl River New Town. *Real Estate Guide, 18.*

Liu, T. (2007). Insight gained from foreign CBD evolution and development for our CBD building. *Journal of Shanghai Technical College of Urban Management, 2.*

Luo, Y., & Zhang, J. (2004). A study on problems in China's CBD development. *Urban Studies, 2.*

Robert, E. P. (1987). *Urban sociology* (pp. 48–62) (J. Song et al. Trans.). Huaxia Press.

Yang, J., & Wu, M. (2006). A study on the index system of the feasibility of CBD development in cities of China. *City Planning Review, 1.*

Yu, H. (2010). *A research on modern service industry agglomeration in CBDs* (Doctorate thesis). Capital University of Economics.

Zhang, J. (2006). Beijing CBD industrial development models and strategies. *Journal of Capital University of Economics and Business, 1.*

Zhang, J. (2007). *A research on the condition and positioning of Chengdu CBD* (Theses). Xi'an Jiaotong University.

---

[33]Ding (2009).

Chapter 10
Township Industrialization: Model and Analysis

The pattern of the industrialization of townships in China generally followed an endogenous model of urban development, which was shaped during the implementation of the strategy of small quasi-city town development and the actual process of township enterprise development in rural areas. In terms of dynamic mechanism, the industrialization model of townships was shaped from the bottom-up by the joint promotion of rural economic forces for industrialization and the influence of local government. However, in terms of space, the industrialization model of townships was mainly applied in rural areas. Therefore, it was, to some extent, the in situ urbanization of otherwise rural areas. Actually, in the Maoist period of the People's communes and collectivizations, researches into the best models by which to shape rural industry and communities had already commenced. It was after 1978, when Mr. Fei Xiaotong proposed the concept of the "small quasi-city town", and conducted a range of in-depth studies, that the urbanization strategy of China was gradually formed as one of "vigorously developing small quasi-city towns" and "encouraging the development of rural industry and the concentration of rural industry in towns" in order, in particular, to avoid "big city disease". Under such a policy, Wenzhou city, in the Yangtze River Delta, several cities in the Pearl River Delta, among other coastal areas took the lead in the in situ urbanization of rural areas. On the one hand, this was facilitated primarily by the development of township enterprises in accordance with then abovementioned urbanization strategy. On the other hand, it was further promoted by the reform and opening policy, which brought with it the introduction of foreign investment and various other factors. When the open door policy was further implemented in Northern China, around the year 2000, Beijing, Tianjin City, the Hebei Province, and the Bohai Coastal Region also witnessed rapid development. In fact, the industrialization of small townships and the in situ urbanization of rural areas ultimately expanded towards Northern China.

© Social Sciences Academic Press 2020
Q. Li, *China's Development under a Differential Urbanization Model*,
Research Series on the Chinese Dream and China's Development Path,
https://doi.org/10.1007/978-981-13-9451-5_10

This chapter will review the developmental process and existing models of the industrialization of townships and the in situ urbanization of rural areas. To this end, two particular township development models are analyzed. Firstly, it shall deal with three types of industrial development and in situ urbanization throughout rural areas in the Hebei Province. Secondly, it shall take Yunfu City in the Guangdong Province as an example, analyzing the bottom-up, endogenous and in situ urbanization of related rural areas. Thirdly, it shall propose the future direction of rural urbanization on the basis of the existing problems in the current model of township industrialization and the in situ urbanization of rural areas.

10.1 The History and Model of in Situ Urbanization in Rural Areas

The industrialization of township in China went through three major phases. The first phase saw a special pattern of development emerge in the Mao era. The second phase witnessed rural industrialization and in situ urbanization under the strategy of developing small quasi-city towns. The third phase showed a new phase of rural development throughout a period in which building a new countryside was the principle intention.

10.1.1 The Rural Development Model in China Throughout the Mao Era

In the early period of the founding of the People's Republic of China, there was very little preexisting basis for development in rural areas. The entire process had to be initiated from nothing while the whole country was faced with a crippling shortage of resources and technology, poor infrastructure, an unskilled population, limited national capital and other problems. Under such circumstances, China took a path characterized by developing heavy industry in cities, a clear urban and rural separation, general regional self-sufficiency and a focus on self-development in rural areas. What's more, after 1955, rural villages began to merge, forming "people's communes" and performing collectivized economic activities on a daily basis. In 1958, meanwhile, the notion of "commune industrialization" was explicitly proposed in the "Resolution on Certain Issues in the People's Communes". This put forward a clear aim: setting up a large number of, to name a few, locally-run chemical, food processing, oil pressing, and tailoring plants. At the same time, efforts were undertaken to refine iron and steel, primarily through the use of the young and middle-aged laborers that made up the backbone of the rural labor force, to realize the modernization of steel production. In the end, the labor force involved in reached a maximum of 60 million.[1] In this sense, it is clear that industrialization was at the core of the Mao era.[2] It was under the system of planned economy and urban-rural separation, then, in China, that the most suitable developmental pathways of industrialization and collective communities for rural areas were extensively explored during that period.

10.1.2   Coastal Areas in China: The in Situ Urbanization in Rural Areas in the Pearl River Delta Region and Its Causation

10.1.2.1   The Strategy of Developing Small Towns and Rural Industrialization

The period from 1978 to 1993 was the first in which the strategy of developing small quasi-city towns was implemented. In 1978, the Third Conference of Chinese City Development set clearly urban development policy of "controlling the scale of large cities and developing more small quasi-city towns". The policy of urban development during that period, then contained two parts. The first was to strictly control the size of large cities and to promote the development of small and medium cities. The second was to strive to develop small quasi-city towns based on rural towns in order to prevent the expansion of big cities and avoid various aspects of the "city disease". Indeed, throughout the 1980s, this concern was the core ideology. In December 1980, meanwhile, "The Summary of China's Urban Planning Conference" advanced explicitly a policy of urban development also focused on "controlling the scale of large cities, rationally developing medium-sized cities, and actively developing small cities". The "Sixth Five-Year Plan" went on to state that the above-mentioned policy should be "conscientiously implemented". Finally, the "Seventh Five-Year Plan" proposed focusing on the development of townships besides the development of small and medium cities. To be more specific, it suggested "preventing resolutely the excessive expansion of large cities, and giving priority to the development of medium and small-sized cities and small quasi-city towns."

The urbanization strategy of prioritizing the development of "small quasi-city towns" began in the 1980s, originating from a 1984 research paper named "Small Towns, Big Issues" by Mr. Fei Xiaotong. Mr. Fei found that previously affluent southern market towns had declined and fallen desolate following the agricultural cooperative and collectivization movement. Therefore, he proposed that agricultural collectivization should be rejected whilst rural commerce and private business

---

[1]Luo (2006).
[2]Dong (2008).

should be restored. In his "Small Towns, Big Issues", Fei also suggested: "The problem of a surplus rural labor force should be solved mainly through developing small quasi-city towns and supplemented by developing large, medium and small cities. Giving priority to building small quasi-city towns was, therefore, inevitable for China's socialist style of urbanization." Influenced by such thoughts, the "Eighth Five Year Plan" advanced that it was necessary to "strictly control the scale of large cities; rationally develop medium cities and small cities and build, based on the rural and township enterprises, a number of new towns, which included reasonable layouts, convenient transportation and local characteristics". Such directives were, in fact, included in the "Urban Planning Law of People's Republic of China" in 1990. During this phase, the scale of setting up new towns gradually reduced. For example, the "Report on the Adjustment of Organizational Standards" was enacted in 1984 and a pattern of developing small quasi-city towns only on the basis of designated towns eventually took shape.

The year 1993, however, saw a turning point for the strategy of developing small quasi-city towns. The development of small quasi-city towns before this was administrative. Nevertheless, it was explicitly defined in the "Decisions on Several Issues of Building a Socialist Market Economic System by the CPC Central Committee" in 1993, that: small quasi-city towns should be the spatial carriers of socialist market economies within rural areas. From that point onwards, the level of urbanization in rural areas would become the criteria for measuring rural industrialization. In the "Decision on Several Issues of a Socialist Market Economic System" it was also clearly stated that efforts should be made to "Strengthen town planning; guide township enterprises to concentrate appropriately; fully utilize and transform existing small towns and build new small quasi-city towns; gradually reform the household registration system in small quasi-city towns; allow farmers to go into small quasi-city towns to work or start businesses; develop tertiary industries in rural areas and, finally, to promote the transfer of surplus rural labor". Since then, small quasi-city towns effectively shouldered the responsibility of rural industrialization and modernization. In 1998, "Decision on Some Major Issues Concerning Agriculture and Rural Work by the CPC Central Committee" stated: "The development of small quasi-city towns is a grand strategy to promote economic and social development in rural áreas". The Fourth Plenary Session of the Fifteenth stated: "To develop Western regions and accelerate the construction of small quasi-city towns are major strategic issues concerning economic and social development in China". In 2000, "Opinions on Promoting the Healthy Development of Small Quasi-city Towns by the CPC Central Committee" stated: "The time has come and the conditions are perfect for speeding up urbanization, so seize the opportunity and timely guide small quasi-city towns to develop healthily. This should be among the important tasks for rural reform and development at present and for a long time in the future". A report of the Sixteenth Congress of the Chinese Communist Party, made in 2002 also noted: "The transfer of surplus rural labor, to non-agricultural industries and cities and quasi-city towns, is an inevitable trend of industrialization and modernization." The national policy after 1993 regarded the development of small quasi-city towns as the solution to the "three issues of agriculture, farmers and rural areas".

10.1.2.2 In Situ Urbanization Driven by Rural Industrial Development and Foreign Investment

After the period from 1992 to 1993, rural industrialization involving township enterprises developed rapidly. For one thing, non-agricultural employment in rural areas grew continuously. The development of township enterprises promoted significantly rural development, as was witnessed in coastal areas, and the desired pattern of in situ urbanization finally emerged. It appeared first in the areas of the Pearl River Delta and the Yangtze River Delta. For instance, in the Pearl River Delta area, investment-oriented economic development gave rise to special rural spatial characteristics, which followed, "neither a city nor a village" model.[3] Two factors constituted the principle causation of in situ urbanization in Eastern rural regions. The first was the rapid development of township enterprises after the 1980s. The second was the economic globalization that had cast its influence over the eastern regions in recent years. Owing to a range of favorable factors, such as location, transportation and policy, including, not least, various preferential policies, the degree of control over exports and imports, as well as more investment, in general, and a larger pool of educated people, the Eastern countryside rapidly became a highly developed and industrialized rural region,[4] In fact, prior to 1998, it was possible for the collectively owned land in townships to be used for non-agricultural construction. Therefore, some township enterprises were, indeed, built on farm land and sprawled out. In recent years, meanwhile, economic globalization triggered the flow of external capital and technology into eastern regions, thereby equipping the region with a clear export-oriented economy.[5] Under such circumstances, the power of local governments and local working units was enhanced and the external economy entering rural areas began to follow a decentralized approach. This approach was often shaped around the collectives of villages and usually operated throughout a spatial pattern of an urban and rural sprawl. Some scholars believed that, the occurrence of in situ urbanization in the rural areas of the Pearl River Delta was due to the limited influence of central cities and the development on the fringes of urban areas and the chronic underdevelopment on borderline agricultural areas.[6] In general, the in situ urbanization of coastal rural areas was characterized by a export-oriented economy, quite similar, in turn, to the phenomenon of "Desakota" observed throughout Southeast Asia.[7]

---

[3]Zhao (2002).

[4]Shen (1998).

[5]Yang and Dan (2006).

[6]Lin (2001).

[7]Deskota proposed by McGee, depicts a geographical landscape different from the spatial centralization of Western cities, but a mixed town form derived from city extending.

10.1.3   Building a New Countryside and the Direction for in Situ Urbanization in the Countryside

Since the mid-1990s, conditions in rural areas has declined while large cities developed rapidly. Many of these large cities find themselves plagued by a host of problems, including social injustice, high population density and elevated levels of risk. At the same time, problems also emerged from the previous stage of extensive small quasi-city town development. The "three issues of agriculture, farmer and rural area" were becoming increasingly serious. In response to this, the central government proposed a series of policies with a view to making an overall planning for urban and rural development and building a new countryside, emphasizing the self-development and construction of rural areas. For example, in November 2002, the Sixteenth National Congress of the Communist Party of China proposed: "speeding up urbanization and making an overall planning for urban and rural economic and social development". In November 2003, the Communique of the Third Plenary Session of the Sixteenth Central Committee of the CPC stated: "In line with the requirement of making an overall planning for urban and rural development, regional development... to a greater extent, the market should be allowed to play a fundamental role in the allocation of resources". In January 2005, "Opinions on a Number of Policies in Further Strengthening Rural Work and Improving Comprehensive Agricultural Production Capacity made by the CPC Central Committee and State Council" stated: "adhere to the strategy of making an overall planning for urban and rural development, giving more, taking less and allowing more flexible policies". Furthermore, in October 2005, the Eleventh Five Year Plan proposed to: "build a new socialist countryside". In February 2006, "Opinions on Promoting the Construction of a New Socialist Countryside by the CPC Central Committee and State Council" stated: "make an overall planning for urban and rural economic and social development, let industry repay agriculture and cities support rural areas". In October 2008, meanwhile, the "Communique of the Third Plenary Session of the Seventeenth Central Committee of the CPC" stated: "sticking to the reform and opening-up policy, making an overall planning for urban and rural reforms". In January 2010, "Suggestions on Making More Efforts in Making an Overall Planning for Urban and Rural Development and Further Consolidating the Foundation for Agricultural and Rural Development by the CPC Central Committee and State Council" stated: we should "increase investment in agriculture and rural areas, promote urbanization, and give priority to the development of small and medium cities and small quasi-city towns". A series of documents issued by the central government, therefore, provided powerful policy support for the rapid development of the non-agricultural economy in rural areas as well as rapid in situ urbanization in general. Above all else, however, the policy of "building a new countryside" led, in 2005, to a new phase of in situ urbanization in rural areas.

10.2   Case 1: In Situ Urbanization in the Rural Areas of Hebei Province Driven by Rural Industry Development

As the opening-up policy spread northward during the mid-1990s, the development of Beijing, Tianjin City, and the Hebei Province, in the Bohai Sea Region, accelerated. During that process, there emerged widespread in situ urbanization within the rural areas of the Hebei Province. This in situ urbanization was based on "bottom-up" industrial development in rural area and generated the spatial aggregation, as was in urbanization, that is, reproducing something like the landscape of industrialization and rural urbanization during the Industrial Revolution in Britain. Pursuant to the degree of spatial aggregation or institutional thickness, the in situ urbanization of the rural areas of the Hebei Province could be divided into three types.

10.2.1   The Form and Motivation of Dispersed in Situ Rural Urbanization

The economic factors and population involved in dispersive in situ rural urbanization were highly decentralized. This was mainly a result of the less outward-oriented economy of these areas and the fact that the introduction of new factors was still in its infancy. That is to say, there was a lack of the impact from the intensification of mass production (market or service) to break the predominant dispersed small-scale family production structure. The rural industry, therefore, generally took the form of low-skilled and labor-intensive light industry, such as the processing of garments, the manufacturing of simple plastics and of rubber products. Relevant to various stages of development and the participants involved, the dispersive in situ urbanization of rural areas could be divided into family-based and village-based processes. In addition, the levels of agricultural industrialization, the part-time employment of farmers and the extent of their reliance on mother villages constituted another dispersive force. Generally speaking, the dispersed state of in situ rural urbanization was caused by a combination of the above-mentioned factors, but, more often than not, with a particular emphasis on just one.

   As for the form of this dispersed in situ rural urbanization, it featured, spatial sprawl of family managed enterprises. The industries undertaken by such enterprises included, mainly, simple, and small-scale machine-based production such as clothing, luggage cases, bags, and footwear. There were, at first, few foreign-funded enterprises or import and export enterprises. They mainly produced low-grade products and imitations of famous-brand, that were then exported through informal channels. As regards the different scale of manufacturing, they could be divided into two spatial units: small family workshops or large family factories.

The production equipment available to small family workshops was, generally speaking, simple and of poor quality. The production of imitation productions constituted most of their workload and they generally received orders or did auxiliary processing for larger factories. There were usually up to 40 employees in such workshops. The workshops themselves, meanwhile, were generally set up either by renovating an old courtyard or building a new courtyard. Typically, dormitories, for employers and employees, were situated, directly opposite a southern gate, in the northern section, whereas work shops where to the west and kitchens and warehouses were positioned in the east. The renovated workshops were built in line with the standards of the old homesteads in their villages, which covered an area of 25×17 m^2 or 20×20 m^2. The newly built workshops were also founded on old homesteads but extended outwards around the village. The larger ones could be as big as 35×35 m^2.

Family factories were similar to family workshops, although with 40 to 100 employees, but, in most cases 50–80 employees. Those with over 200 employees were extremely rare. A typical factory building had three storeys. The first of these was used as storeroom; the second a workshop; the third dormitories. There were often no canteens and these large-family factories, averaging at about 60×70 m, were generally located on the periphery of the village. Among them, 20 factories, with about 100 employees each, gradually emerged in an industrial park allocated by town's government.[8] Despite the fact that they were located in an industrial park, however, their mode of production and management was still family-based. Employees rarely left their employment and the individual units were isolated from one another as well as completely lacking those features of large-scale production and specialty-based work division. Dispersed in situ rural urbanization took place based primarily on the sprawl of the two above-mentioned types of family-run plants (see Fig. 10.1). Meanwhile, populations witnessed slight reductions within the old village boundaries. Since there were numerous renovated family workshops, however, with few courtyards abandoned, overall population decrease was insignificant. The size of those abandoned courtyard, meanwhile, was about 20×20 m^2, which made them hard to transform into family workshops, particularly due to years of neglect and disrepair.

In terms of the overall region, the distance between villages was usually 1000–2000 m. All villages followed the same spatial development patterns. That is to say, they were all based on family plants. These workshops mixed with ordinary courtyards inside the old villages and often extended out from the periphery of the villages to the main roads, thereby forming a plant-cluster along such roads (see Fig. 10.2). Thus, the sprawl along the main roads actually shaped the precise spatial

---

[8]April 10–13, 2007 interviews: Town government plans to include Zhang village and Lai Cheng village into the town area. And they plan to establish 300 acres of industrial zone in in the west of Dianshang village and the East of Zhang Village.

Fig. 10.1 The expanding trends of plants in dispersed in situ rural urbanization

form of dispersed in situ rural urbanization. Specific instances of this type of in situ rural urbanization were mainly found in SanTai Town of Baoding City, Dawang Town of Anxin County and Xiaoli Town of Rongcheng City.

10.2.2   The Form and Motivation of the Concentrated— Dispersed in Situ Rural Urbanization

Concentrated and dispersed in situ rural urbanization refers to a model of urban development that is formed by the activities of larger enterprises. Technical progress and the overall process of economic globalization led to more enterprises which gave rise to centers of economic activity and population influx around the areas in which they located. Counties and towns were the main individual components of economic globalization. At the same time, the locations in which industry naturally clustered became subject to the government's allocation of further resources required for continued industrial development. The technical progress of industry was, then, the main driving force behind concentration. This trend was particularly visible in the clothing, textile, light industry, and metal

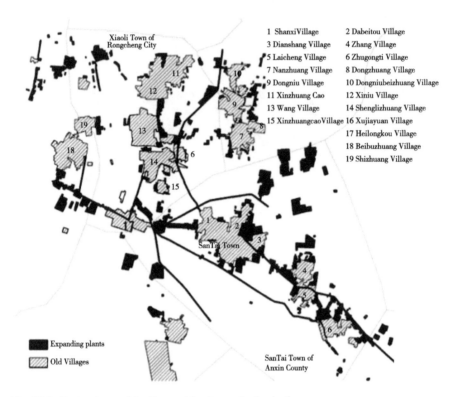

Fig. 10.2 Regional sprawl in dispersed in situ rural urbanization

production sectors. The function of aggregation in in situ rural urbanization was, above all else, to deepen the division of labor and to further enhance the production of modern enterprises. Family factories, for instance, continuously upgraded until they reached a level consistent with modern enterprises, primarily due to the growth of international markets and constant advancements to technology and subsequent productivity. Taking the cashmere industry in Qinghe town as an example, since it first emerged in the 1980s, entering into international market was the driving force behind its subsequent development. To this end, it made continuous efforts to enhance its level of exports. Before 1984, the cashmere industry in Qinghe town had relied heavily on the services of the Import and Export Company of Livestock in Tianjin to meet its own export quotas. In 1984, however, Qinghe Co. Ltd. (Zhuang Rongchang) cooperated with the Xinjiang Livestock Import and Export Corporation and became the first such enterprise to independently export. In fact, throughout the mid-1990s, the Qinghe cashmere industry adopted a variety of additional means of export, such as through the use of agents and further developments as regards independent exports. In the end, the number of licensed enterprises for imports and exports increased to 61 by 2008. Key to it all was the continuous expansion of the international market. This prompted the improvement of cashmere combing technology, including in particular, primary processing and deep processing, as well as the strengthening of subsequent chains, such as the spinning, knitting, clothing and other post deep-processing stages. Besides this, the participation of foreign investment and external companies also guided family factories to adjust to modern production and management techniques, thereby making modern enterprises the dominant industry in Qinghe County.[9] By 2008, 30 cashmere enterprises had attracted foreign investment[10] and large-scale domestic enterprises also maintained branches there. The textile industry, therefore, entered into the stage of qualitative change, gradually giving rise to large industrial clusters with specialized and meticulous divisions.

The gathering of large-scale enterprises in the central region, to a greater extent, reflected the requirements of industrial specialization and large-scaled production, as well as the guidance provided by the government's allocation of resources. During the period of family workshops and small rural factories, cashmere production in Qinghe Town was mainly conducted on a small scale and by means of simple combing machines with low demands for electricity and other facilities. Thus, a small factory, of about 200 m^2, sprawled out, from near its origins of Yang Erzhuang, along the National Highway 308, with a 1 km extension on both the north and south sides, finally reaching Shuangcheng Town, 10 km away from central urban area. Comparatively, the proliferation of small factories was relatively insignificant due to limited traffic and electricity[11] (see Fig. 10.3). After 1998, large-scale factories emerged due to foreign investment and industrial upgrades, but the power, transportation and communications infrastructure needed to support the production in villages was seriously inadequate. So in 1999, the government established the Qinghe International Cashmere Science and Technology Park in Gexian Town and Xielu Town, covering an area of 8 km^2, with a total investment of approximately one- hundred-million yuan to improve transportation, electricity, water supply, pipe networks, and other infrastructure. Needless to say, this project led to the clustering of large-scale plants. Since then, 128 large-scale enterprises have entered the Science and Technology Park. According to interviews, other enterprises in the villages continued to use simple labor-intensive methods for the primary processing of cashmere. Comparatively, the area of aggregated large-scaled enterprises tended to be approximately 200 × 200 m^2, with output values of above 50 million yuan. Meanwhile, only a handful of factories were scattered in the village, covering an overall area of just 2000 m^2.

---

[9]The development of the technology, market and industrial structure of cashmere industry in Qinghe Town under discussion plaese refer to the MS Thesis: "An Empirical Study of the Dynamic Interaction between Social Structural Evolution and the Development of Industrial Technology." by Wang Jici. Tsinghua University, 2000.

[10]Data from the office of Administrative Service Center in Xingtai city. "Analysis and Suggestions on the Development of Foreign Funded Enterprises in 2008". http://www.xtsxzfw.gov.cn/ Broadcast/broadcastview.aspx? Infold = 00090 & type = {InfoType}.

[11]"More than 1000 Cashmere Combing Machines in Shuangcheng Town, but the ' Road Hard to Pass' Prevented Customers from Going to the Region of Shuangcheng Town". http://www.xtnews. gov.cn/node3/xinwen/xsq/qhx/userobject1ai574L.html.

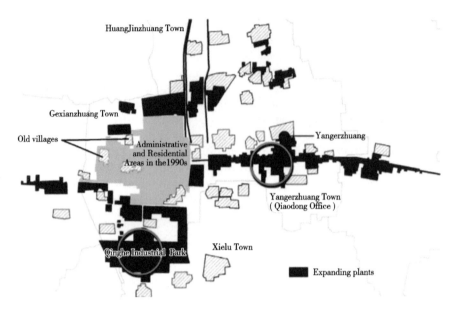

Fig. 10.3 Spatial sprawl pattern of Qinghe town in 2009

The spatial evolution of the central area of the concentrated—dispersed in situ rural urbanization have distinctive features that reflect changing external conditions. Efforts to develop administrative, industrial, commercial and residential areas were the main forces that shaped the different spatial patterns of the "city" at different stages in the central area. By now, the commercial and industrial economy undoubtedly played a most important role in these spatial patterns. Ultimately the aggregate effect triggered by these qualitative changes to the intensification of the Qinghe cashmere industry meant the "village" quickly evolved into a "city". Qinghe City grew up based around an entire group of villages. The administrative, commercial and industrial areas, as well as the residential areas, developed throughout different periods filling the spaces between villages. Whereas the area had previously been shaped by the agricultural economy, via administration, and now, industry and commerce took centre stage. The old center maintained until the end of the 1980s, including, among others, Qinghe No. 1 Middle School, Shanghai Hualian Corporation, the County Government, the County Grain Bureau, and old county hospital. From the middle 1980s to the late 1990s, all administrative centers moved eastward to the Tai Mountain Road area, including the County Government, the Construction Bureau, the Property Management Bureau, Education Bureau, and other administrative units as well as accompanying residential areas (many showed a typical morphology of high walled courtyards such as on Yucai street). Gradually, a commercial street, which were comprised of Jiajiale Supermarkets, Carrefour Supermarkets, theaters and other businesses, (Wusong Street) was formed. From the mid 1990s to the late 1990s, the international market further pushed the development of the cashmere industry. Insofar as the main cashmere industry originally developed at Yang Zhuang and other villages on the eastern side of the railway station, the area around the railway station burst into development. After 1998, a range of large-scaled enterprises moved into the Industrial Park in the South, thereby promoting the gradual development of residential areas and additional businesses in the south. After 2005, real estate started to develop rapidly, and gradually extended its reach to the surrounding villages. The overall spatial development, meanwhile, exemplified various periodical and regional characteristics. The regional center had been a product of the agricultural economy. The eastern part embodied the executive power, while the southern part was host to extensive industrial and commercial development. The outermost circle was evenly scattered by villages and fields (see Fig. 10.4). As a result of this development a

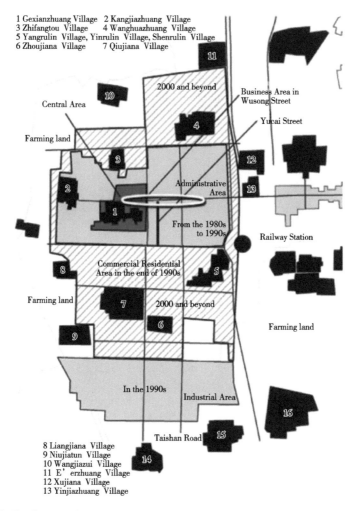

Fig. 10.4 The features of the spatial development of Qinghe town

"City" grew between the villages and, in the end, continuously enclosed the villages, thereby making them "villages in city" or "urban villages".

10.2.3   The Form and Motivations of Concentrated in Situ Rural Urbanization

In an area where concentrated in situ rural urbanization took place, most of the people involved were, of course, local people. Temporary residents, on the contrary, were mainly confined to the central areas. This type of rural urbanization, which gave rise to so-called isolated aggregates, was mainly distributed in Jindian Town, Gengle Town and Cishan Town of Handan City, the Jingxing mining area in Shijiazhuang City, Baicao Village in Wei County of Zhangjiakou City, the Tangshan area, Longhua Town of Jing County and, finally, locations around the Cangzhou area. Such cases of isolated "concentrated in situ rural urbanization" could be divided into two types. The first was the township developed under the direction of the government. the second were those areas developed because of their unique resources or transportation advantages.

The main driving force behind resource-based in situ urbanization was the use of local mineral resources to develop all kinds of metal machinery and equipment manufacturing. The scale and complexity of such industry meant that large and external enterprises were often directly involved. The government's investment inviting policy, which was intended to encourage the processes of economic globalization, actively accelerated this process. Cishan Town, Gengle Town, and Jingdian Town, in Handan city, can be used as examples. The Jingdian Town, located in the She county of Handan city, attracted some major metallurgical enterprises such as "Tian Tie First Rolling limited liability Company", under the "Tian Tie Metallurgy Group Co. Ltd." in Tianjin, and the large metallurgical industry of "Tiantie Chongli Steel Co. Ltd.", a joint venture of local, Tian Tie and foreign investment, as well as Longshan Guodian Electricity Industries based in the "August Fifth Prefabricated Component Factory", that is, a local construction materials industry (see Fig. 10.5). This extensive interest was primarily a result of local resources, including iron ore, and its location near Shanxi, which entailed easy access to abundant coal resources. In order to attract more enterprises, first of all, the government vigorously constructed much-needed roads, power grids and other infrastructure. Take the road network construction project completed in Jingdian town for example. This included the widening of Longjing North Main Street, the construction of Jintan Street, Jinzhong Street and Gongnong Friendship Street. Secondly, the government granted preferential policies in terms of local land use. Many of the new factories were, however, branches of conglomerates, already possessing their own professional and technical workers. What they need was access to local mineral resources, as well as land and power resources. In fact, they had little at all to do with local industry. Instead, these factories were distributed adjacent to the main resources and main roads by separated plants. Plants included various types

Old villages
1 Yijie Village   2 Erjie Village
3 Sanjie Village   4 Sijie Village

Inter-province Highway 309

Chongli Steel Co. Ltd

Tian Tie Group

Residential Area of Tian Tie Group

Fig. 10.5 The spatial aggregation pattern of Jingdian town in 2009

of large-scale workshops, office buildings, canteens, and dormitories (see Fig. 10.5). The supporting facilities for these plants were, meanwhile, mostly completed by the enterprises themselves, and used separately from the local residents.

The direct participation of external factories resulted in increased population concentrations and the gathering of a large number of skilled workers from outside the local area. Although its overall impact on local industrialization was relatively weak, and the share of the local population not employed in the agricultural sector was not large, a strong urban morphogenesis could be observed for the first time. This change was the result, primarily, of various forms of development and construction, conducted by the local government, but with the expenditures paid for by external factories, that is, in return for resources, land and environmental pollution. In fact, over time, land use fees and taxes became, to a large extent, the main source of funding with which the local government could undertake the renovation and construction of the central town area. First on the list was the construction of various types of government offices, such as the expansion and renovation of Jindian's government offices, the police station and the local taxation bureau.

Second on the list were often improvements to roads, the construction of commercial buildings and the introduction of new businesses. Most of the commercial buildings constructed in this area were usually two-story buildings; including the first floor as a shop floor, whilst the second was for habitancy. In fact, they generally took the same form as houses that had been built by villagers along the streets under the modes of dispersed in situ rural urbanization and concentrated - dispersed in situ rural urbanization. Third on the list was the renovation of old villages in the central areas. This was different to the development of commercial residential communities in central areas in accordance with the above-mentioned types of rural urbanization. For one thing, the non-native population generally belonged to industrial systems and, therefore, inhabited the living areas provided by factories under concentrated on-site rural urbanization. Therefore, the renovation and development of central areas was usually conducted collectively in the center of villages as the construction of "new dwelling houses" and "civilized eco-villages", with relatively less commercial development. The funding for the reconstruction of villages, meanwhile, usually came from the compensation provided by factories that occupied and rented the surrounding land.

The development of concentrated in situ rural urbanization relied, to a large extent, upon the aggregation of resource-dependent or traffic-dependent external companies. Nevertheless, this process was often separated from the development of local industries. That it is to say, it lacked in diffusion, failing to influence the spatial situation of surrounding villages in a significant way. Some of the young people from surrounding villages would, of course, go to the central area to work or engage in commercial activities, but the overall industrial structure of the villages would not be altered, but rather still bore the characteristics of agricultural production. These villages lacked the sort of two-story residential houses as were built by the villagers themselves under in situ rural urbanization. Instead, the newly built houses, in these areas, followed the form of traditional one-story courtyards. Only in a select few villages, primarily those in close proximity to coal-mining, or those whose land was occupied, or in gob areas, could one find multi-storey houses built by the villagers themselves. The six five-story residential buildings in Bailonggang Village of Qian'an City and the multistory houses in Banbidian Village in Kaiping District of Tangshan City were typical of this. Perhaps most importantly, since there was no increase to incomes in the surrounding villages, the lifestyles there did not change much either.

10.3   Case 2: The Actions of the "Main Function Zone" and the "Integrated Community" in Yunfu City, Guangdong Province

Most areas that fell under Yunfu City of Guangdong Province were underdeveloped, with a rural population of 60%. In Yunan County, the urbanization rate was only 18.9%, that is, the lowest recorded. Overall urban development was extremely limited. The population in Yunfu City and Luoding City numbered around 200,000, whilst it was 50–100,000 in New Town and Du Town and 10–50,000 in Yaogu Town and other similar semi-new towns. The rest such towns numbered 10,000 or less. There were also no regional urban centers to speak of. As far as the rural population was concerned, according to a sample survey of rural households in "new urbanization", in Yunfu, in 2011, 49% of the labor force chose to go out of Yunfu City to find employment.[12] In light of this, Yunfu City gave priority to the development of the countryside. Then, What, then, will the county-centered urbanization be? Explorations on "new urbanization" in Yunfu focused on three significant aspects that subsequently unfolded here.

Firstly, it was concluded that county-level towns would be the most potential and absorbent places to attract outgoing and back-flowing labor forces. Secondly, the large-scale and modernized management of agricultural production shall become an important method of raising the level of economic development in the countryside and absorbing local labor, surplus labor, and the returning population. Thirdly, the construction of educational, health care and other public facilities within the county-level town and other towns should constitute the core of urbanization.

For this reason, Yunfu City broke though administrative boundaries of planning, designated land as main functional zones and outlined a program "to jointly create a better environment and harmonious society". They also sought to promote, by a development model of "co-scheming, co-constructing, co-managing and co-sharing", on-site rural urbanization, which was both, top-down, that is, launched by the government, but also bottom-up, that is, participated in by the masses.

10.3.1 Urban Spatial Development and Infrastructure Guarantees

Yunfu stated that the urban space pattern and the standard of urban infrastructure shall be the basis of overall regional development. Urban spatial development is, however, a complex process involving a range of factors. For one thing, the development of and protection to sites of a cultural or historical significance, including an extensive planning as regards the detailed classification of these sites, the provincial cultural sites, and intangible cultural heritage. Secondly, utmost importance was also allocated to the protection of the ecological environment. There were, meanwhile, two main priorities as regards the development of infrastructure. The first of these was the equalization of rural infrastructure. This project included planning for irrigation and water conservancy and essential improvements to water supply systems, flood control, drainage works, and sewage treatment plants as well as the planning of power facilities. Secondly, attention was paid to the

---

[12]Data source: the document of *The Overall Development Plan of Yunfu*.

construction of public services. This project included educational facilities, such as junior high schools, which were to be located within the urban area, while primary schools tended to be located within a radius of 2 km, in dense population area.

10.3.2 The Main Function Zone: Transformation of Government Functions and the Construction of Public Services

The expansion of main functions included the classification of particular function zones, adjustments to government functions and priority afforded to governmental work as well as other major measures. What came to be called "main function extension" involved an organic matching between main spatial functions and the subjects involved in implementing these functions. The overall aim was to "let zones be used for what they were supposed to" and to "let people do what they can" as regards these particular functions. Such a functional approach actually started to break spatially organized administrative boundaries and, in the end, altered the blind urbanization by following the same pattern. It effectively functioned to confirm which locations were suitable for and would host which functions. Those areas best suited for urbanization, for instance, became key urbanization areas, those with a strong industrial basis became areas of further industrialization, those with agricultural advantages became specialized agricultural areas and mountainous areas became ecology and forestry conservation zones.

The modernization of agriculture, meanwhile, included the establishment of zones specifically used for the planting of specific crops, the breeding of particular livestock and certain areas allocated to the growth of commercial forests. In addition, agricultural enterprises, leading enterprises, specialized cooperative organizations of farmers and suburban agriculture economies were all rewarded. The development of specific agriculture included the extension of the agricultural production chain, promoting, in the agricultural organization pattern of "company + farming households", the scale and industrialization of featured agriculture, developing an agricultural service economy, supporting rural land circulation and compensation for forest-based ecological development. Crucially, all of this was done with respect to the unique local characteristics of the relevant areas and, in the process, bestowed a degree of local identity to the entire development process. Other incentive mechanisms aimed at financial security and tax sharing were also gradually implemented.

To ensure the locality of development, further reforms were made to the leadership, not to mention the evaluation process, in main function zones throughout Yunfu. The GDP-based assessment of townships, by the government, was canceled. Of utmost importance was the "5 + X"-based standard of evaluation of the township-level authorities. This evaluation was based on the principle that their responsibilities were being carried out in a manner consistent with the rights and interests of all. The "5" here referred to the top priorities of responsibility within townships. These included "social stability, increasing the income of farmers, good public services, policy advocacy and good grassroots social administration". "X" here referred, meanwhile, to the respective functions, responsibilities and economic and social development goals bestowed upon the different villages and towns.[13] This standard of evaluation would gradually change the government's top-down style of implementation to a bottom-based style, thereby further ensuring locality of the development process. To be more specific, "three offices and two centers"[14] were set up in various regions to provide rural social services, develop the agricultural economy and maintain stability, including the establishment of a Land Circulation Service Center, an Entrepreneurship and Employment Service Center, a Center of Agricultural Industrialization, and an SME Service Center. Together, these services represented efforts to become a useful service-oriented government for the local villagers.

10.3.3 Community as the Basic Administrative Unit: The Cultivation of Autonomous Social Organizations

Based on the expansion of these main functions, Yunfu City further planned to build an "integrated community" which would stress issues related to quality of life in the local area, including public spaces, community service systems, social management, perfect infrastructure and community culture with local features. This approach, that was, fostering grass-roots rural communities as the basis of change, effectively paved the way for further local development.

In terms of social management, various autonomous organizations within rural communities were gradually cultivated. Various regions, under Yunfu City, exploratively established such social organization as the three-level of villager councils, they were, the councils at natural village level, that at administrative village level and larger town level. These organizations were tasked with actively participating in and supervising rural public affairs and social management, dealing with affairs that affected the immediate interests of local people. The establishment of the three-level villager councils went through a rather formal process. It was with the guidance of the Party Committee and government, primarily through mass voluntary action, basing on natural village, administrative village and town, that the three-level villager councils ultimately became basic administrative units. These units were afforded legal recognition with a principle of "civil business ran by civilians, civil affairs managed by civilians" and submitted to the County Civil Affairs Bureau for the relevant record taking. Unlike the traditional clan councils that had gone before,

---

[13]Survey on Rural Social Management Innovation in Yunfu City, Guangdong Province. http://www.gd.xinhuanet.com/newscenter/2011-08/26/content_23551395.htm.

[14]Three offices and two centers: the Party and Government Office, the Agricultural Economy Office, the Livable Hometown Office, the Center of Comprehensive Management, the Department of Complaint Dealings and Social Stability and the Center of Social Affairs Services.

these three-level villager councils won the trust and support of the masses and were keenly participated in by leading members from grassroots organizations.

Spatially, these communities preserved some of the distinctive features of rural communities, the natural patterns of historic villages and the tradition of taking ancestral temples as the center of public life. As part of this broader participation, public spaces were created throughout such rural communities for entertainment and learning activities. The roads and drains as well as other essential infrastructure were also renovated. Improvements to the spatial environment, along these lines, actually functioned to promote the development and strengthening of rural communities. In accordance with demand, the priority of infrastructure construction was sewage disposal, the cleaning of rivers and ponds, the repairing of roads and bridges, the building of sports and leisure facilities as well as public service facilities, municipal administrative facilities and, finally, the construction of various types of identification systems.

10.3.4   Action Guidelines

In 2011, the Yunfu Municipal Government promulgated the "Guide to 'Substitute Subsidies with Rewards' for Those Behaviors of Co-creating a Beautiful Environment and a Harmonious Society". This was done with a view to promoting grassroots development within rural areas. It provided comprehensive incentives for the undertaking of as many as 21 rural development projects under four different categories of rural infrastructure construction. They included rural infrastructural projects (including roads, passenger shelters, road management and maintenance, water conservancy and modern-standard farmland construction projects), rural environmental projects (including the construction of brand villages, livable village communities, rural home-inns, forestry, ecological civilization and hygienic villages), rural public service projects (including the integration of the three networks, the construction of entertainment and sports squares, rural home libraries, village cultural clubs, folk cultural activities, popular theatrical and art organizations and the projection of rural movies). Finally, the social management of rural area projects (including the building of communities and of reputable villages).

10.4   Proposals for Township Industrialization and in Situ Rural Urbanization

10.4.1   Common Features and Problems

The in situ rural urbanization in the Hebei Province was, to a large extent, the result of rural industrialization and the gradual development towards modernization and globalization. It was substantially different from other export-oriented development models, that was, the modern industry based directly on investment in urban area, and, to some extent, reflected the characteristics of spontaneous bottom-up rural development. Although rural areas in the Hebei Province had already experienced some spatially in situ urbanization and avoided excessive population concentrations within large cities, the pursuit of modernization by industry did, however, bring with it a variety of problems. The problems that did exist included, among others, the development at the price of agriculture and farmers, the loss of traditional rural society, resource depletion and environmental pollution. To a certain extent, then, in situ rural urbanization in the Hebei Province was not a healthy developmental approach, but rather an inevitable certainty for the modernization of the rural economy.

Relatively speaking, the development model of Yunfu City, Guangdong Province and the model in the rural areas of the Hebei Province bore some similarities and differences. The similarities consisted in the fact that both were reflections of bottom-up rural development. The main difference was that in Yunfu there was a conscious, autonomous and locally-based developmental route based on the spontaneous development model of rural areas in the Hebei Province. Yunfu made an overall exploration as to all aspects of the in situ urbanization of rural life, including the overall spatial layout, the transformation of government functions, the development of local communities and sufficient guidelines. The Yunfu model did not, however, give satisfactory answers as to the pattern of developing the rural economy.

10.4.2 Discussion: Rural Urbanization Should Be Sustainable

The key characteristics of urbanization are different in different countries around the world. Concentrated urbanization in developed countries was often made possible by exploitation of the countryside. Rural areas in developing countries, meanwhile, generally showed a high level of dependency on the process of globalization. In China, during the Maoist era, experiments in the field of rural development were carried out, followed by explorations into locally-oriented development. It was believed that the rural areas should remain independent from external forces such as government guidance and economic globalization. Instead, the emphasis was placed on the local economy and realizing autonomous social development, including, among others, the development of a diversified local economy, a unique rural community and society, and the integration of rural spatial resources.

10.4.2.1 "Non-evolutionary" Diversified Economic Development and Partial Self-sufficiency

The basic problem of Chinese villages, similar to in Western countries throughout early periods of industrialization, was that they were very populous but lacking in land. Even if effective measures were taken to speed up urbanization, such that the rate of urbanization may reach 50–60%, by 2020–2030, there would still be 700–800 million people living within rural areas. That is to say, the absolute number of rural inhabitants would not drop significantly even as urbanization unfolded. Population-to-land ratio, meanwhile, was the foundation for all types of economic development, with the capacity to bind both agricultural development and industrialization. Therefore, the economy in China could only develop on the basis of its own unique conditions.[15] Wen Tiejun, for instance, believed that the present small-scale, highly-dispersed farming economy, with farming households engaged in part-time industrial production, would be the dominant economy category in the Chinese countryside.[16] The concurrence of agriculture and dispersed rural industry was, to a certain degree, inevitable. An autonomous road to development should, then, abandon the standard logic of economic evolution that proceeds from agriculture to large-scale industry and then, finally, to the service-sector. Instead, it must take the approach that allowed multi-economic elements to coexist and promoting "village-town unions".[17] Such an approach would give rise to overall economic development, including agriculture, handicrafts and other traditional economic activities as well as large-scale modern industry and businesses. Zheng et al. also proposed a concept of New Industrialization that involved "completing industrialization through the coordinated development of agriculture, industry and services. In other words, modern industrialization should not be promoted in isolation. Besides, efforts should be made to overcome the shortcomings exposed in traditional industrialization model."[18] The standard format of traditional industrialization was but the blind pursuit of modern industrial evolution.

Rural industries should, then, abandon the predominant model of modern industrialization. In fact, a suitable economic form for the social reality, that is, a vast number of poorly educated farmers, is the coexistence of large-scale modernized industrial production alongside plentiful traditional manual production. Large-scale industrial production, meanwhile, required the transfer of urban industry, demanding the decentralized configuration of resources on the part of government. The development of information technology, however, made it possible for urban industries to establish production processes in rural areas. It was also expected that rural industry had the capacity to mass produce traditional handicrafts with diverse and personalized cultural characteristics, rather, that is, than the large-scale production of the same goods. The potential for this market could be best seen in fair trade[19] shops located in developing countries and regions.

---

[15]Zhu (1996).

[16]Wen (2003).

[17]With regard to village developing after the form of a city, Aristotle believed that the city was the union of towns (Synoecism), namely several adjacent villages unite administratively to form a town, to reach a certain size and achieve self-sufficiency in the community.

[18]Zheng et al. (2004).

[19]Fair trade, that is, anti-capitalist monopoly trade.

For example, the "Earth Tree"[20] organization collected handmade, culturally distinctive, personalized and environmentally friendly products from underdeveloped villages. These were completely different products from the outputs of large-scale industrial production lines. Fair trading practices resulted by virtue of a networked society and all revenues obtained were returned to the underdeveloped areas in order to promote their development. Another example was the "Xingeng workshop" in China.[21] After being founded in May 2007, it integrated production and trade with financial aid to students. It provided employment opportunities for disadvantaged groups in both urban and rural areas. There were, meanwhile, two different sources of its products. One was the handicrafts of villagers. The theme of these products was usually chosen to emphasize Chinese culture or environmental protection. Once samples were designed, the relevant production processes and skills were taught to local women, who would carry out the production themselves. The second was products from remote areas with distinctive local folk characteristics. These products were produced in situ. For those developing rural areas, this might be a new approach, involving sustainable rural economic development which utilized and cherished local resources and culture, developed historical and cultural resources and resulted in much needed cultural reproduction and industries.

These examples show that equal importance should be attached to both agriculture and rural industrialization. Agriculture, after all, meant not only the country's food supply, but also a labor supply for employment purposes. Views of the Physiocrats, presented by Spengler et al. indicated:

(a) Even if people could be employed, national power should not rely solely on the size of the national population.
(b) Population growth depends on the growth of wealth, rather than the reverse.
(c) Wealth growth depends on the expansion of wealth through agricultural production.
(d) Increasing agricultural income expands the size and wealth of the population in both agricultural and non-agricultural sectors.[22]

Crucial to these stages, the realization of agricultural industrialization was considered the best way of ensuring agricultural development, by which agricultural income would then increase. In addition, the role of the government was particularly important during this process. As a result, agriculture should be taken as a matter for public policy. In addition to agricultural subsidies, a more critical role of the government consisted in land management and the cultivation of agro-productive personnel and technology.

To achieve sustainable economic development, the regional economy should also be stressed. In this way, partial self-sufficiency can be realized, that is, instead of being drawn fully into the international industrial division of labor. In other

---

[20]http://www.earthtree.com.tw/.

[21]http://www.xingeng.org/Cn/about.asp.

[22]Klatzmann and Levi (1971).

words, the rural economy should be an organic entirety positioned somewhere between a closed countryside system and a completely opened globalized system, thereby protecting both internal resources and interests. Partial self-sufficiency also meant that rural industrial production and sales should be conducted within local areas, rather than entering into the international division of labor. Failure to do so would surely place these areas at the lowest end of the international division of labor due to the defects as regards productive technology and social characteristics. This would effectively amount to capital exploitation by more developed countries. In fact, regional self-sufficiency was also mentioned by Aristotle in his "village-town union" which included the idea that a supply of collective energy can achieve self-supply to a certain extent.

10.4.2.2   The Development and Application of Rural Community

Equally important to economic development was the self-development and organization of rural communities. An implication of this is that, firstly, the various relevant social forces should intervene in rural areas in order to foster a sense of community. Secondly, there should be considerable self-development implemented by rural communities. Rural construction should not completely depend on the government, but rather the joint efforts of various communities living in the area, including local farmers, enthetic workers, entrepreneurs, who manage nearby enterprises, and all those engaged by local business and services. For example, villagers could build their own roads or some enterprise could invest in the construction of an entertainment activity center. A variety of community forces should be mobilized in order to facilitate the necessary spatial construction. Community building was central.

To foster a community, meanwhile, requires, first of all, a sense of belonging and subjectivity that should be obtained and shared by the various groups of that community. The priority in rural areas was, then, to foster communities composed of various groups of people, thereby giving rise to group-based social forces. Community was, after all, built on the basis of a common identity.[23] Therefore, it became necessary to discover which force of aggregation could give rise to mutual recognition in each community. Farmers and workers should obtain subjectivity, be aware of the importance of the surrounding environment, upon which they depend for survival, and, thus, defend their rights and interests whilst also protecting natural resources and the environment. The forming of communities with distinctive local features would also provide an economic force within rural areas. As far as the past experiences in China were concerned, township enterprises were made successful by overall market-participation by entire rural communities (villages and towns),

---

[23]Castres (2003).

generally under the leadership of grassroots cadres, which was often believed to be formed under the rural collective socialist tradition.[24] Pan Wei, for instance, even believed that "if farmers in China can not become organized, then there is no hope for China's overall modernization." Wen Tiejun also indicated that an economic foundation of small scale farming should be taken as the presupposition to carry out all further organizational and systemic innovation. Development must make use of local social resources. All of these points give rise to considerable demands on the development of rural communities.

10.4.2.3   Resource-Sharing and Regional-Integrated in Situ Rural Urbanization

As to the rural areas of developing countries and regions, when their economy transformed into the non-industrialized, personalized, culturally inherited production using traditional technology, only by sharing productive resources, could traditional culture, production and sales, not to mention the structure of community-based organizations, be formed and all be strong enough to survive the conditions of globalization. Apart from the means of production, in situ rural urbanization should meet actual social and economic needs. In an industrial society, people's day-to-day activities already break through the narrow administrative boundaries of a farming society due to developed transport and infrastructure. This gives rise to the demand for regional spatial integration throughout the process of rural development. That is to say, facilities should not be evenly arranged according to administrative divisions, but rather should be distributed in accordance with the expanded range of socio-economic activities and the radius of supporting service facilities, so as to be regionally shared.

References

Castres. (2003). *The power of identity* (T. Xia. Trans.). Social Sciences Academic Press.
Dong, F. (2008). *Industrialization and China's rural modernization*. St. Martin's Press.; Bo, L. (2008). *Spatial planning and discoursed politics: A reflection on the urbanization strategy in peal river delta.*
Klatzmann, J., & Levi, Y. (1971). *The role of group action in the industrialization of rural areas.* U-nited States: Praeger Publishers.
Lin, G. C. S. (2001). Evolving spatial form of urban—Rural interaction in the Pearl River Delta, China. *Professional Geographer, 53*(1), 56–70.
Luo, P. (2006). *The Whole Story of the People's Commune Movement.* The publishing house of The Party School of Central Committee of C.P.C.
Pan, W. (2003). *Farmers and market—Grassroots regime and township enterprises in China.* Commercial Press.

---

[24]Pan (2003).

Shen, X. (1998). Spatial inequality of rural industrial development in China, 1989–1994. *Journal of Rural Studies, 15*(2), 179–199.

Wen, T. (2003). Three agriculture-related issues and solutions. *China Reform Rural Edition, 2*, 32–34.

Yang, Z., & Dan, Q. (2006). Planning strategies of building a new countryside in the West of Zhuhai City. *Planners, 5,* 27–29.

Zhao, Z. (2002). The strategy of village gathering space and time in rural urbanization process. *The Development of Rural Towns, 10,* 32.

Zheng, F., et al. (2004). *New industrialization road and economic and social development in rural and urban areas.* Shandong People's Publishing House.

Zhu, G. (1996). *On population-land relationship—Systematic study of population and land relationship in China* (p. 143). Fudan University Press.

Chapter 11
Village Industrialization: Model and Analysis

The urbanization of villages is at the core of overall urbanization in China. After all, the essence of urbanization is the transition of population from rural areas to urban areas. In this chapter, the author puts forward the notion that to realize the urbanization of villages, a development model of industrialization should be followed. It is proposed that, through industrialization, the income of villagers can be increased, their lifestyles and ideas can be changed and large numbers of people can be gathered around industrial activities. There are two models of village industrialization that are worthy of attention, namely, village industrialization with an endogenous impetus and village industrialization with an exogenous impetus. These two models are essentially differentiated by the different sources of their respective impetuses. Compared with the exogenous impetus model, it is proposed that village industrialization with an endogenous impetus is more likely to promote the long-term development of a village and bring greater overall benefits to a high number of villagers.

Take Hancunhe, a village located in the suburbs of Beijing, which lacked any significant resources, as an example. Relying on endogenous impetuses, it developed into a so-called "100-million-yuan village". Furthermore, this village presents a good example of village urbanization in general. Of course, its development model also includes a range of limitations and problems. By analyzing this example, this chapter seeks to find a model that might be applied to other villages in China.

11.1 A Rural Urbanization Model Driven by Industry

China's modernization process, as in Western countries, cannot proceed without a transfer of labor forces from agricultural activities to non-agricultural activities. This process is, in many ways, the urbanization process itself. According to primary data from the Sixth National Census, the current rural population of China is about

© Social Sciences Academic Press 2020
Q. Li, *China's Development under a Differential Urbanization Model*,
Research Series on the Chinese Dream and China's Development Path,
https://doi.org/10.1007/978-981-13-9451-5_11

670 million, amounting to around 50.32% of the total population. At the same time, the structure of an agriculture dominant society has transformed into a "semi-urban and semi-rural" one. Nevertheless, China's rural population is still sizeable compared with other developed countries, while the foundation of agriculture in economy remains unshakable. Against this particular background, the Chinese Government has long since prioritized a strategy of assisting small quasi-city town development through the rural-to-urban transition process.

Urbanization is a dynamic process, during which the various elements of rural areas continue to gather together in cities and towns. As part of this process, rural populations migrate to urban areas, changing their household registrations, through the arrangement of China's household registration policy, and in the end, settle down and live in urban areas. In this process, growing urban areas often merge with surrounding rural areas and expand their boundaries accordingly. As a result, the lifestyle and modes of production of farmers undergo a change, that is, from traditional rural ones to modern urban ones. However, to fully realize urbanization, the industrialization of a rural economy is indispensable. This will function as both the motivation for urbanization and the means of providing the resources required to achieve it. By taking the road of industrialization, farmers can be liberated from agricultural production and engaged in the second or the third industries, thereby obtaining greater incomes and benefits in the market competition. After establishing a decent economic foundation, through such industries, the funds required for rural development can be accumulated and the residents of rural areas can look towards improving their quality of life. As population flow increases, more and more farmers will begin to recognize the advantages of urban life, including greater convenience, better public facilities, such as schools, and abundant employment. They will, then, be willing to spontaneously follow the urbanization process themselves. Throughout all of this, industrialization is the key enabling factor.

Before the reform and opening up, China's rural labor force was tied to the land. Private economic activities, of any form, were prohibited by the state, including the self-employment of farmers. Although production teams and the People's Communes could conduct some non-agricultural activities, no wage was ever paid. Instead, the laborers were paid in the form of work points, that was, the measure unit for daily farm work, and any form of non-agricultural industry was effectively nonexistent. With the advent of reform and opening up, the rural economy gradually recovered and came alive. In 1978, the rural economic reform, with the main content of the contract responsibility system, enabled farmers to break the tie of previous inflexible management systems and the constraints of one fold land management. This was, in effect, a prelude to rural industrialization. As township-enterprise development saw three main waves, such enterprises suddenly grew into an important force in the national economy. At this stage, the economy in small towns also grew independently, the impetus of which was, of course, the rise and rapid development of township-enterprises. In the meantime, industrial operations became the main driving-force behind rural economic growth. However, the development of township enterprises was still at the initial start-up stage, so did the urbanization process in rural areas. For one thing, particularly since the mid-1990s, as the market economy continuously infiltrated state-owned enterprises, the seller's market shifted towards a buyer's market, the economic structure was adjusted and upgraded, township-enterprises encountered unprecedented difficulties and challenges as a result of these changes. That, in turn, severely limited the urbanization process in rural areas.

However, in those areas where the township enterprises were well developed, industry-driven urbanization was more successful. For example, some areas around Beijing, in the Wenzhou Region, in the Pearl River Delta and in the southern region of the Jiangsu Province can all be taken as representative cases for successful rural urbanization. On the one hand, because of resource availability, location and differing types of rural industrialization, urbanization in these rural areas can express a range of distinct characteristics. On the other hand, influenced by a common background, that is, China's structural transformation, as well as special institutional and environmental factors, urbanization in these areas also shares some strong common features.

Throughout the suburbs of Beijing, Hancunhe Town presents a prominent case of urbanization. As regards the development of the village's collective economy, an approach dominated by the construction industry, as well as a range of other industries, was taken. This supported development and led to the establishment of the Beijing Hanjian Group co. (hereinafter referred to as the Hanjian Group). A large proportion of the profits generated through enterprise were used for further rural construction and development. For example, a large upscale neighborhood was developed to accommodate much of the local population in relative luxury. As well as providing good living conditions, this project demonstrated that the concept of common prosperity was widely accepted by the local population. The rise of the Hanjian Group not only made Hancunhe grow in leaps and bounds, but also influenced a number of surrounding villages. The development of the Hancunhe Middle-town was to include the surrounding villages in the process of urban development, so as to realize the shift from agricultural production to the secondary and tertiary industrial sectors. This transformation brought with it the start of modern life and modern means of production and development.

The model of development used in Wenzhou has always been praised. Their appeal for accelerating the rural urbanization process was based on the rapid development of rural industrialization. Specialized production by zones and the formation of a market jointly promoted a fundamental change in Wenzhou's industrial structure, as well as a shift in the region's overall spatial economic structure. These rising small quasi-city towns soon became Wenzhou's new economic growth points. In Wenzhou, the number of small quasi-city towns increased, as did their level and quality of development. In the meantime, their aggregation and radiation functions strengthened continuously, such that many production-orientated small towns emerged, including Qiao Tou Town, "the first button market in the east", Liu Shi Town, "the country's largest low-voltage electrical facility city", Jin Xiang Town, "the first trade mark city in China" and Tang Xia Town, "the main production base for auto parts".

By means of export-oriented economic development, especially the development of export-oriented township enterprises, the economic structure of the Pearl River Delta underwent tremendous changes and the regional levels of urbanization were greatly improved. With the rise of export-oriented industrialization in rural areas, the Pearl River Delta became one of the most densely towned regions in China. Compared with the traditional approach of urbanization, this model took the form of urban and rural interaction, which manifested as the interaction between urban and rural areas being strengthened continually. Meanwhile, the development of industry was differential and mixed, but agricultural production was maintained at high levels and the mobility of the population actually increased. The difference between urban and rural landscapes, therefore, became increasingly blurred. In fact, those living in countryside-like areas were engaged in urban activities and enjoyed urban levels of civil development and participation.[1]

Since the 1970s, the rural area in the southern region of the Jiangsu Province has been positively influenced by urban industry and, with urban industrial elements being transferred to rural areas, realized a high degree of rural industrialization. In this process, collective economic organizations and the government, at all levels, have played an important role. Crucially, driven by rural industrialization, small quasi-city towns in the southern region of the Jiangsu Province developed rapidly, becoming an important part of the "South Jiangsu Model". As is well known, the distribution of small quasi-city towns in the southern region of the Jiangsu Province, meanwhile, was very dense, with the distance between them short and the traffic convenient. Therefore, a great deal of the population lived in rural areas, while working in nearby small quasi-city towns. Meanwhile, since the small quasi-city towns had a degree of agglomeration economy effect, a number of township enterprises were also established close to them, thereby giving rise to a landscape of small industries gathered around small quasi-city towns.

After scrutinizing the above-mentioned urbanization paths of different areas, it can be found, in China at least, that the industrialization effect is indeed a common and necessary condition for a countryside area to develop small quasi-city towns. Mr. Fei Xiaotong once said: "Industrial development is different from agricultural development, there must be a place for its concentration. Firstly, the transportation in such a place must be convenient. Secondly, the geographic location of such a place must be appropriate for these village workers who came from various villages. These two requirements made the original decadent small towns became the first choice for the commune-run factories."[2] A key factor was that these towns were not only the direct products of industrialization, but also a form of spatial organization required to realize agricultural industrialization. Industrialization asks for relatively concentrated production and contiguous development, as well as the energy, transportation, communications, finance, water supply, electricity, sewage and other infrastructure and social services that small quasi-city towns can provide.

---

[1]Hu (1998).
[2]Fei (2009).

In turn, the development of industry can guide and push countryside areas towards prosperity, therefore forming a variety of towns of all shapes and patterns. Hence, the development of towns continually depends on and promotes a growing industry and population concentration. It can be seen clearly, then, that the development of industry is an essential factor to promote urbanization in most rural areas. However, a range of problems occurred throughout the process of rural industrialization are also challenges for pushing ahead with the model of rural industrialization. One such problem is the scattered spatial layout of enterprises. It was still necessary, then, for the relevant planning authorities to exploratorily guide the rural industry, such that it may develop in a concentrated pattern, and through an overall planning to combine that process with rural urbanization, such that it may effectively transform the rural industrial and spatial structure.

11.2   The Dynamic Mechanism of Village Industrialization

Although rural industrialization might not necessarily bring about characteristics identical to those forms seen in an urban space, it could still embody the general connotations of urbanization. That is, the essential urbanization of rural life has been changed especially through the development of non-agricultural industries. At present, China's rural population still accounts for a sizeable proportion and the essential position of agriculture cannot be challenged. In this context, the development model of rural industrialization was strategic and significant for China's overall urbanization process. Generally speaking, there exist some overlaps between village industrialization and town industrialization. In fact, village industrialization may only be analyzed as a separate model insofar as the development of industry in villages takes place all on the base of villages. Compared with towns, villages lacked any kind of factors of intensive operation, not to mention a complete lack of prior resources and opportunities. As a result, the process of industrialization with villages generally requires a greater impetus. According to Wang Lijun, on the basis of relevant studies, rural urbanization models can be divided into the following three categories. Firstly, there is a bottom-up rural urbanization model that is primarily driven by private capital. Secondly, there is a synergistic rural urbanization model that is driven by a combination of government forces and private enterprises. Thirdly, there is a rural urbanization model driven primarily by foreign investment.[3] In fact, the second of these has proven to be rare in its implementation. More often than not, rural urbanization is pushed directly by the government. The more important distinction, then, tends to be whether the impetus of rural urbanization is endogenous or exogenous.

---

[3]Wang (2001).

11.2.1   The Model of Industrialization with an Endogenous Impetus

Among the various models of village industrialization driven by an endogenous impetus, the more successful ones tend to be those led by local elites and which depend on local resources, locational advantages and the agricultural or handicraft orientated talents of the local population. Success often depends too on working with the local population to seek common prosperity and achieve significant leaps in development. In such models, most of the village leaders are highly capable, including a good organizational capability and personal charisma. Besides, these models often involve mechanisms that stimulate the vitality of the villagers and lead them to profit financially and realize their other fundamental interests. There is no lack of successful examples of rural industrialization driven by endogenous impetuses in China, including the Huaxi Village, Liuzhuang Village in Xinxiang County and Hancunhe Village, which is investigated by the author. Hancunhe, a village near Beijing and a prominent case of urbanization, followed a path of developing a collective economy and established a construction-oriented development model supported by a multitude of other industries. A large proportion of the enterprise profits were used, in turn, for rural construction and development. This concept of common prosperity was widely accepted by the entire local population. The rise of the Hanjian Group not only made Hancunhe grow in leaps and bounds, but also influenced a number of surrounding villages. The development of the Hancunhe Middle-town was to include the surrounding villages in the process of urban development, so as to realize the shift from agricultural production to the secondary and tertiary industrial sectors. This transformation brought with it the start of modern life and modern means of production and development.

The model adopted in Hancunhe, as it was, driven by local leaders and featured by enterprise repaying village, not only sets an example for other rural areas, but also provides some issues for rethinking, such as the emergence of leaders, the choice of successors, the perfection of systems, equal and democratic elections and the sustainable development of enterprises. If these issues cannot be satisfactorily dealt with and no executive development plan can be made, then the model would be difficult to follow and imitate.

11.2.2   The Model of Industrialization with an Exogenous Impetus

The industrialization of villages with an exogenous impetus refers to the approach of promoting rural industrialization and urbanization via external forces. For instance, foreign funded enterprises greatly promoted the process of rural urbanization in the Zhejiang Province. What's more, Ge Licheng analyzed the rural urbanization of Jiashan County in Jiaxing City. He found that, by attracting foreign funded enterprises and promoting cooperation between foreign funded enterprises and local enterprises, Jiashan County had formed, with those foreign funded enterprises at its core, an industrial cluster, with a supporting chain, engaged in hardware and metal machining with an annual production value of over 5 billion yuan. Jiashan County, then, realized the industrial and population concentration, centered on Weitang Town (now known as Weitnag Street). From a different point of view, Zhu Huachen explored, in depth, the growth of the furniture manufacturing and wood processing industry in Jiashan County. He found that, with the investment of foreign funded enterprises, the speed of technological innovation and the growth rate of the local wood processing and furniture manufacturing industry accelerated markedly. A mechanism for the integration and interaction of private enterprises and foreign funded enterprises was gradually established. This, in turn, became an important impetus for the continuous growth and development of the local wood processing and furniture manufacturing industry clusters, as well as rural urbanization in Jiashan County more generally.[4] Recently, it has become common for government, at all levels, to spare no effort in promoting the industrialization of villages and the exchange for countryside housing land. While a red line was set, dictating that 1.8 billion mu of arable land must be preserved, it was recognized that the land resources of the population at the grassroots level were relatively limited and the use of rural housing land could expand economic development in many ways. Therefore, many regions have proposed a notion of urbanization by means of exchanging for countryside housing land. There were once many examples of village industrialization driven by an endogenous impetus. Yet, in recent years, the exogenous impetus of the government has advanced rapidly. In the actual implementation process, the government usually formulates antecedently a plan, uniformly marks out zones, and invites local farmers, by means of village demolition and mergers, to "go upstairs" (move into tall buildings) and built "new rural communities". Indeed, this model of urbanization, driven by the government, could be practical, that is, if the exchange for countryside housing land could be combined with the promotion of industrial development in rural areas, the employment of farmers, land compensation and the integration of farmers into modern civilized life. Otherwise, just in case these issues are not handled properly, a range of problems may arise. For instance, farmers may be forced to change their original ways of life, but without any development to village industrialization or improvement to the living conditions of the local population.

---

[4]Liu (2011).

11.2.3   *A Comparison Between Endogenous and Exogenous Impetuses*

Firstly, these two impetuses are primarily differentiated by their varied sources. Endogenous impetuses mainly originate from the internal appeal of village elites and villagers, while exogenous impetuses largely depend on foreign investors or higher levels of government. Secondly, the mode of implementation can be different as regards the endogenous and the exogenous impetuses. The implementation of endogenous impetuses depends mainly on the local elites, who often take the lead, and the villagers, who would spontaneously contribute to construction and the transformation of industry based on local conditions. This model is more demanding for the villagers, requiring high levels of self-consciousness and independence. The implementation of exogenous impetuses mainly depends on external forces to promote rural development and industrial upgrades. In this case, villagers may not be enthusiastic about it, especially as they may have a low degree of independence. In general, under such a process of development, the villagers are placed in a passive position, with no appeal or willingness to participate in the process. Thirdly, the effects of endogenous and exogenous impetuses can be very different. The mechanisms of endogenous impetuses often upgrade the industry of a village in such a way as to benefit most local people and allow them to share in the benefits of the village's overall development. Since villagers have greater autonomy, they can determine the pattern of benefit distribution to some extent. Under a development model driven by exogenous impetuses, however, most benefits are gained by the investors, while the villagers only obtain limited benefits throughout the early stages of the process. Furthermore, as the advance stages of development in the village have no connection with the local people, so to do the subsequent profits and benefits have nothing to do with them. Finally, the value of endogenous patterns and exogenous patterns of development vary. From a philosophical point of view, the internal causes of a matter decide the external causes. Sustainable development is only possible when supported and promoted by the strong inner vitality of an area. It is easy to see, meanwhile, that the endogenous impetus model is generally driven by the positive initiative of villagers and, therefore, has stronger vitality and promotional value. When relying on external forces, however, the local population often becomes passive, while only external support and funding, or direct government intervention, can trigger and maintain developmental progress. Such a development model can be difficult for many villages to follow. Therefore, it is better to make good use of the initiative of villagers and to rely on their inner impetuses. Only in this way can there be a reliable and long-term process of development, which may generate abundant benefits for the local population.

In the following parts, an industrial model driven by endogenous impetuses is introduce and highlighted. As the model that has, thus far, promoted the development of rural urbanization, it can provide a number of valuable lessons. Of course, also addressed is the range of problems that may accompany this model.

11.3 The Case of Hancunhe

11.3.1 About Hancunhe

Hancunhe, an administrative village of the Fangshan District, is 40 km to the southwest of Beijing. The village was small in size, only 2.4 km^2 with 2400 mu of arable land. There are, meanwhile, two versions of the history of Hancunhe. The first version takes an ancient monument as evidence. It refers to an ancient monument with inscriptions on it in Hancunhe village. The inscriptions on the stone tablet show that Hancunhe village existed 1300 years ago in the years of Xianqing in the Tang Dynasty. The second version tells a legend about the building of the village being due to a general. It was said that Hancunhe was set in the Liao Dynasty, formerly known as Han Cun or Han Village, after the surname Han. Thousands of years ago, in the Liao and Song periods, the general of State Liao, whose name was Han Chang (also known as Zong Yanshou) was buried there, while the Mangniu River stretched around the village. As a result of this, future generations in the village named it Hancunhe or Hancun River.[5]

Although Hancunhe Village has a history of thousands of years, the people there mainly relied on agricultural production, farming just a few acres of farmland each and living in worn-out houses. Before the reform and opening up, whether compared with surrounding villages or simply viewed in its own right, Hancunhe Village was relatively poor and backward, with much of the land covered by bumps and hollows. A small river, with its source in Longgu Mountain, winded its way through Hancunhe Village, so, when it rained, the village would often become flooded and covered by many ditches and ponds. Local people, therefore, referred to Hancunhe Village as "a bitterly disappointed village". There were even doggerels circulated about the village: "A village run through by a few ditches, muddy hutches built on jutting pieces, every year saw natural disasters, starving people in broken village and homes". "A poor village and broken muddy houses, one year has only half crops, dusty in sunny days while muddy ponds in rainy days". Before the agricultural cooperation movement of China in 1956, every mu of land could only produce 100 kg of grain in Hancunhe Village. It was, however, able to produce 200–300 kg of grain per mu after agricultural collectivization. However, the increased crop production did not result in any improvements to quality of life,

---

[5]The administrative unit of "Hancunhe village" belonged to Dongying township before the year 2000. All the former documents described the development there in the name of "Hancunhe". Since 2000, Dongying town was renamed Hancunhe town, it is not objective and rigorous to use Hancunhe to refer to for Hancunhe village. As "Hancunhe model" is up for an academic discussion, this chapter will still used "Hancunhe" to refer to Hancunhe village. In January 2002, according to the adjustment to Fangshan district administrative divisions, the original Hancunhe town and yuegezhuang town were merged to establish Hancunhe town. The history of the original Hancunhe town is: In 1961, it was separated from Changgou people's commune and established a Zhaogezhuang people's commune. In 1980, it renamed as Dongying Town, and in 2000, it renamed as Hancunhe town.

primarily due to the demands of population growth. According to villagers who were familiar with the past experience of the village, there were over 700 people in Hancunhe village when the P.R. China was established in 1949. Afterwards, due to the nation's policies at the time, which encouraged people to have more children, the village's population continued to grow, amounting to 2300 people when the reform and opening up began.

Surprisingly, such a village, despite its large population, limited land, harsh terrain, and few natural resources, leaped forward. Shortly after the reform and opening up, it became a prime example of redeveloping the countryside and was referred to as "the richest village in the suburbs of Beijing" accordingly. In the meantime, it was also a pioneer as regards the construction of small towns.

11.3.2 Current Conditions

Since the Third Plenary Session of the Eleventh Central Committee of the CPC, especially after 1984, Hancunhe's economic development has accelerated considerably. Hancunhe Village developed rapidly and the living standards of villagers continued to rise. By the end of 2010, the village had 1170 households with 2866 people, while its annual per capita income reached 30,000 yuan. Hancunhe became the richest village in the suburbs of Beijing, being referred to as the "billion yuan village" accordingly. Hancunhe had effectively been transformed from an area of rural countryside to a modern small town with complete infrastructure and a beautiful environment, including wide flat streets, rows of modern cottages and beautiful parks, all of which deeply impressed visitors.

11.3.2.1 Organizations

The organization of Hancunhe was special insofar as the village committee was were under the dual leadership of the Town Party Committee and also the Party Committee of the Hanjian Group. Of the two, the town Party Committee was responsible for conveying and implementing the policies of higher authorities, including ideological construction, family planning, social security, and dispute resolution. The Hanjian Group Party, meanwhile, was responsible for economic and infrastructure construction and public services. In the actual operation, the Hanjianhe Group exerted a greater influence on the village and was more involved in the management of Hancunhe Village.

11.3.2.2 Indicators of Economic Development

According to the official statistics of Hancunhe Town, there were 1170 households in the village in 2010. Among them, 210 households were engaged in agricultural production and management. The total population of the village amounted to 2866 and agricultural households only accounted for 18% of the total number, that is, a very low proportion. It was because the villagers leased their lands to the collective farm of the village, that they could obtain an income according to the size of land leased each year. This income largely replaced the income of farming. Hancunhe had a labor resource of 2052 people. Among them, 1738 were actually employed, including 848 males and 890 females. According to economic sector, 25 people were engaged in the primary industry, 12 people were engaged in the agricultural industry, 13 people were engaged in forestry, 649 people were engaged in construction and 86 people were engaged in industry. Most people were engaged in the tertiary industry, that is, a total of 978 people. Among this latter figure, 110 people were engaged in the accommodation and catering industry, mostly as part of the "agritainment" industry.[6] Those not listed in the above statistics belonged to a range of other categories.

By the end of 2010, the total assets and liabilities of Hancunhe had reached 3.950372 billion yuan and 181,827.7 yuan respectively, accounting for more than 95% of the entire assets and liabilities of the township. Most of this was directly related to the Hanjian Group, which originated from Hancunhe and created an annual profit of more than 400 million yuan.

11.3.3 Agricultural Modernation

Since 1988, the population of Hancunhe had transferred their land to the collective farm for cultivation and established an agricultural company known as "The Farm". Each villager kept only six fens (0.6 mu) of farmland for personal use. Until 1990, all land was owned by the agricultural company. For one thing, the construction industry was developing so rapidly and profitably that few residents were interested in low and hard-won agricultural benefits. They were, then, willing to transfer their land to the collective company. When "The Farm" had all of the farmland concentrated, it was possible for The Farm to carry out large-scale cultivation and harvesting. It was with the support of the Hanjian Group that "The Farm" followed the pattern of modernized agricultural production. For 22 years, the Hanjian Group had invested an accumulated amount of over 10 million yuan in "The Farm", purchasing hundreds of agricultural machines and rolling out mechanized operations to all 2600 mu of cropland in the village. For all of this, only 28 people were engaged in the agricultural operation. In addition, Hancunhe paid more attention to the adjustment of agricultural structure, embracing a program of widespread agricultural industrialization. Since 1996, 30 million yuan had been invested in building a high-tech demonstration zone, with 66 energy-saving solar greenhouses

---

[6]Agritainment is farm-based tourism, includes family style activities, such as corn mazes, haunted hayrides, pick-your-own pumpkins, etc.

and 5 double inflatable plastic greenhouses introduced from the United States. The 260 mu of high-tech vegetable gardens could provide year-round and periodically produced fruit and vegetables that were of a high quality and pollution free. In recognition of this achievement, the high-tech vegetable garden was named as "National Science and Technology Commission's Industrialized and Efficient Agriculture Demonstration Zone" by the State Scientific and Technological Commission.

11.3.4 Building Schools and Cultivating Future Generations

To build a new socialist countryside, abundant ideology and an affluent quality of life were equally important. The Village Party secretary Tian Xiong and his leading group believed that to raise the level of civilization and morality, it was necessary to raise overall levels of education. In 1986, just after it had some money-savings, Hancunhe Village built a new teaching building for an elementary school. In 1995, it invested 15 million yuan in an education center and put it into use. In all, Hancunhe Village made a total investment of 30 million yuan in the construction of an educational zone, including a kindergarten, elementary school, middle school, high school, and college, which together could accommodate 3000 students. At the elementary level tuition fees were covered by the village finances. In addition, the village also offered some subsidies to those students who succeeded in continuing their education throughout middle school, high school, and college. The specific criteria were as follows. Each student was eligible for a one-time subsidy of 3000 yuan subject to their admission to high school or secondary school. Each student was also eligible for a one-time subsidy of 6000 yuan following their admission to a university or college. It was not only the children from Hancunhe itself that could enjoy a full education, from primary school to high school, without ever leaving the village. Children from neighboring villages were also attracted by the standard of education offered, such that schools in Hancunhe became their first choice. In other words, the education zone also benefited these neighboring children and their parents. Over the years, there have been no school drop-outs and many students have been admitted to universities, with some even going abroad to study. Many employees and other adults from the village were also sent to universities and other training centers for further training or study. It is worth mentioning that the village also had its own vocational training school, which was mainly used to train personnel for the Hanjian Group and disseminate up-to-date knowledge to the village people.

11.3.5   A Boomig Tertiary Industry

In order to absorb the surplus rural labor force and accelerate rural urbanization, people in Hancunhe not only focused on the development of the real estate and construction material industry, but also actively developed the tertiary industry, namely tourism and the service industry. The Hanjian Group, taking advantage of its brand awareness, even established the first tourist agency of any Beijing suburb. It invested over 80 million yuan in the building of Hancunhe Villa Convention Center, offering services such as dining, accommodation, transportation, sightseeing, shopping, entertainment and conference facilities. Rooms in Hancunhe Villa Convention Center varied in style, with some imitating antique courtyards, while some were like luxury modern buildings, not to mention the several conference rooms and other entertainment facilities. In order to further promote tourism, Hancunhe rebuilt the old kiln pit into a tree-lined park with a rippling lake. They also took advantage of the land in the village leftover from the planning process to build Luban Park. In order to create panoramic views of the village, a 20 m high viewing tower was also built in Luban Park for tourists. Besides, there was Hancunhe Archives Exhibition Room in the park too, occupying more than 2100 m^2. As a result of these projects, amongst others, rural tourism became a significant new economic growth point for Hancunhe, which received about 500,000 tourists, including 50,000 foreigners, every year.

11.4   Creating Prosperity

11.4.1   The Impetus for Hancunhe' Great-Leap-Forward

Hancunhe's development allowed people outside of the village to see the prosperity of Hancunhe, but only the villagers of Hancunhe themselves could feel how significantly the village had transformed.

Such a rapid and successful transformation raises the question as to what compelled the village to realize these tremendous changes and become so prosperous. According to some of the reviewing literature, as well as the author's personal interviews and surveys, it was the Hanjian Group that helped Hancunhe to make this great-leap-forward. It was the Hanjian Group, after all, that initiated the story of Hancunhe Village and supported financially the village throughout the entire process. The village's annual cost of 3000 million yuan, the transformation of the appearance and environment of the village, small villa for each household, welfare and social services, schools and further education were all funded and organized by the Hanjian Group. It was initially established as a small construction team, which was founded in the village in the early stage of the reform and opening up and developed gradually henceforth. Since then, the Hanjian Group had become a large enterprise, with national level qualifications, attached to the government of the Fangshan District. Its leading business was real estate development and, driven by that, it acted as a prime and professional contractor for housing construction, water conservancy and hydropower projects, highway construction and municipal construction projects. It was responsible for all stages of these construction projects and had a stake in all kinds of relevant businesses, including new building materials, PCCP pipes, and landscaping. All of its operations were supported by the services of its tertiary industry branch and overseas companies. The Hanjian Group's practice demonstrated that a scientific, differential, internationalized domestic development model could be successful. The Hanjian Group had total assets of 4.9 billion yuan and net assets of 2.4 billion yuan, while its highest annual output was 4.85 billion yuan, with as much as 456 million yuan paid to the state by the Hanjian Group in taxes.

Owing mostly to the progressive ideology of Tian Xiong, the founder of the Hanjian Group, ambitious for collective prosperity, the Hanjian Group spent so much, in money and resources, to support and transform the village. The growth and development of the Hanjian Group was, then, the reliable force behind the great transformation of Hancunhe Village.

11.4.2   The Role of Enterprises in Village Development: The Story of the Hanjian Group

The new policy of reform and opening up, announced at the Third Plenary Session of the Eleventh Central Committee of the CPC, triggered new rural reforms, which played a crucial role in the development of rural areas. A conference held by ministers of the State Administration for Industry and Commerce in February 1979, meanwhile, proposed that some idle labor force, with official household registration (Hukou), should be allowed to engage in individual repairs, services and handicraft work, but they should not be allowed to hire employees of their own. This was, in effect, the first stage towards allowing individual economic development after the Third Plenary Session. It was against such a background that the villagers of Hancunhe gradually separated themselves from agricultural production teams and established a "Grade Five Repair Team", engaged in building maintenance, thereby creating a precedent for future self-employment. The secret of the success of village-run enterprises might, then, be found by reviewing the history of the Hanjian Group.

11.4.2.1   The First Phase: 1978–1984

Tian Xiong, the leader of Hancunhe, believed that, despite a lack of natural resources, geographical advantages, arable land (per capita one mu) and prior experience of any kinds except farming, to develop a construction industry would benefit the village greatly, since Hancunhe had a group of masons. The characteristics of the construction industry, meanwhile, dictate that an individual's work is of limited value. Only by organizing the masons of the entire village, collectively engaged in the construction industry, could Hancunhe lift itself out of poverty and prosper. Under the guidance of this notion, Tian Xiong himself studied the basics of construction, consulted experts and practiced, actually starting his career as a bricklayer.

At the beginning of the 1970s, Tian Xiong and several other bricklayers began to help the villagers build houses, but, constrained by the then policies, this was done as a non-profit venture. However, these craftsmen still benefited from their services. Residents awarded them not with money, but rather with work points, so the craftsmen could at least make up for the amount of farming work that they should have been doing. In short, the initial construction team was owned by the production team and their sideline production even took them to the surrounding villages to work.

Later on, the Third Plenary Session untied the economic system and brought vitality to individual economic activity. Therefore, Tian Xiong organized a construction team with more than thirty people, escalating from a "Grade Five Repair Team" to a "Grade Three Repair Team", with their qualifications improved and the team better developed. The impressive performance of this team, as regards both quality and schedule of work, quickly won them a noteworthy reputation. Initially, however, their activities were still limited to the Fangshan District. It was not until 1984, when the construction team took over the Beijing Ziyu Hotel project, a large, complicated project, and completed the project while under great pressure and against a demanding deadline, that Hancunhe construction team became famous and the team enjoyed a turning point.

11.4.2.2 The Second Phase: 1984–1988

Although the Beijing Ziyu Hotel project brought positive attention to the Hancunhe construction team, the team remained stuck at upgrading to the level of a "Grade Two Construction Team". In terms of the construction team's qualifications, this grade rendered them unable to undertake large projects.[7] Fortunately, at this critical point, an opportunity appeared. On October 18th, 1988, following a meeting in the Fangshan Theater, the Fangshan District Government started to organize a "construction enterprise group company", seeking to integrate more than forty small and large construction teams. The Hancunhe construction team seized the opportunity to

---

[7]Ziyu Hotel project was awarded to the Hancunhe construction team through informal channels. Because of the tight deadline of the project, many construction companies were reluctant to take over the project, and because Tian Xiong negotiated with the person in charge of the project, even made a pledge, the project was able to fall into the hands of the Hancunhe construction team.

become a member of this company, becoming, as they did, its second branch and earning the status of a grade two construction team, which was later upgraded to a grade one construction company.

11.4.2.3   The Third Phase: 1988–1994

Instead of being satisfied with simply reaping the benefits of what he had already help built, Tian Xiong had his sight set on something even more ambitious, namely, setting up his own construction group. The establishment of the Hanjian Group was the milestone of this third phase, with the Hancunhe Construction Company separating from the Fanjian Construction Group Company. Numerous obstacles were encountered throughout the process of formalizing this separation, but Tian Xiong remained committed, often going out of his way to improve ties with relevant authorities and departments. In 1994, when the general manager of the Fanjian Construction Group Company was transferred by the Fangshan District Government, Tian Xiong finally got his chance. On August 29th, 1994, in a news conference held in a Beijing Hotel, Tian Xiong announced the establishment of the Hanjian Group which was the first large-scale enterprise rooted in rural areas.

11.4.2.4   The Fourth Phase: 1995–2005

In 1996, the Hanjian Group was ISO certified and became further qualified to undertake a wide range of projects, thereby laying the foundations for its large-scale future development. In 2002, the Hanjian Group was awarded the status of a "Super Grade Construction Enterprise" by the Ministry of Construction of China. There were, at that time, less than thirty enterprises with such a premium qualification, only four of which were located in Beijing. This level of success enabled the Hanjian Group to use its strength and succeed even in a fiercely competitive market.

11.4.2.5   The Fifth Phase: 2006–2011

As the price of construction materials increased and the competition intensified, especially following the introduction of smaller construction teams, the Hanjian Group did encounter some obstacles and setbacks. According to a well placed source, large construction companies generally needed to pay between 12% and 18% income tax, whereas small construction teams, attached to larger construction companies, only needed to pay around 5% income tax. Furthermore, these smaller construction teams generally had lower operational costs, such that they were able to obtain projects by offering lower prices. In fact, this imbalance was responsible for disturbing the entire construction industry during the early stages of its development. Under such market conditions, the Hanjian Group adjusted accordingly. It shifted its focus towards the real estate industry, which had already started to develop itself. In time, the Hanjian Group went so far as to change its leading business area from construction to real estate. With real estate as its main driving force, the Hanjian Group gradually emerged from the prior period of challenges and setbacks. By March 2011, it had been reorganized, with three new groups under the leadership of the chairman of the board, namely, the Real Estate Group, the Construction Group and the Pipe (PCCP) Group, as well as, that is, the Hancunhe Industrial Corporation. The dynamism of these groups was increased insofar as each practiced an independent accounting and management responsibility system.

11.4.3   The Leader of the Hanjian Group and Hancunhe Village

Tian Xiong, the chairman of the Hanjian Group, also the former Party Secretary of Hancunhe Village, once said, "I believe where there is a will, there is a way. I always use this saying to inspire myself. All the things were done for the sake of villagers. Once the people knew that your heart was for everybody, they would support you wholeheartedly. Only by constantly strengthening our capacity in economic development, we can do more practical things and good things for the villagers and improve people's living standards."

Tian Xiong, born in 1946 in Hancunhe, graduated from Fanshan High School in 1967 as one of the Special School Graduates (during 1966–1968). Like the rest of the group, the "Cultural Revolution" ruined his aspirations to attend university. As an educated youth who returned to the rural Hancunhe Village, Tian Xiong was unwilling to succumb to a poor life, as his elder generations had, and remained determined to change the status quo of Hancunhe. Therefore, he studied diligently, seeking to learn from older generations of masons. He labored hard during the day and studied hard at night, taking every opportunity to learn basic skills. Hard work pays off, so, following his rare levels of perseverance and diligence, he quickly acquired excellent skills. Tian Xiong also continued to study academically in his spare time. As such, he was awarded a three-year college diploma in construction management and economic management as well as an undergraduate diploma in construction management. He was also elected as a representative of the 16th National Congress of the Communist Party of China and a representative of the Tenth and Eleventh National People's Congress. He was also the deputy director of the Standing Committee of the People's Congress in the Fangshan District, Party Secretary and the chairman of the Hanjian Group.

After the reform and opening up in 1978, utilizing his extensive experience, and with the support of the village party branch, Tian Xiong organized the Hancunhe collective construction team with over thirty skilled laborers. After working hard throughout the initial period and an additional thirty years of turmoil, Tian Xiong turned the Hancunhe construction team into the pluralistic and integrated Hanjian Group, owning a national super grade qualification, the business of which included construction, municipal construction, irrigation construction, road construction, garden, and ancient style building construction, real estate development, construction material supply, asset management, and others. The once poor and backward Hancunhe Village was subsequently transformed into a new socialist countryside with complete public infrastructure facilities and every household living in villas. Tian Xiong had been engaged in the construction industry for 38 years, 32 of which he lived in a lowly, humid temporary shed for construction staff. He was even the last person in the village to relocate to a high-quality villa, six years later than the first residents were able to do so. That is to say, he clearly insisted on following a pattern of collective economic development, adhering all the while to principles of common prosperity. This view is captured by another of his frequent sayings: "It is worthwhile to bear all the hardships and worries for the fellow countrymen".

11.4.4 The Operating Mechanisms and Management Philosophy of the Hanjian Group

From the very beginning the Hanjian Group rooted itself in rural areas and embraced a pattern of the collective economy, using their profits to build Hancunhe. In the late 1990s, a disavowal of the collective economy occurred, but Hancunhe continued to adhere to the notion and unswervingly pursued common prosperity. At the beginning of the twenty-first century, Hancunhe, following the principles of creating a modern enterprise system, developed and expanded its collective economy and established the Beijing Hanjian Group co. ltd. This approach not only consolidated the collective economy, but also promoted the development of Hancunhe, increased the strength of the Hanjian Group and resulted in benefits for the majority of the villagers.

The Hanjian Group not only served Hancunhe Village, but also actively participated in charitable and social welfare affairs. Since 1989, Tian Xiong, the Party Secretary and Chairman of the Hanjian Group, guided those villagers who became rich first to help the rest of the population towards a common prosperity. The Hanjian Group made numerous positive contributions to society and donated to build Hope Schools. The group also invested in education in Quanshuidi Village, Hami City, Xinjiang Province, Dong Gacha Village and Duilongdeqing County in Tibet as well as remote poor areas in the Yunnan Province. Other forms of financial assistance were also offered to poor students on an individual basis. Besides this, the Hanjian Group also jointly implemented the "Enriching through Education Project" with Hancunhe Town Government, donating to three primary schools in Canzhang Village, Zhao Gezhuang Village and Xidong Village separately. They also helped Lu Zishui Village, Puwa County in the Fanshang District, donating to these poor villages and contributing to the development of the west regions as they did. Sponsorship was provided for training courses for township and village cadres in ten western provinces and autonomous regions. Furthermore, victims were rescued and helped to rebuild their homes in disaster areas. So far, all in all, the Hanjian Group has donated more than 100 million yuan to society and social welfare causes.

11.4.5 Reform of the Hanjian Group

Since its foundation, the Hanjian Group has been a collectively owned enterprise. In 2000, it underwent a reform, not becoming a share-holding enterprise as expected, that is, as its system was not the quantitative shareholding system, but rather transforming into an enterprise contracted production system. Strictly speaking, the relationship between the Hanjian Group and the Hancunhe Industrial Corporation involved Tian Xiong holding contract management responsibility for the Hanjian Group, while the Hanjian Group was responsible for the management of the village. Recently, with the support of the district government, the Hanjian Group aspired to become a real joint-equity company or share-holding enterprise, selecting its candidates for chairman and general manager, such that the Hanjian Group might become a modern enterprise in this way.

The direct beneficiary of the Hanjian Group's growth and development, besides the enterprise's founder and his team, was Hancunhe Village. Tian Xiong, the leader of Hancunhe Village, and the chairman of the Hanjian Group, not only led the villagers to prosperity, but also, responding to the party's call, strived hard for the realization of common prosperity for all villagers. Tian Xiong clarified this approach by declaring that "we work hard away from home to make money, not for ourselves, but for all the villagers. We risk our life to make money, only for our villagers, otherwise we would quit". He made good use of the strength of the Hanjian Group to change the appearance and conditions of the village, building schools and modern housing for the village people. He set up a landscape company and a utility company, among other service sectors, to serve the villagers and resolve issues such as employment and pensions. It was the Hanjian Group and Tian Xiong that effectively built a new Hancunhe Village.

11.5 Building a New Hancunhe Village

Although the level of enterprise and the wealth of the collective economy grew, it did not necessarily mean that all of the villagers became better off. Tian Xiong, as well as other members of village party committees, hoped that the development of enterprise would constitute a process by which all villagers became rich and could enjoy a happy life. To be in line with the development of the new village, they designed commercial areas, industrial areas, cultural and educational areas, office areas and invested 22 million yuan in implementing a "Greening Project", increasing forest coverage around the village to a rate of 60%.

11.5.1 The Transformation of Village Appearance and Environment

Since ancient times, Hancunhe had actually been divided into several small villages by various geographical obstacles such as ditches and pits. When the rainy season came, it was difficult for villagers to move around the village and those houses built on lower grounds were flooded. Needless to say, this problem disrupted the quality of life of the village people considerably.

In the early 1980s, however, the collective economy in Hancunhe Village developed considerably and the living standards improved with each passing day. When the village finally enjoyed enough essentials, such as food and clothing, the improvement of housing conditions become the highest priority. Because the village lacked any kind of unified planning at the time, the houses in the village were constructed in a chaotic and piecemeal fashion. The layout of properties was irrational, the sizes of new and old buildings varied and the boundaries between properties were unclear. Occasionally, some homes had even been built over public roads. In the meantime, influenced by feudal superstitions, some villagers competitively compared the heights of the foundation of their homes, resulting in a degree of disharmony and conflict. Some houses were built and rebuilt repeatedly over a period of many years, causing a huge waste of resources. Outside the fences of some residential houses, dunghills could be found, which often blocked the roads. What's more, firewood was usually placed against walls, constituting a significant fire risk, especially when fireworks were used during festivals. All of these issues not only affected the appearance and conditions of the village, but also created serious security and safety problems.

The chaotic layout of houses in the village greatly damaged the social stability of Hancunhe and hindered, in a variety of ways, its future development. In 1983, for the benefit of the villagers, the Hancunhe construction team, led by Tian Xiong, paid for the construction of the first asphalt road in the village. Unfortunately, this project failed because of unsuccessful negotiation with some of the villagers who had occupied some of the road space by building houses. Tian Xiong's first attempt to implement a strategy of wealth generation through improved communication links had, therefore, been unsuccessful.

In 1988, Tian Xiong was elected as the president of the Economic Association. It was his goal, meanwhile, to solve the contradictions caused by housing building projects in the village, fundamentally improve the living conditions and build a prosperous, civilized and harmonious Hancunhe Village for all. To this end, he

Table 11.1 A schedule of investments in new Hancunhe Village by Hanjian Group

Initial investment
1983 Crossroads construction, being convenient for production and living
1983 Spring. Four towers construction, and have tap water laid on to solve the drinking water problem
1987 Teaching building of primary school construction, the first school buildings in Hancunhe village

Four-year preparation
1990 preparation for building a new village
1991 Theater construction
1992 Water park construction. In the same year, start unified agricultural production by a professional farm, all profits will be returned to villagers, so as to replace the form of each household farms her own land
1993 Gas station construction, be able to use clean energy
1993 Establish water and electricity department, to take care of property management for and serve the whole village

Eleven-year construction
1994 Start to build villa for the villagers
1994 Establish landscaping team
1994 Construction of Hancunhe Villa Convention Center (the first phase)
1995 Education center construction
1996 A local police station construction
1996 Kindergarten construction
1997 Vegetable greenhouses construction
1998 Rural clinic construction
1999 Construction of Hancunhe Villa Convention Center (the second phase)
1999 Farm product market construction
1999 Luban Park construction
2004 Completion of all the projects within 11 years

learnt from the previous asphalt road construction project in 1983 and proposed a plan for the construction of a new village. In 1990, the Hanjian Group underwent a process of rapid development and Tian Xiong worked on a unified overall plan (see Table 11.1).

At the same time, Hancunhe also established a telecommunications branch, a post office, a health-center, a theater, a boiler room, a park, nine roads in the East–West direction, 14 streets in the North–South direction, and other supporting public facilities. After the completion of the new village, the original five small dispersed villages had been transformed into a beautiful and harmonious new countryside with a rational layout and distinctive characteristics. Among all of the work done, a total of 150mus of pits and wasteland and 250mus of trenches were filled up, besides, 80mus of brick factories and four yards, of 120mu were reverted to farm land.

11.5.2   Building Villas and Tall Buildings

In the process of rebuilding the village, house demolition was one of the most difficult tasks, involving not only the costs of housing lands, but also the relocation allowances required for the demolition of old houses, besides those details like the order to move in. At a meeting held by the party branch on June 26, 1986, Tian Xiong announced his plan to the public. To be more specific, he announced that: "Every household in the village would have a villa, with central heating, water, electricity and gas. All the village streets will be re-planned, which should be smooth and wide horizontals and verticals. The village should have complete municipal infrastructure with separate drainage facilities for sewage and rainwater. Three parks will be built in the village and an overall green landscape will be made. In a word, we will make Hancunhe Village a modern, pollution free new countryside!" Initially, Tian Xiong's announcement was controversial amongst the people of Hancunhe. There were even instances of gossip, rumors and hostility, with some village people voicing opposition to the idea of demolishing and rebuilding everything. Others suspected that the project was too ambitious or that Tian Xiong simply wanted to show off his newly acquired wealth.

Indeed, such hostility and suspicion constituted a significant obstacle when it came to actually building the new village. After several attempts by Tian Xiong and the village committee, the new village construction plan did, however, begin to make some progress and, gradually, the demolition phase commenced. Nevertheless, the most difficult work was to mobilize the population for relocation. When the village people explained their concerns and numerous requests, both rational and irrational, Tian Xiong and the committee did their utmost to appease. The primary concern, meanwhile, was the possibility that the price of new homes would be so high that they would be unable to make any kind of purchase. In order to reduce the financial burden on the villagers, after extensive consultation, Tian Xiong implemented an extremely affordable payment plan, including considerable subsidies, thereby effectively winning over the concerned residents.[8]

This payment plan included the following aspects:

1. Measuring all of the houses built before December 31, 1992, and calculating equally the construction area of both new houses and old houses, with a subsequent pricing of 300 yuan per square meter.
2. According to the "Map for Village Residential Buildings", the village's residential buildings were divided into multi-storey buildings and villas, the villagers can voluntarily choose the size and style of their new houses by signing a contract with the collective, subject to the payment of a deposit.
3. For those villagers who previously owned bungalows, but decided to buy a new villa, the area of their former bungalow could be used to offset the value of same area in the new villa, in a 1:1 ratio.

---

[8]Source: Hancunhe Village Archives Exhibition Room.

4. All qualifying households, which completed the required formalities, could collect a one off 30,000 yuan allowance, paid by the collective, within 15 days of moving into their new villa.

5. Due to the varied incomes of different villagers, those households that qualified for purchasing a villa, but instead purchased a multi-storey residential building voluntarily were entitled to a one-time 50,000 yuan allowance.

6. Any households that purchased a multi-storey residential building were entitled to a 5000 yuan allowance, from the Industrial Corporation, subsequent to moving into the new house (this allowance was generally deducted from the amount thus far unpaid).

7. All male villagers aged 18 on December 31, 1998, who were registered as a permanent agricultural resident of Hancunhe Village, were entitled to a one off 5000 yuan housing subsidies when purchasing a multi-story building.

8. All female villagers, who obtained a marriage certificate before December 31, 1998, and were registered as a permanent agricultural resident of Hancunhe Village, were also entitled to purchase a residential building if in need of a house.

9. Villagers could buy a villa by installments. This would require an advance deposit of 10,000 yuan, a 5000 yuan payment upon moving into the new property and a payment of 5000 yuan each year until the total contracted sum is reached.

10. In order to complete the construction of the residential area in stages and groups, those households required to reside in temporary accommodation, according to the relevant provisions, were entitled to a 5 yuan grant per day, again offered by the collective.

11. Finally, the villagers were entitled to compensation from the collective for any advance deposits made, that is to say, from the day of payment to the day of being issued with the key to their new building, at an annual interest rate of 20%

From the above provisions, it is clear that the village collective not only provided the owners of old households with an equivalent offset, but also provided a number of supporting subsidy measures. For instance, both unmarried young men and married young women were also entitled to purchase a building, and villagers, receive considerable levels of compensation from the high interest rates allocated to their advanced deposits. Nevertheless, for a range of reasons, including the abovementioned hostility to such widespread change, many villagers still hesitated to buy into the redevelopment. Later, as a means of further reassuring them, Tian Xiong and the party branch announced that the local elites and village cadres would be the last batch of households to actually move into newly constructed villas.

Table 11.2 List of residential buildings in Hancunhe Village

Style	Quantity	Area (m²)	Purchase price (per m²/yuan)
Ethnic style	475	237	300–400
Continental style	100	260–290	300–400
American style	24	290	350
Multi-storey (building)	180	80–140	240–280

Source Hancunhe Village Archives Exhibition Room

Following this act of selflessness, villagers were, for the most part, finally reassured and they started to move into the new villas and multi-storey buildings. Villagers were thereinafter heard to say: "But for the insistence of Tian Xiong and the village committee, there was no new Hancunhe village".[9]

In 1990, the village committee and the Hanjian Group came up with a design for the construction of a new Hancunhe Village. After four years of preparation, in 1994, the Hanjian Group, invested 530 million yuan and, over a period of eleven years, built 581 villas and apartment-style multi-storey residential buildings, of, in total, 21 entrances, including a total construction area of nearly 200 thousand square meters. All 910 households and 2700 villagers subsequently moved into the new residences. Following this, the village's per capita housing area was around 68 m² (see Table 11.2). Housing and homesteads were, however, still owned by the collective, with the villagers only having the right to use the property.

11.5.3   The Establishment of Sound Social Security and a Welfare System

As regards establishing a social security system, Tian Xiong and the village committee sought to guarantee the basic living standards of the villagers, especially those who were unable to work, including the elderly. The main goal of Hancunhe's subsequent social security system was to set a minimum subsistence level. The levels of financial aid allocated to those in need were raised from 1000 to 1500 yuan per person to the current level of 3600 yuan per person per year. Nevertheless, the personal incomes of most residents were high enough that only four households actually received the living allowance. Assistance for the disabled, meanwhile, was divided into two categories, 100 yuan per month for disabled individuals who were still able to work and 150 yuan per month for disabled individuals who were unable to work.

For individuals with low levels of education and those middle-aged and elderly individuals less able to work, the village committee arranged cleaning, security, facilities maintenance, and other similar roles. The village did not hire a

---

[9]Gao (Gao 2008).

professional sanitation companies, for example. Instead, this role was offered to the villagers themselves, for which they were provided subsidies, not to mention an enhanced awareness of environment protection. At peak there were around 600 people engaged in sweeping streets, that is to say, almost one person from each household. Because of the numbers involved, each participated was allocated only a small public area, requiring just ten minutes a day to finish this job, for which they could earn 260 yuan per month. The team that was responsible for the security of the village was composed in a similar way. There were security booths in the streets, and people on duty inside each booth. All in all, around 80 people were engaged in this security work, including both men and women, each of who could earn 450 yuan payment per month. The village was not, however, responsible for urban migrant workers or young people who were employed outside of the village or in towns.

In terms of community support for elders, the village continued to embrace a traditional family-support system, under which primary means of support for the elderly were provided by the younger generations within the family itself. Nevertheless, villagers aged 60 years old, were eligible for a subsidy of 300 yuan per month from the village collective, a figure that would increase by 5 yuan per month every year thereafter. At Mid-Autumn Festival, each year, elderly residents were even entitled to a 100 yuan subsidy, as well as complimentary moon cakes. This program of subsidies and benefits for the elderly was well received in the village. Firstly, these measures reflected the Hanjian Group's respect and care for the elderly, promoting, in turn, a culture of respect and care for the old throughout the entire village. Secondly, the elderly were provided with their own disposable money, such that they need not rely entirely on their children. This degree of financial autonomy meant that financial conflicts and the related family disputes disappeared accordingly. Finally, these subsidies for the elderly also functioned as an indirect subsidy for children, reducing the overall financial burden on families.

Taking all of these factors into consideration, the support for the elderly in the village was provided to more than satisfactory levels. According to the author's investigation, an elderly individual with a street sweeping role, plus other benefits, could earn around 1000 yuan each month. Lacking serious illness, nor any other noteworthy living costs, one could live a comfortable life with that level of income.

As for health care, the village funded the new cooperative medical insurance for the 2097 villagers who had registered as a permanent agricultural residence in Hancunhe village.[10] The figure paid amounted to 80 yuan per villager annually, that is, the highest standard in the Fangshan District. This coverage meant that 70% of

---

[10]To answer the call of town government and to achieve the goal of urbanization, the village encouraged villagers toregister as a permanent town residence, which two years later will automatically turned to be urban residence and enjoy urban welfare. The villagers registered as residence could still enjoy the village collective benefits. Therefore, there were three types of household registrations in the village: agriculture household registration with 827 households and 2097 people, non-agricultural household registration with 408 households and 645 people, and town household registration with102 households and 162 people.

an individual's medical expenses could be reimbursed, 75% for the elderly. Although the village established a rural clinic, most villagers would pursue better medical care by traveling to the hospitals in towns or larger district hospitals if ever they were sick.

Other benefits included a 10 million yuan investment in heating installations, towards which villagers were only required to pay around 500,000 yuan. If a couple were both only children, then their parents, assuming they were registered as a permanent agricultural residents, were entitled to an "only-child allowance" of 600 yuan annually and an additional pensions saving of 1000 yuan. However, if only one of their parents was registered as a permanent agricultural resident, then they could only enjoy a pension saving of 500 yuan.

The village collective and the Hanjian Group also attached great importance to the living conditions of party members. The party members who joined the party before the foundation of the P.R. China were eligible for a 2000 yuan subsidy per person annually. Younger conscripts, meanwhile, not only benefited from the subsidy issued by relevant authorities, but also received a 2000 yuan subsidy from the village collective, as well as an additional 200 yuan on the Army Day. It is also worth mentioning that there were two water systems in Hancunhe Village. The first of these included groundwater that could be used freely by the villagers. The second was sourced from mountain springs and was intended for use as drinking water. As an additional bonus, 0.5 t of spring water, per villager, was supplied for free each month, while any additional water was charged at a rate of 5 yuan per ton. Finally, every Spring Festival, each villager was entitled to 100 yuan in meat subsidies.

11.6   The Experiences and Future of Hancunhe Village

11.6.1   The Experience of Urbanization in Hancunhe Village

It was, ultimately, down to good leadership, primarily by Tian Xiong, the party secretary of the village, that Hancunhe was transformed from the former "bitterly disappointed village" into "the richest village in the suburbs of Beijing". The leadership carried forward a spirit of selfless dedication, hard work and honesty, seeking, always, to serve the people. Tian Xiong and other leaders emancipated their minds to reform, worked hard with enterprising spirits, rallied the broad masses of the people around the party and put their whole heart into economic construction.

The fundamental goal of developing an economy is to eliminate poverty and achieve a degree of common prosperity. Since the reform and opening up, Hancunhe Village adhered to this goal wholeheartedly. They gave priority to the development of the collective economy, distributed benefits according to workload and fought against idleness and passivity. In this way, they eventually managed to pave the way towards cooperation and common prosperity.

11.6.1.1 Adherence to the Unified Leadership of the Village Collective

Among all of the experiences of Hancunhe's development, one is crucial. So much was achieved insofar as local leaders were able to form unified arrangements and decisions for Hancunhe's future development. Villagers generally accepted these arrangements and decisions because they were themselves the beneficiaries of the village's transformation. Throughout the process of construction, there were, of course, difficult problems. These included the conflicts caused by housing demolitions and merging privately-used land into collective ownership. To solve these problems, Hancunhe adopted an approach that involved combining the village party branch with the Hanjian Group's leadership, forming an overall leadership body, such that the interests of the Hanjian Group were consistent with those of the village. It was, therefore, possible to avoid such problems as "who leads and who obeys" (conflicts of interest and unfair hierarchies). When dealing with the complaints of villagers, the local leaders paid a great deal of attention to the interests of the village as a whole. In the end, the villagers could, therefore, fully enjoy the fruits and benefits of village development. Hancunhe's development thus entered into a virtuous circle. Devotion to the development of the village, on the part of local leaders and the Hanjian Group's directors, was effectively demonstrated through their practical actions. Once the villagers witnessed some of these benefits, they would gradually begin to trust the leaders, including their ideas and decisions pertaining to further development. Therefore all village undertakings were implemented steadily. As a result, contradictions between local leaders and the residents at large rarely existed in Hancunhe and the villagers were, for the most part, completely satisfied. All of these advantages should be credited to the strong village leaders, who were able to draw on everyone's ideas and interests.

11.6.1.2 Adherence to the Dominance of Collective Economy

The development of the collective economy was the material basis for Hancunhe Village to realize common prosperity. Hancunhe's leader, Tian Xiong, realized and held on to this notion. He continuously expanded and consolidated the collective economy, adhering to the principle of accumulating wealth in great quantities, while allocating this wealth in measured quantities, so that the growth in production was always faster than the increase in consumption. Since 1985, the growth of the village's collective annual net income rose by 4.5%, the growth of annual per capita allocation rose by 24.5% and the collective fixed assets reached 68 million yuan. Hancunhe's collective economy accounted for 97.2% of the economic aggregate in the village and becoming a major source of the village income, ensuring the continuous improvement of material and cultural living standards. Throughout the rapid development of the overall collective economy, the development of multiple economic elements was also allowed and encouraged. Villagers who had the technical expertise and ability were encouraged to develop independently. Villagers who lacked management skills and didn't want to be self-employed any more could, instead, find a job within the collective enterprises. As such, not only was the complementary role of a private economy fully utilized, but also the clear superiority and attractiveness of a collective economy was allowed to flourish.

11.6.1.3　The Vision and Ability of Local Leaders

When the residents of Hancunhe were interviewed, they explained the following principle: "To have good rural development, there must be a good leader besides good policies, otherwise the village would be in a state of disunity and villagers would be unable to unify." Much like Wu Renbao navigated Huaxi Village to success, Tian Xiong was Hancunhe Village's captain. Tian Xiong often said that: "We should make people understand our Communist Party through the actions of us communists, so people will follow the party. We communist cadres are willing to be the servant of the people. We should make people really believe that our Communist Party is good". Although Hancunhe village was the richest village in the suburbs of Beijing, Tian Xiong set an example by claiming only the average salary awarded to mid-level cadres. It was, then, clear to all villagers that Tian Xiong was not a greedy or self-serving individual. According to relevant contracts, in the early years, Tian Xiong was entitled to a bonus of a few million yuan. Whilst this bonus was approved of by his superiors, Tian Xiong contributed the money to the collective account, much of which went into developing the public welfare system. The nature of the Hanjian Group, as a collective economy, therefore, remained intact. If the Hanjian Group had reformed and left the countryside, then it could have been rid of the burden of Hancunhe. But Tian Xiong held onto his belief that the Hanjian Group was at the core of the collective and, indeed, the whole village. By branching out, he simply hoped to increase profits in other towns and cities, money which could be used to further develop the village and benefit every villager. Tian Xiong said: "For me, the dedication was a pleasure. It was the communist's responsibility to lead the masses to get rich, if all the masses get rich, can I be poor?"

11.6.1.4　Strengthening Institutional Construction

The reason why Hancunhe's collective economy thrived and that all of the villagers went on to live rich and happy lives was that Hancunhe village had a set of comparatively complete systems, thereby ensuring a suitable range of checks, balances, and rules for all activities. The leaders of Hancunhe Village, at all levels, strictly followed the system of democratic consultation meeting or criticism and self-criticism meeting that was in place. They achieved unity through a process of criticism and, indeed, self-criticism while modestly accepting the opinions of the masses. Major decisions were made by the party committee, strictly implementing administrative and financial responsibility while following the principle of transparency in all matters. Together, these measures formed a strong collective leadership system. What's more, a clear and operable system of supervision and evaluation of leaders was also established in Hancunhe Village. Regular checks on the implementation of responsibilities were carried out accordingly. These checks and balances also meant that research and evaluation could be conducted synchronously, while rewards could be distributed when appropriate.

11.6.1.5   Attaching Importance to Education and Qualifications

The rapid rise of the Hanjian Group, not to mention its dominant place in the construction market, had much to with how it attached importance to qualified personnel. Hancunhe Village faced some challenges due to the low general quality of its workforce and a lack of qualified personnel. When progress finally came, meanwhile, it was, in no small part, due to the presence of highly-trained qualified personnel. Over the years, the Hanjian Group always believed that a high-quality workforce was a decisive factor in economic and social development. Tian Xiong and other decision-makers also recognized that they would not have such a workforce if they did not make any investment. Since 1990, they continuously invested over 30 million yuan into personnel training, for the improvement of their workers through both internal and external training programs. In the meantime, primary school teachers were entitled to a subsidy of 100 yuan per month, and 1.24 million yuan was invested into constructing faculty housing, with an area of 1650 m^2.

11.6.2   Modern Enterprise Management and Organizational Structure

According to the developmental laws of a socialist market economy, Hancunhe Village established and improved its operation and management mechanisms primarily with the unification of incentive and restraint mechanisms.

Firstly, the Hanjian Group introduced competition into its management structure and established an incentive mechanism. It provided equal opportunity for qualified personnel, so each capable employee had an opportunity to display their talents and could earn appraisal through their own achievements. Throughout the process of recruitment and promotion, the Hanjian Group consistently focused on ability, selecting and promoting qualified individuals regardless of age and origin. At that time, the village had more than 1100 management staff and technical personnel.

Among them, those under 35 years old accounted for 80%, while 350 people were introduced from other villages. Such an emphasis on ability facilitated a high-quality, strong capability personnel team. Secondly, in order to encourage the faster development of enterprises, the Hanjian Group stipulated that all engineering departments subordinated to the Hanjian Group could be promoted to an engineering company just in case their annual output value reached 20 million yuan. In addition, all of the able engineering teams, whose annual output value reached the standard of the department, should be promoted in a timely fashion. After the implementation of these measures, an atmosphere of healthy competition, ambition and upwards mobility was formed throughout the entire group.

Besides, the Hanjian Group also established strict rules and regulations and improved the constraint mechanism. As to those kinds of problems, which are often exposed in high-speed economic development, the Hanjian Group insisted on giving priority to education. Any such problems would be solved by establishing and improving a sound system, in which all disadvantages and loopholes were gradually overcome. It successively formulated a "Hanjian Group Constitution", including a "Financial Management System" and an "Internal Audit System", with 36 items and in excess of 180 articles, all of which provided explicit regulations as regards all aspects of management practice and operational procedures. For instance, the Hanjian Group opted to transform its decentralized financial management system into a centralized management system. Each engineering team, under the overall construction company, would have cashier rights only, not a full accounting department. Higher level accounting practices would, instead, be managed by a higher level engineering department or the group's head office. All of the accountants, from the various branches of the Hanjian Group, meanwhile, were instructed to work together. Finally, the parent company of the Hanjian Group would uniformly control and supervise the finances of the village, ensuring that collective investments were not used to benefit only a few individuals, thereby blocking any potential loopholes in the management structure.

11.6.3   The Future of Hancunhe Village

11.6.3.1   Hancunhe's Strategy of Urbanization

Taking a panoramic view of small quasi-city town development, whether following the example of other towns and villages or acting in accordance with the objective conditions of a town itself, a developed and prosperous economy is clearly the key to ensure rapid and successful development. Likewise, prosperous small quasi-city towns are a precondition for further economic development overall. That is to say, without economic prosperity, the development of small quasi-city towns simply cannot be realized. Similarly, without the necessary infrastructure and environment for investment, provided by small quasi-city towns, it is difficult to generate further economic development. For example, the Hanjian Group spent more than

30 million yuan on supporting Hancunhe Village annually. This highlighted an issue, insofar as most other new villages did not require so much financial support. Therefore, the foundation of development in small quasi-city towns must be economic development, the pillars of which are industrial enterprises. The Hanjian Group was, at that time, actively taking responsibility for the small quasi-city town center of Hancunhe Village. It was based on this responsibility that Hancunhe followed a principle of harmonious development, with construction as its leading industry. The construction industry could, it was hoped, drive the primary, secondary and tertiary industries to form an industrial chain and create jointly a multiplier effect. As part of this project, a small, modern quasi-city town center was set up, with administration, healthcare, cultural artifacts, shopping malls and a range of other infrastructural facilities. These services attracted and absorbed neighboring villagers, who elected to work in Hancunhe, thereby giving rise to a small quasi-city town of around 50,000 residents. This growth effectively transformed the village into a small quasi-city town, the residents of which could finally enjoy the benefits of an urban lifestyle.

Even today, the authorities in Hancunhe, with the support of the Hanjian Group, are planning on expanding Hancunhe into a central quasi-city town large enough to integrate a great deal of the surrounding rural areas, with the original Hancunhe Village as the center.

11.6.3.2 The Dilemma for Hancunhe's Development

When summarizing the success of Hancunhe, one of the key factors was that it had a good leader, Tian Xiong. Like Wu Renbao, the leader of Huaxi Village, Tian Xiong, a rural leader aiming for rural development, believed that enterprise will make a village prosperous and drive forward economic and social development. Their actions demonstrated the possibility that, in a socialist country and in accordance with socialist ideology, those who acquire wealth first can help to raise the levels of prosperity of others. However, individuals with the motivation and capability to do so are in short supply. According to Weber's theory, these individuals might be categorized as charismatic figures. This type of leadership is based on extraordinary personal qualities distinguished by high levels of expressiveness, self-confidence, moral conviction, and emotional resonance, resulting in strong follower identification with the leader, alignment with the vision of the leader and inspiration to perform for the leader[11] Weber further analyzed the lifecycle of charismatic leaders, from their emergence and conversion to their extinction. Weber pointed out that this type of rule is temporary in nature. Charismatic leaders can maintain an organization in a state of equilibrium, but potential conflicts in an organization would gradually be exposed when the leaders retreated. Therefore, in order to ensure the stability of an organization, it was necessary, to a certain degree,

---

[11]Su (1988).

to develop appropriate rules and regulations. In the process of transformation, charismatic domination would gradually be transferred to a system of legal or traditional rules. However, from the above-mentioned examples of village transformation, the charismatic managers carried both traditional and legal features. Firstly, as the village elite, they occupied the positions of village party secretary, which empowered them to manage and rule the village, while maintaining order in accordance with the law. It was a legal rule on the basis of villagers obeying the leadership of the Chinese Communist Party and complying with set laws and regulations accordingly. Secondly, as village leaders, they also had a degree of traditionally recognized power and authority that commanded obedience from the village residents. In rural areas, this authority was reflected by a range of widely accepted customs and obligations towards the village leaders.

When these charismatic leaders, who led the villagers to prosperity, retired or otherwise retreated, the question as to who would take over their positions became an issue of public concern. As far as the rich villages in China were concerned, such as in Huaxi Village, the successor was the son of the former leader. The successor of the Hanjian Group, meanwhile, had not yet been appointed. It was said that Tian Xiong's son was destined to become the Hanjian Group's successor. This was above criticism, and it should be remembered that China is a family-governed society after all. The enterprises were created by their leaders and, if their children were competent enough, it would be easily manageable for the leaders to transfer power to their children. Then again, the question of democracy is occasionally raised in this context. As regard this possibility, Hancunhe's leaders did conduct some preliminary investigations. Anyhow, whether family governance was advantageous or disadvantageous, Hancunhe believed that it was best to be tested by practice.

In summary, by running enterprises in rural areas, the village leaders helped the residents of the village to become richer and, in doing so, consolidated the legitimacy of their policy and implementation over village affairs. The relationship of leadership and recognition united the interests of the village and enabled the avoidance of such problems as benefit distribution. If, now, the villagers were asked to vote for the leader of the village, they would still vote for an individual capable of leading the Hanjian Group. Without the support of the Hanjian Group and without the ten million yuan subsidy, provided by the Hanjian Group to support the village, the development of Hancunhe would either stagnate or collapse altogether. Hancunhe has, after all, been sustained by the Hanjian Group. Everything from property management to heating facilities, tourism, and vegetable production has been invested in and supported by the Hanjian Group. Far from being profitable, these investments have actually cost the Hanjian Group. However, they were face-saving projects of Hancunhe. If the money were to stop, Hancunhe's current level of development and the quality of life of its citizens would be unsustainable. In brief, Tian Xiong effectively engineered a "contractual" relationship between Hancunhe and the Hanjian Group, converting the village into a community similar to the social functions of units or corporations that were common before China's reform and opening up. Nevertheless, unlike the social functions of units or corporations, the villagers in Hancunhe were not necessarily working for the Hanjian Group, but still could enjoy the benefits provided. Many of these benefits were accumulated simply because Tian Xiong encouraged villagers to become rich "through their own hard work".

11.6.3.3 How Long Can Hancunhe Village "Lean" on the Hanjian Group

A villager who was interviewed while taking a walk in Hancunhe Park said: "With Hanjian Group's investment, our village would not have any problem. If without their investment, to afford the 10 million yuan heating costs each year alone would be a problem." If Hancunhe Village were able to maintain its current standard of living without the continued investment of the Hanjian Group, then its success would provide many lessons as regards promoting rural urbanization and industrialization. The fact that Hancunhe developed as part of a Hanjian Group led project has, of course, been highly beneficial to the village, especially since the Hanjian Group can provide any follow-up funding that is required. Nevertheless, this is not a permanent solution. To use an analogy, the Hanjian Group should not only "transfuse blood" to sustain Hancunhe, but should also make it so Hancunhe Village can "produce blood", such as through the provision of more opportunities and possibilities.

Based on this school of thought, in accordance with the country's call to develop small quasi-city towns, Hancunhe, led by Tian Xiong, together with the town government, should build Hancunhe into a central quasi-city town within the next few years. Nevertheless, such a project requires huge amounts of capital expenditure. Besides the support of the government, the Hanjian Group would be largely responsible for this project. It also requires that the Hanjian Group develop in a sustainable fashion such that it may supply a steady stream of "blood" into Hancunhe's own developmental process. Problematically, however, the construction and real estate markets are characterized by volatility and liquidity. Herbert Applebaum, for instance, summarized four distinct characteristics of the construction industry.[12] These characteristics highlighted that it was regional in nature, non-standard, subject to time limits and uncertain in duration. For one thing, the regional feature of the construction industry would limit the space for development, determine the available market and influence the operating costs. Nonstandardization, meanwhile, might generate potential threats to enterprise management and control. Moreover, the time limits of construction projects, as well as the operating cycle and capital chain, result in further uncertainty. Recognizing these risks, the Hanjian Group embarked on a process of enterprise restructure and transformation, in order to expand market and achieve long-term development. The stability and harmony of Hancunhe, meanwhile, depended, to a great extent, on the

---

[12]Quoted from a secondary source. Shen (2007).

Hanjian Group's performance. Hancunhe and the Hanjian Group were, in fact, tied together to such an extent that the latter could have been accused of having "kidnapped" the former. Needless to say, then, many villagers were very concerned about the development of the Hanjian Group, primarily insofar as their own futures depended upon the Hanjian Group's success.

11.7 The Evolution of Urbanization Driven by an Industrialization Model

11.7.1 Meditations on the Urbanization Model

Models are approaches and strategies formed from prior experiences. The intention of summarizing and comparing the structures and characteristics of small quasi-city town development models is, in part, to understand the intrinsic link between actions and strategies.[13] The model mentioned here refers to a development model, that is, a distinctive approach formed "in certain areas and under certain historical conditions". Farmers in different regions are under different conditions and, therefore, are likely to have a variety of different methods of making a profit, thus forming different models of rural economic development.[14] The significance of comparing and analyzing these development models consists in the possibility that understanding the inherent logic and law of development could be strengthened through understanding actual facts and experiences. The purpose of doing so is to figure out a suitable and specific development path based on concrete characteristics and conditions. The pattern of developing small quasi-city town adopted in Hancunhe Village is just one of tens of thousands rural urbanization models in China. To make clear the characteristics, the motivations, problems and methods of promotion of this model must all be subject to research. If this model is found to be either too special or too typical, then its promotion and popularization can be queried. In the case of Hancunhe, which is a typical sample of a village supported by enterprise development, various aspects are extensively queried, including the emergence of leaders, the selection of successors, potential improvements to the existing system, holding democratic and fair elections and the sustainability of the enterprise development thus far. If these problems cannot be solved properly and if an executable development plan cannot be provided, then the case in hand can hardly be imitated or learnt from.

On the basis of his field trips to the southern area of the Jiangsu Province (Sunan) and Wenzhou's rural areas, Fei Xiaotong, summarizing his findings and advancing the notion of the "model", proposed the "Wenzhou Model", "Sunan Model" and the "Zhujiang Model". As for the interpretation of the term "model", it

---

[13]Lu (2010).
[14]Fei (1998).

was unnecessary to adhere to or overemphasize the notion that models are samples that can be copied and transplanted. In fact, every model has a degree of particularity, related, perhaps, to its geography, culture, history and certain opportunities. The model of Hancunhe was, therefore, somewhat different from other models of rural urbanization. Although urbanization in both Hancunhe Village and Xiaogang Village, in Fengyang County, Anhui Province, were driven by industrialization, the model of Hancunhe Village was one driven by the local elites, while the model of Xiaogang Village was one promoted by external resources. To compare Hancunhe Village with Huaxi village, though both were, indeed, driven by local elites, there remain essential differences between the two. Both villages were supported by enterprises, but the industry in Huaxi was differential, while there were considerable efforts to make the industries stronger and larger. As a result, it produced a radiation effect that influenced more than a dozen surrounding villages The Hanjian Group, however, could only afford to the support the development of Hancunhe Village. Industries in Huaxi were comparatively stable and well accumulated, with as many as 58 companies in Huaxi Village. Its scale of production covered six major areas, including pipes, belts, wool and textiles. There were more than 1000 categories and over 10,000 kinds of products being manufactured. Such a production chain was not at risk of seasonal variations. As discussed in a previous part, however, the Hanjian Group's main business was real estate development and construction. This industry was characterized by instability and unpredictability, prone to difficulties as a result of market and capital operations. The two villages may, then, have been managed by village elites, but the problems they had to face were subject to their own specific processes of development.

11.7.2   The Features of Models Driven by Industrialization

Urbanization through industrialization was an inevitable process for most rural areas. The characteristics of rural industrial development can be summarized in the following way.

Firstly, rural industrialization depends upon the excavation of certain resources. It is by relying on these resources that villagers can set up their own enterprises, promote the development of related industries and achieve their economic goals. The utilization of resources, meanwhile, can be divided into two types. The first of these is the resource-oriented type. If there are readily available resources in rural areas, suitable for direct use, such as tourism resources, mineral resources, ecological resources and cultural resources, a village may utilize them or, at least, use them to attract investment, so as to achieve a degree of economic development. Nevertheless, this resource-oriented development model had some inherent dangers, primarily due to the risk of short-sighted strategies. Resource exploitation, rarely a sustainable model of development, may, after all, destroy the ecological balance of a rural area. The second method of utilizing resources is the market-oriented type. This type depends more on human resources and the geographical location of the village. For example, in Hancunhe Village, there were no available natural or cultural resources. Instead, a few bricklayers laid the foundation for running an enterprise, forming today's Hanjian Group and expanding the market as they did. Those villages that enjoy a good location often become logistical distribution centers or transit stations. They might even be included in the planning of larger urban development projects, thereby providing more opportunities for interacting with the outside world and setting up industry. Therefore, urbanization in these villages will probably present itself as a smoother process.

Secondly, rural industrialization should be carried out in accordance with the state's overall development. Looking at the successful experiences of different regions, it can be seen that the macro-conditions, as regards nation-wide economic development, can contribute greatly to enhancing rural prosperity, enabling the rise of related industries within villages. Whether it is rural family workshops in Wenzhou or the development of construction teams in Hancunhe, examples of rural industrialization tend to cater to the prevailing trends of national economic development at the time. This enables them to occupy a favorable position in the market, the lack of which would render it highly difficult for them to enjoy any kind of rapid development. Furthermore, low labor costs are often a significant advantage of rural industry, although widespread marketing is a corresponding difficultly. These days, however, the flow of labor has become increasingly frequent throughout China's labor market and the smooth circulation of goods has further enabled the development of rural industry. Rural industry, which relies on local labor and land advantages, can expand its market share with a certain product or industry and, subsequently, develop like rolling a snowball, eventually shifting from workshops to enterprises. As the industrial chains become gradually more complex in rural areas, so too is the demand for labor increased. An industrial aggregation effect may then promote full rural urbanization.

Thirdly, rural industrialization must ultimately rely on towns, to an extent at least. Although the countryside is the birthplace of rural industry, towns are the carriers and supporting bodies for these rural areas. Towns can provide a platform for public services and other basic services such as natural resources, telecommunications, finance and taxation for rural industrialization. With the advantages of location, technology, finance, transportation, culture, and other elements, towns can create the conditions required for the realization of agricultural scale management. For example, in Weihai City, Shandong Province, at intervals of every 60 km, there are designated towns with dense processing industries, convenient transportation and communication networks. The rise of these small towns has played an important and undeniable role in promoting local industrialization.[15] The towns also offer a place where the rural population could relocate, effectively solving the contradiction of large agricultural populations trying to sustain themselves on relatively little land. These towns also expand the market demand for agricultural

---

[15]Liu and Li (2000).

products, optimize the agricultural structure and promote the development and expansion of leading agricultural enterprises. In addition, rural urbanization can promote the shifting of urban civilization and materials to rural areas, transforming agricultural production modes and the lifestyle of rural residents. In turn, this can be helpful for farmers to change their traditional provincialism and lay the foundation for their transformation into modern citizens. Urbanization and rural industrialization are, then, two elements that cannot be separated. They promote each other and develop coordinately because they are both conducive to the rational allocation of resources and make full use of urban and rural resources. In the meantime, they lead to the equal exchange of urban and rural elements so that resource advantages can be turned into economic advantages. In fact, the constant matching and complementation of urban economy and rural economy has been the foundation of urbanization. Whether it was in developed or developing countries, urbanization in practice shows that coordinating the urbanization and industrialization processes can mitigate the tension between urban and rural areas, narrow the gap between them, facilitate productive rural-urban interaction and lead eventually to harmonious development.

References

Fei, X. (1998). *On reality* (p. 201). Beijing University Press.

Fei, X. (2009). *Small towns, big problems. Complete works of Fei Xiaotong* (Vol. 10, p. 215), Inner Mongolia People's Publishing House.

Gao, A. (2008). The impression of Hancunhe village. *China Modern Enterprise Newspaper*, January 22, 2008.

Hu, B. (1998). *Development theory and China* (pp. 168–169). People's Publishing House.

Liu, D. (2011). *A study on rural urbanization driven by private economic—typical cases in Zhejiang province* (p. 12). Ph.D. thesis. Zhejiang Normal Universit.

Liu, X., Li, S. (2000). On synchronized development of agriculture and industrialization in the development of small towns. *Agricultural Economy*, April 2000s.

Lu, Y. (2010). *Peasant China—Study of post-earthbound society and new rural construction* (p. 377). China Renmin University Press.

Shen, Y. (2007). *Market, class and society—Key issues for transitional society.* Social Sciences Academic Press.

Su, G. (1988). *Rationalization and restriction—introduction to Weber's Thought* (p. 191). Shanghai People's Publishing House.

Wang, L. (2001). *A research on the current condition of and countermeasures for rural urbanization in Zhejiang.* Development Research Center of the State Council Network CRCnet), April 10, 2001.